JIM
BRIDGER

By J. CECIL ALTER

University of Oklahoma Press : Norman and London

BY J. CECIL ALTER

James Bridger: A Historical Narrative (Salt Lake City, 1925; Columbus, 1950)

Through the Heart of the Scenic West (Salt Lake City, 1927)

Utah: The Storied Domain (Salt Lake City, 1932)

Early Utah Journalism (Salt Lake City, 1938)

Jim Bridger (Norman, 1962) (New and revised edition of *James Bridger: A Historical Narrative*)

LIBRARY OF CONGRESS CATALOG CARD NUMBER 62-16478

ISBN: 0-8061-1509-2 (paper)

8 9 10 11 12 13 14 15 16 17 18 19 20 21 22 23 24 25

To my three sons: J. Winston, E. Irving, and Marvin S. Alter, who have accompanied me over many of the Old Trails and who furnished the encouraging "drive" for assembling these researches.

JAMES BRIDGER, early western fur trapper, master mountaineer, Indian frontiersman, and U. S. Army scout and guide, was a notable figure in a series of dated pursuits, each one marking a unique epoch never to occur again in American history. A blacksmith's apprenticeship in old St. Louis disciplined him for earning a living the hard way. Nearly half of Bridger's mountain companions succumbed to violent death; only unusual skills and uncanny luck preserved him.

As a Rocky Mountain fur trapper, subsisting solely on game, he was poaching on the rights of the Indians. Buffalo surrounds, deer and antelope kills, elk hunts and grizzly bear encounters, were as frequent as mealtime with him. Residing much of his second twenty years of life with one Indian tribe or another, he came to share the Indians' ways, their religious leanings, and their battles to the death.

His initiative kept sharp by self-preservation impulses, Bridger came to know the Rocky Mountain region and its denizens as a farmer knows his fields and flocks. As an eager explorer, he was among the first white men to use the Indian trail over South Pass of the continental divide—later the Oregon-Mormon-California Trail; he was first to taste the water of Great Salt Lake, first to report a two-ocean creek, foremost in describing Yellowstone Park phenomena, and the only man to run the Big Horn River rapids on a raft. He originally selected the Crow Creek–Sherman–Dale Creek route over Laramie Mountains near Cheyenne, Wyoming, and Bridger's Pass over the continental divide, which were adopted by the Union Pacific Railroad.

Three times a squaw-man and long an influential tribesman, Bridger became an interpreter of both the Indian tongue and the Indian mind, thus rendering valued service at sundry peace conferences. He was counseling aid and guide for U. S. Army Engineers' exploring expeditions and for military officers on Indian reconnaissances and punitive campaigns.

Bridger's conspicuousness as "Mister Rocky Mountains" and his droll humor unwittingly brought to him the character of "hero" in an illegitimate brood of impossible Paul Bunyan tales of the Old West. These were the storyteller's own adaptations and parodies on the still earlier Arkansas traveler's tales. As the reader will learn, however, some of Bridger's adventures would turn the tables on the storyteller, and promote his candidacy for the Rocky Mountain hall of fame.

Having twice exhausted available repositories of "Bridger" materials (Shepard Book Company, Salt Lake City, Utah, 1925, 546 pages; and the same in facsimile, with addenda, Long's College Book Company, Columbus, Ohio, 1950, 601 pages), we here present only events in which the Old Scout had a part. Improbable and uncorroborated tales, howsoever interestingly told, have been omitted, regardless of their popularity.

The present manuscript is based on the original works of 1925 and 1950, though many new facts have been included, mostly affording a new perspective; and some—it was unavoidable—have necessitated entirely new conclusions! My indebtedness to the authorities listed in the bibliography is gratefully acknowledged; through them I have come to know and to appreciate Mr. Bridger.

J. Cecil Alter

LOMITA, CALIFORNIA

⊃ CONTENTS

꒰ ILLUSTRATIONS

xi

JIM BRIDGER

I &sw; BOYHOOD MEMORIES

THE YEAR 1812 was a momentous one for the Bridgers. It was their last in the old home town of Richmond, Virginia. Appropriately, that was where Patrick Henry, in 1775, feeling a bit crowded, shouted to the generations of American people, "Give me liberty or give me death." For a decade the senior Bridger had held a worthy place in the community as a land surveyor, meanwhile leisurely neglecting a starved-out, suburban hill-farm.

Mrs. Bridger presided over a highway inn for dusty travelers. She was also the affectionate mother of three: a toddling baby boy; an ever-busy, inquiring school girl (if there had been a school); and a taciturn young man of destiny, turning eight, whose colorful career we are unraveling here.

Round about Richmond at that time more farmers were abandoning depleted acres than newcomers were requesting land surveys. Moreover, patrons of the Bridger hostelry were fewer than the emigrants camping at the edge of town each night. Dutch, German, Swiss, and other newcomers disembarking at Richmond were unwilling to proceed farther inland, if acceptable opportunities were nearer. The "Star of the West" hovered over Illinois and Missouri.[1]

Young James was curiously interested in the straining ox-teams, the creaking covered wagons, the camping routines, and the preoccupation and gossip of the travelers. He may even have previsioned himself, twenty-five or thirty years later, guiding just such emigrant trains through the Rocky Mountains on their way to Oregon and California.

But if the surveyor's telescope had foreshortened the father's pros-

[1] John Bradbury, *Travels in the Interior of America, 1809-1811.* See Appendix 4, p. 235; Appendix 5, p. 272; and p. 301n. See also "Richmond," in Funk & Wagnall's *New Standard Encyclopedia.*

pect of events that would soon come to pass, he would never have left the Old Dominion, or its unique "Tobacco Town."

Westbound emigrants could hire drivers with teams and wagons as far as the Ohio River, or use their own outfits. There two or three neighbors usually loaded their effects together on a raft, a so-called ark or flatboat, for economical travel. A resident pilot would coax the craft over the falls at Louisville. Barge or keelboat space was available, if broken and irregular, to St. Louis.[2]

Piecing together the scattered bits of James Bridger's recorded recollections, we can only say that in 1812 the family gave way to new managers of the hotel and of the farm and departed toward a bleeding but setting sun. It could have been an omen of their own misfortunes.[3]

A month later, the Bridgers were settling dubiously, like so many migrating wildfowl, on a riverside farmstead near St. Louis. It was on the American Bottoms, also called the Six Mile, or DuPont Prairie, Illinois, if the sources are accurate. Although the soil was deeply fertile, the site had its drawbacks, being subject to flooding and to river fogs. The town of St. Louis was then a rough-and-tumble borough, still learning to look after itself and its uninvited guests.

Even so, opportunity was generous to the senior Bridger. Established surveyors needed an experienced field man. Consequently an occupation and an income were assured; although his assignments were usually toward the settlement frontiers, away from home and family, and out of touch.

From the outset the mother noted that the children seemed to be misfits in a strange environment, in spite of her studied companionship. With further regret, she noted her own increasing frailty in performing some of the outdoor chores she had to undertake. There was money for help, but there was a scarcity of domestic help for any money; likewise a dearth of the store goods, available at Richmond, that had spelled a degree of comfort and convenience. Per-

[2] Leland D. Baldwin, The Keelboat Age on Western Waters, 178, 180, 190, 191.
[3] These family details are from Grenville M. Dodge's Biographical Sketch. The second edition of that pamphlet is reproduced in the original works on Bridger, 493–525. The first printing, by R. M. Rigby Printing Company (Kansas City, Mo., n.d.), was reproduced by the Wyoming Historical Department, Cheyenne, January 15, 1924, in its Quarterly Bulletin. Hereafter referred to as Dodge, Biographical Sketch.

haps the most effective suffocation of her morale was the sheer lone-liness—facing alone the problems and responsibilities usually borne by a devoted father-mother team.

Only a mother's hope kept her from invalidism the first year or two, though the company of the growing children was comforting. Then the cruel consequences began to appear, forcing her into her last confinement the winter of 1815–16. In midsummer of 1816—it would occur while the father was away in the wilderness—messengers sought him out with the sad tidings that his wife had passed away.

It was a distressing bereavement for the family, creating an impossible adjustment. The surveyor's sister came from Virginia to attempt to rescue the children and salvage the farm, with the aid of the surveyor's earnings and encouragement. But the fates still frowned upon them. That winter of 1816 the youngest son was laid beside the mother, they hoped within her arms. Could a rigorous frontier be more exacting and severe? It could! To this broken home, the heartsick father was brought, desperately ill himself, late in the summer of 1817. He died before Christmas.

No wonder James Bridger often spoke tenderly of his sister, a fragment of the mother's love. No wonder he eagerly sought any kind of employment and worked as if he had no other solace.

Master James Bridger would be fourteen in a few months (March 17, 1818). Circumstances had already made him a man in some respects. Tall, strong, and serious, he had the looks and ways of an adult. Such gravity seemed to frown on the diminutive "Jim," but, in time, it admitted him to busy circles everywhere.

With a boy's yearning for adventure, he is said to have acquired a canoe, which he handled well. One could not reach St. Louis from Six Mile without a boat. His most recreative excursions were visiting traps that he set in the bayous in winter. He obtained his traps and traded in a few mink and muskrat skins at Chouteau's. Pierre Chouteau, Jr., was still young, only twenty-nine. Born and reared in St. Louis in a well-to-do family, Pierre had probably trapped some of the same sloughs. On a later occasion he helped young Bridger select and obtain his first gun. The two remained good friends the rest of their lives, though James Bridger thenceforth "paddled his own canoe."

James Bridger's first task was to find a job but in selling himself, he was handicapped by a frustrating shyness. The principal avenues open to him were the few men who knew him. They generously remembered that a tongue-tied timidity never oversold itself.

Elements of St. Louis's early increment of growth came downstream by canoe, pirogue, and raft—Indians and hunters with their furs and skins, but always a goodly proportion of the merchandise came upriver in the tedious, usually tardy flatboats, barges and keelboats.

Every person, animal, vehicle, and pound of freight arriving overland from the east had to be ferried across the Mississippi River to the St. Louis wharves.[4] Ferryboats were already increasing in number and competing for the business.[5]

James Bridger frankly disliked the average riverman. Too often he was a potential vagabond, underemployed (part-time) and overworked while on duty; and he did not have a steady job. The roustabouts at the wharves were of like character.

But the spirit of adventure reposed in the river itself; something new could be expected every day. Thus, the lad must have been a familiar figure at Antoine Dangen's ferry to Old Cahokia (East St. Louis), nearest the Bridger farm home. He could assist with the loading, poling, tying-up, and unloading. Dangen's was the more popular passenger ferry at the time, and young James, with his canoe, undoubtedly took an occasional fare or passenger himself, on special trips. A little later Wiggin's new ferry, with horse-propelled treadwheels, up at Oak Street, could use a horse driver.

It was more than warmth that drew the young man into the St. Louis blacksmith shop that winter. He had often visited there,

---

[4] General Dodge comments that: "After the death of his father and mother, Bridger had to support himself and sister. He got together money enough to buy a flatboat ferry, and when ten years of age made a living by running that ferry to St. Louis." (Alter, *James Bridger*, 500.)

Young Bridger's "Flatboat ferry" service, however, could hardly have been his very own; the ferries then in operation were far out of his financial and operational reach, though, of course, he could have been employed by one or more of them.

[5] Louis Houck, *A History of Missouri*; also I. H. Lionberger, *The Annals of St. Louis* (1928), and other histories give dates and places and other facts about the St. Louis ferries.

6

making himself useful: turning grindstones, handing tools to workmen, holding and soothing horses being shod, pumping the furnace
bellows, assisting with unwieldy wagon tires, removing and replac-
ing wagon wheels, and doing errands on the river front and over
town for the shop or its patrons.

In the gun-repair section, young Bridger affectionately handled
many guns, testing them for heft, feel, and fitness, as companionable,
all-purpose friendly weapons. A gun to him was as personal as a
jacket, and should fit its owner's hands, arms, shoulder, and sighting-
eye naturally.

James Baird (or Beard) was one of St. Louis's pioneer blacksmiths
from about 1811. Subsequent growth of the business provided his
shop with facilities and workmen for other kinds of smithing; also
some wood-working, gunsmithing, and simple manufacturing, such
as of butcher knives.

Available directories and writers of that day do not list Phil
Creamer, who was said by Bridger to have been his blacksmith-shop
foster-father. We can only assume from that, and other circum-
stances, that Creamer was possibly a neighbor of the Bridgers on the
American Bottoms and a leading blacksmith in the Baird shop in
St. Louis. It is only certain that for four years, from 1818, James
Bridger was a blacksmith's apprentice living in Phil Creamer's home.
The apprenticeship would be legally terminated at age eighteen.

We may assume from many circumstances that young James
Bridger, the apprentice, was alert and responsive to men and events;
in the shop, in the town, and in the world about him. He was a
country boy, but he was not a country bumpkin who would let the
horse he was holding step on his feet, or who would hold the swage
askew under the blacksmith's hammer. Continually in danger, he was
almost never hurt in the shop or elsewhere. No word has come down
to us on his skill at helving an axe, nosing a plow, or tempering a
cold chisel; but we have it from acceptable authority that he always
made himself useful around the shop and that the shopmen liked
him.[6]

[6] T. D. Bonner, *The Life and Adventures of James P. Beckwourth*, 33 (all footnote references are to the Leland edition). Beckwourth says he was a blacksmith's
apprentice in St. Louis under George Casner (John L. Sutton, partner) to 1817.
Apparently he did not meet James Bridger until he became a fur-trapper in "Captain
Bridger's Company" (*ibid.*, 94).

Young Bridger felt his inferiority most keenly in chance meetings with young men who spoke familiarly of the Reverend Mr. Niel's academy for "young gentlemen" in St. Louis. There were others—teen-age travelers visiting home at vacation time from college at Bardstown, Kentucky—to accentuate their comfortable, cultural status. Amply sponsored, they were confident and secure, polished sons of officials or businessmen of the city. James Bridger was without even father's counsel or reflected prestige. All his potential accomplishments, his entire career, must come from his own inherent resources, from his opportunities and environment: "The child is father of the man."

THE ST. LOUIS blacksmith shop near the river front was a kind of information exchange for widely traveled visitors. To apprentice Bridger's eager overhearing, this was living history. Although he did not then know it, Bridger would soon become an actor in this captivating scene.

Bridger's own local hunting tours told him the Missouri River could still be as unruly as it had been when discovered by Father Marquette, descending the Mississippi, in June, 1673: "We heard the noise of a rapid; large trees, entire with branches—real floating islands —came from the west so impetuously the water was very muddy."

Old Cahokia (East St. Louis) was established in 1699 as a Roman Catholic mission, but it promptly became a busy trading post. The tradition in Bridger's nearby community was that beaver fur made it so. The Chouteau family of New Orleans established a trading post opposite Cahokia in 1764, which they called St. Louis.

From there, in 1790, a roaming fur trader reached the Mandan Indian villages (present Bismarck, North Dakota). He learned that the villages had been headquarters for fourteen years of a resident trader for Canadian fur companies, that Mexican (Spanish) bridles and saddles were in use by the Mandans, and that white Canadians had already reached the Pacific.

The Missouri River and St. Louis were the natural outlets for this trade. Consequently, the "Company of Explorers of the Upper Missouri" was organized in 1793. In the next few years of inexperience, the leaders of pilot bands, reinforcements, and competitors brought havoc by accusing one another of villainy. They uncovered the disheartening fact that the Indians were improvident hunters and had few furs to trade. After this discovery, "St. Louis merchants were unwilling to expand their efforts to the more remote Indians."[1] The Missouri River region was purchased by the United States in 1803. To explore, map, and appraise the territory, the government sponsored the Lewis and Clark Expedition. This semi-military group moved up the Missouri River in 1804, making examinations, studies, and records of geology, topography, streams, animals, inhabitants—everything that 180 hand-picked experts saw, did, and heard. After wintering with the Mandans, 1804–1805, they crossed the continental divide and wintered in 1805–1806 at the mouth of the Columbia. Returning by approximately the same route, they reached St. Louis in September, 1806.[2]

Their report revealed names and locations of streams and Indian villages and the extent of tribal land possessions, along with descriptions and appraisals of unit areas of the country. They cultivated the good will of the Indians by distributing presents, making friendly speeches, and leaving printed copies as mementos with the Indians. But what they did not do had the most salutary effect: they did not hunt buffalo or trap beaver, or gather elk trophies, or molest Indian women, or steal horses, or antagonize the Indians in any manner.

The Missouri River region thus offered a challenge to any fur trapper–trader who would help himself to the Indians' furs, his game, his women, and his homelands; and would treat any Indians' enemies as friends. This last was especially unforgivable!

The effect in St. Louis was explosive. Manuel Lisa selected forty men from the host of volunteers and proceeded up the Missouri River in 1807. He established Fort Manuel at the mouth of the Big Horn. The Mandans were only a way station to the better beaver lands, but here was virgin beaver country. Thus Lisa returned in 1808 with a rich cargo of furs and a lifetime occupation ahead of him.

Thereupon General William Clark and George Drouillard (of the Lewis and Clark Expedition) with Andrew Henry, Pierre Menard, Thomas James, and others led a formidable company of three or four hundred determined men to another winter at Fort Manuel. Their plans were strategic and farsighted, but in their in-

[1] A. P. Nasatir, *Before Lewis and Clark, Documents, 1785–1804*, I, 92. Also, Paul C. Phillips, *The Fur Trade*, II, 231.
[2] *History of the Expedition of Lewis and Clark, 1804–1805–1806* (ed. by James K. Hosmer).

experience everything seemed hostile and the Indians aggressive.[3]

Using Fort Manuel as a jumping-off place early in 1810, Andrew Henry and Pierre Menard led an eager crew of trappers to Three Forks Basin, having Drouillard and John Colter as guides. While the trappers were getting their bearings, a militant force of Blackfeet attacked, killing two or three isolated men and making off with their property. In a second attack a few days later, other trappers, including Drouillard, were slain. No wonder "most of the Americans prepared to go back to the settlements."[4]

Andrew Henry remained with a substantial, but uncongenial, party, bravely hoping to gather more furs. Instead he promptly lost several more men in a third annihilating attack by the Blackfeet, who meant business. Henry knew when he was licked and hurried over the continental divide to the southward. He established himself for the winter on what has since been called Henry's Fork of Snake River (St. Anthony, Idaho).[5]

Henry's whereabouts and his probable plight were live topics that severe winter of 1810-11, among the Rocky Mountain Indians as well as among the whites at St. Louis. But Henry, after a miserable winter, reached St. Louis in midsummer of 1811 with some forty packs of beaver and "experience" enough to last him exactly eleven years, when James Bridger was to become his protégé.

Major Henry's dejection was like a dash of cold water on fur trapping enthusiasts in St. Louis. For ten long years Astorians spread their traps on the Oregon; the Hudson's Bay and the North West companies continued to slit each other's throats as deftly as they skinned a beaver; and the broken remnants of the Missouri Fur Company remained close to the lower end of the "Big Muddy"—out of respect for the dead.

Politicians, however, were as busy as beavers, and the United States Congress, in 1818, authorized the army to establish a military outpost at the mouth of the Yellowstone River. Accordingly, by early 1819, armed troops in barges and keelboats were working their

---

[3] Hiram M. Chittenden, *History of the American Fur Trade of the Far West* (*1807-43*), 142-44. Also, Phillips, *The Fur Trade*, II, 262-64.

[4] Thomas James, *Three Years Among the Indians and Mexicans*, 80, 83.

[5] Henry built only two or three log cabins for temporary shelter; it was not a trading post.

way upstream at St. Louis before James Bridger's curious eyes. Then, about 1820, Jacob Hawken set up his lathes, drill presses, and other gun-making machinery in St. Louis for producing the so-called Hawken gun in quantity. This is mentioned because Bridger early acquired, and for many years carried, one of these guns, an improvement on the Kentucky rifle.[6]

To bring our historical detour to an abrupt ending in the spring of 1822: Missouri was modestly donning her robes of statehood; Wilson P. Hunt, explorer-merchant, was preparing to become post-master of St. Louis; and, of much warmer concern to readers of this page, James Bridger was completing his apprenticeship in the St. Louis blacksmith shop as of March 17, 1822.

[6] Carl P. Russell, *Guns on the Early Frontiers*, 74–76.

"READ THAT AGAIN," James Bridger must have urged. "To Enterprising Young Men," the St. Louis newspaper notice was addressed on March 20, 1822. "The subscriber wishes to engage one hundred young men to ascend the Missouri River to its source, there to be employed one, two, or three years. For particulars inquire of Major Andrew Henry, near the lead mines, in the county of Washington, who will ascend with and command the party; or the subscriber, near St. Louis.—William H. Ashley."

General Ashley, then forty-four years of age, had recently become lieutenant governor of Missouri and had previously earned his way through the ranks of the state militia to become its top officer. Major Henry was on his staff. Both men were in the lead-mining and powder-manufacturing business. General Ashley was popular and commanded the resources. Major Henry was contributing the experience, attested by eleven-year-old scars on his memory.[1]

Young Bridger did not need to be informed, for it was common gossip, that the employment was hunting and trapping beaver. The wages? Competitor Thomas Hempstead wrote his partner, Joshua Pilcher, of developments: "I am told the Ashley-Henry hunters and trappers are to have one-half of the fur they make; the Company to furnish them with guns, powder, lead, etc. They only are to help build the fort, and defend it in case of necessity.[2]

The notice seemed to be addressed to James Bridger personally. He needed no time to think it over, having already done that many times. His application for enlistment needed no further recommendation: he was strong, agile, unattached, blacksmith's helper, some experience with guns, traps, boats, and horses. Though of the mini-

[1] Chittenden, *Fur Trade*, I, 247.
[2] Dale L. Morgan, *Jedediah Smith, and the Opening of the West*, 28, 29.

mum age, he had some of the skills of an older man. Subsequent references to Bridger's gun lead us to believe he acquired his precious Hawken before he left St. Louis—a personally selected and fitted firearm.

An attempt was made by the leaders to form the applicants into classes, under competent instructors, for screening in regard to capabilities. There was evidence, however, that sheer eagerness for adventure was being offered in lieu of the desired military obedience, leaning, and ability which Major Henry knew were essentials. Consequently the "one hundred young men" mentioned in the advertisement were quietly increased to nearly twice that number.

Years afterward Bridger reflected on that enlistment, which he hoped might bring money to aid his sister.[3] Thus we would like to believe that she and her guardian Auntie shared the going-away arrangements with the Creamers, and that they saw him gleaming in the new buckskin suit the Creamers gave him.

Mr. Creamer seemed glad to give his blessing to the enlistment. Weren't leading families risking their substance and their sons in the fur trade? Referring specifically to the Ashley-Henry enlistees, the St. Louis *Enquirer* said a few days later: "The party is composed entirely of young men, many of whom have relinquished the most respectable employments and circles of society for this arduous but truly meritorious undertaking."[4] As on many another occasion, James Bridger faced the future alone—manfully and unafraid.

Near the end of March, 1822, two sleek keelboats, fresh from the Pittsburgh builders and worth $3,500 apiece, were berthed at a St. Louis wharf for the Ashley-Henry firm. Surprisingly long, sixty-five feet, each boat was about the combined length of three ordinary covered wagons plus teams, and was nearly twice the width of a wagon (fifteen feet). The cargo and cabin superstructures were nearly six feet high; and the indicated loading capacity, when drawing the recommended twenty-five to thirty inches of water, was twenty-five tons, equal to that of an entire train of wagons.[5] Major

[3] Bridger's sister and the guardian aunt may have returned east, before young Bridger went west; there is no record.

[4] Donald McKay Frost, "Notes on General Ashley," *Proceedings of the American Antiquarian Society*, 1945, pp. 68, 69.

[5] Wm. H. Ashley, "Diary and Accounts, 1825" (ed. by Dale L. Morgan), *Bulletin of the Missouri Historical Society*, (October 1954, January and April, 1955). In-

Henry's keelboat was the proper place for James Bridger's beloved canoe. It would serve as a mascot, useful to nearly everybody. But how soon it was to be left behind, like his shop friends and his memories!

On departure day only Henry's boat was ready. On April 3, 1822, the Major spread his ten-foot-square sail from the twenty-foot mast, more to celebrate than to aid; but a brisk south wind had set in, which gave the craft a boost, though presaging inclement weather.[6]

A keelboat was propelled much as a canalboat was drawn, but by men instead of horses. The task was tedious, chiefly as brush, trees, rocks, mud, shallow water, lofty banks, or no banks at all might interfere. Ordinarily a dozen or fifteen men on the cordelle rope would cover eight to twelve miles a day in poor to average shore conditions. They usually halted and sought shelter in pouring rains, and they always laid by at night. (On this voyage of about four months, ten or fifteen days were literally washed off the calendar by rain.)

Only small game, such as squirrels and turkeys, usually fell before the hunters' guns, although an occasional bear, deer, or elk was encountered. The best and most plentiful source of protein, which most of the men seldom got afterward, was bullhead catfish, weighing from fifteen to fifty pounds apiece, found lazying in the quieter side streams of the lower Missouri.

The town of Franklin had branch stores of Chouteau, Carondelet, Pratte, and other St. Louis firms. The *Intelligencer* noticed the

voices include: fusils, muskets, pistols, rifles, flints, fire-steels, gunlocks and other parts, powder, horns, lead, bullets, molds, pouches; butcher, hunting, and jackknives, whetstones, fish hooks, lines; steel traps, trap springs, pack and riding saddles, surcingles, bridles, halters, cordage, spurs, picket pins; axes, adzes, awls, chisels, files, hammers, saws, vises, hatchets, tomahawks, draw knives, gimlets, shovels; pans, cups, kettles, strap iron, tool handles, and pencils.

Jackets, shirts, trousers, belts, buckles, shoes, blankets, hats, caps, breechcloths, handkerchiefs, buttons, thread, needles, twine, combs, razors, scissors, pipes, coffee, sugar, salt, pepper, bacon, ham, flour, meal, rice, beans, raisins, dessicated apples, and other fruit; medicine, tobacco, rum, spirits, oars, nails, pitch, tar, soap, candles, canvas, cloth of brilliant colors; cotton, wool, ribbons, mirrors, metal rings for fingers, wrists, ears, hair, and neck; brass wire and beads.

[6] Boatmen were learning the river at its worst; its roughest water is in the Ozark Hills, and the highest water comes in spring. Modern surveys show the average stream gradient is one-third steeper below Council Bluffs than above, although the Bluffs are only 40 per cent of the way.

passing of the party on April 27, 1822, in its April 30 issue. A wagon road, well worn to St. Louis, had just been opened on to Council Bluffs. Nearby Boone's Lick, across the river, was consolidating its transient population with Franklin. The Daniel Boone family had worked the salt springs there for fifteen years. Farther upstream was a little-used ferry at Arrow Rock and the old Indian trading post (1813–14) of George C. Sibley.

As the party progressed upriver toward the fur country, their encounters with returning river craft, bound for St. Louis, became more frequent. The type of boat and its occupants mattered not at all to the news-hungry men. Each meeting, whether with a lone, furtive man in a canoe or with a flatboat full of furs and jubilant crew, became an occasion for a friendly interchange of information, if not for an overnight celebration. On one of these occasions, a member of Henry's crew, coming upon a homebound acquaintance, chose to return to St. Louis.

Fort Osage was a commanding site, forty miles below the Kansas River on an outer elbow of the stream. Two cannons guarded its bastions. Since 1808 it had been a United States government factory or Indian trading post. Now that it had been ordered closed, its fortunes like its personnel were at a low ebb. Stragglers from the Osage Indian village still loitered about the premises. The young Osage women were clearly interested in the young trappers, but even to men who had not shaved for a month, the Indian women seemed slovenly, untidy, and soiled. Their gargling, throaty conversation did not add to their charm. Obviously the visitors at the wharf, not the Indians on shore, were the featured actors in the scene.

The Kansas River was a popular artery, but the Platte River was a more notable landmark, near the middle of the upriver voyage. It was the Equatorial Zone, usually calling for a hazing, feasting ceremony to initiate the novices, like James' Bridger, who had not been there before. How would a diffident subject such as Bridger respond to such ardent pranksters? They would need his type later.

The ceremony was scarcely out of mind when the keelboat eased up at Fort Atkinson's substantial wharf, May 1, 1822 (ten miles north of Omaha). Representatives of the five-hundred-man garrison welcomed the guests, while scattered Indians stood at "inattention." The cantonment, within a substantial, close-set palisade 520 feet square, consisted of log-and-lumber houses with board floors, shingle roofs, brick chimneys, and a dozen cannons in ominous positions.

Homesickness was contagious. A half-dozen of Henry's men joined up with a small body of soldiers whose enlistments were expiring to seek passage by boat to St. Louis. One or two soldiers reenlisted with Henry, to proceed upriver.

Touring Fort Atkinson shortly afterward, Prince Paul Wilhelm mentions a gristmill and a sawmill, driven by oxen on a treadmill, a gunsmith's smithy, and a Council House about fifty feet in length, where the Indian agent negotiated with Indian deputations.[7]

"Here," says the Prince, "I found Mr. O'Fallon hearing the case of a party of half-breeds and Iroquois Indians, hunters from Montreal . . . . They had started for the sources of the Saskatchewan for beaver trapping.

"As long as they hunted in British territory, everything went well enough. When they crossed into the United States they were attacked by the Crow and Cheyenne Indians. In addition to having several of their number killed, they had to leave some of their women and girls in the lurch. In order to have these women returned to them, the Iroquois and hunters had undertaken the extremely dangerous march to Fort Atkinson at the Council Bluffs."

[7] Prince Paul Wilhelm, *First Journey to North America.*

4 ᘒ THE INDIAN COUNTRY

THE THIRD DAY out of Fort Atkinson young Bridger would have seen Blackbird Hill up ahead. Located within a bend of the Missouri, the hill still seemed nearby after thirty miles of river run. The Indians regarded it with superstitious awe as the mausoleum of Omaha Chief Blackbird, who died of smallpox in 1800. He is said to have correctly prophesied the death of several men he didn't like by the secret aid of arsenic and a trader's formula. He directed that he be interred on this bluff, three hundred feet above the river, sitting astride his horse. From that vantage point he could view the procession of travelers ascending the Missouri River—his idea of a ringside seat. (Chief Blackbird's grandiose plan for "watching the world go by" was ironically reversed in 1832 when his skull was transported, for display, to the National Museum in Washington, D.C.)[1]

Across the river and upward a day's travel was to be seen a knoll similar to Blackbird Hill and containing the mausoleum of Sergeant Charles Floyd. Floyd, who died August 20, 1804, was the only fatality in the Lewis and Clark Expedition.

About a month from Fort Atkinson, the adventurers reached Cedar Fort, or Fort Recovery (near Chamberlain, South Dakota). The country in this area, being dry, afforded little game, while the early excitement of being on the river disappeared as fellow travelers became few and far between. Major Henry was unable either to provide more food for the men or to find some means of improving their morale. D. T. Potts, in his only reference to this phase of the journey, says that he and eight others deserted here, blaming the shortage of food.[2]

[1] George Catlin, *The George Catlin Indian Gallery*, (ed. by Thomas Donaldson), 263.

[2] D. T. Potts, with his meager notes on important matters and his important notes

18

With a reduced burden of grumblers Henry pushed ahead, halting only to purchase horses of the roaming Sioux, Arikara, and Mandan Indians. The men refreshed themselves on the wild berries then ripening in the region.

Young Bridger noticed with eager curiosity that the individual of greatest importance appeared to be the Indian, half-blood, or squawman serving as interpreter or spokesman. This person, necessary to both parties, was master of ceremonies.

By reputation the Arikaras were the "yellow-jackets" of the upper Missouri, without staunch friends or allies chiefly because they were usually belligerent and faithless. The young women were comely, if not seductive on occasion, but the Arikara lodges were like "potato storage holes," says Clyman.

The Mandan villages had been historic meeting grounds for generations. Their hospitality caused the Mandans to be known as the "good neighbors" of the upper Missouri. They offered to the stranger soft, warm beds fitted on comfortable bed frames in improved circular clay hovels. Corn, beans, squash, and pumpkins abounded in their fields and the short, rotund women made good wives, mothers, and housekeepers.

From time immemorial one or more influential white men or half-bloods had resided among the Mandans and had usually risen to the importance of sub-chief or assistant village manager.

Major Henry's party proceeded west from the Mandan villages in two groups, one aboard the keelboat and one on land. The land party was surprised by a roaming band of Assiniboines and, as the men aboard the keelboat were involved in negotiating a long river bend and unable to come to the rescue, the Indians made off with thirty-five horses. The loss rendered impractical Major Henry's design of reaching the Three Forks for an autumn hunt. Moreover, he had no word of Ashley's expected progress upriver behind him.

Arriving at the mouth of the Yellowstone River in late August, 1822, Henry set his men to work constructing a shelter on the wedge of land between the rivers, about a mile above the confluence. Four

on meager matters, becomes one of the most valued sources of fur trapper travels. Potts's letters to his brother were collected and identified by Donald McKay Frost for his splendid compilation "Notes on General Ashley, the Overland trail, and South pass," *Proceedings of the American Antiquarian Society*, 1945 (hereafter referred to as "Notes on General Ashley").

small log huts at the corners of a square were connected by an enclosing palisade.

Joshua Pilcher, of the Missouri Fur Company, still used the post at the mouth of the Big Horn. His St. Louis office, alert to the threat posed by new competition, had kept him informed of the progress of the Ashley-Henry enterprises. Pilcher had also visited briefly with Major Henry on the way up in May. He thus knew that Henry was to erect a depot at the mouth of the Yellowstone, and that he was being drawn upriver by memories of rich furs in the Three Forks country.

Pilcher's daring strategy was soon apparent. A fresh trapping party was being dispatched to the Big Horn post under Michael E. Immel and Robert Jones. They would spend the winter there, and early in 1823 would make a cross-country dash to the Three Forks, ahead of Henry, having only about half as far to travel as Major Henry, who would also be traveling much nearer the hostile Blackfeet. In this somewhat strained atmosphere Immel and Jones, themselves, made a quick courtesy call on Major Henry on their way to the Big Horn post. To James Bridger and other hands, this rivalry was more than a simple card game. To them a career was involved, a livelihood.

Back in St. Louis General Ashley had received a supply of guns from the Mexican Southwest and dispatched the second keelboat on May 8, 1822, only to plunge it into disaster. Near the present Lexington an overhanging limb fouled the mast, turning the boat broadside to the current, thus capsizing the craft and losing its $10,000 cargo. But in three weeks the invincible Ashley had another boat loaded and on the way, himself in command of a crew of forty-six.

Though he little suspected it, the General chanced to recruit three men whose diaries and letters have been a great satisfaction to students of fur trappers' travel and activity. Jedediah S. Smith got his baptism at the sinking of the keelboat, of which only he has given an eyewitness report. His pride in being employed by Ashley as a "hunter" may explain some of Smith's aloofness toward the junior partner, Major Henry. As a hunter he would "avoid the dull monotony of following along the bank of the river entirely dependent on the motions of the boat," he wrote.[3]

[3] Maurice S. Sullivan, *The Travels of Jedediah S. Smith*, 2, 3.

D. T. Potts is another writing man who was out-talked by the enthusiastic Ashley and re-enlisted at Fort Atkinson. James Clyman's brief and intermittent diary is by far the most colorful narrative if the subject was one that interested him.

On the way upriver, General Ashley presided impressively at a horse-trading peace parley with the Arikaras on September 8, 1822; he noted the early migration of the buffalo from Canada to improve his larder, and splashed into the new landing above the Yellowstone about October 1, 1822. "After furnishing the mountain parties with their supplies of goods, and receiving the furs of the last hunt," Smith informs us, "General Ashley started for St. Louis with a large pirogue," laden with the precious first fruits of the Ashley-Henry enterprises.

About the same time, Captain Perkins, of the Missouri Fur Company, went sailing by from the Big Horn post with twenty-eight packs of furs, worth $14,000 in St. Louis. A second consignment of twenty packs, worth $10,000, was following. Ashley and Perkins would reach St. Louis in about four weeks.

MAJOR HENRY, with twenty-one men traveling in a boat and a canoe (presumably Bridger's), was ascending the Missouri at least as far as Milk River in search of a winter encampment nearer the Three Forks, and having ample forage for their animals. With the extra herds of migrating buffalo filling the valleys, this would be a problem.

"Mr. Chapman and myself went with a small party of men up the Yellowstone a short distance for the purpose of procuring a supply of meat for the Fort, and such skins as were wanted for the use of the Company," Smith says. Another party, most likely led by John H. Weber,[1] also went up the Yellowstone, expecting to reach Powder River "and [go] up it as far as practicable" before returning. "We returned to the Fort. . . . Mr. Chapman and myself with a party . . . ascended the Missouri. . . . On our way we met Major Henry on his return. . . . We continued our journey up the river. . . . About the first of November we arrived at the mouth of the Musselshell."[2]

The Musselshell is about the same distance from Three Forks as the mouth of the Big Horn. At the Musselshell camp sweet cottonwood was sufficient for the horses. Smith joined Potts and a dozen others in erecting huts for the winter and subsisting themselves and their animals.

If the winter days dragged for the Major, it was due to his im-

---

[1] This conclusion is based on the biographical sketches of John H. Weber, in the *Salt Lake Tribune,* July 4, 1897, and in Charles L. Camp's essay "The D.T.P. Letters," in *Essays for Henry R. Wagner* (San Francisco, 1947). Weber was one of the oldest (about forty-three), most faithful, and dependable of the Ashley-Henry fur men. He was on his way to the Wasatch Mountains, Utah, and to the Wasatch stream, which, since his visit, has borne his name, and since James Bridger, in the same party, discovered Great Salt Lake.

[2] Sullivan, *Jedediah S. Smith,* 8, 9.

patience to reach the cross-roads of the beaver country at Three Forks. Since he was driven out in 1810, only Hudson's Bay Company and North West Company hunters were allowed to visit the place. The Blackfoot homelands were to the north of the Missouri, extending into Canada. Consequently there were disquieting rumors of an affiliation between the Blackfeet and the British.

The winter was severe, the weather observers at the Musselshell reporting the river frozen strong enough to support the herds of buffalo; Potts says the ice was four feet thick, and did not go out until April 4, 1823.

James Bridger, under Major Henry's tutelage, was to become a stronger man in the organization from that winter. Adaptable, given more to thinking than talking, always obedient to authority, he kept close to the Major and other leaders for such schooling as experience had to offer. They taught him the first rudiments of dealing with Indians, earning the good will of visiting tribesmen and getting rid of a lingering guest, while earning his respect, by foiling his theft of a mount for the ride home.

Major Henry and party reached the Musselshell camp about the first of April, 1823. There they found several men preferring desertion to facing the Blackfeet. Expediency and hindsight would include among the pikers the now celebrated Mike Fink and his companions, Carpenter and Talbot, as we shall see.

Only eleven men accompanied Major Henry out of the Musselshell encampment on April 6, 1823. The defecting remainder agreed to trap the Musselshell and wend their way down to Fort Henry. In alloting the horses and baggage, Potts and a small band drew canoes and an assignment to work the Judith and nearby streams. Potts tells us that while disembarking at the Judith, "I was severely wounded through both knees by an accidental discharge of a rifle, whereby I was obliged to be conducted to our establishment at the mouth of the Yellowstone [Fort Henry]."[3]

With our scribe thus gone from the scene, only a dribble of ghastly fact remains, picked out of subsequent casualty reports.

A short distance above the Great Falls of the Missouri, near the mouth of Smith's River, Major Henry's unit, including James

[3] Frost, "Notes on General Ashley," 60.

Bridger, was precipitately attacked by a horde of angry Blackfeet. In swift and deadly wheeling fire, they fled as suddenly as they came. Four of Henry's men were left dead; a few were wounded; and some of the rest, not surprisingly, had sudden severe symptoms of homesickness.

After burying the dead and administering to the wounded, Major Henry spirited his men carefully away from the hornet's nest and arrived at Fort Henry about the middle of May, 1823. Henry learned later that before he and his disappointed crew reached the fort, a war party of Blackfeet, possibly including some of the same men who fought Henry, attacked and killed the Immel-Jones party returning from Three Forks.[4]

[4] This attack occurred at or near the present Bridger Creek, Custer National Forest, and seems to have been identified by Bridger himself. In Mrs. Carrington's description of Bridger's route to Virginia City (*Ab-Sa-Ra-Ka*, 256), she calls it Emmil's Fork, "named from the massacre of Emmil's [Immel's] party in 1823."

From the painting by George Caleb Bingham in John Francis McDermott, George Caleb Bingham: River Portraitist

Fur traders descending the Missouri. For more than two centuries the fur trader was the most romantic figure in North America.

A mackinaw boat with cordelle, a type of vessel often used in the fur trade.

6 ᘓ⃗ ARIKARAS ATTACK ASHLEY

AT THE SO-CALLED Fort Henry in May, 1823, Major Henry dispatched Jedediah S. Smith down the Missouri with the furs on hand. Smith was to meet General Ashley and apprise him of the need for horses and of the disastrous opposition of the Blackfeet.

Abruptly turning the tables, however, Smith and a companion came racing back to Major Henry about the middle of June, not with the horses needed but with the startling news of General Ashley's own fight with the Arikaras (Smith participating), and requesting every possible aid with all possible speed.

The entire complement of Henry's able men was promptly drafted for the voyage, Henry in command. We may visualize James Bridger carefully fondling his Hawken rifle, sighting, perhaps, at the moving targets ashore to relieve his tension. Only twenty men were left at Fort Henry, apparently in charge of John H. Weber. Some of these men were invalided, among them, D. T. Potts, Mike Fink, and his friends.[1]

Late the preceding autumn General Ashley had reached St. Louis with an appreciable cargo of beaver fur and enthusiasm. Dispatching an order to Pittsburgh for two new keelboats, he forthwith advertised in the newspapers and sent scouts on the streets for one hundred men, to be employed up the Missouri and in the Rocky Mountains as beaver hunters at two hundred dollars a year.

James Clyman says he accepted the employment and began by going "among the grog shops and other sinks of degradation" for hunters, trappers, boatmen, stewards, and others. About seventy

[1] Frost, "Notes on General Ashley," 82. Potts may have furnished the *St. Louis Republican* with news of the killing of the infamous Mike Fink. Mike had aimed too low, by design or accident, when trick-shooting a tin cup from a companion's head. As the companion fell dead, another man of Ashley's expedition "shot Fink dead on the spot."

men, with French "gumboes" as crews, shoved off March 10, 1823, "under sail when winds were favorable; by towline when not."[2]

Adventures at home: "Three men of General Ashley's expedition were conveying [about three hundred pounds of] powder in a cart to the boat, when fire was communicated to the powder by means of a [tobacco] pipe. . . . The men were blown into the air to the height of several hundred feet. . . . One of the men survived a few minutes after his descent to the ground; the others were entirely lifeless."[3]

General Ashley, in tight command of the fleet, met Jedediah S. Smith near the Arikaras on May 29, 1823, with his fresh furs and foul news. By some fast if questionable trading, the needed quota of horses was obtained from the Arikaras, and forty men (including Smith and Clyman) encamped on the sandy beach, ready to get away next morning, June 2.

But at 3:30 A.M. Ashley was awakened and informed that Aaron Stephens had been killed. Then, as Ashley related, "At sunrise the Indians commenced a heavy, well-directed fire. . . . The boatmen were panic struck. . . . In about fifteen minutes the survivors were on the keelboats dropping down stream. Most of the horses being killed . . . I ordered the boats landed, to fortify them. . . . To my surprise and mortification I was told by [most of] the men, that under no circumstances would they return. . . . I called for volunteers, and only thirty volunteered. My loss is fourteen dead and ten wounded, leaving not more than twenty-three effective men."[4]

Clyman adds that on the night of June 1 "several of our men, without permission, went and remained in the Village, among them our interpreter, Mr. [Edward] Rose. About midnight Rose came running into camp and informed us Stephens had been killed in the village, and war was declared in earnest."[5]

Clyman swam to the keelboat, weighted with pistols, bullets, and other "fixins," the pockets in his buckskin suit dipping water, his rifle held high, its muzzle in his belt. He was carried by the current

[2] *James Clyman, Frontiersman* (ed. by Charles L. Camp), 7.

[3] From the *Missouri Republican* March 19, 1823, in Frost, "Notes on General Ashley," 71.

[4] Frost, "Notes on General Ashley" (Ashley to a Gentleman), 74–77; also Ashley to O'Fallon, *ibid.*, 78–81.

[5] *James Clyman, Frontiersman*, 9.

past the keelboat, but was rescued in a hair-grab by Reed Gibson, who was mortally shot just after pulling Clyman aboard.

Landing twenty-five miles downstream, the remainder of the party collected available bodies for a mass burial. Hugh Glass's report of the event mentions the death and burial of Joseph S. Gardner and a "powerful prayer" by Mr. Smith.[6] After the funeral General Ashley dispatched Smith "express" to Major Henry, requesting assistance in demolishing the Arikara road block.

About a month later Major Henry himself, with twenty-odd men, including James Bridger, joined General Ashley at the Cheyenne River. Smith told an army officer that while coming downstream, they disregarded the Arikara signal of friendship and a desire to trade (made with a buffalo robe). Naturally Henry distrusted them.

General Ashley had modestly underrated his plight in his appeals to government officials, and while proceeding in grim desperation with plans to ascend the river on his own resources, he received the news that a scathing speech by O'Fallon to Ashley's deserters had resulted in a score of re-enlistments.

News of Ashley's defeat reached Colonel Leavenworth at Fort Atkinson, June 18, 1823. About the same time, an "express" from the upper river reached him, reporting the disaster to Immel and Jones. The Colonel was thus doubly convinced; the Arikaras needed a sound thrashing.

He made ready at once, setting out June 22, 1823, by land and water with 220 officers and men, equipped with cannon, shoulder guns, and ammunition. Joshua Pilcher, of the Missouri Fur Company, eager to participate, followed with 40 men and about 700 Sioux Indians at war with the Arikaras. All were commanded by Henry Vanderburg and Moses B. Carson.

[6] John G. Neihardt, *The Splendid Wayfaring*, 240.

AS AN UNNOTICED PRIVATE in an improvised army, James Bridger helped to stop the Arikara advance when the weary Sioux withdrew to eat; and Bridger did it on an empty stomach. He later saw the Arikaras gesture for peace, and he saw the Indians flee from their flaming village at nightfall. But Bridger's particular part has not been specified.

One of Colonel Leavenworth's keelboats was snagged and sunk near Fort Vermillion, July 3. Seven men were drowned in the accident, and considerable quantities of provisions, ammunition, and equipment were lost. General Ashley and party joined Colonel Leavenworth's forces at the Teton (Bad) River about July 30, 1823.

The Colonel was pleased to approve the organization already achieved by Ashley and Henry: Hiram Scott and Jedediah S. Smith, captains; Allen and Jackson, lieutenants; Cunningham and Edward Rose, ensigns; Fleming, surgeon; Thomas Fitzpatrick, quartermaster; and William L. Sublette, sergeant-major; supported by young James Bridger and other privates in the ranks. For them it was a thrilling moment for contemplation, their initiation into Indian warfare on a grand scale.

Completing the socalled "Missouri Legion," Colonel Leavenworth bestowed on Mr. Pilcher the everlasting title of "major," making Vanderburgh and McDonald captains and Carson and Gordon lieutenants. They all disembarked a few miles below the Arikara towns on August 8 (seven miles above Grand River).[1]

From here we follow Colonel Leavenworth's official report, written at Fort Atkinson, August 30, 1823.[2]

[1] Chittenden, *Fur Trade*, 591.
[2] Frost, "Notes on General Ashley," 98–102.

We arrived before the Arikara towns on the 9th. The Sioux Indians met the Arikaras a half mile from their towns for a skirmish. The Arikaras drove the Sioux back until the regular troops, and General Ashley's men, arrived and formed their line. The Arikaras were immediately driven into their towns.[3]

The Sioux meanwhile were gathering and carrying off the Arikara corn. . . . The troops were ordered to form, for the purpose of collecting corn for their own use, as General Ashley's men had been destitute of provisions for two days.

At this time a party of Sioux and a party of Arikaras both on horseback, were discovered holding a parley on the hill beyond the upper town . . . . The Sioux were going off . . . . The Arikaras came and begged for peace. They said that the first shot from our cannon killed the celebrated Chief called "Grey Eyes," who caused all the mischief; and we had killed a great many of their people and horses. . . .

Supposing that the Government would be better pleased to have Indians *corrected* than *exterminated* . . . it was thought best to listen to the solicitations of the Arikaras for peace. . . . Our men were frequenting the town for the purpose of trading for moccasins, etc. . . . I sent word to Little Soldier that I would not attack them. Early on the morning of the 13th we found the Arikaras had left their towns during the night. . . .

It was now evident that our artillery had been served with very great effect. The towns had been completely riddled. It is supposed that more than fifty Arikaras were killed, and a great number wounded. . . . On the morning of the 14th, we placed the mother of the late Chief Grey Eyes (An aged and infirm woman, whom they left in their flight), in one of the principal lodges, gave her plenty of provisions and water and left her in the quiet possession of the towns.

About ten o'clock on the evening of the 15th the troops were embarked to descend the river, and our guard withdrawn. All the boats were got under way nearly at the same time. Before we were out of sight of the towns, we had the mortification to discover them to be on fire. There is no doubt but that they have been consumed to ashes; nor is there any doubt but that they were set on fire by one M'Donald,

---

[3] Chittenden, *Fur Trade*, 687. The Colonel wrote on October 20, 1823: "I had not found any one willing to go into those villages, except a man by the name of Rose. . . . He had resided for about three years with them . . . but was with General Ashley when Ashley was attacked. . . . The Indians at that time called to him [Rose] to take care of himself, before they fired upon General Ashley's party."

a partner, and one Gordon, a clerk, of the Missouri Fur Company. . . .

We sustained no loss in men, and had two wounded. . . . I have been highly gratified . . . with General Ashley and his command, and intend to do myself the honor to make a more detailed and circumstantial account of what was done by each.

Colonel Leavenworth skated warily over the thin ice of the peace conference of August 10–11. It was during those parleys the disgusted Sioux, in full-chested contempt for their lagging White allies, were making off with seven of the trappers' horses, and six army mules! That the Indians considered Pilcher to be in command was, according to Pilcher, the reason for Leavenworth's enmity toward him.

On Joshua's "Long Day" of August 15, 1823, the Colonel composed a couple of documents that may properly go here:

> August 15, 1823, On Board Keelboat No. 1, Below the Arikara towns, headquarters 6th Regiment. The Colonel commanding will not further cooperate or receive the services of any of the Missouri Fur Company; they were pledged by their agent and acting partner to obey orders. The Colonel commanding is extremely mortified to say that he has too much reason to believe that the Arikara towns have been set on fire by that Company, contrary to the most positive orders; with such men we have no further intercourse. Signed:
>
> H. Leavenworth

> August 15, 1823, Arikara Towns, Mr. Pilcher, Sir: The Sioux Indians, for whom you are subagent, have taken six mules belonging to the United States. I have to request that you will be pleased to take measures to have them returned.
>
> Resp. H. Leavenworth[4]

"Major" Pilcher's public letter to Colonel Leavenworth, dated August 26, 1823, from Fort Recovery (Cedar Fort),[5] completes the record of the ugly Arikara affair, which to this day rates as one of the West's worst Indian fights of the fur trading era:

> After my having declined any participation in your proposed treaty

[4] Frost, "Notes on General Ashley," 104, 105, 108.
[5] *Ibid.*, 104–14.

with the Arikaras, you seemed determined on support from some one, and called on Major Henry, in my presence, who most positively refused even his opinion or advice upon the subject. . . .

As to the burning of the Arikara towns: The guarding of a few miserable, smoky cells of iniquity, inhabited by one old squaw, one chicken cock, about 40 or 50 Indian dogs, and containing a few willow baskets and some corn caches, are objects well worthy of your genius. The Arikara fortifications were such as schoolboys make and call them play houses. These huts are fortified with pieces of driftwood, poles of different sizes, brush, willows, etc. Here for the first time you met Little Soldier; the affectionate manner in which you embraced him done credit to the goodness of your heart. The negotiations appeared to be carried on principally through a celebrated outlaw (who left this country in chains some ten years since) by the name of Rose, and Little Soldier.

After two days labor a treaty was signed. . . . I immediately informed you that neither of the principal chiefs of the nation had signed it. You did not condescend to notice the information I gave you.

You called on me to attend a council; we met, and you suggested the propriety of postponing the charge until morning for the purpose of giving Little Soldier an opportunity of getting his family out of the village; and also the probability of having many wounded in the charge; and if so, that it would be difficult to dress their wounds after night.

It was my object and my aim to make my decision evasive; to leave it to your discretion; to the inexpressible astonishment of all, you abruptly concluded with these remarks:

"The Little Soldier has used every effort to induce his people to comply with the treaty; he is unable to make good the property; and I have therefore determined to abandon the charge." Rest assured, sir, that you have left things in a state ten times worse than you found them. You came to restore peace and tranquility to the country, and leave an impression which would insure its continuance.

Your operations have been such as to produce the contrary effect, and to impress the different Indian tribes, with the greatest possible contempt for the American character. You came (to use your own language) to open and make good this great road; instead of which, you have, by the imbecility of your conduct and operations created and left impassible barriers. I am Sir, not as I was once and ever wished to be, your friend and humble servant, but quite the reverse.

31

In later missives Pilcher adds: "I will do all in my power to obtain the mules." And: "The jealousy and suspicion rose in your breast when you detected the best Sioux interpreter on the continent, of telling the Sioux that: 'Pilcher is the big chief of the expedition.'"

8 ❧ INTO THE WILDERNESS

ALWAYS A GENTLEMAN, General Ashley did not take sides with the critics of the army in the Arikara debacle. But to Ashley the fur trader one fact was obvious, as he wrote on the seventh of June, 1823: "If our government does not send troops on this river as high as the mouth of the Yellowstone, or above that place, the Americans must abandon the trade in this country. The Indians are becoming more formidable every year."[1]

The sinking of his own and a government keelboat were redoubtable deterrents. Surely these hazards pointed to a less concentrated mode of transportation than a keelboat, which puts so many precious eggs in one basket.

Besides this, Major Henry had twice tested the temper of the Blackfeet, and the survivors of the Immel-Jones massacre had reported the Three Forks trapped out. Henry's own winter of 1810–11, on Henry's Fork of Snake River, and his most probable exit by way of Jackson Hole and the Big Horn River certainly introduced him to other beaver regions comparable to the Three Forks.

These were all matters for executive discussion in the last days General Ashley and Major Henry were together. The parting conference between them at Fort Kiowa (Fort Lookout), attended or shared by Clyman, Bridger, Fitzpatrick, Smith, Sublette, and others, built up intriguing prospects. Necessity was driving them into a new fur-bearing world, preferably a more negotiable distance from St. Louis. Although one of the younger members of the party, James Bridger could sense the challenge.

General Ashley was soon off to St. Louis, freighted with the new company's frustrations. Major Henry gathered his party of twelve

[1] Frost, "Notes on General Ashley," 77.

or fifteen men,[2] including Johnson Gardner, Daniel S. D. Moore, Moses (Black) Harris, Milton Sublette, Hugh Glass, and James Bridger, and left Fort Kiowa in late August, 1823. Jedediah S. Smith, Thomas Fitzpatrick, James Clyman, William L. Sublette, and others, guided by Edward Rose, would scour the local countryside for more horses and proceed due westward to winter with the Crows.

Henry's party obtained only enough horses to carry the baggage; but by cautious travel they expected to reach the Yellowstone post 350 miles distant, in ten or twelve days. On the way up, while yet below the Mandan Villages, the trappers were mistaken for enemies by a roving war party of Mandans. They killed two trappers (James Anderson and Auguste Neill), wounded two more, and got two horses, losing only one warrior to the whites.[3]

The dispirited trappers met a further delay when Hugh Glass was mauled by a bear, leaving him a hero, though not a cripple.[4] After turning up Grand River to avoid the Arikaras, Allen and a comrade preceded the party to kill meat. Allen explained later to Yount:

> Glass, as was usual, could not be kept in obedience to orders, with the band, but persevered to thread his way, alone, through the bushes and chaparral. As the two hunters were wending their way up the river, Allen discovered Glass, dodging along in the forest alone,[5] and said to his companion "There, look at that fellow, Glass; see him foolishly exposing his life. I wish some grizzly bear would pounce upon him, and teach him a lesson of obedience to orders, and to keep his place. He is ever off, scouting in the bushes, and exposing himself to dangers.
>
> Glass disappeared in the chaparral, and within half an hour his screams were heard. The two hunters hastened to his relief and discovered a huge grizzly bear with two cubs. . . .[6] The whole party were soon there; the monster and her cubs were slain, and the victim cared for in the best degree possible.
>
> A convenient hand litter was prepared and the sufferer carried by

[2] *James Clyman, Frontiersman,* 15.
[3] Frost, "Notes on General Ashley," 127–29.
[4] Examined in the next chapter; only firsthand witnesses, other than Glass, are heard here.
[5] The only forests on Grand River watershed are fifty miles above the Forks.
[6] Hugh's injuries are reviewed in the next chapter.

his humane fellow trappers, from day to day. . . . Day by day they ministered to his wants. After having thus carried Glass [six *is crossed out*] several days[7] it became necessary for the party to crowd their journey.[8]

The bear fight occurred after the entire party turned up Grand River; consequently they must have been traveling up North Fork when the detachment with Glass readied itself to proceed west to the previously planned Powder River rendezvous. Using this route, they would avoid driving the pack horses and conveying Glass the long way around. The distance by direct travel to the mouth of Powder River was less than half the distance Major Henry would travel by way of the mouth of the Yellowstone River. The detached party, with Glass and the luggage, would, of course, not retrace their steps to Fort Kiowa, but would push forward, carrying Glass by travois or litter as necessary and convenient.

On reaching the Yellowstone post, Henry received from Captain John H. Weber the unwelcome news that, owing to the reduced quota of horse guards, about thirty horses had been lost in recent Indian raids Henry thereupon decided to abandon the place. He grimly loaded every piece of property on the boat and set the men to towing it up the Yellowstone, perhaps attempting to evade further acts of a plaguing Nemesis.

Awaiting Major Henry at the mouth of Powder River were Smith's men with a few furs, a Crow Indian village with horses to trade, and the pack horse detachment with Hugh Glass, signifying a busy week end. Glass would accompany Henry to the Big Horn by boat for the winter; and Moses (Black) Harris, with Fitzgerald and another man named Harris, would depart at once for St. Louis by pirogue with the mail and twenty-eight fur packs.

Most momentous of all, Captain John H. Weber and party, impatient for action, were the first to depart up Powder River for the pressing business of fur trapping. With Weber were D. T. Potts and James Bridger, as well as forty-seven newly acquired Crow horses.

[7] Edmund Flagg, "History of a Western Trapper," in the *Literary News-Letter*, September 7, 1839. Flagg says Hugh was carried on a litter for three days. Hereafter referred to as Flagg, "History of a Western Trapper."
[8] George C. Yount, *Chronicles of George C. Yount* (ed. by Charles L. Camp), 26.

Longest to linger and last to leave, Major Henry ascended Wolf Rapids, near Powder River (which had stalled first arrivals), by the simple expedient of crossing to the left bank of the Yellowstone with his cordelles. After a fortnight of towing, his party settled itself at the Big Horn.

The site had several bleak aspects; Henry's winter cantonment was to be about the fourth to rise there and . . . quickly fade away, the first having been Fort Manuel in 1807. These forts stood on the rocky promontory southwest of the confluence. Henry, himself, had wintered there in 1809–10, prior to his disastrous defeat at Three Forks, and he sojourned there on his way out in 1811. Now there were other problems and an entirely new post to be erected, this one two miles below the Big Horn.

Hugh Glass was hardly happy at the Big Horn. Convalescing from injuries attributable at least in part to his own delinquencies, he did not fraternize as freely as usual with other trappers, but he seemed to be moodily incubating his plan for the future.

It happened, a few weeks after the bear attacked Hugh, that Jedediah S. Smith was frightfully mauled and lacerated by a grizzly not so very far away, according to Clyman. Three ribs were broken, his scalp slitted entirely across the head, and an ear torn off.[9]

Thus the honors for heroics must have fluctuated that winter. In one camp Jedediah had surgical stitches and scars to exhibit, while in the other (and trappers did visit) Hugh had to wrestle with his self-esteem. It was Hugh's last season with the Ashley-Henry concern, although it wasn't his injury that caused him to leave. Moreover, both Hugh and Henry left the Big Horn post in 1824, but not together.[10]

Some of Hugh's best friends have characterized him: "In point of adventure, dangers and narrow escapes; and capacity for endurance,

---

[9] *James Clyman, Frontiersman,* 18.

[10] An unidentified "Mr. Vásquez" offers this somewhat garbled account: that Glass was killed by Arikaras on the Platte (although the Arikaras, according to Harris, were still in Dakota); that a "Mr. Wheeler" was killed by a bear (an obvious transposition of names, or a misunderstanding, inadvertent or intentional); that Smith "had crossed the mountains," rather than "intended to cross the mountains." "Vásquez" gave only the surnames of the other men, none of whom were ever actually identified except by this misinforming canard. "Vásquez's" report appears in Frost, "Notes on General Ashley," 132.

and the sufferings which befell him, this man [Hugh Glass] was pre-eminent. He was bold, daring, reckless and eccentric to a high degree; but was, nevertheless, a man of great talents, and intellectual as well as bodily power."[11]

They add: "Hugh had a 'passion for traveling alone. . . . He would never encamp with his fellows, but always miles distant, roaming solitary, and sleeping in silent loneliness,' often not being seen for many weeks."

Hugh was celebrated for his marvellous repertoire of personal adventures, including superhuman exploits, captures and punishments, death sentences, Providential help, and escapes. No account of him is without them and some accounts are replete with them, but all of them duly authenticated—by Hugh Glass![12]

Hugh learned by button-holing tenderfeet which subjects were of most interest—and about how far a narrator could go in describing them. In this manner, during his recovery from the bear fight, Hugh undoubtedly contributed a share of hope, courage, and good cheer; if he did not, in this form of delirium, concoct the West's most famous bear story.

11 Yount, *Chronicles*, 29–31.
12 *Ibid.*, 25–32.

HUGH GLASS has been kited to a questionable fame as the party of the worst part in a grizzly bear fight, and certain modern versions of the tradition have implied that James Bridger was one of the victim's unfaithful caretakers. A critical examination of the legend is therefore due.

There was only one contemporary account of the bear fight, in James Clyman's journal near the end of September, 1823, at Fort Kiowa, South Dakota. Reviewing other news from Major Henry's group, Clyman continues:[1]

"Amongst this party was a Mr. Hugh Glass, who could not be restrained and kept under subordination. He went off the line of March one afternoon and met a large grizzly bear, which he shot and wounded. The bear, as is usual, attacked Glass. He attempted to climb a tree but the bear caught him and hauled him to the ground, tearing and lacerating his body in fearful rate.

"By this time several men were in close gunshot, but could not shoot for fear of hitting Glass. At length the bear appeared to be satisfied and turned to leave, when two or three men fired. The bear turned immediately on Glass and gave him a second mutilation. On turning again, several more men shot him, when for the third time he pounced on Glass, and fell dead over his body. This I have from information, not being present. Here I leave Glass for the present." Clyman did not refer to the affair again.

The second written version of the story is by an anonymous contributor to the *Philadelphia Port Folio*.[2] He picked up Hugh's well-bandied tale during the summer of 1824, and published it as "The Missouri Trapper," in March, 1825. As it was a dramatized feature,

[1] *James Clyman, Frontiersman,* 15.
[2] "The Missouri Trapper," *Port Folio,* March, 1825, pp. 214–19.

local newspapers did not use it as news, probably having already heard grogshop versions of it. The article is prefaced with this disclaimer of responsibility: "The following is his own account of himself for the last ten months of his perilous career."

The writer closes the unlikely tale by admitting he did not see or interview the adventurer, though "my informant" did. The *Port Folio* version is therefore entirely in the language of its unknown author. Careful of his own reputation, the writer slyly warns the reader that he may be accused of concocting a whopper by the use of tongue-in-cheek sentences (in quotation marks in the following condensation).

Hugh Glass "supposed some time since to have been devoured by a white bear, but more recently reported to have been slain by the Arikara Indians," while hunting on Grand River, came upon a grizzly. Before he could "set his triggers or turn to retreat, he was seized by the throat, and raised from the ground. Casting him again upon the earth, his grim adversary tore out a mouthful of the cannibal food which had excited her appetite, and retired to submit the sample to her yearling cubs."

During the bear fight "he had received several dangerous wounds. His whole body was bruised and mangled." Major Henry induced two of his party to remain until Glass should expire. They remained five days and cruelly abandoned him, taking his rifle and ammunition, and reported his death and burial.

Meanwhile Glass crawled to a spring, "where he lay ten days," subsisting on cherries and buffalo berries. He then set off for Fort Kiowa, 350 miles distant. Fortunately he got "in at the death of a buffalo calf" (by wolves). The "fatted calf" was served raw. "With indefatigable industry he continued to crawl, until he reached Fort Kiowa!"

Before his wounds were healed, he joined a party for the Yellowstone to obtain his rifle and seek vengeance. Approaching the Mandans, "Our trapper of hair breadth 'scapes' " landed for a shorter route to Tilton's Fort, whereupon the party of five was massacred by angry Arikaras. The Arikaras pursued Glass, but Mandan warriors hoisted him onto a fleet horse, miraculously brought for the purpose, and, instead of killing him as he expected, set him down unharmed at Tilton's Fort.

That same evening Glass crept out of the fort and in thirty-eight days, alone, he reached Henry's establishment. The trapper with Hugh's gun was at Fort Atkinson, and Hugh started to go there with five other men on "February 29, 1824" (a false date). Below the Black Hills on the Platte, they met a remnant of Gray Eyes's band of Arikaras, under Chief Elk's Tongue (sounds phony).

The chief professed friendship, as "Glass had once resided with this '*tonguey*' old politician during a long winter; had joined him in the chase, and smoked his pipe, and cracked many a bottle by the genial fires of his wigwam." The whites were off their guard, but Hugh noticed Indian women making off with trappers' property, and the fight was on.

Hugh's companions were all killed in this complex action, but "versed in all the arts of border warfare, our adventurer was enabled to practise them in the present crisis, with such success as to baffle his bloodthirsty enemies." A pity it is that none of these "arts" was particularly described and thus preserved for posterity, save the one most clearly implied—the art of "drawing the long bow"!

In fifteen days Hugh was at Fort Kiowa, fed up on buffalo veal, having found his knife, flint, and steel in his shot pouch. Descending thence to Fort Atkinson at the Council Bluffs, Hugh surprised his "old traitorous acquaintance," obtained his rifle, and with it a gift of other appliances needed to take to the field again.

Hugh then filled his lecture engagement, and the story ends: "This appeased the wrath of Hugh Glass, whom my informant left, astounding the gaping rank and file of the garrison, with his wonderful narration."

The next version is George C. Yount's recollection of what Hugh told him the winter of 1828–29, when they were together at Sweet Lake (Bear Lake, Utah).[3] In spite of the frequent avowals of its authenticity, the text was prepared by a writer who had not known or seen Glass, being entirely hearsay and research with several inconsistencies. The chief error is in taking two years for the Hugh Glass story instead of one, as indicated by dated, printed sources.

The rattlesnake steaks "jambed" off as needed are as difficult for the reader to swallow as they must have been for Hugh, though he had buffalo berries for dessert. This morsel was not on the *Port Folio*

---

[3] Yount, *Chronicles*, 24–32.

menu. That, or some other good protein, was his fare in the spring of 1825, for, "He knew no fatigue; but after a day's travel, could leap and frolic," Yount tells us. After the Arikara sham battle, the cache of provisions on which Dutton and Glass "lived sumptuously," was more providential than the manna found by Moses and the children of Israel—it hadn't spoiled.

Yount's version shows a greater divergence in the description of the bear fight, but claims to have Allen's eye witness confirmation:[4]

"The monster had seized him, torn the flesh from the lower part of the body, and from the lower limbs. He also had his neck shockingly torn, even to the degree that an aperture appeared to have been made into the windpipe, and his breath to exude at the side of his neck. It is not probable, however, that any aperture was made into the windpipe. Blood flowed freely, but fortunately no bone was broken, and his hands and arms were not disabled." This extraordinary feature was not recorded by the *Port Folio* writer.

Yount says, in a footnote: "An account given by Pattie appears to refer to Glass. . . . A bear attacked one of the party, who may not have been Glass; but the date, place and circumstances do not agree with other sources."[5] Hugh had reached Fort Atkinson in June, 1824, and Pattie left there July 30, 1824. Glass is next reported working out of Taos, New Mexico. It is therefore possible that Glass was with, or traveling near, or later saw, the Pattie party, though Pattie does not mention Glass. The Pattie story is digested here.

In southwestern Kansas, September 11, 1824, a bear attacked one of Pattie's men at night.[6] "Our companion was literally torn in pieces. The flesh on his hip was torn off, leaving the sinews bare, by the teeth of the bear. His side was so wounded in three places, that his breath came through the openings; his head was dreadfully bruised, and his jaw broken. His breath came out from both sides of his windpipe." No one supposed he would recover.

"We remained in our encampment three days, attending on him. . . . We then concluded to move . . . leaving two men with him, to each of whom we gave one dollar a day for remaining to take care of him, until he should die; and to bury him decently." Pattie found

[4] *Ibid.,* 26.
[5] *Ibid.,* 24.
[6] James O. Pattie, *Personal Narrative,* 37–38, 51.

a new camp, then: "Our companions, with the wounded man on a litter, reached us." When they reached the Arkansas River: "We were detained here until the 4th [of October]. . . . Awaiting the arrival of the two men we had left with our wounded companion. They came, and brought with them his gun and ammunition. He died the fifth day after we had left him."

Philip St. George Cooke wrote a pretentious literary version of the Glass-bear opus about 1830,[7] designating "A man named Fitzgerald and a youth of seventeen" as caretakers. He did not identify anyone, but inserted human-interest phrases into a lofty unbelievable tale.

Colonel Leavenworth wrote General Atkinson, December 20, 1823, that a man named "Fitzgerald left Major Henry's party at Powder River and came down in a canoe,"[8] with Moses (Black) Harris and another man named Harris. "John S. Fitzgerald" enlisted in the army at Fort Atkinson, April 19, 1824.[9] This very nearly closes the circuit of circumstantial, if not corroborative, evidence that Fitzgerald could have been the elder caretaker, not necessarily an "unfaithful" one. However, the historical narrative is still far behind Hugh's fictional image in its development.

Edmund Flagg fathered a fourth dramatized version in 1839, saying a consultation resolved Glass should be left with "Fitzgerald and Bridges."[10] It is a short jump from "Bridges" to James Bridger, and General Chittenden says Captain La Barge almost accomplished it. ("Captain La Barge, who remembers the tradition well, says it was James Bridger.")[11] But Chittenden omitted the reference from his subsequent life of La Barge. He was not using historical facts shot at him half-cocked. Besides, a trapper named "Bridges" was reported by Lewis H. Morgan on the Missouri;[12] and Alpheus H. Favour reveals that "James Bridges" (not Bridger) was a contemporary frontiersman on the Missouri.[13]

Moses (Black) Harris, "who appears to be a correct and intelli-

[7] Philip St. George Cooke, *Scenes and Adventures in the U. S. Army*, 139.
[8] Morgan, *Jedediah Smith*, 102–103.
[9] *Ibid.*, 391.
[10] Flagg, "History of a Western Trapper," 326.
[11] Chittenden, *Fur Trade*, 704.
[12] Lewis H. Morgan, *The American Beaver and His Works*.
[13] Alpheus H. Favour, *Old Bill Williams*, 43.

gent young man," was interviewed that winter by down-river news-papers, but did not mention the bear fight, though one, and possibly both, of the caretakers were with him.

In all his narrations and interviews Hugh was careful not to divulge the names of the discredited caretakers. He well recalled that other fellow trappers aided him generously when he was in actual need, but that no real person ever took care of a man in the dire plight he described. Hugh did not give the names of the care-takers because they did not belong in his invented screed. None of his imaginary tales ever had identifiable characters, and there were never any heroes in them but himself. The villains of those days, when too clearly identified, sued for libel with a rifle.

The greatest need—the story's outstanding defect—now that it has endured so long, is not the names of the caretakers, but the stories of the caretakers; that is, their versions of this unique recital.

Hugh Glass was not the only frontiersman who loved a joke and was a story in and of himself. The Glass bear story is clearly a product of the school of frontier braggarts, and its original author, Hugh Glass, far from meriting pity for being neglected, rightfully becomes instead a distinguished raconteur.

The story of Hugh Glass and the bear has many authors. In the present century alone their number is legion. Versions are quite as numerous as narrators. A popular treatment from the beginning has been to consolidate all previous versions, slanting the rewrite to the new writer's predilection. If any part of the snowballed story needs improvement, it gets it, to become the bear-fighter's masterpiece. Any western roundup without Hugh Glass and the bear would be like a zoo without an elephant.

JAMES BRIDGER, on Powder River, was being initiated into the mysteries of a fur trapper's life, as well as the life of the Indian and of the beaver. It was a congenial, well-equipped brigade which had been shaped and left by Major Henry, presumably headed by the seasoned and likable former sea captain, John H. Weber. Portions of a Crow Indian village dragged along with the trappers to hunt buffalo for winter meat.

Young Bridger was not accustomed to the clicking military routines of Major Henry, but he liked the effective timing and enforced industry. Without such pressures one could become too relaxed, like the Indian. But such a state of purposelessness would be difficult with a leader like Captain Weber, and especially for such a dedicated, "enterprising young man" as James Bridger.

Captain Weber sought to maintain the high spirit of the group at subsequent campfire seminars. The results were apparent in improved skills and increasing beaver takes. It was not by accident, the trappers learned, that the beaver thrives and produces its finest furs in subarctic latitudes, especially in the similar climatic zones of the loftier Rocky Mountains. The beaver had before its virtual extermination by the hunters, been forced to adapt itself to a wide range of climates and foods, but the beaver naturally produces its richer, more colorful furs at elevations of 6,500 to 10,500 feet above the sea.

A mature mountain beaver weighs twenty-five to forty pounds, its pelt about one-twentieth as much. The thick, coarse hide has no use other than holding the fur. At home either on land or in water, more beaver families live in land apartments than in water lodges for security reasons. They require a water-sealed entrance-exit to effect this privacy and protection.[1]

[1] Morgan, *The American Beaver*.

44

The beaver subsists mostly (in the Rocky Mountains) on the twigs and bark of the quaking aspen, but it is also nourished by cottonwood, poplar, and willow saplings. For obtaining this diet and for cutting timber for its dams, the beaver has four large curved chisel-tipped incisors and a set of grinding molars with roughened surfaces similar to those of the horse.

The small forelegs and forepaws, with their long, strong digging claws, are for burrowing, for carrying earth, mud, rocks, sticks, and debris, held against its body, and for fixing these materials in the dam or lodge. In swimming the forearms are folded, not used. The hind legs and feet are large, the toes tipped with heavy claws. A wide-spreading, nearly full, webbing between the hind toes aids in swimming and other water maneuvers. The large paddle-shaped tail is used chiefly as a rudder in swimming (and is a choice morsel of food for the trapper).

The beaver's keen sense of smell cannot be surpassed, unless by its own acute hearing. Its eyes are small and little used, as the beaver works chiefly at night through shyness or caution. Several beavers in a lodge upper-chamber will betray their presence by their body warmth and breathing, which melts the snow from the lodge, giving a tip to the trapper.

The beaver requires for his domicile a tolerably level mountain meadow, plentifully set with quaking aspens (or cottonwood or willow) and with a live stream nearby. These features naturally invite the trapper's attention. Contemporary generations of beaver only maintain, remodel, and perfect the dams, water lodges, and land burrows initially designed by their ancestors.

Beavers fell saplings or trees by gnawing them around and around. This symmetrical chipping leaves a pointed stump above the ground or crusted snow and a pointed butt on the trunk. The limbs are then gnawed off in convenient sizes for moving. The lighter branches are dragged in the beaver's mouth and borne lightly across its back. The use of long grasses and weeds indicates the work of young beavers.

The huge moose may forage at will, and the muskrat and otter may have their abode in these magnificent swimming pools of the beaver without objection from the docile proprietors. Beaver lodges in a pond, usually placed near the bank, are of similar construction to the dams: brush foundation, weighted and surmounted by a structure of mud, rocks, sticks, and debris. The burrow opening is always in a foot or more of water. The passageway leads to the spacious living chamber under the closed dome of the lodge and above the permanent water level. Similar passageways lead to the living apartments in the bank.

The burrow openings are usually found near or under a root, log, rock, or other fixed object, potential sites for the hunter's trap. An exposed burrow opening is sometimes obscured by a small pile of brush. All beavers are, by instinct, self-appointed patrolmen examining the community dam regularly for weak or leaky places. The patrolling path is nearly always in the water, along the upper face of the dam. Here the trapper notes other sites for his trap, usually where the trail rounds an obstacle or point of ground.

A goodly pile of limbs for food is gathered by the beaver from September to November and stored in an ungainly collection under water, between the lodge and the bank. The hungry beaver (which may suspend breathing several minutes) proceeds to the submerged brush pile in winter as one might fill a breakfast tray at a cafeteria. The limb selected is dragged to the dry living apartment to be eaten. The discards, or large debarked sticks, are deposited on the top of the lodge and on the dam.

The beaver does comparatively little work in winter and, as it does not hibernate, is usually fattest in winter. Thick ice interrupts trapping, but even at high elevations and in more northern latitudes beaver ponds seldom freeze solid to the bottom. Trappers are surprised to note that there is no frost in the ground under deep snow cover or broad bodies of water because of the rising warmth from the earth's deep interior.

A limited amount of trapping was done through the ice in winter, especially when the beaver's brush-food pile dwindled. At such a time, a freshly cut aspen stick, thrust through a hole in the ice, was as tempting to the beaver as candy to a baby. It did not awaken the resistance and caution of the beaver who did not suspect a steel trap was hidden under it.

Each trapper carried half a dozen six-inch smooth-jaw, double-spring steel traps, each with a three-foot chain and a four-inch ring at the end, in his leather saddlebags. The business of the trapper was to sequester the open trap in a slight depression on a beaver trail, lightly covering it with siftings of soil and debris. The chain ring was slipped over a smooth anchor pole, set firmly aslant in deeper water, the merciless intent being to drown the beaver.

Alexander Ross pointed out that when warm days and cold nights alternate, the water level fluctuates several inches, and the beaver may swim over the trap; or, more likely, if caught, since he cannot dive into deep water, he will frantically twist a foot off to escape. Ross had just written: "Between feet and toes, we took no less than 42! We put 170 traps in the water and got 15 beaver."[2]

The trapper worked a beaver village until six or eight merchantable skins were taken from each beaver lodge: two adults, two or three two-year-olds, and two or three yearlings. A final stratagem was to make a slight opening in a beaver dam. This would disturb the water a little and the remaining beavers a lot, for they would all appear at dusk to find and repair the damage, and inadvertently "throw" a few open traps.

Gum camphor, cinnamon, clove, or oil of juniper, when reduced to a paste in alcohol, made an excellent scented beaver-bait. A particle of the paste would be put on a stick placed over the trap. But the most potent "medicine" comes from the beaver's own body, the castoreum. The pod-shaped glands just beneath the skin in front of the genital organs of both sexes were removed and their outlets tied to prevent leakage. The beaver was never shot because of the risk of damage to the skin, and also because he might yet be lost by lodging, or drifting away in the stream. The excited beaver does straight-dive and strikes the surface with a resounding smack of the tail as a signal he has sensed danger.

Mrs. Beaver has a visit from the stork about May of each year, after three or four months' gestation. The mystic bird brings two or three, sometimes four or five, roly-poly bright brown bundles, although the mother has room for only four at her breast. The cubs are weaned readily in about six weeks, turning to aspen bark as readily as the trapper turns to tobacco.

The beaver youngsters have an affectionate home life and take their time to grow up, attaining adulthood in about two years. At

[2] Alexander Ross, *The Fur Hunters of the Far West* (ed. by Kenneth A. Spaulding), 246, 256, 257.

that time, say in June of their third summer, they are off on a honey-moon with a neighboring mate, or they are forced out by the sub-sequent visit of the stork. The departing honeymooners usually go downstream—a honeymoon should be a pleasant journey! But the old folks are apt to remain or move higher among the smaller waters where it is easier to find a living. The grandparents, whose aging is often related to incisor trouble, finally drop away to Elysium at twelve or fifteen years of age, barring that more dreaded tragedy, the hunter's steel trap.

Captain Weber's men had noticed a young beaver kept as a family pet by visiting Indians at Powder River. It was friendly, harmless, and enjoyed being petted; but it was a mischievous busy-body, sharing the Indian baby's food, snoozing at the Indian mother's side, and nosing around the camp like a puppy, manifesting no desire to pick a quarrel or to avoid one. It even seemed to enjoy traveling in a saddlebag. A bit of sugar sent it into an uncontrollable ecstasy of de-light—something for the men to chuckle about for time to come.

The baby beaver at home, like the human infant, is inclined to cry its way out of trouble, and the earnest hunger cries of the beaver baby sound very much like the cries of the human baby. Even the ambitious trapper is touched on discovering a wandering, crying baby beaver, calling in vain for the mother beaver detained in the hunter's trap.

In a study of beaver habits and populations, with the beavers fully protected by game laws (Utah), Rasmussen counted 380 beaver colonies (about 1,976 beavers) on 620 miles of streams be-tween 6,500 and 10,300 feet above the sea (headwaters of Duchesne, Provo, Weber, and Bear rivers).[3] This averages only three beavers per stream mile in beaver country. Thus the early fur trapper had to make Brobdingnagian strides to find, capture, and peel his precious peltrys.

General Ashley wrote Senator Benton, November 12, 1827: "After trapping beaver, where plentiful, until they are so diminished as not to justify continuation; and leaving the streams undisturbed five or six years, beavers will be found as numerous as when first

[3] D. I. Rasmussen, "Beaver-Trout Relationship," *Transactions of the North American Wild Life Conference* (Washington, 1940), 256, 263.

trapped. Under suitable regulations, the practise would afford a great quantity of furs for centuries to come."[4]

[4] 20 Cong., 2 sess., *Sen. Doc.* 67, pp. 11, 12 (Ashley to Benton, November 12, 1827).

THE UPPER POWDER RIVER was not heavily stocked with beaver, and Captain Weber, sooner than he wished, crossed the south end of the Big Horn Mountains and descended into the upper Big Horn Basin. Trapper Potts remembered it thus:

> A large and beautiful valley, adorned with many flowers. At the upper end of this valley on the Horn is a boiling spring at the foot of a small burnt mountain, about two rods in diameter, discharging sufficient water for an overshot mill . . . .[1] [This was Thermopolis Hot Springs, Wyoming, "largest mineral hot springs in the world."]
>
> From thence we crossed the [Owl Creek] Mountains to Wind River Valley. In crossing this mountain I unfortunately froze my feet and was unable to travel from the loss of two toes. Here I am obliged to remark the humanity of the natives to me, who conducted me to their village and into the lodge of their chief, who regularly twice a day divested himself of all his clothing except a breech clout, and dressed my wounds until I left.

Potts was writing from a long memory, with many events intervening, and may have telescoped some incidents. His flowers and frozen feet are pretty close together.

Related facts convince us that Captain Weber led his men south from the mineral springs, on a much used Indian trail along the Big Horn where it breaks through Owl Creek Mountains. They continued to the present Riverton, Wyoming, where Wind River irrevocably surrenders its name as in marriage to the Big Horn River. In confirmation, a map, issued in "Washington, 1839," shows, near the mouth of Wind River, "Oil Spring" and "Rendezvous."

[1] Frost, "Notes on General Ashley," 61, 133-34.

In this sheltered valley of about five thousand feet elevation, with a genial climate similar to that of Fort Collins, Colorado, Captain Weber was welcomed by the Crow Indians and by Captain Jedediah S. Smith and his party. Potts further describes it: "Wind River is a beautiful, transparent stream with hard gravel bottom, about seventy or eighty yards wide. . . . The grass and herbage are good and plenty. . . . The snow rarely falls more than three or four inches deep and never remains more than three or four days. . . . There is an oil spring in this valley which discharges sixty or seventy gallons of pure oil per day." This spring was on the Little Popo Agie, ten miles southeast of the present Lander, Wyoming. The spring ceased to flow when the first wells began to produce in the 1880's. The field is still in production with about thirty wells.

Captain Weber dispatched couriers to Major Henry at the other end of the Big Horn. This "express" seems to have included James Bridger. The couriers returned before Christmas, 1823, with a couple of packs of goods for the Crow Indian trade. They also had a note from Major Henry. This was devoid of the instructions expected from a leader, but suggested a rendezvous after the spring hunt at the Wind River–Big Horn elbow. What the Major did *not* say was to become the biggest news of the season.

James Bridger's homing instinct, no matter how confusing the trail, how winding the stream, or how blinding the brush or weather, was making him a safe scout to follow; he never got lost. He had a way of mapping the country in his mind, unrolling and completing the map as he progressed by frequent studies of the scenes to left, to right, and, especially, behind. This gave him a seat on the informal committee on geography for the encampment. The Crow Indians were also helpful in mapping the streams and mountains, some of which the trappers had not yet seen. James Clyman says he piled little ridges of sand on a blanket for the mountains and made finger marks for the streams.

The Wind River Mountains form the western horizon at Riverton rendezvous, half a dozen peaks piercing the sky above thirteen thousand feet. One of them, Gannett Peak, elevation 13,785 feet, is the highest point in the entire northern Rocky Mountains.

These mountains are appropriately named. The wind almost

ceaselessly pours through the lofty teeth of this comblike crest. Under special conditions, the wind descends Wind River Canyon to produce the region's well-known Chinooks. At Dubois, seven thousand feet elevation, a "snow-eater" Chinook may run a fever of several degrees in a winter balmy spell. But ordinarily Dubois is comparatively cold in winter, the lowest temperature of record, east of the mountains, in Wyoming, having occurred at Dubois.[2]

The Crow Indians were feuding country cousins of the great Sioux Nation. They could ride, shoot, make good clothing, useful implements, and weapons. They were usually rich in horses but poor in beaver. The Crow men were dapper but belligerent, and some of them were always failing to return from war-party forays. The result: a surplus of Crow Indian women. These women were not handsome, but many were cultured in their way and they were about the best-dressed Indians in the early West.

Their skin dressing and tanning was even better than that of some professional whites. These industrious women usually had for sale, or would tailor for a visitor, plain or fancy moccasins, blouses, skirts, and shirts of gleaming white leather from the skins of bighorn, antelope, or deer. The clothes were decorated and tastefully colored with attached tassels, rosettes, quills, and feathers. Their buffalo robes were dyed and ornamented, and their tipis substantially constructed of buffalo hides, almost exactly like the stately tents of the Sioux.

Bridger and other trappers noted the indifference of the Crow women to the attentions of Edward Rose, the guide. His personal friends were few, although he once stood high in Crow councils, having earned the soubriquet "Five Scalps." Instinctively an Indian, with flashes of Caucasian shrewdness, he was distrusted in time by both. With a Negro-Cherokee half-blood mother and white father, Rose easily passed for an Indian.[3]

Rose became guide for Wilson Price Hunt to Astoria, by way of the Big Horn and Wind rivers. Distrusting Rose, Hunt discharged him in September, 1811, at the Crow village. He married a Crow

---

[2] United States Weather Bureau *Summaries of Climatological Data for Wyoming*.
[3] Reuben Holmes, "Five Scalps (Edward Rose)," *Glimpses of the Past*, 1938. Hereafter referred to as Holmes, "Five Scalps (Edward Rose)."

woman in 1813, but is said to have been taken to New Orleans as a prisoner on a liquor charge about 1815–16. He rejoined the Arikaras in 1819.

James Bridger was interested in the Crow leader's ministrations over trapper Potts's frozen feet, especially in the results. The Indian medicine man claimed he attracted the attention of a superior power or intellect. This seemed as reasonable as any religious notions Bridger had heard concerning a Lord-of-All. Indeed, here was a possible improvement—the medicine man was apparently making it work.

To Bridger it also seemed rational to seek the friendship and influence of a Manitou that could influence an enemy, understand any language, establish the intertribal Peace Pipe having the force of an oath, cast its favors on the buffalo hunt and the beaver take, the migration of the herds, and the forage on the plains. All this was an interesting realm for meditation to young Bridger. There had been no storybooks in Bridger's youth, no children's games, no church, no school; in fact, no spiritual influence at all.

Roving Indian scouts visited the rendezvous, bringing the news that Alexander Ross, of the Flathead post of the Hudson's Bay Company (Eddy, Montana, elevation 2,437 feet) was on the march, as weather allowed, towards Henry's Fork of Snake River (St. Anthony, Idaho) for his spring hunt. These tidings made Jedediah S. Smith's sore ears tingle. Mountaineers generally were aware of the vaguely defined international jurisdictions—American, Mexican, and British—also the more realistic but poorly defined Indian provinces. Smith was eager to do a little probing.

Ross's journal[4] incorporates his weather records, from which we note that Ross's weather one day on the Bitterroot became Weber's weather at the Wind–Big Horn rendezvous the next. About mid-February violent weather set in, swamping Ross's caravan in eight to ten feet of snow and freezing many hands, feet, ears, and noses. Almost simultaneously the same protracted snowstorm foiled Jedediah S. Smith's attempt to cross Wind River Mountain crest in February, 1824.

Smith's party returned to camp and pushed stubbornly southward

4 Ross, *Fur Hunters of Far West,* 222–27.

with Clyman's sand map in mind. But on emerging from the shelter of the mountains in the South Pass region, Smith was suddenly caught in a phenomenon of weather not possible elsewhere in the world in such intensity. It was a frigidly cold jet-stream of destructive wind from the west, which at the whip-cracker end of a severe winter has in more recent years (1917) stalled railroad snowplows, locomotives, and freight and passenger trains, and, still more recently, reduced to zero the speed of early westbound airplanes.

A mountainous cold air mass over the Northwest was draining eastward in a Niagara of power through the one-hundred-mile gap between Wind River and Medicine Bow Mountains. Surface velocities reached forty or fifty miles an hour for days on end, with higher speeds aloft. Stalled trainmen, caught in a similar blast, melting samples of driven snow that sealed the roadway on nearby Laramie Plains (1917), reported them to be 10 to 20 per cent desert sand.

Neither men nor animals could face such a devastating sandblast. It literally blew Jedediah S. Smith and his party directly away from the plainly marked buffalo-and-Indian trail across the South Pass into the slight and inadequate shelter of the Sweetwater and the hill country about thirty miles east of the South Pass. After two or three weeks the winds slackened and the party found its way westward, reaching the mouth of the Big Sandy, March 19, 1824.[5]

It is only thirteen comparatively level miles (a half-day's team travel) from the Sweetwater to Pacific across the South Pass top-of-the-world, 7,550 feet elevation, the route Smith attempted but could not then negotiate.

A similar near-disastrous experience is related by James P. Beckwourth.[6] He says these storms, called "Poo-der-ee" by the Crows, "have proved fatal to great numbers of trappers and Indians." A number of subsequent travelers bemoaned these winds, though none of them were there as early as Smith and Fitzpatrick. James Bridger was to seek shelter from such a wind on June 16, 1866, as we shall see.[7]

The dividing of Smith's party at this time, Fitzpatrick heading the alien, independent faction, was as hard to understand as the weather

---

[5] *James Clyman, Frontiersman*, 25; some of his weather, 22–24.
[6] Bonner, *James P. Beckwourth*, 238, 239.
[7] Agnes Wright Spring, *Casper Collins*, 117.

was for them to endure. But, like freemen, they could hardly be rated deserters. Having cached some of their goods on the Sweetwater during the storm, Smith and Fitzpatrick agreed upon that site as a rendezvous for June 1. Major Andrew Henry, the owner-partner, could forget any plans he might have made!

Smith hunted towards the Uinta Mountains of Utah, going far enough and remaining long enough to get his name on the region's longest stream, Smith's Fork, later homesteaded by Uncle Jack Robertson. One of Smith's men was similarly memorialized by Black's Fork, future site of Fort Bridger. Fitzpatrick, Clyman, and party trapped on the upper Green River. Both parties met, as planned, on the Sweetwater with a revolutionary scheme; they constructed and loaded skin boats, and the fleet set off for the Platte, Fitzpatrick in command. Most of the cargo was lost at the Platte, and the rest was cached nearby. Fitzpatrick, Clyman, Branch, and Stone reached Fort Atkinson that autumn in a pitiable state of physical exhaustion. William L. Sublette apparently joined the Smith party, which proceeded directly northwest, determined to pay a visit to Alexander Ross.

Captain John H. Weber and his men had observed the plans and the plight of the Smith-Fitzpatrick contingents; thus when Major Henry arrived, it was made very clear that the Weber minority was henceforth to provide the thread of life-continuity for the Ashley-Henry enterprises in the Rocky Mountains. Henry's sole business, according to the buzz of gossip in the camp, was to organize a pack train of the furs on hand and lead the caravan homeward. Fitzpatrick had demonstrated the way *not* to do it. Henry would pack only to the mouth of the Big Horn, where his keelboat lay. Johnson Gardner may have been second-in-command, for he next appears with a following fully detached from Captain Weber's precious minority.

Major Henry's various vexations may have stemmed from the independent spirit of the freeman in himself, as well as in others. Freemen always posed an enigma to organized fur traders. Nobody could get along with them, and no company could get along without them. Alexander Ross complained that they would not willingly guard horses or take assigned camping sites or trapping territory. They complained of company trade prices, and were forever seducing or alienating good company men. But their numbers were always needed in an Indian fight, and their furs were always needed for quotas. James Bridger was becoming a dependable integer in some larger plans, but he was never a captious freeman at heart.

Major Henry's arrival in St. Louis was quite inadequately covered by the newspapers. The Arkansas *Gazette* of September 21, 1824, carried an item dated at St. Louis, August 30, 1824: "An arrival from the Mountains; After an absence of nearly three years, we are happy to announce the safe return of Major Henry (of the firm of Ashley and Henry) with a part of his company, from the Rocky Mountains. He descended the Missouri in boats to St. Louis, with a considerable quantity of valuable furs."

And on November 16, 1824: "By the arrival of Major Henry from the Rocky Mountains, we learn that his party have discovered a passage by which loaded wagons can at this time reach the navigable waters of the Columbia River. This route lies south of the one explored by Lewis & Clark, and is inhabited by Indians friendly to us."[8]

[8] Frost, "Notes on General Ashley," 133–34.

From an original drawing by Mary Baker

The beaver, prime animal of the fur trade.

From the water color by Alfred Jacob Miller
Courtesy of the Walters Art Gallery

Trapping beaver, this mountain man sets his bait. Indian traders became trappers and began to do their own hunting when they lost patience with the Red Men.

CAPTAIN JOHN H. WEBER led his trappers around the Wind River Mountains to the southwest, crossing the Sweetwater where they came to it and likewise the isthmus of land known as South Pass. For a few miles here the slender Sweetwater runs only a few feet lower than the surface of South Pass.[1]

To James Bridger the South Pass was a portal of much importance —the entrance to a new life. Too bad he could not have seen posterity's tribute facing him at that great moment! "Bridger National Forest" drapes the western slope of Wind River Mountains, and blankets the upper Green River Valley, 2,700 square miles in extent. Within this "Forest" is the dedicated "Bridger Primitive Area," containing about one thousand natural lakes and ponds, a potential beaver haven. Instead, it is today populated by 20,000 deer, 5,000 elk, 1,000 moose, 450 bears, 400 bighorns, plus antelope, small game, birds, and fish.[2]

The forest is suitably constituted, including almost every typical feature, and it is most appropriately named. If James Bridger had any prominent characteristics, his phrenological eminence of Locality, on the forehead, must have been as conspicuous as Gannett's Peak, overlooking Bridger Forest.

Sea Captain John H. Weber was not impressed by the mirage of the future, just unfurled, prophetically emblazoning Bridger's humble name as if in mile-high letters of gold. That particular event did not occur until March 11, 1941. Weber apparently led his party, by way of the Little Sandy, to the mouth of Big Sandy for crossing the Green River.

"We proceeded southwesterly from Green River," Potts con-

[1] Frost, "Notes on General Ashley," 61–63.
[2] United States Forest Service, maps and circulars, for Bridger National Forest.

tinues, "over an inconsiderable ridge [Ham's Fork, near the present Kemmerer] when we fell on a considerable river, called Bear River, which rises to the south in the Utaw [Uinta] Mountains, bears north eighty or ninety miles, when it turns sharp to the southwest and south. We first approached Bear River at a small sweet lake about 120 miles in circumference, with beautiful, clear water, and when the wind blows, has a splendid appearance [Bear Lake, Utah-Idaho]."

They touched Bear River at what has since been known as Bridger Creek, coming in from the east-southeast. Sage Creek comes in from the west nearby. The lake was also known as Weaver Lake, that being the Indian pronunciation of Captain Weber's name. At the south end of the lake extensive meadowlands made the region a popular summer gathering place for Indians and, later, for the fur trader's rendezvous. A trailway to the north led along the eastern lake shore, at the base of Lake Mountain.

"There is also to be found in this valley," says Potts, "a considerable sour spring near the most northerly swing of the river [Soda Springs, Idaho]. The second or Willow Valley [Utah and Idaho] has been our chief place of rendezvous and wintering ground [from the autumn of 1824]. Numerous streams fall in through this valley which is surrounded by stupendous mountains."

The casualty reports of later dates, made by Indian agents and others, include for the year 1824: "Thomas, a half-breed, was killed by Williams, on the waters of Bear River."[3] Bridger was in the only party of Americans on Bear River, but there it is, an alluring story, reduced to a mere statistic. Most of the trapper casualties however, did not get that much notice.

The winter rendezvous of 1824–25, according to prevailing tradition, was on Cub Creek where it joins Bear River, near Richmond, Utah. Both the Bear and her Cub have here dug rather deep channels for themselves, thus affording natural protection for an encampment. The Bear bends accommodatingly toward the east, more convenient to timber in the adjacent canyon. Early Mormon settlers of the 1850's report having found old stumps and woodpiles hereabouts.

As none of the trappers had yet been to the mouth of the Bear, its course was an enigma of no ordinary importance. Green River flows southward, around the eastern end of the Uinta Mountains,

[3] Morgan, *Jedediah Smith*, 343.

while Bear River, a neighboring stream of similar size, flows north-ward from the western end of the same Uinta Mountains. The westerly trend of the Bear, near the north end of Bear Lake, sug-gested it supplied Snake River. But the trappers saw it belying these appearances, and turning south into Willow Valley, headed for goodness knows where.

Indian rumors placed the estuary in a lake within fifty miles of the trappers' encampment on the Cub and said the lake waters had a nasty taste. The trappers only knew that Bear River broke away from the peaceful restraints of Willow Valley to roar its noisy way through rocky cliffs only fifteen miles distant. James Bridger's opinion was respected, but his prowess was at stake. A wager brought his curiosity to the boiling point. The incident is amply documented by Robert Campbell, an Ashley fur trader, who wrote to G. K. Warren, United States government geographer, as follows:[4]

St. Louis, April 4, 1857

Dear Sir:

Your favor of the 25th ultimo reached me at a very fortunate period to enable me to give you a satisfactory reply to your inquiry as to who was the first discoverer of the Great Salt Lake. It happened that James Bridger and Samuel Tullock both met at my counting room after a separation of eighteen years, and were bringing up reminiscences of the past when your letter reached me. I had it read to them, and elicited the following facts:

A party of beaver trappers who had ascended the Missouri with Henry and Ashley found themselves in pursuit of their occupation on Bear River in Cache (or Willow) Valley, where they wintered in the winter of 1824 and 1825; and in descending [discussing?] the course which Bear River ran, a bet was made between two of the party, and James Bridger was selected to follow the course of the river and de-termine the bet. This took him where the river passes through the mountain, and there he discovered the Great Salt Lake. He went to its margin and tasted the water, and on his return reported his dis-covery. The fact of the water being salt, induced the belief that it was an arm of the Pacific Ocean; but in the spring of 1826, four men went in skin boats around it to discover if any streams containing beaver

---

[4] G. K. Warren, "Warren's Memoir," *Pacific Railroad Reports*, XI, 35. Hereafter referred to as Warren, "Memoir."

were to be found emptying into it, but returned with indifferent success.

I went to Willow or Cache Valley in the spring of 1826, and found the party just returned from their exploration of the Lake, and recollect their report that it was without outlet. Mr. Tullock corroborates in every respect the statement of James Bridger, and both are men of the strictest integrity and truthfulness. I have known both of them since 1826. *James Bridger was the first discoverer of Great Salt Lake.*

I am happy in being able to give you the information and of the character that you wished for.

Your obedient servant,
(Sgd) Robert Campbell.

To "follow the course of the river," how did Bridger travel, and when? If he was in a bullboat, he portaged the difficult two-mile gorge through Bear River Canyon. The river freezes over about mid-November in a normal season. The ice goes out towards March 15, when melting snow from the countryside swells the stream to twice its autumn volume and turbulence. Bridger would need to go two or three miles out into the lake from the stream to dip salt water.

Using a bullboat he would have walked part way down and all the way back. He could about as well have traveled on foot the entire round trip. Using his customary method of travel, on horseback, Bridger could have examined the stream in less time and with greater safety. He could have dipped saline water on the eastern shore anywhere between Bear River and Weber River, or anywhere along the western, or Promontory Mountain shore, of Bear River Bay. In that year, 1824, the lake level stood at an unusually high stage, covering shorelands that are swampy at lower stages.[5]

The document says Bridger went alone, thus allowing his curiosity to outweigh his caution in strange Indian country. In case of trouble he would have fared better with a mount. Also, "he went to its margin and tasted the water." On this fuller analysis, I conclude he rode a horse.

Forty years' residence in that climate convinces me that Bridger made the journey in the autumn, because of the preponderance of

[5] *James Clyman, Frontiersman,* 218.

fine weather as compared with the more inclement conditions in the spring. Moreover, the winter's campfire gossip brought news of seven trappers' deaths at the hands of hostile Indians in the region. Bridger would not have ventured down Bear River "alone" after such an epidemic of casualties nearby.

General Ashley was duly proud of this and other discoveries. In his "Narrative,"[6] he says intelligence concerning the "Grand Salt Lake" and its incoming streams "was communicated to me by our hunters who had crossed this region in the summer of 1824 . . . and from their own observations, and information collected from the Indians, they supposed it to be about eighty miles long and fifty broad. They represented it as a little brackish, though in this latter quality, the accounts differ; some insist that it is not brackish."

The salinity varies, being lowest near the discharging streams and during the higher lake stages. The belief that it was an arm of the ocean was an unthinking remark of someone else, and does not square with the trapper's general knowledge of the great length and descent of the Missouri, Green, and Snake rivers to the ocean, nor with the Indians' reports of the lake.

It was long ago when Baron Lahontan, pushing westward from the upper Missouri in May, 1689 [*sic*], got wind of the Great Salt Lake from his curious Mozeemlek Nation of Indians. Their "principal river empties itself into a Salt Lake." Father Escalante, while visiting the Timpanogos Indians on Utah Lake, forty miles south, wrote on September 25, 1776: "The other Lake, with which this one is connected, so they informed us . . . . Its waters are harmful or extremely salty."

Lahontan and Escalante only heard of Salt Lake and roughly indicated its position and shape on their maps, which they drew largely from Indian hearsay. J. Arrowsmith, official cartographer, did quite as well on his western United States map of 1802, carrying forward his predecessor's traditions. In the blank space, beyond all co-ordinated tracings, he inserted a lone plus mark, and the note: "Pearl Shell Lake is hereabout, according to the Indian accounts, nearly a hundred miles long S.W. and N.E. The water is brackish."

After visiting the lake and tasting its waters, James Bridger returned to the trappers' rendezvous in Willow Valley, Utah, with the

---

[6] Harrison C. Dale, *The Ashley-Smith Explorations*, 153–54

first eyewitness account of a white man's visit to the once fabled, but now real, Great Salt Lake. Bridger's trapper friends were appreciative and proud of him and his achievement. The distinction has clung to him like a scholastic degree.

THE HOTTEST GOSSIP in Willow Valley that winter concerned the deadly attack in the late autumn on Étienne Provost and party of ten or twelve, who were trapping on Provo River (formerly Timpa-nogos River). A band of Snake Indians, led by "Bad Gosha" (Gotia), invited the Provost party to smoke. The crafty Gosha insisted, how-ever, that it was against his "medicine" to smoke near anything made of metal. Not wishing to offend, Provost and his men set aside their guns, seating themselves alternately in the Indian ceremonial circle.[1]

As if by a signal, the interspersed Indians attacked the trappers with concealed hunting knives. Provost and three or four trappers extricated themselves and escaped, but seven were slain and their property was taken. Provost and the other survivors hastened east-ward, wintering, as before, in a semipermanent encampment at the confluence of White River with the Green (Ouray, Utah).

Other casualties Weber's men would have heard about are given in this report: "The Missouri Fur Company had a man killed on Weber's Fork by the Snakes; and in 1825, Marshall was lost in Willow valley near the Salt Lake."[2]

Both reports are sorely deficient in the six standard news cate-gories: Who? What? Where? When? Why? and How? They are worthy of note, however, because the victims were Bridger's fellows.

Captain Weber had an uneasy winter in Willow Valley, and he trapped it only superficially that snowy spring of 1825. He then followed James Bridger's trail to Great Salt Lake, having in mind a

---

[1] Chittenden, *Fur Trade*, 276. See also Morgan, *Jedediah Smith*, 401–402. The Jordan River, between Utah Lake and Great Salt Lake, is an intermittent, sluggish stream, neither a fishing nor a beaver stream, a most unlikely place for beaver trappers.

[2] *United States Indian Agents' Reports*, XLII; see also Morgan, *Jedediah Smith*, 342, 345.

midsummer trading rendezvous, probably on Green River. Captain Weber and his party thus ascended the larger stream coming into Great Salt Lake from the east (present Ogden, Utah), which has since been called Weber River.

On the upper reaches of the river he met Étienne Provost, boldly returning to the vicinity of his recent disaster. Johnson Gardner and other Ashley men joined the Provost party for a brief excursion, while Captain Weber pushed eastward up Chalk Creek with his bundles of furs.

Provost and his main group, some of them deserters from Hudson's Bay Company, were eager to look in on the Britons, reported to be approaching under the leadership of Peter Skene Ogden. Provost's Ute Indians knew the route, and Johnson Gardner felt sure of effecting more defections with proper pressure. He would accompany Provost just for the fun of it. They were all on Mexican soil.

The Provost-Gardner men turned up Lost Creek (Old Pumbars), spreading out somewhat for search and trapping. In early May, 1825, they chanced to meet Jedediah S. Smith, and Zachariah Ham, who, it seems, joined Provost and Gardner on their way to the proposed brawl with Ogden. Smith had only recently left Ogden on Bear River. Bridger, as a sight-seer, drifted with the crowd.

For perspective: Alexander Ross, of Hudson's Bay Company, left Flathead House (Eddy, Montana) the preceding spring, February 10, 1824. It was his bad weather of one day that was at Wind River the next, and it was he whom Jedediah S. Smith had wished to meet. Traveling with Ross were fifty-five men with twenty-five wives and sixty-four children, carrying 75 guns, a brass three-pounder, 212 traps, and 392 horses; a band of flighty Iroquois under Pierre Tivanitogan marched with them, in all making a cavalcade nearly two miles in length.

At Henry's Fork (St. Anthony, Idaho), in June, 1824, the Iroquois proceeded to Bear River because "we have already trapped that country for two years," said Pierre. Ross led the main party westward, attended the Fishing Fair at Twin Falls in August and returned through the present Sun Valley to meet the perverse Iroquois, as planned, at Canoe Point (Salmon City).

With a knack for picking up trouble, the Iroquois came, accompanied by Jedediah S. Smith and six associates, openly spying out

Hudson's Bay Company's men and methods. The Iroquois were practically destitute—an Iroquois had given a horse for a Snake wife, but refused to give two horses as requested. When the woman deserted, the Indians clashed.

"We had 900 beaver, 54 traps, 27 horses and 5 guns, besides our clothing, all of which the Snakes took," admitted Pierre, who said they then met the Americans fresh from the Sweetwater-Platte rendezvous. Smith said he had received 105 beaver skins for escorting the Iroquois out of trouble. Smith forthwith considered he had earned the right to accompany the Britons for a winter sojourn among them.

The winter was short. The Ross-Smith-Pierre cavalcade reached Flathead House on November 26, 1824, where Peter Skene Ogden was already booking men for the Snake River expedition of 1825.[3] They left December 29, 1824, Smith's unwelcome group doggedly trailing the company of "Twenty-five lodges, two gentlemen, two interpreters, 71 men and lads [ladies?], 80 guns, 364 beaver traps, and 372 horses."

The clerk, Kittson, the other "gentleman," voiced Ogden's sentiments: "Jedediah S. Smith is a sly, cunning Yankee", and Ogden asked Kittson "to notice the way the Americans went." Ogden explains why: "These fellows, by going ahead, will secure the beaver. . . . We must endeavor to annoy them as much as we possibly can."

They reached Bear River (Grace, Idaho) April 26, 1825, "which the deceased Michael Bourdon named Bear River [1819] from the great number of those animals on its borders," Ogden divulged. Kittson adds: "Here the Americans have gone upwards; and we are to follow it downward." Ogden also furnished news of Weber's party.

By May 2, 1825 (at present Preston, Idaho), the beaver take jumped from forty to seventy-four, including one pelican. On Cub River seven Snake Indians reported that a party of Americans (Weber's party) had wintered just below, but had already gone south. "The Snakes displayed four brand new guns of the Barnet type, one dated 1802, and another 1817; they also had plenty of ammunition, obtained from the Americans," writes Ogden.

May 8, 1825, Kittson's route map places the campsite dot near the

3 Morgan, *Jedediah Smith*, 145, 403.

present Logan, Utah; and Ogden's journal mourns: "The Americans have taken nearly all the beaver. They are a selfish set. They leave nothing for their friends; we act differently." May 9: "Bear River takes a great bend west." Continuing southward, the Ogden party reached Little Bear River (Paradise, Utah).

May 11, Ogden left Little Bear, ascending the largest of Three Forks (East Fork) six miles; buffalo scarce, grizzlies numerous, seventy beavers, "a convincing proof the Americans trapped only the lower parts of these forks. From the quantity of snow at the time, it was impossible for them to proceed to their sources."

May 12: "I sent two men to the sources of Middle Fork [through Scare Canyon]." May 13: Ascended Middle Fork, as nearly all the traps are ahead of us. Encamped near a lofty range of mountains. 79 beavers. Course Southwest [should read southeast]. eleven miles [old service roads still follow the original trails]." May 15: "Awaiting men in the rear." May 16: "Crossed the summit and descended; 10 miles; camped [on Rock Creek of Beaver Creek, on Forest Service maps]."

"It does not appear the Americans have come this way," Ogden is happy to report, and Kittson adds: "We are in a hole, as I may say, surrounded by lofty mountains; Mr. Ogden named it 'New Hole' [since then it has been known as Ogden Hole]." May 17: "Moved 6 miles southeast for grass; crossed three forks rich in beaver. All trappers in; 244 beavers in three nights; great success." (Camp near the present "Camp Kiesel" on South Fork of Ogden River.)

"It is to be regretted this spot is not ten times as large. I presume the Americans intended returning this way; but they will be as we were on Bear River, *taken in*. They ought to keep at home, not infringe on their neighbor's territories." It is noted that both Ogden and Kittson recorded topographical facts furnished by trappers, along with their own observations, to account for some inconsistencies in their journal entries.

May 22, 1825: "Our course this day South, over a hilly country, for ten miles, when we again reached New River (Ogden River), but there is nothing but stones and gravel, without any appearance of beaver." Of course the writer of that sentence meant his course was mainly southwesterly. It is not his first error of the kind in reworking his field notes for permanent record. Ten miles "south" from any part of New River here would have brought them to Weber's Fork, a stream exactly four times the volume of New River, and he would have been on the wrong side of it. Ogden's description of the terrain that day agrees with the land he would encounter traveling "southwestward." A distance of ten miles would have brought him to the lower Three Forks (present Huntsville), where Kittson correctly spots the encampment on his map.[4]

May 25, 1825 (Huntsville): "Early in the day a party of fifteen men, Canadians and Spaniards, headed by one Provost; and François, one of our deserters, arrived. Also in the afternoon arrived, in company with fourteen of our absent men, a party of twenty-five Americans, with colors flying, the latter party headed by one Gardner. They encamped within 100 yards of our encampment, and lost no time informing all hands in the camp that they were in the United States Territories, and were all free, indebted or engaged; and to add to this, they would pay cash for beaver 3½ dollars p. lb. and their goods cheap in proportion."

Kittson adds a detail: "The strong party of Americans" were "bearing flags" (plural), "and were under different heads; one of them, Gardner," becoming spokesman. This "strong party of Americans" was comprised of volunteer guests or spectators from Weber's, Ham's, and Smith's commands, including William L. Sublette, Milton Sublette, D. T. Potts, James Bridger, and other Ashley men. They were not necessarily participating in Gardner's endeavors to embarrass Mr. Ogden.

Gardner had a grievance: Ogden had snared nearly five hundred beaver skins from under his nose while Gardner noisily quibbled about "rights." He could have used some of Smith's diplomacy.

> May 24, 1825: Gardner came to my tent and questioned me: Do you know in whose country you are? To which I made answer that I did not, as it was not yet determined, between Great Britain and America, to whom it belonged. To this he made answer, that it had been ceded to the latter; and as I had no license to trap or trade, to return from

4 Peter Skene Ogden, *Snake Country Journals*, Hudson's Bay Record Society Edition, 40–54; also in same, Kittson, Appendix A, March 18, April 26, May 16 and 23, 1825. This edition is hereafter referred to as Ogden, *Journals*.

whence I came. To this I made answer: When we receive orders from the British Government we shall obey. Then he replied: remain at your peril; he then departed.

The Americans, headed by Gardner, advanced to assist all who were inclined to desert. Lazard now called out: "We are superior in numbers; let us fire and pillage them." On saying this, he advanced with his gun cocked and pointed at me; but finding I was determined . . . they desisted, and we secured the ten Company horses, but not without enduring the most opprobrious terms they could think of, from both Americans and Iroquois.

To remain in this quarter any longer would merely be to trap beaver for the Americans," Ogden consoles his diary, as crocodile tears fall on his rich take of beaver skins. Ogden retired from Ogden Hole by ascending Middle Fork and thence following his incoming line of campsites.

James Bridger, like most of the visitors, did not have much to say in the brisk battle of the braggarts. To them it did not matter what was said; Peter Skene Ogden was carrying away the beaver harvest which the Americans should have gleaned.

General Ashley commented in the Cincinnati *Gazette* of December 31, 1827:

> Messrs Jedediah S. Smith, William L. Sublette, and several others of the American party, intelligent young men of strict veracity, had visited the British Camp and reported to their comrades that the British flag had been repeatedly hoisted during their stay there. The Americans, indignant at such impertinence, and understanding, too, that the British Camp was within eight miles of them, resolved to proceed to the place, and tear down the flag, even at the risk of their lives.
>
> Twenty-two of them, with the American flag hoisted, advanced to the spot, but no British flag was to be seen. They made known their business to Mr. Ogden, and protested in threatening language against a recurrence of the insult offered them; they also required of Mr. Ogden to remove his party from that vicinity without delay. Mr. O. at first hesitated, calling upon his men for protection, but ultimately finding there would probably be much danger in delay, he lost no time in getting under way, and has kept at a respectful distance ever since.[5]

[5] Courtesy Cincinnati Public Library. The item in the *Gazette*, is "From the Missouri Observer."

ABOUT THE TIME James Bridger was discovering the Great Salt Lake in the autumn of 1824, his employer, General William H. Ashley, with dogged determination, was outfitting himself in St. Louis for an abysmal plunge into the wilderness. Only Ashley's defeat for the Missouri governorship could have steeled him for such an ordeal.

Leading a pack train of fifty horses and twenty-five or thirty men up the Platte from Fort Atkinson, Ashley ascended the South Platte about Christmastime of 1824, and was on the Cache La Poudre from February 4 to 26, 1825. After rounding Medicine Bow Mountains, crossing Laramie Plains, and descending the North Platte, he turned up the Sweetwater. Already plagued with more trouble than was his share, Ashley lost seventeen horses to Crow Indians in April. Caching some packs and loading others on broad shoulders, Ashley crossed South Pass and gathered his broken ranks on Green River at the Sandys, April 19–22, 1825.[1]

Ashley's men killed six buffalo and constructed a bullboat for the packs; then the trappers dispersed. James Clyman with six men, including James P. Beckwourth, went to the upper Green; Zachariah Ham with seven men went west, working what became Ham's Fork (and falling in with Smith); while Thomas Fitzpatrick preferred to go south to the Uinta Mountains, with six men.

General Ashley with seven men went down Green River in the

---

[1] Dale, *Ashley-Smith Explorations*, 117–61. General Ashley's diary, March 25 to June 27, 1825, masquerading as the diary of William L. Sublette, was identified by Dale L. Morgan, and edited and published in the *Bulletin* of the Missouri Historical Society, October, 1954, and January and April, 1955, St. Louis, Missouri.

A picturesque narrative of this journey is in Bonner's *James P. Beckwourth*, chapters 4 to 7, inclusive, pages 50 to 90 inclusive. Bonner's pages bristle with anger and get soggy with tears, but it is remarkable how closely historians follow him new boat. They were all to meet before July 10, west of the Green and north of the Uintas. After killing four more buffalo for another bullboat, they deposited the principal cache May 1–4, 1825, on what they named Henry's Fork, although the Major was not there to appreciate the honor.

Embarking May 5, 1825, on the harmless-looking Green River in their buffalo-hide boats, Ashley and his men drifted innocently into a series of adventures that make the average Indian fight a picnic in comparison.

The stirring story of this first known passage of the cruel canyons of the Green did not mention Flaming Gorge, Brown's Hole, Lodore Canyon, Disaster Falls, Hell's Half Mile, Whirlpool Canyon, or Split Mountain, all of whose names, and attendant fame, came from later hairbreadth adventures of other daring voyagers.

But the two simple words, "Ashley 1825," inscribed in black paint on a boulder under a cliff wall near Ashley Falls—although not mentioned in the diary—have brought to him as much acclaim as all his other writings combined, etched as they were on the portals of all Grand Canyon literature.

The doughty General and his bedraggled crew emerged from the canyon at Father Escalante's crossing of 1776 (now the Dinosaur National Monument, Utah) on May 16, 1825, ending the most strenuous and exciting decade of the General's entire life. Finding and visiting Provost's post (Ouray, Utah) for refreshment and advice, Ashley followed the trail west around the Uinta Mountains. He met Provost returning from the Peter Skene Ogden conference with further news of Ashley's mountain men.

Provost and the Hudson's Bay Company deserters joined Ashley to attend the trading rendezvous, which they reached near the end of June.[2] "On the first day of July [1825] all the men in my employ or with whom I had any concern in the country, together with twenty-nine who had recently withdrawn from the Hudson's Bay

---

when other sources give out. The leading fault of the Bonner-Beckwourth team is in misdating events from memory years after they happened. The next fault might be their recklessness with statistics. Even so, thank goodness for Beckwourth!

[2] The Ashley diary ends June 27, 1825, on Big Muddy Creek, ten miles northwest of Fort Bridger and sixty miles northwest of the 1825 rendezvous site.

Company, making in all, 120 men, were assembled for the appointed rendezvous."[3]

Only in our imagination can we see James Bridger striking hands with Thomas Fitzpatrick and James Clyman after a year's absence, welcoming into the fraternity of mountaineers the one and only James P. Beckwourth whom he was meeting for the first time, and engaging in friendly conversation with General Ashley.

General Ashley's appreciative interest in James Bridger's discovery of Great Salt Lake is apparent in his "Narrative."[4] Bridger was, in turn, concerned with the General's recent passage of the canyons of the Green. Twenty-two years later Bridger told the Mormon Pioneers: "It is impossible for wagons to follow down the river, neither can it be followed by boats. Some have gone down with canoes, but had great difficulty getting back on account of the rapid current and rough channel. Cannot pass the mountains close to the river even with horses."[5]

While General Ashley had no competition in the purchase of furs at the rendezvous, some of the accounts indicate payments of about $3.00 a skin to Ogden's deserters, not $3.50 as Gardner promised, according to Ogden. Ashley's men were credited with $2.00 or $2.50 a skin, which is about what Ogden was paying.[6]

General Ashley's own men were credited as follows: Fitzpatrick, 140 skins; Gardner, 132; Sublette, 166; Clyman, 155; Zachariah Ham's grand total was 461 skins; Jedediah S. Smith's, 668; and Smith's men, 675. A stray figure of 3,100 in one account has been attributed by editor Morgan to J. H. Weber and his party of seven. That would be about 440 skins apiece, or $1,100 at $2.50 per beaver, for each contracted man like Potts, Beckwourth, or Bridger.[7]

[3] Dale, *Ashley-Smith Explorations*, 156. Bonner, *James P. Beckwourth*, 79: "We constituted quite a little town, numbering at least 800 souls, of whom one-half were women and children."

[4] *Ibid.*, 153.

[5] William Clayton, *Journal 1846–1847*, with the Mormon Pioneers, Nauvoo, Illinois to Utah, 174.

[6] *Missouri Historical Society Bulletin*, April 1955, pp. 291, 292, Prudhomme and Montour; also pp. 296, 298, Eddy and Sublette.

[7] John H. Weber's subsequent whereabouts and biographical data are rather scarce and doubtful, like his much-needed attendance at Ashley's first trading rendezvous. Could he have given his name to the river by being buried there?

Summarizing the sales at rendezvous: there were twenty-six orders for coffee in varying amounts; twenty-four for sugar; seventeen for knives; fifteen for colored cloth, mostly red or blue; fifteen for beads; fourteen for powder; thirteen for lead; twelve for earrings; eleven for tobacco; eight for ribbons; seven for awls; six for gun flints; six for fishhooks; five for flannels; five for buttons; and five for combs. Fewer orders were for blankets, kettles, chisels, axes, files, gunlocks, and pistols. Mentioned were pipes, razors, soap, thread, paper, mirrors, scissors, and lead pencils. In the twenty-odd accounts there are only two liquor sales: "Old Pierre, one gallon rum [no price]; and Gardner and Williams, 10 gallons rum, at $10 . . . $100."

James Bridger remained on the payroll and accompanied General Ashley to the lower Big Horn, according to the Ashley "Narrative": "On the 3rd day of July I set out on my way homewards with fifty men, 25 of whom were to accompany me to a navigable point on the Big Horn River, thence to return with the horses employed in the transportation of the furs." Subsequent developments indicate that Jedediah S. Smith, James P. Beckwourth, Zachariah Ham, and James Clyman accompanied General Ashley to St. Louis.

> I had 45 packs of beaver cached a few miles east of our direct route. . . . I took with me twenty men and raised the cache . . . But was attacked by a party of about sixty Blackfeet.
>
> They made their appearance at the break of day, yelling in the most hideous manner, and using every means in their power to alarm our horses, which they so effectually did that the horses, although closely hobbled, broke by the guards and ran off. The Indians succeeded in getting all the horses except two. . . . I sent an express to secure horses from our men who had taken a direct route. . . . In two days I received the desired aid and proceeded about ten miles, when, at midnight, we were again attacked, [this time] by a war party of Crow Indians, two of whom were killed and two wounded, but without loss to us.

The General leaves us wondering whether Bridger was among those who went for or sent the aid. Under the goading of the Blackfoot thieves, those stolen horses traveled far. Peter Skene Ogden, on

September 30, 1825, in faraway western Montana, tells us: "McKay met with eight Piegans, horse thieves, [Blackfoot federation] who were in quest of the Flatheads. They had one horse loaded with cords and provisions. They informed McKay that a party of Blackfeet had lately arrived in camp with 53 horses, stolen from the Americans on Bear's River."

General Ashley rejoined his main party and proceeded to the Big Horn at Wind River Bend. Being short on horses and long on experience (Fitzpatrick had been wrecked on the Platte, and Ashley had descended Green River), they constructed a few bullboats to convey part of the load down the Big Horn, while most of it continued by pack-horse caravan. At the Big Horn Canyon, or "Bad Pass" of the Indians (at the Wyoming-Montana state line), they gathered for a conference.

While advance scouts proceeded on land, James Bridger, alone on a small but sturdy raft of driftwood, ventured a pilot voyage through the twenty-mile "Bad Pass." He succeeded, unwittingly performing a feat never equaled in western travel annals except by General Ashley's descent of the Green. Captain W. F. Raynolds (1859) says: "Bridger claims to have descended the lower Big Horn Canyon some years since on a raft, during his service as a trapper. . . . His descriptions of the grandeur of the scenery along its banks are glowing and remarkable. He portrays a series of rugged canyons, the river foaming among jagged rocks, between lofty overhanging precipices, whose threatening arches shut out all sunlight; interspersed with narrow valleys, teeming with luxuriant verdure, through whose pleasant banks the stream flows as placidly as in its broad valleys below."[8]

Washington Irving says: "Its passage through this chain is rough and violent; making repeated falls, and rushing down long and furious rapids, which threaten destruction to the navigator; though a hardy trapper is said to have shot down them in a canoe. At the foot of these rapids is the head of navigation."[9]

It is no wonder maps began to show such legends as: *"Bad Pass—*

[8] William F. Raynolds, *Report on the Exploration of the Yellowstone River, 1859-60,* 56.

[9] Washington Irving, *Adventures of Captain Bonneville,* 172, 177. He says it is "a rugged and frightful route, emphatically called the 'Bad Pass.'"

Here for 40 miles the river runs through a narrow gap in the mountains, the precipices on both sides 1,000 feet high."[10] In August, 1833, N. J. Wyeth, portaging the Bad Pass section said: "The River here looks tranquil, but flows between two perpendicular banks of stone perhaps five hundred to eight hundred feet high. The chasm, even at the top, is of no great width."[11]

G. I. Powers of the Crow Indian Agency went through the canyon in a motor boat in August, 1954. He says:

> The gorge meanders constantly and turns back on itself, with rarely more than a thousand yards of straight course. It deepens and widens to a maximum near the Wyoming-Montana State line, of a mile in width and two thousand feet in depth. Elsewhere the walls are three to six hundred feet in vertical height; and there are numerous places where they rise directly from the water on both sides. In these narrows the rapids are quite turbulent. The average current is slow.
>
> There are hundreds of spires, chimneys, caverns, windows and figures, of all imaginable shapes, in the colorful sandstone, limestone, dolomite and granite; the colors being as rich and numerous as in the Grand Canyon of Arizona. Where the slopes and banks admit, deer, elk, bobcats, mountain lions, bear, beaver and racoon, are evident from their tracks, at the water's edge.
>
> The river is treacherous for navigation, due to short but perilous rapids; rock-ledge drops or falls of three to five feet; and to submerged and protruding boulders. Rubber rafts negotiate the rapids safely in skilled hands; but rigid craft are risky. Our ten-foot motorboat was swamped and sunk, with resulting hull damage that rendered it useless. Bridger's voyage on a raft must have been exciting indeed!

General Ashley reached the "Bad Pass" portage August 7, 1825, with the land caravan. The next day they all detoured the Canyon, evidently having had word from Bridger warning them not to attempt the canyon voyage with their packs of furs. Below the Pass, towards the Little Big Horn, Beckwourth relates they set about killing buffalo and preparing bullboats for the voyage down the Yellowstone. That required only five days, he says. Ashley hitch-hiked a safe ride from Fort Henry, according to Indian Agent

[10] That legend is on a map identified only, "Washington, 1839."
[11] Nathaniel J. Wyeth, *Correspondence and Journals*, 209.

O'Fallon's report: "On August 19, 1825, General Ashley arrived from across the Rocky Mountains, by way of the headwaters of the Yellowstone, which he descended in skin canoes. On the 27th of August, General Ashley and his party of twenty-three men, with one hundred packs of beaver, being taken aboard the [Army] transport . . . reached Council Bluffs, September 19, 1825," and St. Louis on October 4. The newspapers estimated the value of this load of furs at $50,000.[12]

12 *Annual Reports of Indian Agents, 1825.* O'Fallon.

RUNNING THE RAPIDS of the "Bad Pass" of the Big Horn won for James Bridger the acclaim of the Indians, who had always feared the passage. From them, in turn, he acquired a fund of intelligence about the Absaroka country which the trappers were now ready to explore. They had already excited his curiosity by reports of hot-water fountains, stinking springs, roaring waterfalls, and colorful canyons.

The natives further confirmed Bridger's own conclusion that the Seedskedee (Green), the Lewis or Snake (Columbia), and the Missouri (Yellowstone) headed near one another. The tradition among the Canadian trappers was equally insistent that the Yellowstone had been visited by French fur men long ago who had named it "Rochejaune," (Rock Yellow, or Yellowstone).[1]

William L. Sublette had earned his right to head the trappers, and Thomas Fitzpatrick had also been trained by experience to serve as first lieutenant. James Bridger, though five years their junior, was a capable brigade leader and a strong man out in front of any group. When General Ashley departed, "Captain" Sublette's company was near the foot of the two-prong Shoshone trail, one side leading westward through the present Sylvan Pass, the other angling southwestward to the Wind River Mountains. Charles G. Coutant, Wyoming's early historian, says this about their route:

> During the same season [1825] Fitzpatrick and Bridger, with a detachment of thirty trappers went up the Snake (Shoshone) River and trapped in all the tributary streams of that locality. Bridger, with a small party, followed the Snake [Shoshone] River to its very source, and wandered around for some time in what is now known as Yellow-

[1] Hiram M. Chittenden, *The Yellowstone National Park*, 2.

stone National Park; and he evidently became fascinated with the wonders of that country. He talked with many persons about it, but as in Colter's case, his stories were laughed at by the trappers.

The next year [1826] he happened to be at the trading post of the American Fur Company on the Yellowstone, and there met a young Kentuckian, Robert Meldrum, who came out to be employed as a blacksmith at the post. He was a good workman, but soon imbibed the love of adventure and went out as a trapper. During Bridger's visit to the post he told Meldrum what he had seen the year before; and that young man was fired with an ambition to go into that country.

He soon after joined the Crows, and it was while living with these people that he found an opportunity to investigate the wonders around Yellowstone Lake. In later years he often talked with Army officers and others about the geysers, and for a wonder, his stories were believed.[2]

On that first visit, Bridger seems to have led his curious trappers through Sylvan Pass to the canyons of the Yellowstone River. In a truly wonderful region to the west, he afterward told many friends, there was a river that was hot at the bottom (Fire Hole), petrified tree trunks still standing, and a dark glass cliff (Obsidian Cliff).

Captain Gunnison spoke of Bridger's descriptions: "A picture most romantic and enticing . . . A lake sixty miles long, cold and pellucid . . . . The river issues from this lake, and for fifteen miles roars through the perpendicular canyons. . . . Waterfalls are sparkling, leaping and thundering down the precipices, and collect in the pools below.

"On the west side . . . the ground resounds to the tread of horses. Geysers spout up seventy feet, with a terrible hissing noise, at regular intervals. In this section are the great springs, so hot that meat is readily cooked in them; and as they descend on the successive terraces, afford at length delightful baths."[3]

In the course of time these phenomena, to Bridger, became as commonplace as cumulus clouds. They filled Bridger's hunger for discovery quite as full as Yellowstone Lake, which seemed to be spilling over the entire horizon, lying on the very top of the world.

Terminating his initial excursion through the park at the Lake

[2] Charles G. Coutant, *History of Wyoming*, 126.
[3] John W. Gunnison, *A History of the Mormons*, 151–52.

Outlet (Fishing Bridge), Bridger was convinced that this bulky stream bespoke an equal incoming stream on the Lake's remote boundary.

A day's travel to the south along the Indian trail bordering the eastern shore brought them to the seemingly separated but very much alive tail-section of the Yellowstone River, some fifty-odd miles in length, flowing north. One more day's journey would bring the trappers into a welcome encampment at a pond-sized lake, since named by all map-makers "Bridger Lake," nestling outside the present boundary of Yellowstone Park.

The following morning, following two hours on the Indian trail to Jackson Hole, Bridger's luck, plus his discerning understanding of the unique, brought him to Two Ocean Creek, which ambiguous phenomenon seemed to spew a lying split tongue at him, as if saying in Indian language: "There ain't no such thing!" But there it was and still is, and it is the living heart of the "Teton Wilderness Area," within the Teton National Forest, Wyoming. Forest Supervisor H. H. Van Winkle describes it in a letter:

> Two Ocean Creek is approximately three miles long, flowing southward along the Pacific side of the Continental Divide. In lowest water stages the Creek is four or five feet wide and about six inches deep where it divides into two approximately equal streams. Atlantic and Pacific Creeks. The division takes place in the timber, rather than in an open park, about a hundred yards above a marshy type of meadowland, through which both streams meander some distance before breaking away from the Divide.
>
> High water stages do not overflow the banks above the marsh; and the streams have never gone dry; thus it is not apparent that the "Y" or division point has been moved by floods or erosion. From all appearances, and considering the size and age of the trees on the banks, the "Y" has remained where it is for several hundred years. The Old Trail across the Continental Divide, from Jackson Hole to Bridger Lake, which approximately follows Pacific and Atlantic Creeks, crosses both creeks about fifty feet below the split or division of the main stream. Fish can cross the Continental Divide in the two creeks.
>
> The "Y" or dividing point is partly shaded or obscured in the forest, and does not always show up well in photographs.

We may follow James Bridger and his trapper friends through Jackson Hole, up Salt River, and down the Bear to Willow Valley to join their fellows for the winter encampment. But always we will find James Bridger's spirit lingering in the vicinity of Two Ocean Pass. It is Bridger's very own, as if he had created it instead of merely finding it.

At the campfire, Bridger and others pondered and perfected traffic regulations, as necessary then in Indian country as today on the highways. General Ashley was always a proud spokesman for his mountaineers. In a letter to General Macomb, commander-in-chief of the United States Army, Ashley described his method of equipping and moving parties in Indian country:[4] Mules were better for heavy packs, and each man had two, also one horse to ride. Each man received one saddle and saddle blanket, one bearskin cover for pack or saddle, packstraps, bridle for mount, and one heavy halter with sixteen-foot rein strong enough to hold under any circumstances, for each animal. A two-foot picket pin was provided with pointed iron socket and ring at the top.

In a party of sixty to eighty men, four of the most trustworthy and competent were selected to aid the command; the rest were divided into messes of eight or ten men, each headed by a suitable man, who reported the needs of his men. He received and distributed their supplies, observed their conduct, and enforced order. Every article issued to each man was entered in a record.

In Indian country strict vigilance was required. The line of march was preferably along a watercourse, and the encampment was laid out in a square, the waterway forming one side. The enclosure had to be large enough for all the animals, allowing a circle of thirty feet for each animal.

The position of each mess was then designated, and there the packs and saddles were removed and arranged in a breastwork in case of Indian attack. The animals were watered and delivered to the horse-guards, who kept them on the best grass outside, but near, the encampment until sunset. Each man brought in his own animals and picketed them within easy reach.

At daylight two or more mounted men examined the ravines,

4 21 Cong., 2 sess., *Sen. Doc. 39,* (Ashley to Macomb), 6, 7.

hills, and woodlands within striking distance; if all appeared to be safe, the animals were given to the care of the horseguards and allowed to graze until the men had breakfasted. The first mess ready to march took position behind the leaders, the other messes falling in line as they got ready. They marched in that order all day. Scouts were kept several miles ahead to examine the country near the route, and other guards were kept half a mile or more in front, on the flanks, and in the rear within signal range.

An old fur press, a device employed to squeeze furs into bundles of convenient shape and weight for haulage to market.

Buffalo Hunting Near Independence Rock, 1837, from a water color by Alfred Jacob Miller.

WHAT HAPPENED in Willow Valley that winter of 1825–26, only the "spirit guides" and James P. Beckwourth know, and only Mr. Beckwourth has spoken. Returning from St. Louis towards Christmas, probably in company with Jedediah S. Smith and party as far as Wind River, Beckwourth bore an important message to William L. Sublette in Willow Valley.

No one knows what was in that message besides the $1,000 Beckwourth says Ashley gave him for bringing it, but suddenly Mr. Sublette became important and took most of the trappers including Bridger and Beckwourth, to the Ogden-Weber junction, fifty miles distant, for its slightly milder climate. There Sublette began spreading word of a mid-July trading rendezvous at Bear Lake and assigning trapper territory.

The Snake Indian village was near Sublette's encampment on the Weber; the presence of these Indians should have been a protection, but it wasn't. Additional pasturage was sought for the horses in the meadows north of the Snake village. About eighty of these isolated horses were promptly stolen by Bannock Indians. A pursuit party headed by Fitzpatrick, Beckwourth, and Bridger followed the trail to the Bannock camp (Malade City, Idaho). The stolen horses were found grazing in the Indian herd.

"We then divided our forces, Fitzpatrick taking command of one party and a James Bridger of the other," says Beckwourth. Fitzpatrick was to charge the Indians and cover Bridger's party while they stampeded all the horses they could get away with. "I formed one of Captain Bridger's party, this being the first affair of the kind I had ever witnessed. . . . We rushed in upon the horses and stampeded from 200 to 300. The Indians recovered a great number of the horses from us, but we succeeded in getting off with the number of our own missing, and forty head besides. In the engagement six of the enemy were killed and scalped, while not one of our party received a scratch."[1]

The Snake Indians at the Ogden-Weber encampment constructed a medicine lodge that winter, a kind of tabernacle in the wilderness—a habitation for the Great Spirit—in which religious services were conducted, Beckwourth tells us. The medicine man was a high priest, his utterances sacred. When his presentiments were verified, confidence in the prophet exceeded all belief. Similar supernatural proclamations were made for prominent whites worthy of the shaman's attention.

These occult practices were rather serious business to the inquiring and vulnerable James Bridger. The attention he paid to them and the confidence he placed in them resulted in part from the uncanny premonitions given by the shaman in behalf of Thomas Fitzpatrick that winter. Beckwourth furnishes them (here digested):

"Where are you going?" the Prophet asked Fitzpatrick.

"We are going to the country of the Blackfeet."

"No," said the Prophet, "You will go to Sheep Mountain [Alexander, Idaho]. There you will find the snow so deep you cannot pass; you will then go down Portneuf to Snake River. . . . 'Bad Hand' [Fitzpatrick], I tell you there is blood in your path this grass. If you beat the Blackfeet . . . You will retrace your steps and go to Bear River whose waters you will follow until you come to Sage River. There you will meet two men [presumably not Indians but white men] who will give you news."[2]

As open waters appeared in early spring, Sublette, apparently working hand in hand with the Indian prophet, sent Thomas Fitzpatrick and James Bridger, with brigades, to Cache Valley to work Bear River around to Bear Lake.

"Soon after we arrived," says Beckwourth, "we commenced digging caches for the seventy-five packs of beaver skins on hand. While digging a cache in the bank, the earth caved in, killing two Canadians. The Indians buried them by hoisting the bodies up in trees." Tradition says that cache was near the entrance to Blacksmith's Fork canyon.

[1] Bonner, *James P. Beckwourth*, 92–94.
[2] *Ibid.*, 95–96.

"I had engaged to the fur company for the spring hunt of 1826, for the sum of $500, with the privilege of taking for servant the widow of one of the men killed in the bank. She was of light complexion, smart, trim and active, and never tired in her efforts to please me, she seeming to think that she belonged to me for the remainder of her life. I had never had a servant before, and I found her of great service to me in keeping my clothes in repair, making my bed, and taking care of my weapons."[3]

Beckwourth had told his sweetheart in St. Louis that he would be free to return to her when he delivered the thousand-dollar message to Captain Sublette. What Beckwourth did not foresee was this offer of five hundred dollars for the spring hunt, and a comely blond Indian woman eager to serve him as valet.

Parenthetically, James P. Beckwourth called it Cache Valley (not Willow), the name it has borne since then. Historians have overlooked the matter of bestowing on Mr. Beckwourth the honor of naming the valley.

As the Fitzpatrick and Bridger brigades worked their way north in Cache Valley, they found their way blocked by deep snow at Sheep Mountain, precisely as the medicine man had predicted. Crossing to the Portneuf, they descended into a hornet's nest of roving Blackfeet near the present Pocatello, Idaho. Consolidating their forces and keeping strict guard, they nevertheless noticed next morning three tether ropes cut and three fine horses missing. The alarm rang out: "The ropes are cut; stop the Indians; shoot them down!" Beckwourth duly noted.

Six Indians fell forthwith, "five of whom were scalped while warm, the sixth victim having crawled into the river to drown, taking his scalp with him." Hastily breaking camp, Fitzpatrick's men fled up the Portneuf. It had been exactly as predicted.[4]

Peter Skene Ogden, encamped nearby, tells his journal: "April 9, 1826. Portneuf River. About 10 A.M. we were surprised by the arrival of a party of Americans, and some of our deserters of last year, twenty-eight in all. If we were surprised, they were more so, from an idea that the threats of last year would have prevented us from returning to this quarter; but they find themselves mistaken. They

3 *Ibid.*, 96–98.
4 *Ibid.*, 99.

camped a short distance away; all quiet." (Ogden had written, March 24: "The American camp of twenty-five tents were on Bear's River, and it is a month since they left.")

April 10, 1826, Ogden concludes: "The strangers paid me a visit and I had a busy day settling with them, and more to my satisfaction and the Company's than last year. . . . Our deserters are already tired of their new masters, and from their manner, will soon return to us."[5]

While the Americans were moving up the Portneuf to cross the low divide to Bear River, "a party of fur trappers consisting of twelve men under the charge of one Logan, left our company to try their fortune; but [four of them] were never heard from afterward."[6] Evidently they were victims of Blackfeet. Subsequent casualty reports identify them as Ephraim Logan, Jacob O'Harrer, William Bell, and James Scott. They concern us, for they had been with either Bridger's or Fitzpatrick's brigade. .

When Fitzpatrick and party followed the medicine man out of Camp Weber that spring, Captain Sublette was arranging to reach Provost's post on the Green and assign trappers to the Wasatch streams. Bear Lake would be easier reached than Henry's Fork, had much better pasturage, and was more central and accessible. If Smith had reached Wind River, he could cover the upper Green. A considerable curiosity had grown up about Great Salt Lake, and four or five men delegated themselves (no doubt with Captain Sublette's knowledge and consent) to explore the lake and its beaver resources.

Fitzpatrick, Bridger, Beckwourth, and company returned to lower Cache Valley to confer with Sublette, lift the caches, and work the Cache Valley streams, where previously snow had prevented. Fitzpatrick and Beckwourth, with some of the trappers, may have then departed up the Bear River for trapping. Didn't the shaman say they would?

In early June, Robert Campbell and party reached Cache Valley fresh from St. Louis. Accompanying Ashley and his trading caravan, Campbell had hurried ahead from the Platte to notify Sublette and Ashley's trappers.

In his letter to G. K. Warren, April 4, 1857, naming James Bridger

---

[5] Ogden, *Journals*, 35–36.
[6] Bonner, *James P. Beckwourth*, 100.

as the discoverer of Great Salt Lake, Campbell adds: "In the spring of 1826 four men went in skin boats around it to discover if any streams containing beaver were to be found emptying into it, but returned with indifferent success.

"I went to Willow or Cache Valley in the spring of 1826, and found the party just returned from the exploration of the lake, and recollect their report, that it was without any outlet."[7]

What the explorers told Campbell and the company, Campbell told Ashley and the newspapers and others. The Alexandria *Gazette*, December 28, 1826, says Great Salt Lake "was coasted last spring by a party of General Ashley's men in canoes, who were occupied four and twenty days in making the circuit. They did not exactly ascertain its outlet, but passed a place where they supposed it must have been."

James Bridger told the Mormon Pioneers in 1847: "Some of his [Bridger's] men have been around the Salt Lake in canoes; they went out hunting beavers, and had their horses stolen by the Indians." Captain Bonneville wrote on July 29, 1833: "The Big Salt Lake I have never seen, but am told it has never been travelled around; five trappers once attempted to coast it, and were near dying from hunger and thirst."[8]

Who coasted the lake? James Clyman wrote in his journal for June 1, 1846 (southeast shore): "I observed that this lake . . . had nearly wasted away one half of its surface since [1826] when I floated around it in my bull boat." Moses (Black) Harris told the Mormon Pioneers on June 26, 1847, that he had traveled the whole circumference of the lake. (Beckwourth may have misdated his meeting with Harris at Sage River, southeast of Bear Lake, not 1826.) Louis Vásquez told a feature writer on the San Francisco *Bulletin* for October 29, 1858, that he had built a boat and circumnavigated the lake in 1826. D. T. Potts has been nominated as a fourth voyager, on account of his familiarity with the western shores of the lake, and H. G. Fraeb has also been named.

None of these navigators seem to have had any grave sense of the dangers courted. Great Salt Lake, far from being a popular pleasure-

[7] Warren, "Memoir," 35.
[8] Irving, *Captain Bonneville*, 390.

boating water, is extremely hazardous, especially for such light craft as individual bullboats. The voyagers' wisdom, or sheer good luck, lay in coasting the lake instead of crossing it.

Captain Sublette led his trapping band east to Bear Lake, probably along the route used by Campbell westbound. The old Indian trail between Cache Valley and Bear Lake has its eastern terminus in the well-grassed meadowlands at Meadowville and Laketown.

Fitzpatrick, Beckwourth, and company reached Sage River, fifteen miles southeast of Bear Lake. Here the leader was surprised to meet two men on their way to the rendezvous. They were Moses (Black) Harris and Beckwourth's old friend, Portulese. The incident completed the verification of the medicine man's prophecies. Fitzpatrick took up his traps and accompanied them to Bear Lake.

GENERAL ASHLEY's second and last fur-trading rendezvous, held June-July, 1826, appears to have been attended by all of the hunters under contract to him—James Bridger and the rest. General Ashley informed the press later that there had been no losses during the year by death.[1]

When Jedediah S. Smith joined General Ashley in 1825 as Major Henry's successor, James Bridger and the other hunters were blanketed into the new Ashley-Smith firm. Their contracts ran until July, 1827.[2]

Smith had left St. Louis October 30, 1825, "as a partner of General Ashley's in the fur trade," with sixty men and $20,000 worth of supplies and equipment for two years. The date coincides approximately with that of James P. Beckwourth's delivery of the message from Ashley to Sublette; possibly he and Smith traveled together. Beckwourth got through, but Smith's only record skips eight months' time; presumably he was wintering (Wind River? Riverton?) during this period and trapping the upper Green. He merely says his party "arrived at destination in June, 1826."[3]

General Ashley himself left St. Louis on March 8, 1826, with a

[1] Alexandria *Gazette*, December 28, 1826, quoted in Frost, "Notes on General Ashley," 147–48.

Ashley's caravan did not reach Great Salt Lake; but the newspaperman got the impression that it did, or that Bear Lake was the same as Great Salt Lake. A few years later, General Ashley wrote to General Macomb: "I have marched parties . . . to the vicinity of the Grand Lake, which is situated about one hundred and fifty miles down the waters of the Pacific Ocean, in seventy-eight days [in 1827]."

Bear Lake is about 140 travel miles from the Continental Divide at the South Pass. Great Salt Lake's nearest shore is about 200 travel miles from South Pass.

[2] Morgan, *Jedediah Smith*, 190, 411–12 (Ashley to Pratte).

[3] *Ibid.*, 331. See also: *Missouri Republican*, October 31, 1825; Philadelphia *National Gazette*, December 5, 1825; and Frost, "Notes on General Ashley," 143.

party of twenty-five men handling a lengthy merchandise caravan. Their travel route was along the North Platte River, across the South Pass, to Bear Lake. "He traveled the whole way by land, with pack horses going and coming, and has performed the trip in a shorter time [including several weeks spent there] than was ever known before. Wagons and carriages could go with ease as far as General Ashley went."[4]

For Robert Campbell, David E. Jackson, and several others it was the first trip west. To welcome and initiate them, all of Ashley's field men reached Bear Lake by June, 1826. "It may well be supposed that the arrival of such a vast amount of luxuries from the East did not pass off without a celebration." Beckwourth assures us that mirth, singing, dancing, shouting, trading, running, and jumping were indulged in, "medicine water" heightening the festivities.[5]

By letter of July 16, 1826, at Bear Lake: "We celebrated the Fourth of July, by firing three rounds of small arms; and partook of a most excellent dinner; after which a number of political toasts were drunk."[6] For such a program, General Ashley was undoubtedly master of ceremonies, and the refreshments came unquestionably by the new caravan. The newspapers later said Ashley remained at the lake "several weeks."[7]

The General's contract, signed "near the Grand Lake west of the Rocky Mountains," on July 18, 1826, by "J. S. Smith, D. E. Jackson, and Wm. L. Sublette," transferred only his mountain interests and activities; he agreed to supply the new three-party firm exclusively, retaining other related business.[8] By "Grand Lake" Ashley meant Great Salt Lake, about 60 trapper's travel miles from Bear Lake. The latter is about 140 miles west of the continental divide or Ashley's "Rocky Mountains."

By this document the new firm was to have possession of what

[4] Missouri *Republican*, September 21, 1826, and Alexandria *Gazette*, December 28, 1826, quoted in Frost, "Notes on General Ashley," 146–47.

[5] Bonner, *James P. Beckwourth*, 105.

[6] Frost, "Notes on General Ashley," 63.

[7] Missouri *Republican*, September 21, 1826, quoted in Frost, "Notes on General Ashley," 146.

[8] Chittenden, *Fur Trade*, 280.

remained of the contracts of the forty-two hunters, including James Bridger, and $16,000 worth of merchandise remaining unsold at the 1826 rendezvous. Ashley had brought more merchandise than the hunters brought furs, thinking of the competition of Peter Skene Ogden and Étienne Provost.

Additional trade goods could be ordered by express in St. Louis by March 1, from General Ashley. They were to be deposited "at the west end of the Little Lake of Bear River [Bear Lake], a water of the Pacific Ocean, by July 1, 1827." Furs would be traded in at $3.00 a pound, transportation was $1.125 a pound.

General Ashley's return march to St. Louis occupied about seventy days and was attended only by those who conducted the Smith and Ashley caravans to the mountains. Many of the trappers, including James Bridger, "have been out four or five years, and are too happy in the freedom of those wild regions to think of returning to the comparative thraldom of civilized life."[9] The General reached St. Louis around September 26, with about 125 packs of fur valued at $60,000.[10]

When General Ashley started for St. Louis on July 19, 1826, the new firm of Smith, Jackson and Sublette divided the men according to desires and needs, then apportioned the territory, comparing and adjusting plans and commitments. Smith with twelve or fifteen men would explore the southwestern deserts and coastal California, possibly, later, the entire Pacific Coast. Jackson and Sublette, having a large and competent band, would reconnoiter the Blackfoot lands. It was the summer season, and several men had not yet seen the Yellowstone country. The party gained courage from such members as Robert Campbell, D. T. Potts, James P. Beckwourth, and James Bridger.

Advancing through the Snake River region, "we were daily harassed by the Blackfeet," Potts wrote. He grew eloquent about the well-watered flat top of the world around Yellowstone Lake, writ-

---

9 Alexandria *Gazette*, December 28, 1826, quoted in Frost, "Notes on General Ashley," 147–48.

10 Missouri *Intelligencer*, September 28, 1826, quoted in Frost, "Notes on General Ashley," 146. None of these newspaper notices mention Ashley's withdrawal from the fur-catching part of the business or the existence of the new firm, Smith, Jackson and Sublette.

ing the first description of Yellowstone Park phenomena that is known to have been printed, as James Bridger had been first to describe them orally.

> On the border of this lake is a number of hot and boiling springs, some of water and others of most beautiful fine [white and pink] clay, resembling a mush pot, and throwing particles to the immense height of from twenty to thirty feet. There is also a number of places where pure sulphur is sent forth in abundance. One of our men visited one of these whilst taking his recreation; there, at an instant the earth began a tremendous trembling, and he with difficulty, made his escape, when an explosion took place resembling that of thunder.[11]

James Bridger seems to have met Robert Meldrum of the American Fur Company on this excursion, somewhere on or near the Yellowstone River, as historian Coutant informs us. Meldrum's company was investigating sites for trading posts to connect the Columbia Fur Company with the Hudson's Bay Company posts in an interlacing of ownership.

Traveling northwest and crossing the headwaters of the Missouri River, James Bridger, while trailing a bear, saw "smoke," according to Robert Campbell's Reminiscences (prepared in 1870 and furnished here by prospective editor, Dale L. Morgan).[12]

"Sublette, Bridger and myself . . . came to a place where Indians had camped . . . leaving some burned logs from which the smoke still issued." In camp this rather empty exploit was afterward called "the battle of the burned logs," which didn't even turn out to be steaming hot springs. However, it confirms Bridger's presence in company with the party leaders, also their cultivated caution in stealthily creeping close to a smoking log.

Beckwourth recollected that the company fell in with a roaming village of Flathead Indians enjoying the high country in the summertime. Jackson seems to have arranged with them for his winter's board and lodging, but if James Bridger manifested any warmth of interest in the young Flathead women, it was more than fifteen years breaking into flame for his first marriage. It is possible, how-

[11] Frost, "Notes on General Ashley," 63–64.

[12] Information furnished by letter from Dale L. Morgan, whose manuscript, "Robert Campbell's Reminiscences," is in preparation.

ever, that the discerning young woman who dragged her hope chest into Fort Bridger in 1843 was among the maidens lighting candles for Bridger in 1826.

Leading Blackfoot Indians, friends of the Flatheads, came to see Captain Sublette and invited him to establish a trading post among them. The Blackfeet were hungry for the white man's goods and "had many people and horses, and plenty of beaver." Sublette asked for volunteers, and Beckwourth responded, taking only his boy and one man to the Blackfoot camp. We may suspect that this "one man" was in charge.

Their success was rather phenomenal; in twenty days' time they had traded for thirty-nine packs of beaver fur and several fine horses. "Many times I bought a fine beaver skin for a butcher knife or a plug of tobacco," says Beckwourth. But his really wonderful feats were in the alleged conquests of the chief's daughters and the thrilling narration in fond recollection afterward.[13]

We begin to understand why a company captain required an efficient sergeant major like James Bridger to supervise and discipline the personnel. Beckwourth closes the episode: "I received a severe lecture from Mr. Sublette for my rashness while at the trading post!"

Returning in the early autumn towards Bear Lake, Captain Sublette visited a Snake Indian village and learned that the doubtful Pun-naks (Bannock) were nearby on Salt River, and with them a thieving band of renegade Snakes. Sublette sent a warning through the Snake villagers that if the Pun-naks stole anything from him, he would "rub them out." As a taunting reply, the Pun-naks killed a Snake guest and sent two trappers back wounded.

Sublette's call for volunteers brought 215 men, over whom Sublette appointed James Bridger as leader. When Bridger reached the site of the Pun-nak village, the Indians had fled. Bridger pursued them hotly, racing them forty-five miles to Green River. Here the Pun-naks, by quick maneuver, gained an island in the stream.

"What shall we do now, Jim?" Bridger asked Beckwourth.

"I will cross to the other side with one-half of the men," said Beckwourth, "and get abreast of the island. Their retreat will thus be cut off, and we can exterminate them in their trap."

13 Bonner, *James P. Beckwourth,* 110–16.

"Go," said Bridger. "I will take them if they attempt to make this shore."

Beckwourth finishes the gory story abruptly: "We carried back 488 scalps; and as we then supposed, annihilated the Pun-nak band. On our return, however, we found six or eight of their squaws who had been left behind in the fight, whom we carried back and gave to the Snakes."[14]

Moving together towards the upper Green River, Beckwourth says the Crows, Snakes, and whites made quite a village until the dispersal of the trapping teams on the fall hunt. Instructions had been issued to report in by a certain date to winter headquarters, which this time was to be on the lower Weber (Ogden, Utah).

[14] *Ibid.*, 124–25.

CAPTAIN SUBLETTE'S MEN were restless that mild winter on the Weber (1826–27). The mountaineers' order for supplies was due in St. Louis on March 1, and only Captain Sublette and Moses (Black) Harris had traveled the route lately. Consequently, "Colonel Sublette [and Harris] started on the 1st of January, 1827, from the valley of the Big Salt Lake. On snow shoes part of the time . . . an Indian broken dog carried a pack of fifty pounds . . . Ham's Fork . . . Carrying meat from Bear River."[1] They reached St. Louis on March 4.

Thomas Fitzpatrick was in charge of the Weber camp. From Bridger's subsequent statements, he seems to have accompanied D. T. Potts on an excursion into central Utah.

Having but little or no winter weather, six of us took our departure, about the middle of February, 1827, and proceeded . . . by way of the Utah Lake . . . thirty miles long and ten broad. . . . Utah Lake is plentifully supplied with fish. . . . On its banks were a number of buildings constructed of bulrushes, resembling muskrat houses. These we soon discovered to be wigwams. . . . As there is not a tree within three miles, their principal fuel is bulrushes. . . . The grass is, at this time [July 8], from six to twelve inches in height, and in full bloom. . . . The Utah Lake lies on the west side of a large, snowy mountain [Timpanogos], which divides it from the Leichadu [Seedskadee or Green].

From thence we proceeded due south about thirty miles to a small river [Sevier]. . . . We descended this river about fifty miles to where it discharges into a Salt Lake [Sevier Lake]. . . . From thence we went east across the snowy mountain above mentioned, to a small river

1 Matthew C. Field, *Prairie and Mountain Sketches*, (coll. by Clyde and Mae Reed Porter; ed. by Kate L. Gregg and John Frances McDermott), 165.

which discharges in the Leichadu [Strawberry River]. Here the natives paid us a visit, and stole one of our horses. Two nights afterward they stole another, and shot their arrows into four horses, two of which belonged to myself.[2]

In apparent confirmation James Bridger told the Mormon Pioneers in 1847: "There is no timber on the Utah Lake, only on the streams that empty into it. . . . The Utah tribe of Indians inhabit the region around the Utah Lake, and are a bad people. If they catch a man alone they are sure to rob and abuse him, if they don't kill him; but parties of men are in no danger. . . . He never saw any grapes on the Utah Lake, but there are plenty of cherries and berries of several kinds. He thinks the Utah Lake is the best country in the vicinity of the Salt Lake. . . . There is an abundance of fish in the streams . . . timber all around the Utah Lake, and plenty of good grass. . . . We will find another river which enters into another lake about fifty miles south of the Utah Lake."[3]

"In the month of March 1827," wrote General Ashley, "I fitted out a party of sixty men; mounted a piece of artillery [a fourpounder] on a carriage which was drawn by two mules. They marched to [Bear Lake] or near the Grand Lake, beyond the Rocky Mountains," arriving June 13, 1827.[4] James B. Bruffe and Hiram Scott were in charge of the caravan, but William L. Sublette and his brother, Pinckney W. Sublette, accompanied them.

Of special interest to James Bridger and the rest was the arrival of the senior partner, Jedediah S. Smith. The preceding summer, his fifteen once-hardy men were saved from pitiful starvation by Mohave melons, grains, and garden vegetables. In primitive Los Angeles they were frowned upon as unwelcome and told to get out. Proceeding to the San Francisco district, twelve of the party remained. Smith and two companions crossed the Sierras and by chance came upon a miserable band of Indians as destitute as themselves (June 27, 1827). "The Salt Lake was a joyful sight. . . . My home of the wilderness."

A few days later Smith turned into Cache Valley and found two

[2] Frost, "Notes on General Ashley," 66, 67.
[3] Clayton, *Journal*, 275.
[4] 21 Cong., 2 sess., *Sen. Doc. 39* (Ashley to Macomb).

hundred lodges of Indians on their way to Bear Lake. Using the Indian trail up Logan River and its right-hand fork, they then descended through Temple Canyon to the Round Valley meadowlands (Laketown-Meadowville), July 3, 1827. Smith admits he "caused a considerable bustle in camp, for myself and party had been given up as lost. A small cannon, brought up from St. Louis, was loaded and fired for a salute."[5] This caisson was the first wheeled vehicle to cross South Pass, but it was needed most for the fur caravan, and we do not hear of it again.

How attentively James Bridger listened to Jedediah S. Smith's story is indicated in Bridger's statements, twenty years later, to the Mormon Pioneers: "The desert extends from the Salt Lake to the Gulf of California. . . . He supposes it to have been an arm of the sea [Imperial Valley]. The Indians of that country [Mohaves] make farms, and raise an abundance of grain . . . persimmons, grapes, corn, wheat, pumpkins and produce in abundance. . . . It is about twenty days' travel from the Salt Lake. . . . He supposes there might be access from Texas."[6]

At Bear Lake in 1827 the new firm of Smith, Jackson and Sublette sold to "W. H. Ashley & Co.," seven thousand four hundred pounds of beaver, at $3 a pound; ninety-five pounds of castor at $3 per pound; and one hundred and two otter skins at $2 each, totaling $22,690.[7] But their purchases of supplies from General Ashley's representatives came to about the same amount!

James Bridger's status as a fur hunter is fairly represented in General Ashley's letter of November 12, 1827, to Senator Thomas Hart Benton: "The products of the American hunters (about a hundred in number), for three years, averages about $600 annually each. That the same water courses, when first trapped, furnished double the quantity of furs in the same time with the same labor, I have not the least doubt."[8] Thus the trapper, like the trapped, was in process of decline to extinction.

Writing from the Bear Lake rendezvous, July 8, 1827, D. T. Potts says: "There is a poor prospect of making much here, owing

---

[5] Sullivan, *Jedediah S. Smith*, 23–26, June 22, 28, July 3, 1827.

[6] Clayton, *Journal*, 276–77.

[7] Morgan, *Jedediah Smith*, 233.

[8] 20 Cong., 2 sess., *Sen. Doc.* 67 (Ashley to Benton).

to the evil disposition of the Indians, and the exhorbitant price of goods." For example: powder, $2.50 a pound; lead, $1.50; coffee, sugar, and tobacco $2.00; three-point blankets, $15.00; cotton and calico, $2.50 a yard; blue and scarlet cloth $8.00 to $10.00 a yard; horses, $150.00 to $500.00 each.[9]

James B. Bruffe and Hiram Scott led the fur caravan away from Bear Lake July 13, 1827, presumably safeguarded by the four-pound cannon. William L. Sublette, always the motive power of the new firm, seems to have journeyed to Flathead House of Hudson's Bay Company to succeed Jackson as official observer. Smith and a small party departed again for California.

Robert Campbell, James Bridger, and a dependable band of trappers worked the Wasatch Mountain streams before settling for the winter on the lower Weber. They little suspected that an accumulated scarcity of meat animals, the continued concentration of Indians and whites, and an abnormally severe, snowy winter would combine to cause for them all the worst suffering they had known for years.

[9] Frost, "Notes on General Ashley," 66, 67.

PETER SKENE OGDEN's rich haul of furs at Ogden Hole in 1825 was never forgotten or forgiven, by the Americans. Smith, Jackson, and Sublette had all taken turns eavesdropping on the British at Flathead House. In further retaliation, William L.. Sublette had recently (March 26, 1827) taken out a license for his company to hunt on the potentially American waters in the Briton's front yard; specifically on the chimericial "Bonaventura," an eastern affluent of Great Salt Lake; on Horse Prairie Creek, in far southwestern Montana; and on Clark's Fork of the Columbia, or Flathead House itself.[1]

A much-used source of the history of the American Fur Trade is Peter Skene Ogden's "Snake Country Journals" (Idaho),[2] wherein a wily competitor keeps a jealous eye on American personalities, movements, and circumstances. The two most frequently mentioned Americans striding through Ogden's journal in the winter of 1827–28 are Robert Campbell and Samuel Tullock, each inclined to be friendly with James Bridger.

Ogden encountered a company of American freemen trapping on the Snake, near the Weiser, September 25, 1827. They claimed a force of forty, but only five joined Ogden on the Malade (Big Wood) in October for trade and safety. When they left for Salt Lake on November 30, Ogden reported they had caught only twenty-six beavers in the two months, but had traded to him more than a hundred.

[1] 20 Cong., 2 sess., *Sen. Doc.* 67, pp. 12–15. "Coty's Defile," named for Joseph Coty, whose death Ashley reported to Benton, "under the immediate command of Mr. W. Sublette," is shown on early maps to be the southernmost tributary from the west of the present Birch Creek.

[2] Peter Skene Ogden, "Journal," 1827–28, *Oregon Historical Quarterly*, Vol. XI, No. 4 (December, 1910), 361–96. Quoting extracts only. Hereafter referred to as Peter Skene Ogden, "Journal."

While encamped near the outlet of the Portneuf, Ogden further reports that two of a party of seven Americans visited him on December 20, 1827. They had met Ogden's aide, McKay, two days earlier in Day's Defile (of Little Lost River). The Americans had traded forty-nine horses from the Nez Percés, averaging $50 apiece, lost nineteen crossing the plains from Day's Defile, were obliged to eat six, and had ten stolen by hostile Snakes.

On December 24, 1827, Ogden wrote: "The American party of six joined us, their leader, a man named Tullock, a decent fellow." From Tullock, Ogden learned: "With them, beaver, large and small, are averaged at $5 each; with us, $2 for large, and $1 for small. Here is a wide difference. All to their liberty to trade with the natives. It is optional with them to take furs to St. Louis, where they obtain $5.50. One third of the American trappers follow this plan. Goods are sold to them at least 150% dearer than we do; but they have the advantage of receiving them in the waters of the Snake Country.

"For three years prior to the last ones, General Ashley transported supplies to this country; and in that period has cleared $80,000 and retired, selling the remainder of his goods in hand at an advance of 150%. . . . Three young men, Smith, Jackson and Sublette, purchased them [the supplies] who have, in this first year, made $20,000. It is to be observed, finding themselves alone, they sold their goods one-third dearer than Ashley did."[3]

On January 1, 1828, Ogden writes: "The Americans leave for Salt Lake," that is, they tried the deep snow at the head of the Portneuf. But they were all back again at the mouth of the Portneuf, January 16, 1828, when Ogden reveals, "The Americans are anxious to procure snowshoes, and I am equally so they should not. . . . I have given orders to all not to make any for the Americans."

Ogden feared the Salt Lake trappers, if they came, would overwhelm him. Tullock's men had only ten traps. But Ogden's greatest fear was American liquor. "I know not what their intentions, but had I the same chance they have, long since I would have had a good stock of liquor here, and every beaver in camp would be mine," he admits. The fact is, Tullock was not trying to trick Ogden; his horse-buying excursion fitted with the spring trapping plans out of

[3] Peter Skene Ogden, "Journal," January 5, 1828, pp. 368–69.

Camp Weber and possibly also with Sublette's operations in the far north.

On January 20, 1828, Ogden wrote: "Tullock, the American, who failed to get through the snow to Salt Lake, tried to engage an Indian to carry letters . . . to Salt Lake." Three days later: "The American is now very low spirited. He cannot hire a man to go to his cache, nor [obtain] snow shoes, nor does he suspect that I prevented. This day he offered eight beaver and $50 for a pair, and a prime horse. . . . I have supplied the Americans with meat, as they cannot procure it without snowshoes. The Americans are starving on Bear River, according to report; no buffalo in that quarter; they are reduced to eat horses and dogs."

January 25, 1828: "Snow and storms continue; a terrible winter. A man who went in quest of lost traps arrived with reports of fearful distress of the Americans. Horses dead, caches rifled. I believe this, as a trapper saw calico among the Snakes."

The Americans (with Ogden) "are making snowshoes themselves, which they ought to have done two weeks ago." January 28: Two Americans started for Salt Lake. "Wretched snowshoes; and this is the first time they ever used them. . . . The ice is very weak" (on Snake River under deep snow). "An American had a narrow escape; a minute more and he would have gone. He made a noble struggle for his life."

February 4, 1828. "The two Americans who left January 28th, unexpectedly made their appearance. Most agreeable to me, but a cruel disappointment to them. They could only reach the sources of Portneuf River." February 10: "The two Americans again set out for their cache." February 12: "A war party of Blackfeet has taken the direction of Salt Lake. The Americans left here are alarmed at the news, not only on account of the two men, but for their camp in that quarter. The Americans [with Ogden] have only twenty-four horses left; the rest dead from cold; and of the fifty they brought, I have no hope one horse can escape, though covered with robes each night."

February 16, 1828: "The two Americans arrived this afternoon, accompanied by one of their traders [Robert Campbell], and two men they met on Portneuf River near the source." One of these newcomers must have been James Bridger. They reported a recent fight with Blackfeet and the killing of Old Pierre Tivanitogan. The 1828 supplies of the Americans did not arrive owing to bad weather.

"It was a novel sight in this part of the world to see a party arrive with dogs and sleds; for seldom are two inches of snow to be found here," says Ogden, as he apprehensively reports the arrival of eight new packs of playing cards. He sees no solace in the Americans' losing $400 to the British card sharps.

February 19, 1828: "The Americans are making preparations to go to the Flatheads," evidently transferring the loads from dogs to horses. "Their trader, Mr. Campbell, informed me two of their trappers, Goodrich and Johnson who joined my camp last fall, are heavily indebted to his concern. . . . My conduct to them was far different from theirs to me four years since. He said it was regretted; that there was no regular company, otherwise I should have received compensation."

February 23, 1828: "The American party left for the Flatheads, and perhaps to the Kootenays. They have a long journey but are well provided, though very silent regarding the object of their journey. I believe they intend trapping the Forks of the Missouri, for which they are strong enough in numbers." March 26, 1828: "The Americans, [now five in number] . . . with us since December, departed for Salt Lake."

May 10, 1828: Plains Snakes, returning from Henry's Fork, reported, "Two days since, raiding a party of Blackfeet. In the loot were clothes, hunter's hats, shoes, etc., horses belonging to the Americans who wintered with us [Tullock's party]. The furs were left on the Plains, a convincing proof the Americans have been murdered and pillaged. . . . The Snakes are on the way to Salt Lake to find the Americans there, and obtain reward for restoration of property."

In corroboration, General Ashley wrote to Senator Benton, January 20, 1829: "Mr. Tullock states, that after he had left Mr. Ogden's camp some three or four days, but while within twenty miles of it, he was attacked by a party of thirty or forty Indians, who killed three men [P. Sublette, J. Johndron, and P. Ragotte], plundered him of about $4,000 worth of furs; forty-four horses; and a considerable quantity of merchandise."[4]

---

[4] 20 Cong., 2 sess., *Sen. Doc.* 67, 14.

HIRAM SCOTT, with the sidetracked caravan of supplies for 1828, "returned to the mountains," presumably at Wind River (Riverton), in late November, 1827.[1] There he fought a vicious winter, if not an uglier foe. His party must have furnished most of the "twenty white men" who joined Meldrum, Beckwourth, and the Crows in a bitter battle with Blackfeet.[2]

Continuing with his caravan, Scott reached Bear Lake in early June, 1828. While he was making his merchandise display, another Indian fight occurred, which Beckwourth describes at length. We follow, attentively, for James Bridger participated, we understand.[3]

Some Flathead Indians brought the news that "thirty white men, with women and children, were encamped on a creek twelve or fifteen miles distant [Cokeville]. They had twenty-six guns, but their ammunition was expended." Gallantly Beckwourth offered to take the party some ammunition. "Provo, Jarvey [Gervais], and myself, mounted on our fleetest steeds, found the party in camp. As we had expected, we found they were Campbell's party, among whom were many of our personal friends," including James Bridger.

"We encamped with them that night, and escorted them to the rendezvous next day." On the way they heard voices, which proved to belong to Blackfeet, advancing menacingly. Directing the women and children to make all speed to a grove of willows six miles ahead

---

1 In Ashley's letter to Macomb (March, 1829), concerning the sending of a cannon to Bear Lake in 1827, Ashley adds that the fur caravan of 1827 "returned to Lexington, in the western part of Missouri, in September, where the party was met with everything necessary for another outfit, and did return (using the same horses and mules) to the mountains, by the last of November, in the same year," with the 1828 supplies.

2 Bonner, *James P. Beckwourth*, 168.

3 *Ibid.*, 100–105.

(South Eden Canyon, east side of Bear Lake), "we formed to hold the Indians in check. . . . Situated as we were, it was impossible for them to surround us, for we had a lake on one side and a mountain on the other. . . . When they approached too near, we used our rifles, and always with effect. . . . It was a running fight through the whole six miles.

"On the way we lost one man, who was quite old. . . . I tarried with him, urging him on, until I found it would be certain death to delay longer. My horse had scarcely made three leaps in advance, when I heard him cry, 'Oh, God, I am wounded!' . . . I returned to him and found an arrow trembling in his back. I jerked it out and gave his horse several blows to quicken his pace; but the poor old man reeled and fell from his steed, and the Indians were upon him in a moment to tear off his scalp.

"Our ammunition now grew very short . . . at length we gained the willows . . . Eroquey led the charge. In our fierce onset . . . my beautiful horse was killed in its tracks, leaving me alone amid a throng of Indians. I was wounded with an arrow in the hand. . . . My Boy, Baptiste, seeing my danger . . . rode up to me; I sprang on the saddle behind him, and retreated in safety to the willows. . . . The foe pressed us sorely . . . their shots cut off the twigs of the bushes concealing us.

"Campbell then said that two had better go, for there might be a chance of one living to reach the camp. Calhoun volunteered to accompany me. . . . Disrobing our selves, then, to the Indian costume, and tying a handkerchief round our heads, we mounted horses as fleet as the wind, and bade the little band adieu. . . . We dashed through the ranks of the foe. The balls and arrows flew around us like hail, but we escaped uninjured.

"When about five miles from the camp we saw a party of our men approaching us at a slow gallop. We halted instantly, and, taking our saddle blankets, signalled to them, first for haste; and then, that there was a fight. Perceiving this, one man wheeled and returned to camp, while the others quickened their pace, and were with us in a moment. . . . Soon the road was lined with men, all hurrying along at utmost speed. . . . My companion and I returned with the first party . . . into the willows. The Indians were surprised at the reinforcements . . . instantly gave up the battle and commenced a retreat.

"We followed them about two miles, until we came to the body of Bolliere [Boldue], the old man that had been slain. We then returned, bringing his mangled remains with us. . . . On our side we lost four men killed and seven wounded. . . . From the enemy we took seventeen scalps. . . . We also lost two packs of beavers; a few packs of meat; together with some valuable horses. . . . The battle lasted five hours. At rendezvous, the scalp dance was performed by all the half-breeds and women, many of the mountaineers taking part in the dance. . . .

"The reader will wonder how a contest could last that length of time, when there were but thirty to oppose five hundred men, and we not meet with greater loss. It is accounted for by the Indian mode of warfare. The Indian is a poor marksman with a gun, more especially on horseback; and to kill with their arrows, they must be near their mark. . . . Unlike the Indians, we seldom discharged our guns unless sure of our man."

The report of this fight, relayed from Campbell and his men to Captain Sublette and General Ashley, was in turn relayed by the General to Senator Benton on January 20, 1829: "Lewis Boldue belonged to a party of eighteen men, under the direction of Mr. Robert Campbell, Clerk for Smith, Jackson and Sublette, who was on his way from the Flathead nation of Indians to a place appointed by Messrs. S. J. and S. as a general rendezvous in June, last.[4]

"It was well known by the H. B. Company traders (some of whom were trading with the Flatheads) as well as by the neighboring Indians, that Mr. Campbell had a valuable collection of furs, and intended, about this time setting out to join the rest of the Americans; this circumstance induced Mr. C. to use all possible expedition on his march.

"Notwithstanding, when within a few miles (perhaps about fifteen) of the rendezvous, he discovered two or three hundred Indians in pursuit of him; he and party [Boldue excepted] succeeded in reaching some rocks near at hand, which seemed to offer a place of safety. The Indians, who proved to be Blackfoot warriors, ad-

---

[4] 20 Cong., 2 sess., *Sen. Doc.* 67 (Ashley to Benton, January 20, 1829), 13–14.

vanced, but were repulsed, with the loss of several of their men killed; they would, no doubt, have ultimately succeeded in cutting off the whites, had they not been so near the place of rendezvous, where, in addition to sixty or seventy white men, there were several hundred Indians friendly to them, and enemies of the Blackfeet.

"This fact was communicated to the assailants by a Flathead Indian who happened to be with Mr. Campbell, and who spoke the Blackfoot language. At the same time, the Indians saw two men mounted on fleet horses, pass through their lines unhurt, to carry the information of Mr. C.'s situation to his friends. This alarmed the Indians, and produced an immediate retreat.

"Lewis Boldue, being an inactive man, was overtaken and killed before he had reached the rocks; several others were wounded while defending themselves among the rocks. This party lost about five thousand dollars worth of beaver furs; forty horses; and a small amount of merchandise."

Even an Indian fight did not cause the men to forget why they were there. The Sublette Papers, in the files of the Missouri Historical Society, St. Louis, credited Smith, Jackson and Sublette with 7,107½ pounds of beaver at $5.00 a pound; 49 otter skins at $3.00 each; 27 pounds of castoreum at $4.00 a pound; and 75 muskrats at 25 cents each; total $35,810.75.[5]

Captain William L. Sublette and Hiram Scott led the fur caravan from Bear Lake. On the way to St. Louis, Scott became desperately ill, and, in the style of early western tales, was abandoned. His bleaching bones gave his name to Scott's Bluffs, Nebraska.[6]

Joshua Pilcher, with a party of forty-five, including Lucien B. Fontenelle, William Henry Vanderburgh, and Andrew Drips, attended the rendezvous as potential competition, then proceeded to the Northwest.[7]

Robert Campbell, with James Bridger and a party of thirty-one,

[5] Morgan, *Jedediah Smith*, 302; and Missouri Historical Society, Sublette Papers file.

[6] Merrill J. Mattes, "Hiram Scott, Fur Trader," *Nebraska History*, July and September, 1945, pp. 127–62. Hereafter referred to as Mattes, "Hiram Scott, Fur Trader."

[7] 21 Cong., 2 sess., *Sen. Ex. Doc. 39* ("Joshua Pilcher's Report," St. Louis, December 1, 1831).

went east to trap Powder River. James P. Beckwourth, a member of the party, has made a spectacular event of the excursion, with himself in the role of hero and James Bridger as material witness.

Meeting a delegation of Crow Indians on Green River, a trapper among them named Caleb Greenwood (married to a Crow) invented the fiction that Beckwourth was in fact a Crow Indian who had been lost in a great conflict. Because of their inordinate credulity, Beckwourth tells us, the Crows believed the tale.[8]

Trapping with Bridger one morning, Beckwourth missed one of his beaver traps. "Captain Bridger (as skillful a hunter as ever lived in the mountains)," Beckwourth tells us, "offered to renew the search with me, expressing confidence that the trap would be found. We searched diligently along the river and the bank for a considerable distance. The float-pole was also gone—a pole ten or twelve feet long and four inches thick. We at length gave it up as lost.

"The next morning the whole party moved farther up the river. To shorten our route Bridger and myself crossed the stream at the spot where I had set my missing trap. It was a buffalo-crossing and there was a good trail worn in the banks, so that we could easily cross with our horses. After crossing and traveling on some two miles, I discovered what I supposed to be a badger, and we both made a rush for him. On closer inspection, however, it proved to be my beaver, with trap, chain and float-pole.

"It was apparent that some buffalo, in crossing the river, had become entangled in the chain, and, as we conceived, had carried the trap on his shoulder, with the beaver pendant on one side, and the pole on the other. We inferred that he had in some way got his head under the chain, between the trap and the pole, and, in his endeavors to extricate himself, had pushed his head through. The hump on his back would prevent it passing over his body, and away he would speed with his burden, probably urged forward by the four sharp teeth of the beaver, which would doubtless object to his sudden equestrian (or rather bovine) journey. . . . We killed the beaver and took his skin, feeling much satisfaction at the solution of the mystery. . . .

"The same evening Captain Bridger and myself started out with

[8] Bonner, *James P. Beckwourth,* 129–37.

our traps, intending to be gone three or four days. We followed up a small stream until it forked, when Bridger proposed that I should take one fork and he the other, and the one who had set his traps first should cross the hill which separated the two streams and rejoin the other. Thus we parted, expecting to meet again in a few hours. I continued my course up the stream in pursuit of beaver villages until I found myself among an innumerable drove of horses, and I could plainly see they were not wild ones.

"The horses were guarded by several of their Indian owners, who had discovered me long before I saw them. I could hear their signals to each other, and in a few moments I was surrounded by them, and escape was impossible. I resigned myself to my fate . . . . I was marched to the camp, and ushered into the chief's lodge," and there examined for resemblances and birthmarks. Plenty of signs were found.

Thus was Beckwourth established in the Crow Indian fold, eagerly allowing this mistaken identity to gain for him the place he secretly coveted. That his real mother was a quadroon and his father a planter did not matter, nor that he had Indian wives elsewhere and a betrothed lady, color not stated, in St. Louis. Given the finest Crow woman in the village and married in state, Beckwourth became, and for some years remained, to all appearances, a Crow Indian.

To add to Beckwourth's stature, he was promptly paid by Kenneth Mackenzie—to use his Crow Indian influence to work directly with Fort Union, Fort Clark, and the new post at the mouth of the Big Horn. Beckwourth would not be the one to announce it, but he probably operated as a subordinate to Robert Meldrum, mostly on Powder, Tongue, and Little Big Horn rivers.

We prefer to believe that James Bridger was aware of the Indians' strategy, if not a party to it; also that he knew a "Chi-an" from a Crow. Bridger rejoined Captain Robert Campbell to report Beckwourth's new honors and to resume his trapping. After this, Campbell's Company settled for the winter (1828–29) at the Wind River–Big Horn elbow. The winter village of the Crows was usually in this vicinity. As a kind of chieftain in this tribe, Beckwourth fraternized freely with his former trapper friends.

On January 6, 1829, at Wind River, Beckwourth signed (by mark) a promissory note, witnessed by Robert Campbell, acknowledging his indebtedness to Smith, Jackson and Sublette, for $275.00, payable in beaver at $3.00 a pound.[9]

[9] Missouri Historical Society, Sublette Papers file; also Morgan, *Jedediah Smith*, 305.

ROBERT CAMPBELL, James Bridger, and their trappers made spring hunt, 1829, on the upper waters of the Wind and Big Horn rivers. The casualty lists show that four men were killed near "Bad Pass": Ezekiel Abel, Philip Adam, Luke Lariour, and Peter Spoon. They were undoubtedly members of the Campbell-Bridger party. Thus Campbell's cup of frontiering was filling rapidly, and the future for Bridger was not clear.

As clerk for Smith, Jackson and Sublette, Campbell had been the only visible head of the concern for many months, and the responsibilities were tremendous at times: refereeing controversies, keeping the peace among the Indians and freemen about the camp, apportioning hunting and grazing areas, efficient teaming and congenial grouping of trappers, and the orderly, safe movement and encamping of such a chaotic army.

In St. Louis, William L. Sublette had wintered with relatives and friends—and signed up a fifty-four-man crew of packers, mountaineers, and adventurers. Among the trappers were Joseph L. Meek and Robert Newell, whose memoirs have greatly aided researchers who are trailing the fur trappers. Sublette's pack-horse caravan left St. Louis on March 17, 1829, and unloaded at the Oil Spring (Lander, Wyoming), July 1, 1829. Messengers had preceded the supply train to Wind River, Green River, and Bear Lake, announcing the time and place of rendezvous.

But rendezvous trade was rather light. The books were soon closed, and the surplus goods cached. No one was surprised when Robert Campbell rode away at the head of the returning caravan. He reached St. Louis on September 5, 1829, with his forty-five packs of beaver fur.

At the Oil Spring, Captain William L. Sublette arranged for his brother, Milton G. Sublette, Henry Fraeb, Jean Baptiste Gervais, and party to make the fall hunt on Big Horn waters as a cleanup squad. The Captain himself, assisted principally by James Bridger, but accompanied by Meek, Newell, and others, set out toward the west to meet Jedediah S. Smith and David E. Jackson as they had agreed upon long ago.

Ascending Wind River and entering what has since been known as Jackson Hole, they learned from the natives that Jackson had spent some time there in the autumn of 1828, but had proceeded to the far northwest for the winter. Sublette forced his way through Teton Pass down the Teton River, and to Henry's Fork (St. Anthony, Idaho).

Here the sky was opened, and both Jedediah S. Smith and David E. Jackson were let down to meet Captain Sublette on August 5, 1829. Accidental as it seemed to be, this was the first meeting of the trio since their names had been linked together in partnership.

Both parties needed supplies. An express returned for the goods cached at the Oil Spring, and Pierre's Hole was designated as the site for this belated rendezvous. Newell says it was held August 20, 1829, for about 175 trappers.[1]

After the Pierre's Hole trading rendezvous, Newell says they "separated for beaver hunting. . . . It fell to my lot to go with Smith and Sublette [James Bridger as pilot].[2] We went up Henry's Fork of Snake River; on to Lewis's Fork; crossed the mountain; on to the waters of the Missouri; took up winter quarters on the Big Horn; then went to Powder River and remained until spring. That winter Mr. Sublette went to St. Louis."[3]

To amplify: They went up Henry's Fork, Falls River, Lewis's River, Two Ocean Pass, Yount's Peak, Shoshone Basin, Shoshone or Grey Bull river, and the Big Horn to Wind River junction.

A campfire pleasantry on this journey, featuring James Bridger, is related by Meek.[4] Bridger is supposed to have been waylaid by

[1] Robert Newell, *Memoranda of Travel in Missouri*, 31.

[2] Frances S. Victor, *The River of the West*, (*Joseph L. Meek*), 85.

[3] Newell, *Memoranda*, 31.

[4] Victor, *River of the West*, 81. John E. Sunder, *Bill Sublette, Mountain Man*, 84; Bonner, *James P. Beckwourth*, 146; and Newell, *Memoranda*, 35.

Blackfeet, who shot and injured his horse. That caused the animal to rear and pitch, and Bridger dropped his rifle. In the story, an Indian snatched up the gun. There was nothing to do but run, which Bridger did, on horseback!

At a later camp, Bridger was making the rounds, inspecting trappers' equipment, and found Mahoney's weapon very dirty. "What would you do with a gun like that, if Indians were to charge the camp?" scolded Bridger. "Be Gorra, I would throw it at them and run, the way you did!" answered the Irishman.

Meek's dictated recollections imply that it was along about this time that James Bridger acquired the soubriquet "Old Gabe." As a lieutenant under Captains Smith and Sublette, Bridger had some success at communicating the word of authority to subordinates. The angel Gabriel, in the Bible, had the mythical duty of revealing Jehovah's will and purpose to various individuals. Jedediah S. Smith's familiarity with the Bible enabled him to see in Bridger the image of "Old Gabriel."

In January, 1830, Jedediah S. Smith moved the camp from Wind River to Powder River for buffalo meat and better forage. Here the trappers shaved sweet cottonwood bark from the trees and cut twigs from the tips of limbs for horse feed, says Meek. This roughage was tied in bundles or in blankets for use as needed. In the spring the trappers went "from Powder to Tongue, Little Horn, Clark's Fork, through Pryor's Gap, to the Yellowstone River. Returned to Wind River in July 1830," says Newell.

Meek further relates that thirty horses and three hundred beaver traps were lost in the crossing of a fork of the Yellowstone during flood stage. Returning from the Yellowstone, Tullock, Meek, and Ponto were delegated to lift a cache on the Big Horn. The bank caved in and killed poor Ponto, who was "rolled in a blanket and pitched into the river"[5] alone at his funeral. Meek was hurt at the time and was carried to camp but soon recovered.

Captain Sublette reached St. Louis on February 11, 1830, and announced an innovation. He purchased ten heavy-duty, farm-type wagons, with canvas covers on frames and wide tires on the wheels. Two Dearborn buggies were included, "four wheels; top, with curtained sides." The Captain had made visual reconnaissance of the

5 Victor, *River of The West*, 88.

route, and had plans for excavations of stream banks and hillsides with extra men and tools.

This first wagon train left St. Louis, April 10, 1830. It consisted of 10 wagons, 2 carriages, 150 draft and riding mules, and 12 beef cattle, in care of eighty selected men. There is little record of this unique enterprise, the participants being too busy getting there to write about it day by day. But Sublette's biographer, John E. Sunder, says one man was killed and another injured by the caving of a bank of earth during the excavation of a difficult piece of road.[6]

This extraordinary wagon train reached what has since been called Independence Rock on July 4, 1830. Captain Sublette, acting as master of ceremonies, conducted a christening ceremony, naming the huge boulder "Independence Rock." He had an audience of eighty men, most of them seated in the first wagons to reach the crest of the continent.[7] The wagons drew into Wind River rendezvous, at the mouth of the Popo Agie River, on July 16, 1830, having averaged about ten miles a day.

These famous white-top wagons framed the picture of the retiring firm of Smith, Jackson and Sublette transferring their mountain interests to their leading associates: Thomas Fitzpatrick, Milton G. Sublette, Henry Fraeb, Jean Baptiste Gervais, and James Bridger, named in that order on the papers which were signed August 1, 1830. The property value given was about $16,000. The new firm would continue to carry the informal name, "Rocky Mountain Fur Company."

The returning wagons left Wind River August 4, 1830, with the three retiring partners riding in the Dearborns. Two beef oxen and the milk cow also went back to St. Louis. The party, arriving October 10, 1830, averaged nearly fifteen miles a day. As if in explanation of their action, the retiring firm announced that the fur country was "nearly exhausted of its beavers."[8]

---

[6] Sunder, *Bill Sublette*, 85.

[7] "Diary of Asahel and Eliza Munger," *Oregon Historical Quarterly*, December, 1907, entry for June 25, 1839, 391. See also Field, *Prairie and Mountain Sketches*, 117 (1831 should read 1830; Sublette was in Santa Fe, July 4, 1831).

[8] 21 Cong., 2 sess., *Sen. Ex. Doc. 39*, (Message of January 24, 1831. Letter of October 29, 1830, to the Hon. John H. Eaton, Secretary of War, signed by Jedediah S. Smith, David E. Jackson, and W. L. Sublette.) See also William Waldo, "Recollections of A Septuagenarian," *Glimpses of the Past*, April–June, 1938, 86 (hereafter referred to as Waldo, "Recollections").

The new firm faced a dwindling of the buffalo, important for subsistence, and an increasing restlessness on the part of the Indians, who were fully aware of the danger, to them, in the loss of the beaver, the buffalo, and other game. Fortunately, the casualty lists were also diminishing, in spite of the almost magic increase in the number of trapper-adventurers. The West was not as wild as it used to be!

James Bridger (1804–81), from a drawing by C. M. Ismert.

Bridger's Hawken rifle, said to have been made in 1820.

AN AMERICAN FUR COMPANY merchandise caravan consisting of forty-five men and one hundred pack animals, sneaked through South Pass on June 20, 1830, nearly a month ahead of Captain Sublette's wagon train. Its leaders, Andrew Drips and Lucien Fontenelle, searched Green and Bear River basins in vain for customers who were not there.[1]

Fraeb and Gervais of the reorganized Rocky Mountain Fur Company, yearning for the headwaters of the Platte (in northern Colorado), selected a company of twenty-two trappers and ten Iroquois with wives and children. The fickle Iroquois were of Hudson's Bay Company origin and knew the country, but the petticoats were in the saddles, and they preferred Big Snake River. As a consequence Fraeb and Gervais, only pretending to be leaders, reluctantly followed the Iroquois across Green River to share the beaver streams with Joseph Robidoux and their ill tempers with everybody. They finally settled in Cache Valley for the winter (1830-31).

Thomas Fitzpatrick, Milton G. Sublette, and James Bridger organized a splendid force of ninety-one men, not counting freemen, for the still dangerous but ever tempting country of the Blackfeet. From the "Bad Pass" of the Big Horn, they waded Clark's Fork at Bridger's favorite ford (now Bridger village). Crossing the Yellowstone in the Big Timber–Livingston area they proceeded to the Smith River.

Tightly organized and highly cautious, they trapped Smith River to its junction with the Missouri above the Great Falls. With sor-

---

1 Warren Angus Ferris, *Life in the Rocky Mountains,* 39. Footnote references are to Denver edition.

rowful recollections, Bridger viewed the burial site of his comrades who fell in the foray of the spring of 1823. But Major Henry was still there in spirit, and his strategy, followed by Fitzpatrick, was to trap the entire Missouri to its head at the Three Forks, keeping the trappers virtually under armed guards. The party returned to take up winter quarters on the Yellowstone, where forage for horses and buffalo was available.[2]

Early in "the spring of 1831 Mr. Fitzpatrick went to St. Louis for supplies," wrote Newell. "Mr. M. G. Sublette and Bridger proceeded from Yellowstone River, south; came to Tongue River; lost fifty-seven head of animals by the Crow Indians." Meek says most of the stolen mounts belonged to the freemen. Antoine Godin, an unhorsed freeman, led a coterie of volunteers in pursuit. Bridger, for the company, accompanied them to ascertain the true facts as Meek had reported three hundred horses stolen. Fortunately the thieves employed the same kind of horse guards as the freemen. Godin and Newell therefore cut out the trappers' horses and distinguished themselves as bareback riders, herding the horses back to camp.

Moving to Powder River, "Bridger and Sublette separated," wrote Newell. "Sublette went to the Park on the Platte [New Park, Colorado]. I being one of Bridger's number, went with him to the head of Laramie's Fork [also Colorado]. Met Sublette in the Park; from there to the Snake country on Bear River, near the Big Lake [Bear Lake]." There, continues Newell, they "took up summer quarters to wait the arrival of Mr. Fitzpatrick with supplies, but in vain!"

As Newell implies, the biggest news in camp was no news at all concerning Thomas Fitzpatrick. In an earnest conference held by Sublette, Bridger, Fraeb, and Gervais, Bridger agreed with Fraeb that the Crow medicine man should be consulted.

The medicine man went to work. In a clairvoyant trance, he divulged that Fitzpatrick was not dead, he was on the road, but it was the wrong road; they would find him if they searched. The message was worth the horses they paid for it.

Henry Fraeb was the man to go. With him went Meek, Ebberts, trapper Reese, a hunter, a scout, and an Indian interpreter. They

[2] Newell, *Memoranda*, 31.

were to make a clean sweep of Bear River, Ham's Fork, Green River, Wind River, and the Platte. Two wagon trains had made the road fast so that they were soon in Laramie River's Black Hills (now the Laramie Mountains). To their astonishment they came upon Fitzpatrick with thirty men and a pack train, making all possible speed west.

If Fitzpatrick's face was red, it was from explaining to a worried associate how he happened to be in Santa Fe, New Mexico, on July 4, 1831, the day he should have been on Green River. His ruddy face turned a shade redder from talking Fraeb into exchanging places—Fitzpatrick to return to St. Louis for the mountain goods for 1832, and Fraeb to conduct the pack train to the trappers.

Fitzpatrick then related to Fraeb the interesting story of what had detained him. At Lexington, Missouri, he noticed the assembling of an extraordinary wagon freighting train. For a wonder, Jedediah S. Smith was in general charge of the expedition, and for a greater wonder Smith was assisted by William L. Sublette and David E. Jackson. The layout, "to a man up a tree," looked very much as though the new Rocky Mountain Fur Company was "holding the bag."[3]

However, since Smith was freighting goods to New Mexico, arrangements could be made at Santa Fe to load a pack train for the Rocky Mountain Fur Company, if Fitzpatrick wished to accompany them to Santa Fe. He did.

J. J. Warner, one of Smith's men, said they left Lexington on May 4, 1831, with eighty-five men and twenty-two wagons:

> Mr. Fitzpatrick, one of the partners, successor to Smith Jackson & Sublette, who, with one man, had come from the rendezvous on the Yellowstone in the winter, reached Lexington while our party was at that place, with two or three others, accompanied the party to New Mexico.
>
> On the morning of the second day after leaving the Arkansas River [May 27, 1831], Mr. Smith rode in advance in search of water. He did not return. Soon after the arrival of the party at Santa Fe, July 4, 1831, some New Mexican Indian traders came in bringing the rifle

[3] Waldo, "Recollections," 86–88.

and holster pistols of Mr. Smith, which they had purchased from the Indians, who stated that they had killed the owner on the Cimarron.[4]

David E. Jackson thereupon dissolved his partnership with Captain Sublette and joined William Waldo and Ewing Young in the southwestern mule trade. Captain Sublette's first business was to consign, equip, staff, and dispatch Fitzpatrick's caravan. He then disposed of the rest of his goods and returned to St. Louis.

After Fraeb's departure, Milton G. Sublette and James Bridger had set out on the fall hunt. Fur-trapping territory was shrinking, and fur hunters were multiplying like mosquitoes. Hudson's Bay Company had forty men in the area, the American Fur Company thirty, and the woods were full of freemen. Having informed Fraeb that they would winter on Salmon River, Sublette and Bridger proceeded northward over the divide, descending Gray's Fork. About daylight of August 15, while the horses were being turned out to nibble their breakfast, a hundred Blackfeet, supported by a yelling group of Cree Indians, made a sweeping charge on the Sublette-Bridger herd.

Afterward a self-selected committee of Crees, unarmed, strode nonchalantly into the trapper's camp, begging food and gifts. "Sorry," they had mistaken them for Snake Indians. Neither Sublette nor Bridger was "born yesterday." They knew the Crees were Canadian compatriots of the Blackfeet and well established as the world's worst Indian neighbors. The trappers presented their guns menacingly, in sharp reply to this impudence, and the Crees retired.[5]

The disappointed Indians caught four of Bridger's trappers on Gray's Creek, as they risked a night away from the main camp. At daybreak of August 19, the trappers were attacked, and it looked like a fight to extermination.

The trappers wisely lay low, agreeing to keep three guns in readiness for an all-out attack. They would fire only one gun at a time, and only when they were certain of execution. In this deadly manner the more daring warriors were dropped one by one. Finally

---

[4] J. J. Warner, "Reminiscences 1831–1846," *Historical Society of Southern California Publication*, 1907–1908, pp. 176–93. Hereafter referred to as Warner, "Reminiscences."

[5] Ferris, *Life in the Rocky Mountains*, 121.

short of ammunition, the Crees retired. The Indian dead were estimated at thirty; marksmanship had paid.[6]

Newell gives the trappers' travel route: "To Gray's Fork . . . a scrimmage with Blackfeet . . . . On to Salmon . . . on to Deer Lodge River; and on to the head of Flathead River [far northwestern Montana] . . . called a fork of the Missouri by Bridger and Sublette." Northward from Flathead Lake, Flathead River rises in a beautiful Canadian basin. "We returned to Salmon River," stopping on the way while Sublette and Bridger paid their first visit to Flathead Post of Hudson's Bay Company (Eddy, Montana).[7]

The Flatheads and Nez Percés were not unique in their chosen winter rendezvous. Ferris says his unit of Drips's American Fur Company was already there when Sublette and Bridger arrived in force. The increasing population of men and animals called for some moves and adjustments to trial locations such as Big Hole Valley and Horse Prairie. Sublette and Bridger first settled in the present Salmon City site.

Henry Fraeb arrived with the pack train on November 5, 1831, ending an unheard-of and never-to-be-repeated journey. From Santa Fe to Salmon City—Santa Claus coming in from the south! But the ensuing hilarity was short-lived before the "liquor kegs were bunged," Ferris informs us.

Kit Carson was in Fraeb's party, having enlisted with Fitzpatrick at Taos. Carson remembered it: "We traveled north till we struck the Platte River and then took up the Sweetwater. . . . We trapped to the head of the Sweetwater, and then on to Green River, and then on to Jackson Hole . . . and from there on to the head of Salmon River. Then we came to the camp of a part of our band that we had been hunting; then we went into winter quarters on the head of Salmon River. During the winter we lost some four or five men . . . killed by the Blackfeet Indians."[8]

After Christmas, Sublette and Bridger moved upriver opposite Horse Prairie entrance, accompanied by forty or fifty lodges of

[6] *Ibid.,* 123.

[7] Newell, *Memoranda,* 32.

[8] Kit Carson, *Carson's Own Story of His Life* (ed. by Blanche C. Grant and Charles L. Camp), 21.

self-invited Flatheads and Nez Percés. "Horse Prairie" had been used by the Blackfeet as a horse trap, and already twenty of Bridger's horses had been stolen through Lemhi Pass. The very next day a wily party of Blackfeet came to the Sublette-Bridger camp, brazenly cutting the tethers on seven or eight horses belonging to the Flatheads. Appropriately it was a Flathead who killed and scalped a visiting warrior within the campsite.[9]

It happens that leaders of these same Flathead–Nez Percés Indians were at that time (winter 1831–32) visiting Captain William Clark, Indian superintendent at St. Louis, inquiring about the white man's "Book of Heaven." The religious press of the nation rang with the Macedonian cry of these spiritually hungry Indians. This marked the beginning of a new wave of missionary work among the American Indians.

Robert Campbell, former fur trapper, vouched for them, but he warned that cultured missionaries would be subjected to inconceivable privations and hardships, living and migrating with the Indians. Although these particular Indians were eagerly inquiring about the "Book of Heaven," missionaries would find them in dire need of clothing, food, morals, skills, and occupations.

On March 1, 1832, James Bridger led his men east across Horse Prairie and Red Rock Creek, which had only been skimmed by the trappers because of the Blackfoot bugaboo. Working only the more westerly affluents, he crossed the continental divide (Monida), to Cassia Creek and Gray's Lake Outlet.

Here, on May 15, 1832, "in a narrow bottom, beneath the walls of Gray's Creek, we found a party of trappers, headed by [James] Bridger. Their encampment was decked with hundreds of beaver skins, now drying in the sun. . . . There were [in addition] several hundred skins folded and tied up in packs."[10]

At this meeting, Bridger heard the sad news that a new brigade of American Fur Company men, under William Henry Vanderburgh, had come up the Yellowstone, wintering in Cache Valley, Utah. Blackfeet had already slain four of their trappers, and four others had not returned from a hunt.

Vanderburgh was to meet Andrew Drips at Bear Lake, then both

[9] Ferris, *Life in the Rocky Mountains*, 129.
[10] *Ibid.*, 144.

leaders would attend the general rendezvous at Pierre's Hole. Drips brought only some liquor and his own supplies, but Fontenelle and Étienne Provost, of the same company, were bringing a supply pack train to Pierre's Hole.

Bridger led his own men directly over to Pierre's Hole to lay out the central encampment near the middle of the valley in readiness for the Rocky Mountain Fur Company's fresh pack train, which he, of course, expected Fitzpatrick would be bringing soon. It was one of the great assemblies of record during the fur era, Newell estimating 350 whites and 250 friendly Indians in attendance.[11]

[11] Newell, *Memoranda*, 32.

BECOMING APPREHENSIVE, Milton G. Sublette and James Bridger dispatched scouts towards the Platte about June 15, 1832, to look for and assist their oncoming pack train. A few days later leaders of the American Fur Company sent out couriers in quest of their caravan. On June 29, 1832, the Sublette-Bridger camp was startled by the excited return of their somewhat dilapidated scouts. At Laramie's Fork they had been robbed of their mounts by Crow Indians, but had no word of the pack train.

A small pack outfit under Alexander Sinclair reached Pierre's Hole, July 3, 1832, having wintered on Popo Agie or Wind River. They had fallen in with O'Fallon and Harris, who had six or seven Mexicans with them and the same number of pack animals laden with liquor, blankets, and knives, bound for the rendezvous. As a suitable celebration of the national birthday, July 4, 1832, an American Fur Company scout returned to Pierre's Hole to report that Captain William L. Sublette was approaching with the Rocky Mountain Fur Company's pack train from St. Louis.[1]

Everybody was in a high state of expectancy when, on July 8, 1832, Captain Sublette's cavalcade pulled into Pierre's Hole with about one hundred pack mules in the competent care of about fifty hostlers, packers, and hunters.

Accompanying them, as traveling companions only, were about twenty Oregon-bound opportunists and adventurers, whose senior leader was Nathaniel J. Wyeth.[2] A similar body of fur trappers and traders from Taos, New Mexico, outfitted by Gantt and Blackwell but led by A. K. Stephens, were transferring themselves by some

[1] Ferris, *Life in the Rocky Mountains*, 151.
[2] Nathaniel J. Wyeth, *Correspondence*, 159.

veiled transaction to the Rocky Mountain Fur Company. This group included Zenas Leonard.

Captain William L. Sublette had quit New Mexico for good in 1831, and, meeting Fitzpatrick in St. Louis, readily adjusted his pursuit of opportunity by taking charge of the 1832 merchandise caravan for the Rocky Mountain Fur Company. Too many mountaineers owed him too much money for that business to be delegated to anyone else; besides, he longed for the mountains. He left St. Louis, March 13, 1832, with Thomas Fitzpatrick "second in command," Nidever says.

On the last day of June, at Laramie's Fork, we hear of them from Zenas Leonard: "Mr. Fitzpatrick and a company of 115 men came to our camp. . . . This company informed us that the firm of Gantt & Blackwell had become insolvent. At this news we all became discouraged and . . . agreed to join Fitzpatrick . . . . Mr. Stephens took 120 beaver skins which belonged to Captain Gantt and sold them to Fitzpatrick. For this Fitzpatrick was to furnish him with horses, and equipment."[3]

Fitzpatrick had rushed ahead from the Sweetwater to herald the forthcoming news—not to make the news.

After a week of baffling search and anxious inquiry, George Nidever and a hunter named Poe returned to Pierre's Hole from a meat hunt, escorting a bedraggled Fitzpatrick, practically incoherent from exhaustion. A band of roving Blackfeet had pursued him, captured him, and held him prisoner for several days in a rocky crevice.[4]

Nidever adds: "We met Fitzpatrick crossing Lewis Fork. He was mounted, having by the merest chance, caught a horse saddled and bridled, that had escaped from one of the men at Pierre's Hole. Fitzpatrick was shoeless, hatless and almost naked. In crossing a river his powder horn was lost; and this rendered useless his gun and pistols, which he threw away. For ten days or thereabouts he had wandered about, having in that time eaten no food excepting a very small piece of dried meat."

While Fitzpatrick was being fed and nursed back to health, the

---

[3] Zenas Leonard, *Leonard's Narrative*, 92.

[4] George Nidever, *Life and Adventures of George Nidever* (ed. by W. H. Ellison), 24–25.

store goods were being opened and passed out in exchange for peltry, first to the needy men of the Rocky Mountain Fur Company, next to their collaborating freemen and friendly Indians, and then to others in need, as few other goods had arrived.

It seemed to be a turning point for several members of the Wyeth family and party. They wished to break with their leader and to organize for the return to St. Louis. N. J. Wyeth himself, with eleven followers, was eager to get on the way to Oregon. Captain William L. Sublette arranged with Wyeth for his brother, Milton G. Sublette, to accompany the Wyeth party out of range of the Blackfoot Indians.

This group, with Milton as escort, would be in trapping territory on the lower reaches of Snake River when the hunting season opened. On July 17, 1832, Wyeth moved southward towards an opening in the mountain girdle of Pierre's Hole. The following morning a party of travelers was observed entering the valley.[5]

A fleeting hope that it was Fontenelle's belated pack train turned quickly to consternation when Wyeth's spyglass revealed a belligerent-looking band of Blackfoot Indians. There were possibly fifty warriors in war regalia, accompanied by their women and children, as if on some casual or peaceful errand. Signs of friendship were exchanged, and emissaries advanced for a parley. The trappers' representative was Antoine Godin, a freeman, and he was accompanied by a leading Flathead Indian. On nearing the Blackfoot (Gros Ventres) couple, Godin recognized the murderer of his father, Pierre Godin. Distrusting them, Godin promptly shot the chief dead and retreated, after snatching the royal robe as a trophy.

The Blackfeet fled at once to the shelter of some small fallen timber nearby, the warriors fiercely occupied with their weapons, while the women scooped firing depressions and placed barricades. A white courier was rushed back to the rendezvous, six or eight miles distant, where Captain William L. Sublette, Thomas Fitzpatrick, and James Bridger went into a hasty conference and called for experienced volunteers.

The leaders suspected that the mixed party of Indians was merely

[5] John B. Wyeth, *Oregon: A Short History of a Long Journey*, 69–74; see also Irving, *Captain Bonneville*, 57; Newell, *Memoranda*, 32; and Victor, *River of the West*, 111–18.

executing a diversion to draw the guards away from the merchandise, furs, equipment, and animals for a larger force poised for attack. It was decided that Fitzpatrick and Bridger would secure the safety of the rendezvous by doubling the horse guards and rushing sentries to every likely approach.

Captain Sublette selected about thirty whites and as many friendly Flathead and Nez Percés Indians, then galloped to the battle scene. A cursory examination indicated that an attacking posse would be dangerously exposed. Thus restraint was more in order than encouragement. The battle was for that reason confined to a random fusillade. This continued until dusk, when the Indians on both sides stealthily retired. The whites did likewise, and Wyeth's entire party returned to the rendezvous.

Captain Alexander Sinclair and one of Fraeb's Iroquois Indians were killed in the engagement. Several whites were wounded, Captain Sublette worst of all, with a ball through his shoulder. Five allied Indians fell and eight Blackfoot Indians were scalped, three bodies being found on the field next morning. About twenty-five of the Indians' horses were killed, but one of the live horses taken belonged to Fitzpatrick.

A week's rest under the professional care of Dr. Jacob Wyeth, Nathaniel's brother, brought improvement to most of the wounded at the rendezvous. The doctor's own delicate health, however, had already forced him to join the faction of his cousin, John B. Wyeth, determined to return to St. Louis with Captain Sublette's pack train.

Nathaniel's party of eleven, escorted by Milton G. Sublette, Henry Fraeb, and their trapping party (Meek included),[6] moved for the second time out of Pierre's Hole on July 24. The remaining sixteen members of Captain Sinclair's crew accompanied Wyeth only as far as Raft River, going thence to the Humboldt (Nevada).

Wyeth's escort descended Snake River with him to the Boise–Payette region, turning east on August 28 for the autumn trapping.[7]

At Pierre's Hole, several documents were signed by Captain Sublette and the Rocky Mountain Fur Company, on July 25.[8] These transactions triggered another move on that same day. A party of

---

6 Victor, *River of the West*, 119.
7 John Ball, *Autobiography*, 79.
8 Sunder, *Bill Sublette*, 110–12.

seven under A. K. Stephens departed in a huff, some of the party being defecting Wyethites in frail health.

Zenas Leonard says: "A violent dispute arose between Stephens and Fitzpatrick, about the price of horses," in exchange for the 120 beaver skins presumably cached at Laramie's Fork. "Finally he [Stephens] succeeded in hiring four men and started back to the mouth of the Laramie, to secure the fur which he had sold to Fitzpatrick."

The next day, July 26, twenty Blackfoot Indians attacked the departing seven in Little Jackson Hole, killing George More and William Nud. Captain Stephens and another, wounded, were brought back to Pierre's Hole on July 27 for a sad readjustment.

Captain Sublette moved out of Pierre's Hole after a warm shake of James Bridger's hand, on July 30. With him were sixty assistants, and a handful of returning members of the Wyeth party. The Captain was under contract with the so-called Rocky Mountain Fur Company, to deliver a herd of horses for them in St. Louis and to transport 169 packs of beaver fur, weighing 11,246 pounds, at fifty cents a pound. The wounded and frustrated Captain Stephens, who attempted the journey with Captain Sublette, was in worse condition than had been apparent. He died as the caravan trailed out of Pierre's Hole and was buried by the way.

In Captain Sublette's mail bag was a letter from John Robertson to his father, who lived near St. Louis, dated July 15, 1832. Robertson was an employee, a personal friend, and later a neighbor of James Bridger. "Uncle Jack's" letter read in part: "I am now about to make a fall hunt, having bought horses and traps. . . . I should have come down this fall but Sublette and Fitzpatrick persuaded me to stay out this year; and besides, I got to be lazy, and do not believe I could go to work. I have sent down $100 by Mr. Sublette, to pay for the land."[9]

Washington Irving, returning from his "Tour on the Prairies," September 23, 1832, wrote near Lexington, Missouri: "We remember to have seen . . . their long cavalcade stretched out for nearly a half mile. Sublette still wore his arm in a sling. The mountaineers in their rude hunting dresses, armed with rifles and roughly mounted, and leading their pack horses down a hill of the forest, looked like

[9] Elizabeth A. Stone, *Uinta County: Its Place in History*, 42.

banditti returning with plunder. On the top of some of the packs were perched several half-breed children, perfect little imps, with wild, black eyes glaring from among elf locks. These, I was told, were children of the trappers; pledges of love from their squaw spouses in the wilderness."[10]

[10] Irving, *Captain Bonneville,* 66.

THOMAS FITZPATRICK and James Bridger broke camp at Pierre's Hole on July 31, 1832, having organized a large, partly trained, semi-military unit to guarantee safety and efficiency. Current reports indicated that Blackfoot warriors were nearly everywhere, and concomitantly, fear of them was intense and widespread. With the Blackfeet on the prowl, the Missouri River sources adjoining their homelands would be no more hazardous than Pierre's Hole or Green River.

With Polaris as their guiding star, Fitzpatrick and Bridger crossed Henry's Fork and Camas Creek, filing into the lengthy Lemhi Valley to Salmon River, according to Newell.[1] Turning eastward into Big Hole, towards Beaverhead and Jefferson rivers, they expected to find Nez Percés and Pend d'Oreille Indians with beaver furs to trade, as these Indians had not attended rendezvous.

It became more evident, about this time, that the Blackfeet were not the only foes operating against the Rocky Mountain Fur Company. The American Fur Company, as registered at Pierre's Hole, was in two or three units, each working independently. Captain Vanderburgh had a speaking affiliation with Drips; and both were expecting to be re-supplied by Fontenelle. They left Pierre's Hole together, August 2, 1832, and luckily fell in with Fontenelle and Provost on Green River, August 8, with about 50 men and 150 horses.[2]

Fontenelle had but recently conferred with Captain Benjamin L. E. Bonneville, yet another newcomer, who, with a force of 120 men, 20 covered wagons, several pack horses, and a large remuda of horses and mules, was erecting a fort headquarters a few miles down

[1] Newell, *Memoranda*, 32.
[2] Ferris, *Life in the Rocky Mountains*, 158–59.

Green River. After the trading was completed at Pierre's Hole, Fontenelle departed for Fort Union with a thirty-man pack train on August 12. At the same time Vanderburgh and Drips took about 115 men northwest to Horse Prairie and Salmon River, trusting their guides to find beaver.

Fitzpatrick and Bridger knew the fur country stream by stream. They also knew the Indians, and they knew the art of living in the open. But they recognized the probability of competitive superiority in business strategy. For that reason they had discussed with the American Fur Company the dividing of the fur territory.[3]

The newcomers, however, may have suspected they would be given the less desirable areas by the more experienced hunters. Thus, no deal. Some sort of contest was obvious, however, when Fitzpatrick and Bridger reached Big Hole in the early autumn of 1832. There they heard that Vanderburgh and Drips were approaching. In fact, as Fitzpatrick and Bridger moved out, Vanderburgh and Drips moved in; and forthwith the latter two conceived the very logical idea that Fitzpatrick and Bridger would be good "guides."

Out of Big Hole Valley, across the Deer Lodge and Clark Fork, the new hunters pursued their "guides." They were all taking a few beavers, but were feeling the shortage of protein for themselves. They were off course for buffalo at that season, and there were too many hunters for the wary game animals. Fitzpatrick and Bridger were at the Deer Lodge, August 31, while Vanderburgh and Drips were there September 4.[4]

In a special effort to "lose" their followers, Fitzpatrick and Bridger penetrated the very front yard of the militant Blackfeet by reaching the upper filaments of the Blackfoot River. They then proceeded over the divide to Dearborn River, descending it to the Missouri (midway between Helena and Great Falls). Arriving there on September 14, they were surprised to find Vanderburgh and Drips arriving at the same time. They had accepted the challenge of a race, instead of a beaver hunt.

In a falsely friendly hand-shaking conference, it developed, when

---

[3] Victor, *River of the West*, 108. Mrs. Victor often adds material obtained from sources other than Meek, and registers or records her own conclusions or background, instead of Meek's.

[4] Ferris *Life in the Rocky Mountains,* 166.

anyone was caught speaking candidly, that their mutual heart interest, in painful fact, was a little lower in the anatomy—they were all hungry, starving. Bridger assured them the Three Forks Valley was the nearest place promising both furs and game, if there were not too many trappers already there.

Vanderburgh was ten or twelve years older than Bridger and had a few years' trapping to his credit. He could read between the lines; there were few furs to be found on Bridger's trail. With the instincts of a gentleman and the initiative of a freeman, Vanderburgh broke away entirely, on September 16, with a force of about fifty men, to operate on his own.

Vanderburgh's departure left the atmosphere of the double encampment stormy, both mentally and meteorologically. When Bridger directed the scouts to advance southward up the Missouri in the face of a biting sleet storm, Andrew Drips and about fifty American Fur men reluctantly fell in line to follow. Forced marches, in a three-day storm, were an ordeal even for experienced legs, but they brought them to Three Forks valley by September 21.

On the way the scouts and hunters had glimpsed occasional elk families in the timbered outskirts, as well as a few antelope and deer which had sought quieter natural shelters from the storm and deepening snow. But Bridger had held his course to the open country for speed. Here the camp dogs jumped an occasional rabbit, but heavy barbecuing game was scarce, and buffalo nonexistent.

The weather and human tempers gradually improved together, although as Bridger had correctly anticipated, the game, the forage, and the beaver were not abundant in the face of such a large and sudden demand. Moreover, some of the trapping teams had sighted Blackfeet in war paint sneaking close enough to make still closer bed-fellows out of men who weren't. Nevertheless, Drips very soon came to the conclusion that it was time he, too, struck out for himself. This he did, moving up the Jefferson with fifty or sixty men. It was exactly what the Rocky Mountain Fur Company leaders had been listing in their prayers.

Having appraised the beaver prospects, Fitzpatrick and Bridger set out to trap systematically, under diligent guard, the Gallatin and then the Madison, from Three Forks. The upper Madison was nearer their proposed winter rendezvous on the Salmon River. They made rapid headway, but Ferris reported delaying snowfalls on October 4 and 6. On a sunny October 9, they met Vanderburgh's party and camped with them on the Madison. The next day it snowed again, good weather for visiting, comparing notes, and renewing friendships by the men.

Vanderburgh had crossed Deer Lodge Plain, after parting with the Rocky Mountain trappers, then journeyed to the Jefferson, reaching it about thirty miles below Beaverhead on September 30. He then traced Philanthropy to its sources and moved over to the Madison, descending it for this two-day meeting. From here Vanderburgh rode directly into trouble. His party traveled down the Madison some fifteen miles on October 12, turning into a tributary of Philanthropy (present Ennis–Alder Gulch area). On the fourteenth, hunters reported a nearby Indian campsite that looked as if it had been abandoned in haste.

In order to make an investigation before settling his own camp, Vanderburgh, with a few volunteers, proceeded to examine the still-warm Indian campsite, three miles upstream. Pushing on another two or three miles, looking for Indian signs, they crossed a small wooded bottomland. Suddenly a score of rifles thundered from the gulley ahead, and most of the trappers turned and fled in panic. Only two remained: Pillon, who was dying, and Vanderburgh, whose horse was killed.

The courageous leader partially rose on his dead mount, carefully aimed his gun, and dropped the nearest Indian. At that instant a second volley from the advancing horde returned the fire and felled him. Tomahawks and spears completed the gruesome orgy to the victorious screams of exulting Blackfeet. Searchers subsequently buried Pillon where he fell. Vanderburgh was not to be found, probably having been thrown in the stream. Later examiners (Indians) came upon what they presumed were his bones, and buried them nearby.[5]

After the memorable meeting with Vanderburgh, Fitzpatrick and Bridger pressed forward, October 11, to cover the upper branches not already closed by snow and ice. Accomplishing these activities under the hardships of winter, they fell in with another touring

[5] *Ibid.*, 177–78, 181.

band of trappers, separated earlier from Drips's troops near the Three Forks. (Newell implies this was Craig's brigade.)[6]

Fitzpatrick and Bridger, trailed by the new group, then struck westward into Pierre's Fork of the Jefferson. Here they encountered a formidable band of Piegans (of the Blackfoot family). Two of the Indian leaders gingerly approached, unarmed, pleading a peaceful purpose and a desire to trade with the whites. They claimed all other Piegans had decided on this new attitude. They departed, apparently happy, with some minor gifts from Fitzpatrick. But in going, they warned Bridger that a horde of roving Bloods (also of the Blackfoot family) was lurking in the region and might show fight.

Confirming the word of the Piegans, more than one hundred Blood Indians appeared ahead on October 25. An advance guard fired a warning shot on the Bloods, who surprised everybody by hoisting a white rag on a stick.[7] Friendly signals were exchanged, and two or three from each group advanced cautiously. Meeting midway, they formed a circle and passed the pipe from hand to hand, each man smoking it solemnly.

A Mexican among the freemen trappers was accompanied by his wife, a Blackfoot woman. Noticing her brother among the Indians, she pushed forward to greet him affectionately, Washington Irving tells us. Sensing possible trouble, James Bridger "left the main body of trappers and rode slowly towards the group of smokers, with his rifle resting across the pommel of his saddle. The Chief of the Black-feet stepped forward to meet him.[8]

"From some unfortunate feeling of distrust Bridger cocked his rifle just as the Chief was extending his hand in friendship. The quick ear of the savage caught the click of the lock; in a twinkling he grasped the barrel, forced the muzzle downward, and the contents were discharged into the earth at his feet. His next movement was to wrest the weapon from the hand of Bridger, and fell him with it to the earth.

"He might have found this no easy task had not the unfortunate leader received two arrows in his back during the struggle. The Chief now sprang into the vacant saddle and galloped off to his

---

[6] Newell, *Memoranda*, 32.

[7] Ferris, *Life in the Rocky Mountains*, 184.

[8] Irving, *Captain Bonneville*, 94–6.

band. A wild hurry-skurry scene ensued; each party took to the banks, the rocks and trees, to gain favorable positions, and an irregular firing was kept up on each side without much effect. . . .

"The approach of night put an end to the skirmishing fire of the adverse parties, and the savages drew off without renewing their hostilities." Bridger carried a metal arrowhead in his hip until Dr. Whitman removed it in August of 1835. Otherwise no part of this incident has been denied or corroborated; Bridger might have recovered the gun and horse.

HORSE PRAIRIE, the present Grant-Brenner area of Montana, had neither enough game nor enough forage to support its overly heavy population. Captain Bonneville had arrived there September 26, 1832, and erected temporary shelters for his men, along with pens for his goods and animals.

The Flathead, Nez Percés, and Pend d'Oreille Indians had for generations used the region as a seasonal abode; and were, at the moment, present in considerable numbers. The lower elevation, milder climate, and lighter snowfalls drew them there. But now, "The climate be hanged!" declared the seasoned leaders. It would be pleasanter to freeze to death in some other place than starve to death here. Moreover, Bonneville's aide, Matthieu, and Milton G. Sublette, each with a trapping party, were not yet in.

Fitzpatrick and Bridger, with their close-knit organization, arrived at Horse Prairie in late October. They found there both contingents of the American Fur Company. As if to pre-empt a place for winter rendezvous, Drips and party departed on October 24 for Henry's Fork of Snake River. The melancholy Vanderburgh division followed shortly.

But even with this relief, Fitzpatrick and Bridger were still uneasy about food and forage. After securing the remuda of horses under guard, they drifted to the forks of the Salmon for a social call on the Flatheads.

Captain Bonneville was wisely releasing about fifty men under J. Reddeford Walker, with ample packs and mounts, to proceed to the mouth of Blackfoot River for the winter. Fitzpatrick then decided to investigate other wintering possibilities on Snake River. Walker and Fitzpatrick departed October 31, leaving Bridger in charge on the upper Lemhi.

On November 7, Milton G. Sublette with his brigade trudged into Bridger's encampment. They had had a poor hunt, but an interesting journey, "almost to Walla Walla." Fitzpatrick had passed down Day's Defile (present Birch Creek) a few hours before Sublette reached it. Bridger, Sublette, Fraeb, and possibly Gervais settled themselves in Eighteen Mile Valley, adjacent to Horse Prairie, to await Fitzpatrick's return and report.

About December 1, "Five men left the Rocky Mountain Fur Company on Gordiaz [Godin] River in quest of meat; but were never afterwards heard of."[1] They left property with the company worth several hundred dollars. These may have been buffalo hunters from Bridger's camp, or from Milton G. Sublette's band.

Thomas Fitzpatrick traveled extensively in his sweeping examination of Snake River. He remained longest with Andrew Drips at Henry's Fork, catching up on news. But he got no intelligence concerning his own company's supplies for 1833. The American Fur Company could make no commitments. After spending Christmas with Walker at the mouth of the Blackfoot, Fitzpatrick reached Bridger's camp about New Year's Day, 1833.

Momentous meetings were now in order for the new proprietors of the Rocky Mountain Fur Company. Apparently all five of the partners were present. Their business: to segregate their several congenial groups, plot their spring travel and trapping routes, and discuss means of supplying themselves, since definite arrangements had not been concluded. Moreover, the bulk of the winter lay before them, and occupants of Horse Prairie and the upper valleys nearby were facing a famine if all the trappers remained there.

"I left Mr. Fitzpatrick the 25th day of January [1833] and joined Captain Bonneville," says Newell, and others may have been similarly alienated.[2] The directors decided that Milton G. Sublette, with Gervais and their own crowd, would remove to the Snake River, at the mouth of the Portneuf, to wear out the rest of the winter.

According to Joseph L. Meek, Milton had additional reasons for the move: He had not fully recovered from a stabbing injury, and he had, for a year or two, been espoused to and accompanied by a

[1] Ferris, *Life in the Rocky Mountains*, 191.
[2] Newell, *Memoranda*, 33.

Snake Indian woman. Mrs. Sublette, with her lusty baby, pined to rejoin her people in the Snake-Portneuf section. Meek has much to say of this woman for another special reason: after Milton died, a couple of years later, the woman became Mrs. Joseph L. Meek.[3]

At that conference of the executives, it was agreed that Henry Fraeb, with an escort, should proceed towards St. Louis to search for the 1833 supplies. It was further decided that Fitzpatrick would assume charge of the fur packs and meager stores on hand, and accompany Fraeb as far as Green River. His trapping would be on the Black's Fork and adjacent streams.

James Bridger was to organize the remaining trappers for the spring hunt on the Grayling, Gibbon, and Firehole sources of Madison River, in what is now Yellowstone Park. He departed by way of Shoshone Lake, Snake River (Lewis), Jackson Hole, and Hoback River, reaching the rendezvous site on Green River.

Milton G. Sublette must have wintered well among his wife's people, for on April 6, 1833, at the south end of Godin's Defile (Big Lost River) Captain Bonneville found "twenty-two prime trappers, all well appointed, with excellent horses in capital condition, led by Milton Sublette and an able coadjutor named Gervais, in full march for the Malade [Idaho] hunting grounds."[4]

Captain Bonneville seems to have had a housekeeper forced onto him on this journey. "At the camp on Henry's Fork, July 7, 1833, when all hands had assembled for the evening, a clatter of hoofs beat the way into camp, and a solitary young woman of the Nez Percé tribe strode into the trappers' midst and quietly seated herself, still holding her horse by a long tether."

Was the throng curious, interested? Every man had a close look and a long one, and everyone had a guess, if not a wish. It was Captain Bonneville's prerogative to approach the visitor with his modest inquiry: "Why?" Her answer was assuring and final: "I love the whites; I will go with them." She was accordingly assigned to a lodge, "and from that time, was considered one of the camp." Hadn't the Captain just recently lost a secretary in Mr. Walker?[5]

However, there seem to have been other ways for the lonely

[3] Victor, *River of the West*, 107.
[4] Irving, *Captain Bonneville*, 134.
[5] *Ibid.*, 148.

trapper to acquire domestic assistance—using the example of the associates of James Bridger:

William H. Gray journalizes, July 6, 1837, at Green River rendezvous: "Today I was told, in conversation with Messrs. McLeod, McKay, Walker and McLane, that Indian women are lawful commerce among the men that resort to these mountains. . . . They named to me a man by the name of Dr. Newell, as he is called, who won a woman on a wager. On hearing that his old Flathead wife was coming with McLeod's party, he said he must get rid of the woman. Accordingly he went and sold her to her previous owner, for one hundred dollars."[6]

Captain Bonneville saved the following anecdote for Washington Irving. Among the Indian beauties at rendezvous, two free trappers discovered their two "whilom" (former) squaws, one a Utah and the other a Shoshoni. The trappers wanted the women, and the women wanted the wardrobe finery of the freemen. Consequently, the "pert little Eutaw wench . . . was readily ransomed."

But the Shoshoni "had become the wife of a Shoshoni brave . . . who had another wife of older date." All attempts to bargain were useless. The freeman suggested an elopement. The Shoshoni woman listened and began to lean a little, but feared the fury of a Shoshoni husband. At night she stole away to the trapper's tent, and they fled on horseback. The desperate Shoshoni brave followed them to their camp, where the local populace interested itself, and the Shoshoni brave acquired "two good horses . . . for one bad wife!"[7]

[6] William H. Gray, "Unpublished Journals of William H. Gray," *Whitman College Quarterly*, June, 1913. Hereafter referred to as Gray, "Journals."

[7] Irving, *Captain Bonneville*, 357–59.

A FLOWERY SPRINGTIME was unfolding at Bonneville's so-called "Fort Nonsense" (Daniel, Wyoming, seven thousand feet elevation), when James Bridger trudged in with his fur brigade about July 1, 1833. Rendezvous had been a single trading center with comparable prices to all, but the 1833 rendezvous, when beaver skins were harder to get, had competitors hard to count, promising prices still harder to understand.

Units of the American Fur Company were encamped about four miles down Green River. Captain Fitzpatrick had placed the Rocky Mountain Fur Company four miles farther south, where Green River could be forded. But Fitzpatrick, himself, had departed eastward in response to an express courier from Robert Campbell, who was approaching with a supply caravan. Campbell wanted to know where to find an assured market and thus urged Fitzpatrick to meet him in the Black Hills.

Bridger had some misgivings about Fraeb, who should have intercepted Campbell or his courier. Somewhere about the Black Hills, they did meet, however, and a voluble partisan says Mr. Fraeb was "going to St. Louis to purchase goods, with the intention to return to the mountains in the fall. . . . [Instead] Mr. Fraeb made some arrangements with Mr. Campbell on which he bought the outfit, with the exception of ten mules and ten barrels of liquor and two bales of goods."[1]

In a few days, "Mr. Fitzpatrick arrived with three men and six mules loaded with beaver," says Larpenteur. "The following day they settled all their affairs and started" for the rendezvous, but

[1] Charles Larpenteur, *Forty Years a Fur Trader* (ed. by Elliot Coues), 25, 27. Parts of a parallel "Original Journey" are carried in the footnotes.

Fraeb had to detour for beaver to trap or trade. Accompanying the forty-man and one-hundred-mule pack train, were young Benjamin Harrison, adventurer; and Sir William Drummond Stewart, sportsman, with his own outfit. They made quite a stir on arrival at Green River, July 5, 1833.

Surely William L. Sublette had arrived, in spirit if not in flesh, to direct and dominate the apparently headless Rocky Mountain Fur Company. "The day after we reached the rendezvous, Mr. Campbell with ten men, departed to raise a beaver cache at a place called Pierre's Hole," Larpenteur informs us. Campbell got back about July 15, with ten packs of beaver.[2]

Nathaniel J. Wyeth arrived that same day. According to his diary about five hundred white trappers had chased the beaver during the year, and among the companies about twenty-five men had been killed. The losses of furs, equipment, and especially of horses had been crushing.[3]

Wyeth wrote on July 18, 1833, to Francis Ermatinger, of the Hudson's Bay Company, that the American Fur Company obtained 51 packs of furs; the Rocky Mountain Fur Company 55 packs from 55 men, Fraeb and company not in; Bonneville's company of 125 men had 22½ packs; and Harris, 7 packs. A party under Bridger and Fraeb also lost their horses. "In my opinion you would have been robbed of your goods and beaver if you had come here. . . . There is here a great majority of scoundrels."[4]

Larpenteur says Campbell's liquor was placed on sale at Green River under the supervision of Fitzpatrick, but was dispensed in Campbell's absence by a Mr. Redman (who was not an Indian) and by Larpenteur. During the last week of the rendezvous, a hydrophobia scare swept the camp, although it was without serious consequences. The epidemic was apparently caused by some sickened wolves that had overindulged as camp scavengers. In their own stupor, they had bitten an unsheltered bibulous mountaineer or two, a thankless repayment for their rare fare.

[2] *Ibid.*, 34. The caches raised by Campbell probably included the one ordered by Captain William L. Sublette, referred to by John B. Wyeth in his *Oregon*, 61–62.
[3] Nathaniel J. Wyeth, *Correspondence*, 205.
[4] *Ibid.*, 69–70.

Fitzpatrick, Sublette, Bridger, Gervais, and possibly Fraeb, Harris, and others herded their animals over to Ham's Fork for better forage. And, "On July 22, 1833," says Larpenteur, "Mr. Gervais started with thirty men to trap the Root Digger's country," meaning the headwaters of Raft and Humboldt rivers.

On July 24, Joseph Reddeford Walker and about forty men left under orders from Captain Bonneville, who outfitted them, to explore Great Salt Lake. They traveled instead to far-away California for an extended sojourn. They returned by a remote southern route a year later from "this most disgraceful expedition" and broke Bonneville's heart by having no knowledge of Great Salt Lake.[5]

The rendezvous broke camp July 24, and Thomas Fitzpatrick, as pilot, led the procession by way of New Fork, crossing the low continental divide to the Sweetwater on July 26. But while scouting the way to the head of the Big Horn, they got lost.

During this delay four of Fraeb's men applied to James Bridger at Ham's Fork for directions to overtake Fitzpatrick's column. Bridger detailed their route to the Wind–Big Horn bend (Riverton), where he assumed Fitzpatrick would be. On July 31, Fitzpatrick's scattered forces came together near the Oil Spring. Here they fell in with Fraeb's four men, one severely injured, all of their horses stolen by Indians.

Wyeth explains: "August 1, 1833: The case was this: Mr. Bridger sent four men to this river to look for us, viz.: Mr. Smith, Thompson, Charbonneau, a half-breed; and Evans. . . . Thompson [picketed?] his horse to the others . . . sat down . . . having been on guard much of the time previous, fell asleep.[6]

"He was awakened by a noise among the horses . . . and opening his eyes . . . on the muzzle of a gun in the hands of an Indian. It was immediately discharged, and so near his head that the front piece of his cap, alone, saved his eyes from being put out by the powder. The ball entered the head outside of the eye, and breaking the cheek bone, passing downward, and lodged behind the ear in the neck. This stunned him, and while insensible, an arrow was shot into him, on the top of the shoulder, downward, which entered about six inches. The Indians got 7 horses, all there were."

[5] Irving, *Captain Bonneville*, 296.
[6] Nathaniel J. Wyeth, *Correspondence*, 207–208.

Reaching the lower Big Horn valley (Montana) while the hunters were killing buffalo for their hides and making bullboats for the fur-pack cargo, Milton G. Sublette and Thomas Fitzpatrick, for the Rocky Mountain Fur Company, on August 15 signed an agreement with Nathaniel J. Wyeth for $3,000 worth of supplies to be delivered at Green River in July 1834. Wyeth wrote later (November 8, 1833) that the contract was made "when I was in doubt whether I would be able to pay the forfeit."[7]

Fitzpatrick and Captain Stewart moved eastward on the Little Big Horn to Tongue River through Crow Indian lands. Fitzpatrick's old side-kick, James P. Beckwourth, then resided with the Crows. But a legion of surly Crows challenged the party on Tongue River, September 5, 1833, and invited Fitzpatrick to talk to their chief.

Placing Captain William Drummond Stewart in charge of the camp, Fitzpatrick made the courtesy call on the Crow Chief. Meanwhile the visiting Crows overpowered Captain Stewart's forces and pillaged the camp completely. The raiding Crows on their return met Fitzpatrick between camps and rudely took from him his mount, gun, capote (overcoat with hood), and even his watch. Returning indignantly to the Crow chief, Fitzpatrick effected partial restitution.

Convinced the strategy had been insipired by white men, Fitzpatrick applied to Samuel Tullock, at Fort Cass, three miles below the Big Horn outlet, for the return of the furs stolen by the Crows and sold to Tullock. The response, dictated by Kenneth Mackenzie of Fort Union, on January 4, 1834, belongs here:

"The forty-three beaver skins traded, marked 'R. M. F. Co.,' I would in the present instance give up, if Mr. Fitzpatrick wishes to have them, on his paying the price the articles traded for them are worth on their arrival in the Crow Village, and the expense of bringing the beaver in and securing it. My goods are brought in to the country to trade, and I would as willingly dispose of them to Mr. Fitzpatrick as to any one else for beaver or beaver's worth if I get my price. I make this proposal as a favor, not as a matter of right, for I consider the Indians entitled to trade any beaver in their possession to me or to any other trader."

Despite the loss of his overcoat, Fitzpatrick marched into James Bridger's camp on Ham's Fork on October 26, burning as with a

[7] *Ibid.*, 77.

fever. But being left in charge of the camp, in a few days he cooled off, in part, by means of the following letter, written to Milton G. Sublette, in St. Louis:

Ham's Fork Nov. 13th 1833.

Dear Sir,

I am sorry to have to relate to you I unfortunately met with the Crow Village who robbed me of everything I had with me save Horses and a few traps and by that means lost all my fall's hunt which you know was an inestimable loss. The Indians were pushed on to rob me by the American Fur Co. and I wish you to find out whether or no we can obtain any redress for such proceedings. If not we will have to seek it ourselves. I am now about to write to Gen'l. Ashley for advice on this subject, whom I hope will assist us if anything can be done to our benefit. Harris & Dr. Harrison is now about to leave here for St. Louis which I suppose you will see and receive all information respecting our Situation.

However, it is not quite so bad as you may suppose. Bridger and Myself have on hand about twenty three packs of Beaver furr. Fraeb with about 20 men is gone down the SeesKeedee with Bil Williams for pilot and intends not to return before March 1st. I think they may do well. I have not heard from neither. The understanding between you and my self will have to remain in the same state you left it until our meeting next summer as the parties are absent.

I have been uneasy ever since we parted about our arrangements with Wyeth. However, it may terminate well, but still I dread it. I have an idea we will stand in need of a large supply of Madze [mdse?] at rendezvous as the Spanish Companies will meet us there and there is now a party of them with Fraeb. I wish you to work Wyeth as advantageous and secure as possible, Studdy well the articles of profit.

Liquor will be much wanting, I well know; and indeed all groceries. Come as soon as possible to the rendezvous and look out for the Crows on your way up. I believe they will be hostile to all parties hereafter. They have good encouragement from the A F Co; perhaps they may not kill but they will certainly rob all they are able and perhaps murder also.

I intend to winter here and here abouts and will hunt nearly in the same section where I did last spring; don't you go high up on Seetskeddu as horse Creek; Strike somewhere about the mouth of Sandy and remain until we come. Harrison is going after a small equipment; you will, if you alow him to take up, make terms with him about it; he will be owing us considerable.

Now I have given you a short sketch of the whole situation of our affairs and I expect you to act hereafter although according to your own dictations; Mr. Guthery was killed last fall by lightning, and Biggs since supplies his place.

Yours,

Thos F.[8]

Certain facts concerning Bridger's own firm at this time (November 8, 1833) were written by Nathaniel J. Wyeth to his backers: "Smith, Jackson and Sublette sold out to Milton Sublette, Fraeb, Gervais, Bridger and Thos. Fitzpatrick . . . for $30,000, dividing among them about $60,000 for, I think, three years' business. This last firm . . . have paid the purchase money and have cleared their stock of goods and animals. . . . But not being business men, and unknown where the goods are to be bought, have been dependent on others for their supplies, for which they have paid enormously to Mr. Wm. L. Sublette. . . . They have been together three years and have made two returns amounting to 210 packs of furs, value, net, about $80,000; and received two outfits of goods, first cost about $6,000, for which they have paid about $30,000; and for returning their furs, about $8,000, leaving them, after paying the first purchase, about $12,000."[9]

No man gets anywhere without his detached seasons of prayer and meditation, a spiritual vacation of sorts. James Bridger knew it was the fur that was disappearing, not the men or means for gathering it. He also knew something of the Indians' predicament; they wanted to keep on eating and living. Bridger could see the handwriting on the Rocky Mountain walls and could readily read that kind of text. William D. Stewart had come into camp with Thomas Fitzpatrick and was in a mood for a change.

The evidence indicates that Stewart and Bridger journeyed to the Spanish Southwest for the winter of 1833–34. Bernard De Voto gives authenticity to a footnote in William Drummond Stewart's fictional work, *Edward Warren*: "It was in the spring of 1834. I was

[8] Photostat of the original letter in the files of the Missouri Historical Society, St. Louis, Missouri.

[9] Nathaniel J. Wyeth, *Correspondence*, 74.

with Jim Bridger, and one of the bravest and most dashing hunters of the day, Captain Lee, of the U. S. Army, in a range of mountains whose western slopes give birth to the waters of California, and near the city of Taos."[10]

Bridger told Captain John W. Gunnison that he had "traversed the region from the headwaters of the Missouri to the [Río Grande] Del Norte and along the Gila to the Gulf. . . . His graphic sketches are delightful romances. With a buffalo skin and a piece of charcoal he will map out any portion of this immense region, and delineate mountains, streams and the circular valleys called 'holes' with wonderful accuracy (at least the portion we traversed).

"Another region he visited and trapped in lies to the west of the [Río Grande] Del Norte [headwaters], and north of the Gila. This he represents as once the abode of man, where there are gigantic ruins of masonry [Mesa Verde and others], which he describes with the clearness of a Stephens. Trees have grown over these destroyed towns, and fruits and nuts load thir branches."[11]

Joseph L. Meek, who accompanied Walker on his "round robin" to California, claims to have met "Frapp . . . on Williams Fork of the Colorado," in western Arizona. The Meek and Fraeb parties advanced to the Moqui villages, where they all disgraced themselves—except Meek.[12] On their way to the headwaters of the Río Grande, they picked up Kit Carson. Moving northward, Meek and Fraeb traveled by way of Little Snake River, to the Green River rendezvous of 1834.

Kit Carson says:

In Taos [October 1833] I found Captain Lee of the U. S. A., a partner of Bent & St. Vrain. He purchased goods to trade with the trappers. I joined him, and in the latter part of October we started for the mountains to find the trappers. We followed the Spanish Trail that leads to California till we struck White River; took down the White River till we struck Green River [Ouray, Utah]; crossed Green River to the Wintey [Uinta] River.

There we found Mr. Robidoux. He had a party of some twenty men that were trapping and trading. . . . We passed a very pleasant

10 Bernard De Voto, *Across the Wide Missouri*, 429.
11 Gunnison, *A History of the Mormons*, 151–52.
12 Victor, *River of the West*, 152.

winter, and in March [1834] we heard of Mr. Fitzpatrick and Bridger being on Snake River [Colorado-Wyoming boundary].[13] . . . Some trappers came to our camp and informed us that Fitzpatrick and Bridger were on the Snake River encamped. In March we struck out for the purpose of finding their camp. In fifteen days we found their camp. Then Captain Lee sold his goods to Fitzpatrick to be paid in Beaver. When paid, Lee started for Taos.

I joined Fitzpatrick and remained with him one month. He had a great many men in his employ, and I thought it best to get three men and go hunt by ourselves. I done so. We passed the summer trapping on the head of Laramie and its tributaries, keeping to the Mountains, our party being too weak to venture on the plains.

One evening when we were on the route to join Bridger's party, after I had selected the camp for the night [Carson experienced and survived his "worst difficult" bear fight] . . . . We remained in this place [head of the Laramie, Colorado] some ten or fifteen days, when Bridger came, making his way for the summer rendezvous [1834]. We joined him and went to Green River . . . .

They arrived about May 26, 1834, says Irving.

Carson's "Snake River," from his context, was always Little Snake River in northwestern Colorado and on the Wyoming boundary. Carson often visited Idaho's Snake River, and was always careful to designate it "Big Snake River." Parenthetically, a western map of 1839 identifies Bear Lake as "Little Snake Lake."

13 Carson, *Own Story*, 30–33.

It looked like the beginning of the end for several mountain enterprises. James Bridger had been aware of this as he stood aloof in 1833 observing the trends. There were now nearly as many trappers and traders as beavers. All of these men were traveling farther and coming in with less; some of them were willing to make their pile from the other fellow's mistakes or misfortunes. As a partner, Bridger was carrying some of this worry load, and it rested no easier than the metal arrowhead curled against his hip bone.

Bridger had already concluded, probably before 1834, to marry the discerning daughter of the Little Chief, Insala of the Flathead Nation. They were a good and ambitious people, and Bridger stood well among them. Hadn't Beckwourth, Fontenelle, and even Milton Sublette married Indian women? And weren't Newell, Meek, and others contemplating similar marriages?[1]

Mountaineers began arriving for the rendezvous in early June, 1834, including such leaders as Fitzpatrick, Fraeb, Bridger, Meek, Carson, and Walker, as well as Sir William Drummond Stewart and others. William L. Sublette and Nathaniel J. Wyeth, wily competitors, were hurrying from the East with their supplies, traveling independently.

The Little Chief, an early arrival, had dutifully pre-empted the valley of Ham's Fork for Bridger's brigade. Louis Vásquez had wintered with Campbell at one of Sublette and Campbell's new competing posts on the Missouri at the mouth of the Yellowstone. He was here to see the fireworks and to deliver the following letter to James Bridger:

[1] Robert Newell's editor, Dorothy O. Johansen, annotating his *Memoranda* for the spring of 1834, writes: "Newell was married to Kitty M., a Nez Percé, on the Green River, probably at Ham's Fork" (p. 43).

144

Fort William, February 28, 1834. Mr. James Bridger, Dear Sir: Last season whilst in the mountains it was not in my power to meet you, but I had some conversation with Mr. Fitzpatrick respecting you, in which I told him, in case of any change in your affairs, it was my wish that you and him would come in here and join us; and that I had no doubt we would make some arrangement for your advantage.

As Mr. Vasquez is now going to meet you, I thought better to address a few lines to yourself, and to offer anything in our power to do for you. I hope your hunt has resulted favorably. Respectfully, Your obedient servant, Robert Campbell. To Mr. James Bridger, Rocky Mountains.[2]

Nathaniel J. Wyeth had hounded the limping Milton Sublette from New York to Boston and back again to get his order for goods as agreed upon at the Big Horn. But Milton's leg wound had developed a fungus, and Captain William L. Sublette was engaged on some counter plans, which worried Wyeth.

Wyeth and Milton left Independence April 28, 1834, accompanied by naturalists Nuttall and Townsend along with five missionaries led by Jason Lee. The company totaled 70 men with 250 horses. But on May 8, at Little Vermillion River, Wyeth wrote his backers, Tucker and Williams: "I am very sorry to say that Mr. M. G. Sublette's leg has grown so troublesome that he is today obliged to turn back, and by him I write this."

William L. Sublette was not far behind with a lighter load in a speedy caravan. After leaving the Blue River on May 12, Wyeth got an "express" off to "Thomas Fitzpatrick or Co., in The Rocky Mountains." The letter informed Fitzpatrick that Sublette had passed Wyeth, but "You may expect me by the 1st July at the rendezvous named in your letter to Milton [November 13, 1833]. . . . N. J. W."

Wyeth wrote from the "Sweetwater, June 9, 1834. Mess. Thomas Fitzpatrick & Co. Gent. I send this to inform you of my approach with your goods. I am now two days behind Wm. Sublette, who I presume is with you by this. Milton informed me that you would rendezvous near the mouth of the Sandy. In case you do not, I wish you would immediately inform me by Express. I am now one day's march above Rock Independence, and shall continue to come on at a

2 Missouri Historical Society, St. Louis, Missouri, in the Sublette Manuscript file.

good rate, and for the present follow the same route which I came by two years since.

"I wish you would defer making any contract for carrying home any surplus furs that you have, or for a further supply of goods, until I come, as I have sent a vessel to the mouth of the Columbia with such goods as you want and am ready to give you a supply for winter rendezvous if you wish, or for next year; and also to send home by her, at a low rate, such furs as you may have and can make you advances in St. Louis on them to pay men etc."[3]

William M. Anderson wrote at the rendezvous: "I raised the 'Star Spangled Banner.'" Instantly "four men were seen darting like Cossacks over the plains, wild with amazement and delight. They screamed and shouted . . . and into our tent they rushed. . . . Somehow I learned their names. They were Vasquez, the long lost Vasquez; Fitzpatrick; Gray, and the Little Chief [Insala]. Vasquez and Sublette are shaking hands with their right, and smacking and pushing each other with the left. They both ask questions . . . ."

Anderson wrote from Green River, June 14, 1834: "Three camps are now within fifty or sixty miles of each other"—American Fur Company on Green River; Rocky Mountain Fur Company moved to Ham's Fork; and Bonneville and Company on Bear River, near present Montpelier, Idaho. June 16, 1834: "Mr. Sublette has just returned from Fitzpatrick's camp [Rocky Mountain Fur Company], bringing with him the Little Chief." June 17: "We have moved our camp a few miles up the river where we were joined by Fitzpatrick . . . .

"Mr. Sublette has met here an old acquaintance and friend in 'Rotten Belly'; a tall, commanding looking fellow [Indian] who was wounded in the same Blackfeet fight where the former received a ball in his arm and side. [Pierre's Hole, 1832.] The 'bread-basket' of the Nez Perce [Rotten Belly] was so seriously damaged that he has ever since borne a name indicative of that fact. It was curious to see how those two iron men enjoyed their wounds. For a short time the scene was uproarious. Shouting, laughing, slapping and joking each other; then winding up by cursing the Blackfeet with a hearty and vicious eloquence."[4]

[3] Nathaniel J. Wyeth, *Correspondence*, 132–33.

[4] William M. Anderson, *Narrative of a Ride to the Rocky Mountains in 1834*, 9–10. Anderson was accompanying Sublette as a guest adventurer.

Wyeth, June 19, 1834: "Found rendezvous about twelve miles up, and much to my astonishment, the goods which I had contracted to bring up to the Rocky Mountain Fur Company, were refused by these honorable Gentlemen."[5] That evening and the next day most groups moved over to Ham's Fork, near the present Kemmerer, Wyoming, "to recruit our jaded animals."[6] Here it was that Mr. Wyeth broke the bad news to his backers in lengthy letters, and here the demise and the re-creation of the Rocky Mountain Fur Company occurred.

The governing spirit of the Rocky Mountain Fur Company, after William H. Ashley departed, was Captain William L. Sublette, whose mere suggestions carried the force of decrees. He doubtless had a hand in the writing of the document dissolving and reconstituting the firm:

> Whereas, a dissolution of partnership having taken place by mutual consent between Thomas Fitzpatrick, Milton G. Sublette, Henry Fraeb, John Baptiste Jervais [sic] and James Bridger, members of the Rocky Mountain Fur Company, all persons having demands against said company are requested to come forward and receive payment; those indebted to said firm are desired to call and make immediate payment, as they are anxious to close the business of the concern.
>
> Ham's Fork, June 20, 1834.
> [Signed]

Thos. Fitzpatrick,		*His*
M. G. Sublette,	James X Bridger	
Henry Fraeb,		*Mark*
J. B. Gervais,		

> Wit. Wm. L. Sublette, for Bridger and Fitzpatrick.
> Wit. J. P. Risley for Fraeb and Gervais.
>
> The public are hereby notified that the business will in future be conducted by Thomas Fitzpatrick, Milton G. Sublette and James Bridger, under the style and firm of Fitzpatrick, Sublette and Bridger.
>
> Ham's Fork, June 20, 1834.
> [Signed]

Thos. Fitzpatrick,		*His*
M. G. Sublette,	James X Bridger	
Wit. W. L. Sublette.		*Mark*

[5] Nathaniel J. Wyeth, *Correspondence*, 225.
[6] D. Lee and J. H. Frost, *Ten Years in Oregon*, 118.

(The signature of M. G. Sublette in both places is in different ink as if added at a later date.)

That same day Henry Fraeb withdrew from the firm, and the remaining four partners (Fitzpatrick, Sublette, Gervais, and Bridger) paid to Fraeb "forty head of horse beast, forty beaver traps, eight guns, and $1,000 worth of merchandise." Then, in turn, Gervais withdrew, his receipt showing that only three partners (Fitzpatrick, Sublette, and Bridger) paid to Gervais "twenty head of horse beast, thirty beaver traps, and $500 worth of merchandise."[7]

Divulging his own intentions, Nathaniel J. Wyeth wrote: "Ham's Fork of the Colorado of the West, June 20, 1834. James Fenno, Boston . . . . Our getting no furs as yet renders it quite probable that the business may be given up soon. . . . The Companies here have all failed of making hunts; some from quarreling among themselves; some from having been defeated by the Indians; and some from want of horses; and what few furs have been taken, have been paid to the men for their services. . . . I shall build a fort on Lewis River [Fort Hall] . . . and there deposit my goods for sale when there is beaver to pay for them."

Mr. Wyeth's dealings with the Rocky Mountain Fur Company were not exactly fruitless, as is attested by the following: "Ham's Fork of the Colorado of the West, June 30, 1834. Mess Von Phull & McGill, Gent. I herewith indorse draft, Fitzpatrick, Sublette & Bridger, on Sublette & Campbell, $1002.81, twelve mos. from date, dated July 1, 1834. Also, on same parties, four months $864.12, same date. These drafts, or the proceeds of them, you will please collect, or hold subject to the directions of Mess. Tucker & Williams of Boston."

Wyeth wrote Tucker and Williams: "The Rocky Mountain Fur Co. refused to receive the goods, alleging that they were unable to continue business longer, and that they had dissolved, but offered to pay the advances made to M. G. Sublette and the Forfeit. These terms I have been obliged to accept although they would not even pay the interest on cash advances, for there is no law here."

Wyeth's touching finale: "Ham's Fork, July 1, 1834. Mr. M. G. Sublette, Dear Sir: I arrived at rendezvous at the mouth of Sandy on

[7] Missouri Historical Society, St. Louis, Missouri, in the Sublette Manuscript file; see also Chittenden, *Fur Trade*, illustration, 864.

the 17th of June. Fitzpatrick refused to receive the goods; he paid, however, the forfeit and the cash advance I made to you. . . . I think he has been bribed to sacrifice my interests by better offers from your brother. Now, Milton, business is closed between us, but you will find that you have only bound yourself over to receive your supplies at such prices as may be inflicted; and that all you will ever make in the country will go to pay for your goods; you will be kept as you have been, a mere slave to catch beaver for others. I sincerely wish you well. . . . I hope that your leg is better and that you will be able to go whole footed in all respects."[8]

Captain William L. Sublette left Ham's Fork July 9 with about sixty packs of fur. A small surplus of trade goods was taken by him and left at Fort William (Laramie), and a quantity of furs already left there were taken by him to St. Louis, where he arrived in late August.

Arrangements had been made between William L. Sublette, the American Fur Company, and the Rocky Mountain Fur Company (Thomas Fitzpatrick, Milton G. Sublette, and James Bridger) for Fitzpatrick to become resident manager of the new Fort William that winter for the American Fur Company.

Reporting to Pierre Chouteau, of St. Louis, by letter dated September 17, 1834, at Bellevue, Lucien Fontenelle says: "The heretofore arrangements between William L. Sublette and Messrs Fitzpatrick, Milton Sublette and others [Bridger, Fraeb, and Gervais, as a firm] having expired last spring, they have concluded not to have anything more to do with William L. Sublette.

"I have entered into a partnership with the others [Fitzpatrick, Bridger, and M. G. Sublette], and the whole of the beaver caught by them is to be turned over to us. . . . William Sublette has built such a fort as Fort Clark [Mandans] on Laramie's Fork of the River Platte and can make it a central place for the *Sioux* and *Cheyenne* trade."[9]

8 Nathaniel J. Wyeth, *Correspondence*, 133–34, 138, 140.

9 Missouri Historical Society, St. Louis, Missouri, in the Sublette Manuscript file; see also Chittenden, *Fur Trade*, 304–305n.

JAMES BRIDGER moved out of Ham's Fork encampment September 1, 1834, with a colorful crew, including Kit Carson, Joseph L. Meek, Robert Newell, and groups of Flathead and Nez Percés Indians. Newell said they "returned with goods to the Flathead Indians" on Salmon River, but part of the trappers sojourned on the way. "Bridger came to us from the Flatheads, on Pierre's Fork, near Horse Prairie [Brenner, Montana]. . . ." He was on the way to Henry's Fork of Snake River for the winter.[1]

On Christmas Eve, 1834, Captain Thyng arrived from the Columbia with a pack train of supplies for a new post to be called Fort Hall, owned by Nathaniel J. Wyeth. Joseph Gale had been hired by Wyeth to trap in Bridger's domain. In fact, Bridger unwittingly became chief contributor to Gale's outfit when a dozen of his trappers deserted to the new leader.

Left with a small crew and an unorganized village of Indians, Bridger knew it was good time for a bad time! Sure enough, a clique of Blackfeet came through Monida Pass on snowshoes, cut out eighteen of Bridger's horses, and fled with them into the Sand Dune country to the west.

Kit Carson, Joseph L. Meek, and a dozen others were in pursuit at once, overtaking the thieves about fifty miles distant. They proposed a parley, and the Indians agreed; one man from each side would openly and cautiously advance. The Blackfeet claimed they thought they were stealing from the Snakes. But when only five of the poorest horses were fetched in restitution, Carson says, "We broke for our arms; and they for theirs." The ensuing fight continued until dusk.[2]

[1] Newell, *Memoranda*, 33.
[2] Carson, *Own Story*, 33–35.

Carson was the only white man injured, suffering the only wound in his entire trapping career—a fusee ball, like a marble, in his neck and shoulder. After a miserable night, with Carson suffering from cold and pain, the defeated trappers returned to Bridger's camp. Forthwith Bridger himself and a posse of about thirty men galloped in pursuit of the fleeing Indians, but they could find neither Indians nor horses.

Comparing versions of the story, this seems to have been the time and the place (not two years earlier) when Bridger's favorite race horse, "Grohean," "a Comanche steed of great speed and endurance,"[3] was stolen for keeps. The Indians got away because they were mounted on the swiftest steeds—formerly the property of the trappers.

Bridger prudently followed the migrating moose and elk into the higher grazing meadows of Henry's Fork. The beaver haul had been fairly good, measured in beaver per man, when they turned back to Snake River on the way to the rendezvous site near Fort Bonneville, on Green River.

While ascending Salt River (Star Valley), they met Captain Gale, whose course had included Cache Valley, the Salt Lake depot, and Bear Lake. Gale's destination was Fort Hall. Bridger reached Fort Bonneville about May 31, 1835.

Francis Ermatinger and William D. Stewart, hailing from Fort Vancouver, reached Fort Bonneville on June 30, having left Wyeth at Fort Hall.[4] Captain Bonneville, his resources as well as his ambitions exhausted, had spread himself, with some pretense of luxury, on the southern shore of Bear Lake among the Ute and Snake Indians. There he sensibly busied himself with collecting his memories and memoranda preparatory to launching the great literary project which Washington Irving would complete. In the early summer Captain Bonneville drifted eastward, avoiding Fort Bonneville. After a fortnight of good-byes and a Fourth of July celebration at Wind River, he headed home, the "Blue Devils" of disappointment leading the way.

Washington Irving informs us in understandable but unbelievable

[3] Victor, *River of the West*, 141.

[4] Near the junction of the Portneuf River with Snake River and the present Pocatello, Idaho.

language, that Captain Bonneville's immense inventory of equipment was cached in crevices, pits, and other secret places by confidential men working at night, who obliterated all sign afterward. They are thus supposed to have disposed of camping and trapping equipment for one hundred men, harnesses, saddles, and other gear for two hundred horses, and twenty-eight huge covered wagons, with extra wheels, tongues, and other parts.

Farther east, Thomas Fitzpatrick welcomed Robert Campbell at Fort William (Laramie) in May, and they completed the transfer of management of the fort to Fitzpatrick, Milton Sublette, and Bridger. Campbell returned to the settlements with a burden of buffalo robes. On June 27–29, he met the Drips and Fontenelle supply caravan near the Elkhorn.

The Reverend Samuel Parker, guest traveler, was with Fontenelle, who traveled slowly with heavy wagons, reaching Fort William on July 26, 1835 for a week-end layover. Dr. Parker was surprised "to see tall young chaps, well dressed in their own mode, walking arm in arm with their ladies."[5]

August 1, 1835: "Our wagons were left at the fort . . . and all our goods were packed upon mules. . . . Mr. Fontenelle stopped at the Fort, and Mr. Fitzpatrick took his place in charge of the caravan." August 12, 1835: "We came to the Green River . . . where the caravans hold their rendezvous. . . . Here were assembled many Indians, belonging to four different nations: the Utaws, Shoshones [Snakes], Nez Percés, and Flatheads, who were waiting for the caravan. . . . I was disappointed to see nothing peculiar in the Flathead Indians to give them their name. . . .

"While we continued in this place, Doct. Whitman was called to perform some very important surgical operations. He extracted an iron arrow, three inches long, from the back of Capt. Bridger, which was received in a skirmish, three years before, with the Blackfeet Indians. It was a difficult operation, because the arrow was hooked at the point by striking a large bone, and a cartilaginous substance had grown around it. The Doctor pursued the operation with great self-possession and perseverance; and his patient manifested equal

[5] Samuel Parker, *Journal of an Exploring Tour Beyond the Rocky Mountains in 1835*, 49–50.

firmness. The Indians looked on meanwhile, with countenances in-
dicating wonder; and in their own peculiar manner expressed great
astonishment when it was extracted. The Doctor also extracted
another arrow from the shoulder of one of the hunters, which had
been there two years and a half. His reputation becoming favorably
established, calls for medical and surgical aid were almost incessant."[6]

An echo of this incident appears in Stewart's *Edward Warren.*
Speaking of Whitman, he says: "A most excellent man . . . and a
most bold operator, for he, without hesitation . . . cut out an arrowhead with a butcher knife, which had been for years wandering
about in Jim Bridger's back and hip, which I have in my pocket
while I write."[7]

Rendezvous over, Fitzpatrick led the caravan to Fort William for
Fontenelle. Andrew Sublette, who had come out with Campbell,
joined Louis Vásquez on a trapping enterprise on the South Platte.
Milton G. Sublette was at home trying to learn to use an artificial
leg after amputation. Dr. Marcus Whitman, Henry Fraeb, J. Baptiste
Gervais, Robert Newell, William Drummond Stewart, and several
others accompanied the caravan to St. Louis.

James Bridger had found a new interest in the mountains, and
Dr. Samuel Parker, one of the best of travel narrators, seemed glad
to accompany Bridger's party a few days. Dr. Parker writes:
"August 21st, commenced our journey in company with Capt.
Bridger, who goes with about fifty men, six or eight days' journey
on our route.

"On the 22d. . . . Today we arrived at what is called [Little]
Jackson's Hole[8] . . . one of the upper branches of the Columbia River
[Bondurant–Triangle F Ranch area, near the headwaters of Hoback
River.] . . .

"The Indians were very attentive to all my wants—took the
entire care of my packed animals, cooking &c. They preserve particular order in their movements. The first chief leads the way; the
next chiefs follow, then the common men; and after these, the
women and children. The place assigned to me was with the first

[6] *Ibid.,* 72, 79–81.
[7] De Voto, *Across the Wide Missouri,* 254.
[8] Parker, *Journal of an Exploring Tour,* 87.

chief [Later references indicate he was with Nez Percés]. . . . The principal chief of the Flatheads kindly furnished me with a horse to relieve mine.

"Two little girls brought me a quart of strawberries, a rare dish for this season of the year. And an Indian brought me some service berries, which are large, purple and oblong, of a pleasant, sweet taste, similar to whortleberries. We encamped upon a fertile plain surrounded by mountains, where three years before three men were killed by a small war party of Blackfeet Indians. There were seven of the hunters; and when they saw the Blackfeet they all fled in different directions, and by so doing, emboldened the Indians to the pursuit. Had they stood firm and combined, it is probable they would have escaped unhurt." He had learned this much from Bridger.[9]

"We traveled four hours on the 25th, to another branch of Lewis or Snake River, and encamped in a large, pleasant valley, commonly called Jackson's large hole [6,200 feet elevation]. . . . A branch of some magnitude coming from the North-east which is the outlet of Jackson's Lake . . . .

"We continued in this encampment three days to give our animals opportunity to recruit; and for Captain Bridger to fit and send out several of his men into the mountains to hunt and trap. . . .

"Tai-quin-su-wa-tish [Nez Percé chieftain] took me to his company of horses and gave me one in token of his friendship, and probably not without the motive to enlist me in his favor. The horse was finely made, and of the beautiful color of intermixed cream and white.

"On the 28th we pursued our journey and passed over a mountain so high that the banks of snow were but a short distance from our trail [Teton Pass, 8,431 feet elevation]. . . .

"On the 29th we removed our encampment and traveled five hours along the valley to a place where, two years before, two fur companies held their rendezvous [it was in 1832]. Pierre's Hole is an extensive, level country, of rich soil. . . . The valley is well covered with grass, but is deficient in woodland, having only a scanty supply of cottonwood and willows scattered along the streams. . . . Between this and our last encampment, I was shown the place where the men of the fur companies, at the time of their rendezvous two [three]

9 Wyeth, *Oregon*, 72–76.

years before [Driggs-Tetonia area], had a battle with the Blackfeet Indians.

"Of the Blackfeet party there were about sixty men, and more than the same number of women and children. Of the white men in the valley there were some few hundred who could be called to action. From the information given me [undoubtedly by James Bridger] it appeared that these Indians were on their way through this valley, and unexpectedly met about forty hunters and trappers going out from rendezvous to the southwest on their fall and winter hunt.

"These Indians manifested an unwillingness to fight, and presented tokens of peace; but they were not reciprocated. Those who came forward to stipulate terms of peace were fired upon and killed. When the Indians saw their danger, they fled to the cottonwood trees and willows which were scattered along the stream of water, and, taking advantage of some fallen trees, constructed as good defense as time and circumstances would permit. They were poorly provided with guns, and were still more destitute of ammunition.

"The trappers, keeping out of reach of their arrows, and being well armed with the best of rifles, made the contest unequal; and it became still more unequal, when, by an express sent to rendezvous, they were reinforced by veterans in mountain life. The hunters keeping at a safe distance, in the course of a few hours killed several of the Indians, and almost all their horses, which, in their situation, could not be protected, while they themselves suffered by small loss.

"Those killed, on both sides, have been differently stated; but considering the numbers engaged and the length of time the skirmishing continued, it could not have been a bloody battle; and not much to the honor of civilized Americans. . . . When night approached, the hunters retired to their encampment at the place of rendezvous, and the Indians made their escape. Thus the famous battle of Pierre's Hole began and ended.[10]

"In this place I parted with Captain Bridger and his party, who went northeast into the mountains to their hunting ground, which the Blackfeet claim, and for which they will contend. The first chief of the Flatheads [Insala] and his family, with a few of his people, went with Captain Bridger, that they might continue within the

[10] Parker, *Journal of an Exploring Tour*, 94–95.

range of buffalo through the coming winter. The Nez Perces, and the Flatheads, with whom I go, take a north-west direction for Salmon River, beyond which is their country."

Bridger told General Dodge that his first wife was the daughter of a Flathead chief, and his eldest child, Mary Ann, aged eleven years, was in the Waiilatpu (Walla Walla) Mission School at the time of the Whitman Massacre in 1847. Thus we may arrive, if only approximately, at the beginning of Bridger's family life, in 1835. We may conclude that Chief Insala was Bridger's father-in-law and that the Bridgers were then on their honeymoon, leading a long procession, which continues today, of couples who have chosen Yellowstone Park as their seat of bliss.

Rendezvous. Segment of a water color by Alfred Jacob Miller showing Jim Bridger in Sir William Drummond Stewart's suit of full armor.

The Trapper's Bride. From a water color by Alfred Jacob Miller.

JAMES BRIDGER'S beaver hunters found few beaver sign on the steep streams west of the Grand Tetons and the present Yellowstone Park. But this only shortened the journey to the headwater lakes of Henry's Fork, where Bridger established a work center. Few men dared to cross the continental divide to the Madison feeders. It was here that Osborne Russell, trapping under Joseph Gale, met fourteen of Bridger's men. Scouts announced that Bridger's central encampment, twenty miles south, would soon consolidate with his other camps.

The consolidation was too late; eight men started down the Madison and were instantly challenged by about eighty Blackfeet. The whites rushed back to Gale's camp and prepared for a siege, their best riflemen keeping the Indians at long range. Brush fires set by the Indians confined the whites; but in return the whites set backfires to baffle the Blackfeet. Towards evening a leading Indian was signaling for his men to retire "by taking hold of opposite corners of his robe, lifting it up, and striking it three times to the ground."[1]

Gale was an unpopular leader and had lost several men by desertion. He consequently sought and gratefully received Bridger's permission to combine parties while they were making their exit from the danger zone. Both were aiming for Henry's Fork at Snake River.

Bridger's company moved westward onto the Madison, visiting with a large encampment of Flatheads and Pen d'Oreilles, greeting Ermatinger's company westbound; and turning thence southward, Bridger crossed Monida Pass on September 27, 1835, to Camas Creek. Gale dispatched Russell to Fort Hall for mounts and pack animals, "contrary to the advice and remonstrance of Mr. Bridger and his

[1] Osborne Russell, *Journal of a Trapper, 1834-43* (ed. by Aubrey L. Haines), 30-31. All footnote references are to 1955 edition.

men," Russell complained. Bridger moved his own men down Snake River to the Blackfoot River for the winter.

Russell rejoined Bridger's party in February, 1836. "Mr. Bridger's men lived very poor, and it was their own fault, for the valley was crowded with fat cows [buffalo] when they arrived in November; but instead of killing their meat for the winter, they began to kill by running on horseback, which had driven the buffalo over the mountain to the headwaters of the Missouri."

Kit Carson corroborates the shortage of food. From the Humboldt River, Nevada, his party went to Fort Hall. "On our march we found no game; the country was barren. For many days the only food we had was roots, and we would bleed our horses and cook the blood. . . . We then started to hunt buffalo . . . a couple of days travel from the Fort. We killed a good many buffalo and returned to the Fort."

Russell says Bridger's party "killed plenty of bulls but they were so poor that their meat was perfectly blue; yet this was their only article of food." The camp keeper or cook used a club to jostle off the ashes before carving the meat in pieces suitable for eating. "Come Major, Judge, Squire, Dollar, Pike, Cotton and Gabe, won't you take a lunch of Simon?" "Gabe," of course, is Bridger.[2]

In March, 1836, Bridger moved over to the Muddy, sending teams to the headwaters of Gray's and Blackfoot rivers. He fell in with Drips, who had a large crew with several hundred lodges of Snakes, Bannocks, Flatheads, and Nez Percés on Bear River. Bridger settled on Ham's Fork, May 11, 1836. Towards July they all headed for Horse Creek meadows, near Old Fort Bonneville, for the summer trading fair.

An incident, occurring about this time, reported by Meek concerning himself and Bridger, belongs here. Bridger had been a kind of "best man" witness when Milton G. Sublette moved into the leather Indian tipi occupied by the lonely Shoshoni maiden, Umentucken Tukutsey Undewatsey; he had noted Milton's mountain career ending with an amputated leg, and had finally noticed, no doubt with approval, that Joseph Lafayette Meek took no detours on his way to the vacant pillow.

[2] *Ibid.*, 39–41.

Meek, with Mrs. Victor's assistance, makes a pretty tale of it all. And while in the mood, the literary pair do as much for Bridger: A party of Crows visited, bringing skins to trade. One young, inquisitive brave, nosing about the premises, in a spirit of exuberance struck the comely Umentucken with a small whip, in a temptingly exposed area.

Only the original narrator knows how precipitately that mischievous Indian went to his ultimate reward on the wings of Meek's rifle ball. Of course, a general melee was called for in the script, also a few additional casualties. It was then that Mr. Bridger, the Booshway, invited Mr. Not-So-Meek on the carpet:

"You've raised a heck of a row!" Meek heard the ominous rumble.

"Very sorry, Captain Bridger; just couldn't help it!"

"But you got a man killed," pressed Bridger.

"Sorry for the man; but no Devil of an Indian should strike Meek's wife!"[3]

By this time Bridger's own marriage in the Indian style and his status as a squaw man were generally accepted. Lately, also, a redskinned baby in the customary carrying capsule was being nuzzled by everyone, as a gesture of welcome to the little lady. But this was another subject that Bridger did not talk about. On his part, there were no cigars, no comment. He was thirty two and had a full load of responsibilities.

The rendezvous of 1836, like that of preceeding years, was held on the strip of land two to four miles wide and six or eight miles in length between Horse Creek and Green River, west from the present Daniel, Wyoming. Bridger and Drips allocated the Flatheads and Nez Percés to the upper end of the area (above Bonneville's "fort"); and the Utes and Shoshonis (Snakes) to the lower end, near the river junction. The central portion of the rendezvous encampment would thus be at the old trading hut, standing a little nearer to Horse Creek, which was a natural protection against surprise attack.

The trading hut, or headquarters, was merely a log pen about eighteen feet square and ten feet high, with poles and brush for roof shade. A piece of canvas covered the merchandise piled within. The

[3] Victor, *River of the West*, Chapter 12, especially 179–80.

chinks between the logs served as windows, and a six-foot cut-out of the fifth and sixth logs answered as a service opening or counter over which trades were made. That opening was also a crawl-hole for the clerks, there being no door. The pack and riding saddles and other caravan equipment were stored on the ground nearby. Adjacent were the leather sleeping tents of the company leaders.[4]

Nathaniel J. Wyeth and the Hudson's Bay Company leaders, John McLeod and Thomas McKay, were early arrivals from Fort Hall, mainly for purposes of observation. Wyeth was on his way to the States and to retirement from the fur trade.

James Bridger's main concern was the forthcoming merchandise caravan, which proved to be a memorable one. The caravan was sent by the American Fur Company at Council Bluffs (Bellevue), but William L. Sublette still held a heavy hand on their business, by reason of their unpaid notes. That might explain why "Fitzpatrick headed the caravan this year," as Dr. Whitman wrote the American Board from Vancouver, September 18, 1836. "We traveled hard, but more comfortably than last year, as we always took breakfast before starting in the morning. Captain Fontenelle had become so intemperate that the company had disposed of him."[5]

Moses (Black) Harris, as pilot, was Captain Fitzpatrick's chief assistant when they left Bellevue, May 14, 1836. There were seven wagons for the fur company, two for William Drummond Stewart, two for the missionaries (total, eleven wagons), "and one cart," wrote Mrs. Whitman, "drawn by two mules (one in the shafts and one ahead), which carries a lame man, one of the proprietors of the Company."[6]

This was unquestionably Milton G. Sublette. After a second amputation of the same leg, and while trying out another artificial limb, he had chosen this superhuman journey rather than further incarceration as an invalid at his brother's farm near St. Louis.

Trailing the caravan, came the Presbyterian missionaries: Dr. and Mrs. Marcus Whitman and Dr. and Mrs. Henry H. Spalding, honey-

[4] William H. Gray, *History of Oregon*, 121–22.

[5] Archer B. and Dorothy P. Hulburt, *Marcus Whitman, Crusader*.

[6] Myron F. Eells, *Marcus Whitman*, 60–61, 67; see also Gray, *History of Oregon*, 115.

mooning newly-weds, but all very seriously intent on their mission work. These ladies were by chance set apart from all womankind, as the first white women to cross the continent. With them was William H. Gray, secular aid to the missionaries.

On arriving at the rendezvous, Mrs. Whitman wrote: "As soon as I alighted from my horse, I was met by a company of matron native women, one after another shaking hands, and saluting me with a most hearty kiss. This was unexpected, and affected me very much. They gave sister Spalding the same salutation. . . . After we had been seated awhile in the midst of the gazing throng, one of the Chiefs, whom we had seen before [Insala], came with his wife, and very politely introduced her to us. They say they all like us very much; they thank God that they have seen us, and that we have come to live with them."

Mr. Gray writes: "Among the hunters, a tall man with black hair . . . and a lively manner . . . paid his respects to the ladies . . . . Mrs. Whitman asked if he ever had any trouble with Indians. . . . 'That, we did,' he assured her. 'One time I was with Bridger's camp, and Blackfeet were sighted. The rest of our party put whips to their mounts and were gone; but my old mule wouldn't budge, with all the beating I gave her. . . . But when she saw the Blackfeet herself, she got out of there like a streak. As I passed the other boys I sang out: "Come on; we can't fight 'em here." ' "[7]

Captain Wyeth graciously introduced the missionary party to Messrs. McLeod and Mckay; James Bridger welcomed Doctor Whitman with special warmth, remembering the removal of the arrowhead from his back the year before. Bridger is also said to have promised Dr. Whitman that when his little girl came to school age, he would send her to Dr. Whitman's mission school—and he did.

On their own initiative the four Indian tribes represented at rendezvous joined their talents and numbers for a grand parade in honor of their unusual guests on July 9, 1836. Some groups were singing, others were dancing or otherwise showing off, but many were only marching. All were gaily painted or dressed, in brilliant animal skins. The warriors, hardly dressed at all but gruesomely painted, were bearing their weapons and displaying their regalia

[7] Gray, *History of Oregon*, 124–25.

in mock threatening style, while equestrian performers skillfully displayed their tricks and abilities at riding.

The missionaries left rendezvous accompanied by Mr. Drips on July 18, 1836. Drs. Whitman and Spalding overcame objections again and loaded their baggage in the light wagon for the journey westward. At Fort Hall they reduced the wagon to a cart, loading the other wheels in the cart; but at Fort Boise the cart and contents were abandoned.

Milton G. Sublette may have returned to Fort Laramie after an upset or two in order to seek relief for his physical suffering. There he remained. Even Fort Laramie, however, afforded no hospital care, no physician, no nursing, no surcease. There, the sufferer's only sedative was alcohol, though his suffering was at times almost unbearable. Would he be criticized for becoming an alcoholic?

Mrs. Victor writes, filling out Meek's memory: "About the first of January [1837] Fontenelle, with four men and Captain Stewart's party, left the [trapper's] camp [on Powder River] to go to St. Louis for supplies. At Fort Laramie, Fontenelle committed suicide, in a fit of *mania a potu* [mania resulting from alcoholic excess—*delirium tremens*] and his men returned with the news."[8]

The newer evidence is that Lucien Fontenelle was not in the mountains that winter. He attended rendezvous and trapped with Bridger in 1837, bought a horse of Elkanah Walker at Fort Laramie, May 30, 1838, and wrote a letter to P. A. Sarpy August 5, 1838, which is now in Missouri Historical Society files.

But Milton G. Sublette did die at Fort Laramie, his passing being reported in the St. Louis *Missouri Republican*, June 16, 1837: "Died —on the 5th of April, last, at Fort William, River Platte, Milton G. Sublette, long known as one of the most enterprising Indian traders of the Rocky Mountains . . . ."[9] His remains lie buried near the fort. Joseph L. Meek's mountain memories clearly but inadvertently transposed the names.

[8] Victor, *River of the West*, 224.
[9] Field, *Prairie and Mountain Sketches*, 75.

AFTER WITNESSING the spectacle of a fragment of civilization passing in review, Bridger needed the uplift of the best of his own realm.
Thus he led his family and his beaver hunters away from the 1836
rendezvous, through Jackson Hole, over the Two Ocean Pass Trail
to Lake Bridger and to Lake Yellowstone.

In modern days, appropriately enough, the higher part of this
landed area is maintained by the government as the Teton Wilderness Area, exactly as Bridger knew it, with its moose, elk, deer, and
grizzly bears, and also a plenty of bighorn sheep, black bears, and a
few beavers. The rare trumpet swan of the Arctic is at home on
Jackson and Bridger lakes. The Teton Wilderness is virtually a
northern extension of the Bridger Primitive Area, in the heart of the
Bridger National Forest.

The first general get-together of Bridger's forces was on the
northern shore of Yellowstone Lake, August 19, 1836. Trapping
squads went out in various directions, principally to trade for skins
with friendly Indians. They would gather again in Gardner's Hole,
on the twenty-seventh.[1]

Below Gardner's Fork, Meek says he was captured by a war party
of Crows, but was ingeniously liberated by Captain Bridger. Determined to make an expensive "last stand," Meek leveled his gun
at the Chief named "The Bold." The Chief calmly called to him to
put down his gun and live, gesturing towards the armed warriors
around them. "The Bold" picked up Meek's gun and shamefully
put the prisoner in care of three tyrant Indian women.

---

[1] Russell, *Journal of a Trapper*, 46. Frances Victor, in *River of the West* (written
for Joseph L. Meek), spelled it "Gardner" (220) and for many years she was the
sole authority. It is generally claimed that the stream and the "Hole" were named
for trapper Johnson Gardner.

"What is your captain's name," asked The Bold. "Bridger is my captain's name; or, in the Crow tongue, Casapy, the Blanket Chief." Then he asked, "How many men has he?" I said forty, a tremendous lie, for there were 240. "You shall live; but they shall die," he said. He then asked where I was to meet Bridger's camp; and I answered truly, for I wanted them to find the camp. Two big Indians mounted my mule; the women made me carry moccasins.

On the fourth day spies reported white men on the Yellowstone bottoms three miles ahead. The Crow chief stood with his hand on his mouth in amazement. Bridger's horse-guards came near, and The Bold ordered me to tell them to come up. Instead I howled at them to stay away or be killed; and to tell Bridger to try to treat with them and get me away.

In a few minutes Bridger appeared on his large white horse. . . . he called to me, asking who the Indians were. He then asked me to say to the Crow chief he wished him to send one of his sub-chiefs to smoke with him. The Bold ordered "Little Gun" to smoke with Bridger. When "Little Gun" got within a hundred yards of Bridger, each was forced by the Crow laws of war, to strip himself, and proceed the remaining distance in a state of nudity, then kiss, and embrace so all could see.

During this ceremony five of Bridger's men had followed him keeping in a ravine until they got within shooting distance, when they showed themselves, moved in and cut off the return of Little Gun, thus making him prisoner. Suddenly about a hundred of our trappers appeared and Bridger called out for me to propose to the Crow chief to exchange me for "Little Gun." The Bold in a sullen mood, consented.

That evening the Crow Chief, with forty of his braves, visited Bridger, professed their friendship for the whites, and made a treaty for three months to fight the Blackfeet together. As evidence of their good faith, they returned Meek's mule, gun and beaver pelts.[2]

Meek's mention of Bridger's name, "Casapy, the Blanket Chief," is clarified by Burnett: "Kash-sha-peece," meaning "fine cloth." Bridger's woman sewed together yard-wide strips of red and blue cloth, beading the seam with quills. It was a kind of full dress, for

[2] Victor, *River of the West*, 189–94. This quotation is paraphrased in parts.

show-off or party occasions. Hence his nickname: "Fine Cloth, the blanket Chief."[3]

Proceeding down the Yellowstone, the trappers were working the tributaries "leaving Mr. Bridger with twenty-five camp keepers to travel slowly down the river." At the mouth of Twenty-Five-Yard River, the brigades reported again to Bridger. The next reunion was on Rocky Fork (present Red Lodge), September 7, 1836. Here, trouble raised a hostile head.[4] A trapping brigade reported that Bodah (Baudin, Boudair) had been killed by Blackfeet, and that a Delaware Indian had received a hip wound in the skirmish. Mark Head later told Matthew Field that Bodah's body was riddled by five balls and two arrows. He also gave Field a good account of the winter's activities.[5]

"Gabe," said Meek, "You remember where Pryor leaves the bluffs, and plum trees three miles up on a branch?" Bridger did. "Well, we set traps there yesterday, and went to eating the best plums I ever ate; large, sweet; no wonder the Savages liked the place." Meek's narrative runs on like a waterfall. "I heard a rustling, and pop, pop, went the guns, so close I see the wads coming out of their muzzles. 'Two Shebit' [his white horse] got a ball in the neck, but raised a-runnin, and I on his back, till I overtook Dave."

Bridger then moved camp to the mouth of Rock Creek, at Clark's Fork, and ran into the open arms of about sixty Blackfeet, wildly racing to retaliate. They drove a pair of trappers into the river and shot after them as their mounts swam the stream. Howell was severely wounded by two balls in his body. Green almost reached camp with him, but Howell died next morning and was buried there, in what was afterwards called "Howell's Encampment."

Bridger decided to resist, and twenty picked whites and allied Indians, scouring the vicinity, drove the Blackfeet to an island in the river. Here sniping trappers harassed them until dusk. The Blackfeet got away in the night, secretly carrying off their dead and wounded, if any.

Bridger then moved down to Pryor's Fork, September 11, 1836,

[3] Robert B. David, *Finn Burnett, Frontiersman.*
[4] Russell, *Journal of a Trapper*, 47–48.
[5] Field, *Prairie and Mountain Sketches*, 152–53.

to investigate the plum crop, while Meek recovered his courage and his abandoned beaver traps.

From a few delicious, overripe plums to frigid snowdrifts was a quick transition and sent the camp to the best available forage, on the Yellowstone and Clark's Fork bottom lands, for wintering. Buffalo were too numerous for the forage available. The trappers were back on the Yellowstone bottoms at Christmas, where sweet cottonwood bark served as forage for the horses.

Here, then, convened the second semester of what Osborne Russell called the Rocky Mountain College, where the camp-keepers made things cosy for the trappers and leaders and participated at the councils of the larger lodges in debates, storytelling, arguments, adventures, and reminiscences. Here also Booshway Bridger discussed the route, the beaver take, and the spring plans; and took his turn at baby-sitting and doing the supper chores at home.[6]

On January 28, 1837, Bridger dispatched half a dozen hunters up Clark's Fork for meat, buffalo preferred. The junket took them over to Rock Creek, where, of a sudden, about eighty Blackfoot savages showered leaden balls among them, breaking the right arm of a trapper (identified later as Isaac P. Rose) and taking his gun. New strategy was in order. The Blackfeet apparently needed neither food nor sleep.

"February 22, 1837. Mr. Bridger, according to his usual custom, took his telescope and mounted a high bluff near the camp, to look for 'squalls,' as he phrased it. About one o'clock he returned, somewhat alarmed; said the plain below was alive with savages, crossing to the timber about ten miles below." He set all hands to work erecting log and brush breastworks, actual and camouflage, 250 feet square around the camp, 6 feet high, with sloping "palisades" laid on the inside.

The twenty-second happened to be a clear cold night highly favorable for a resplendent display of the aurora or northern lights. "On February 23, about 2 P.M. Mr. Bridger and six men galloped out to reconnoitre; they reported the enemy encamped near the river three miles below." About sunrise, February 24, a solitary savage crept up behind the trees and took a wild shot at Bridger's cook, who was cutting breakfast fuel. A Spaniard was dispatched to the bluff to spy

[6] Russell, *Journal of a Trapper*, 51.

out the enemy and was met by an Indian scout, already there. The scout was hit in the heel by a ball, as he exposed the heel while fleeing down the bluffside.

The Blackfeet were already advancing on the ice, the chief, signaling with a white blanket that they were not fighting, but were returning to the Three Forks. Bridger and his scouts picked up the news that the brilliant aurora borealis of the previous night had frightened the Blackfeet out of their wits. To them it was a signal from the skies, warning them to give up the fight before it began.[7]

On February 28, Bridger led his troop toward the Big Horn. Halting on Bovey's Fork to fill their empty larders with buffalo meat, they had a visit with Crow Chief "Long Hair." On March 25, Bridger led his fellows west. Halting at Howell's Camp to raise a cache of beaver furs on April 10, they proceeded to trap the waters of Twenty-Five-Yard River and the Musselshell.

Roaming Blackfeet killed an isolated trapper and wounded his Delaware teammate; the Blackfeet still had their stingers out. Thus Bridger called it quits for the season, and turned southeast. After crossing Clark's Fork, Stinking River, Greybull Fork, and Medicine Lodge Creek, his party reached the Big Horn. Halting for a respite at Oil Spring, May 24–26, by June 10 they were laying out the encampment on Green River, twelve miles below Horse Creek. Here the hunting parties were already assembling to await the trading caravan.

The atmosphere seemed charged with trouble, especially among the Indians. Certain Bannock Indians had stolen several horses and beaver traps from a French brigade on Bear River. The thieves were brazenly encamped near the rendezvous and were in a defiant mood. On June 15, two Nez Percé Indians, backed by a handful of whites, visited the Bannock section and retrieved the stolen horses and traps while the Bannocks were absent on a buffalo hunt.

Toward midafternoon about thirty overheated Bannocks dashed headlong into the Flathead camp at rendezvous, demanding the horses—diplomatically declaring as an afterthought that they were not fighting the whites. David L. Brown, who reached the rendezvous a month later was told that "the Bannocks had stolen a very fine stallion belonging to the principal Chief of the Flatheads [In-

---

[7] *Ibid.*, 54.

sala]." For safety, Insala had quietly slipped the halter to son-in-law James Bridger, who, at the moment, stood before his own lodge.

Brown learned that "a Bannock Chief impudently demanded the restoration of the brute, as belonging to his tribe. This was denied on the part of the Flatheads, and the horse was finally given into the hands of Bridger for security and safe keeping. As this person was leading off the disputed property, the Bannock Chief stepped resolutely forward and attempted to wrest the halter from Bridger's hand, by which the horse was confined, when a scuffle ensued, in which Bridger's rifle was either intentionally, or accidentally discharged."[8]

Meek's version: "At this unprecedented insult to his master, a Negro named Jim, cook to the Booshway [Bridger], seized a rifle and shot the Bannock Chief dead." Brown's narrative: "This served as the signal for a general onslaught. The hunters and trappers, who had gathered around at the commencement of the difficulty, from motives of curiosity, now poured in a murderous fire upon the surprised and astonished Bannocks, who had been calmly awaiting on horseback, the result of their Chief's interference.

"Nine saddles were immediately emptied of their occupants, and probably as many more persons were mortally wounded, but who were still able to retain their seats and escape. The poor wretches who had fallen in the commencement of the affray, were tomahawked and scalped on the spot, and their disfigured and mutilated remains were dragged about a mile from the encampment, and there left to be devoured by the wolf . . . and vulture."

Obviously chronicler Brown was not informed of the pathetic sequel. Joseph L. Meek had good reason to remember the occasion, if not the precise date of its occurrence, for in the melee against the Bannocks, a stray arrow struck the lovely Umentucken in the breast and the joys and sorrows of the "Mountain Lamb" were forever ended. There is little question that she had been with the Bridger beaver trappers during the previous winter, squired by the ever loyal Joseph L. Meek. Her death occurred almost coincidentally with the newspaper announcements, in faraway St. Louis, of the death of her beloved first husband, Milton G. Sublette.[9]

[8] David L. Brown, *Three Years in the Rocky Mountains*, 17; see also Russell, *Journal of a Trapper*, 63.

[9] Victor, *River of the West*, 197–98.

JAMES BRIDGER insisted it would be dangerous for the missionary William H. Gray to depart with his own small company. Gray should await the strongly manned returning fur caravan. Gray had reached Green River, June 26, 1837, eastbound from Oregon, by way of "Tom Ham's Fork," for that very purpose, but the caravan had not arrived and Gray was impatient. He confided to his journal: "Mr. Harris [Moses B.] came to our camp," July 1, express from the supply caravan to explain the delay.

"July 18, 1837. The Company from St. Louis have arrived. Captain [William Drummond] Stewart, and others, are with the Company; also, a Mr. [Alfred Jacob] Miller. They have been since the 27th of June coming from Fort William, on Laramie's Fork. . . . Mr. Miller, who is a portrait painter, called at tea or supper.

"July 19, 1837. This morning I learned that the Company would probably remain at this place till the 5th or 10th of August. . . . I have concluded to proceed as soon as possible. A number have engaged to go with me—Captain Fontenelle [caravan leader] took dinner with me; I rode up to Mr. McLeod's camp to let him know my determination."

"July 23, 1837. Confusion, anxiety and perplexity have filled my mind. The news of the Blackfeet has caused a great panic in camp. Five Flatheads came to visit; they wish to go to the States with me— They wish me to delay . . . . July 25, 1837. We are to leave this morning, after breakfast. At 8 we were on our way."[1]

Fully conscious of his responsibility for four Indian boys, an Iroquois guide, Messrs. Callaghan, Forsyth, Grimm, and an "indolent" one, at least ten in all, Gray passed from the rendezvous with Bridger's disheartening warning ringing in his ears. He made forced

---

[1] Gray, "Journals," 54-55.

marches under grueling conditions, goaded by fear all the way. At Fort Laramie, August 2, 1837: "A half-breed has been killed by a Sioux, below the Chimney. My Indians and men are fearful about proceeding. In my own mind, these circumstances have cleared our way of Indians, rendering it less dangerous for us."

On August 7, while still above the forks of the Platte, Gray's little party was attacked by a band of Sioux Indians. Gray received wounds in the scalp and on the temple. The Sioux then "rushed upon my Indians [three Flatheads and one Nez Percé boy], and butchered them [as members of enemy nations] in a most horrible manner." Gray's party was then plundered of its useful goods and ordered to depart, lest a worse fate befall them. It was a distressing, humiliating experience.

David L. Brown, in the Cincinnati *Atlas* of September, 1845, wrote that he had attended the 1837 rendezvous (probably as a guest of William Drummond Stewart). He observed that "Mr. Gray, contrary to all advice, and to every consideration urgently laid before him by the most experienced men, persisted in his purpose of proceeding alone on his route to the States, without waiting for the escort and protection of the Company. The result of this course was precisely what had been anticipated. . . ."[2]

"Bridger's remark to Mr. Gray, when the latter was about to set out on his ill-omened expedition, struck me forcibly at the time. It was in answer to some of the other's foolish and fantastic dogmas. 'Sir,' said the old hunter, slapping his right hand heavily on the breech of his rifle, 'the grace of God wont carry a man through these prairies; it takes powder and ball!' "

Bridger was not being irreverent; he just knew what would stop a marauding Indian and what would not. He also remembered that Jedediah S. Smith, the devout fur trapper, trader, and explorer, suffered the Mohave massacre of ten of his men, the Umpqua massacre of fifteen fellowmen, and met his own death, alone, at a Comanche water hole, aged thirty-four years.

Brown's narrative continues: "On the second evening after our arrival at the general Rendezvous, I attended an entertainment given

[2] David L. Brown, *Three Years in the Rocky Mountains*, 19–20. The original manuscript reads 1836, but research indicates that it should be 1837, as corrected in the "Introduction" of the reprint.

by Capt. Stewart to the mountain trappers. . . . The entertainment was given in a large tent . . . containing some twenty-five or thirty persons. . . . Most of these were noted characters in the mountains. . . . To an ample supply of fresh buffalo meat [served on the grass] the Capt. had added some choice old liquors. . . .[3]

"On the right of Captain Stewart sat, or rather squatted in oriental fashion, one of the most remarkable men of this remarkable assemblage. This was Mr. James Bridger, or 'Jim' Bridger, as he was always termed who had come to that country in the first instance, in the employment of General Ashley, and after having acted for a series of years as a caterer or hunter for that gentleman's mess, was finally engaged, and after many a shifting and turning of Dame Fortune's wheel, by the North American Fur Company to fill the difficult and hazardous position he now held as a partisan or leader of beaver hunting parties; for which he was admirably adapted from his wide and thorough acquaintance with the whole mountain regions from the Russian settlements to the Californias, and every nook by hidden lake and unfrequented stream where these singularly shy and sagacious animals 'most do congregate.'

"Bridger had likewise, in addition to the above mentioned qualifications, other qualifications, other qualities of scarcely less importance, and without which the former would have been of comparatively little value. These were a complete and absolute understanding of the Indian character in all its different phases, and a firm, though by no means over cautious, distrust with regard to these savages, based upon his own large experience of their general perfidy, cunning and atrocity. To sum up, his bravery was unquestionable, his horsemanship equally so, and as to his skill with the rifle, it will scarcely be doubted, when we mention the fact that he has been known to kill twenty buffaloes by the same number of consecutive shots.

"The physical conformation of this man was in admirable keeping with his character. Tall—six feet at least—muscular, without an ounce of superfluous flesh to impede its forces or exhaust its elasticity, he might have served as a model for a sculptor or painter, by which to express the perfection of graceful strength and easy activity. One remarkable feature of this man I had almost omitted, and that was

[3] *Ibid.*, 11–13.

his neck, which rivalled his head in size and thickness, and which gave to the upper portion of his otherwise well-formed person a somewhat *outre* and unpleasant appearance. His cheek bones were high, his nose hooked or aquiline, the expression of his eye mild and thoughtful, and that of his face grave, almost to solemnity.

"To complete the picture he was perfectly ignorant of all knowledge contained in books, not even knowing the letters of the alphabet; put perfect faith in dreams and omens, and was unutterably scandalized if even the most childish of the superstitions of the Indians were treated with anything like contempt or disrespect; for in all these he was a firm and devout believer.

"Next to Bridger, sat Bill Williams, the Nestor of the trappers. . . .

"On the opposite side of the table, or whatever the reader may choose to call that portion of the greensward that served as such, was placed Joe Meek, or 'Major' Meek, as he was indifferently called. . . . Meek's real history and adventures, if fairly and honestly written out, would be a book to make the fortune of its author."

Posterity had a picture-maker at the rendezvous in Alfred Jacob Miller, guest of Captain William Drummond Stewart. As an aspiring professional frontier artist, Miller spent a busy month sketching, outlining, studying, and making memoranda of scenes, groups, and busts of travelers, frontiersmen, animals, and Indians. These illustrations, which were destined to be filled out and finished as needed in the years to come, were inexact roughs when compared to photographs, but with the notes to accompany them, they became unique contemporary interpretations.

In 1842, Miller settled down as a journeyman artist with a flair for frontier, Indian, and other western scenes. But "as time went on," writes Bernard De Voto, "Miller took increasing liberties with western subjects, conventionalizing them entirely out of agreement with his observations. The process of deterioration may be clearly seen in a large portrait of a man in buckskin. . . . A family tradition holds the subject was Jim Bridger; but the portrait is not in the least a likeness."[4]

Mrs. Frances Fuller Victor, describing the 1837 rendezvous for Joseph L. Meek, says: "The Shawnees and Delawares danced their great war-dance before the tents of the missionaries; and Joe Meek,

[4] De Voto, *Across the Wide Missouri*, 410.

not to be outdone, arrayed himself in a suit of armor belonging to Captain Stewart, and strutted about the encampment; then mounting his horse, played the part of an ancient knight, with a good deal of eclat."[5]

For a field sketch entitled "The Rendezvous near Green River, Oregon," Miller wrote as follows:

"Here we rested for a month . . . encamping among 3000 Snake and other Indians, who had all assembled . . . to trade buffalo robes and peltries for dry goods, ammunition, tobacco . . . . The white lodges of the Indians stretching out in vast perspective, the busy throng of savages on spirited horses moving in all directions, some of them dressed in barbaric magnificance . . . . On the bluff in the sketch, our Commander, after making valuable presents, is smoking the Calumet with some warriors; and being very popular, the Indians composed processions in their war dresses to do him honor. . . .

"Our Commander [Stewart] at this rendezvous presented Pilcher, a distinguished mountaineer with a full suit of steel armor, such as is worn by the Horse Guards of London and which he had imported for this purpose. It is sad to record the infirmities of great men but my impression is that we saw Pilcher one evening reeling from the Commander's tent where *high jinks* had been held, evidently having eaten too much dinner."[6] Other views of the subject were made as experience and demands for Miller's pictures increased.

Revising and condensing this title at another time, the artist wrote: "The scene represented is the broad prairie; the whole plain is dotted with lodges and tents, with groups of Indians surrounding them. In the river near the foreground Indians are bathing; to the left rises a bluff overlooking the plain whereon are stationed some braves and Indian women. In the midst of them is Capt. Bridger in a full suit of steel armor. This gentleman was a famous mountain man, and we venture to say that no one has traveled here within the last thirty years without seeing or hearing of him. The suit of armor was imported from England and presented to Captain B. by our com-

[5] Victor, *River of the West*, 238. Some of these events were inadvertently dated 1838 instead of 1837.

[6] Carl P. Russell, "Wilderness Rendezvous Period of the American Fur Trade," *Oregon Historical Quarterly*, March, 1941, pp. 38–39; see also De Voto, *Across the Wide Missouri*, Plate LXXXV, 74.

mander; it was a fac-simile of that worn by the English life-guards, and created a sensation when worn by him on stated occasions."[7]

Eventually, it is apparent, the artist fancied that a painting of James Bridger in armor might be more salable than one of Meek or Pilcher, or he may have been averse to duplicating the title. It is noted that "James Bridger in Armor" (Plate LXXIV, *Across the Wide Missouri*) has a different helmet from that in Plate LXXV—or a different hair-do. The more conspicuous figure strides a white horse in the scene. Although white horses were rare, James Bridger's white horse was well known in that year.

On occasion Bridger had serious need of a steel suit of armor, impervious to Indian arrowheads if, in the sunshine, it did not become a solar cooking stove! But while thanking his friends for the compliment, Bridger had a queer presentiment that they were laughing at him. Without confirming or denying any evidence, it can only be presumed that James Bridger, like Joseph L. Meek, may have modeled the suit just to see if it fit at the clavicle.

Congenial trapping brigades were forming to work Old Park (the present Colorado) and to visit the Spanish Southwest. Newell and his Indians connections would call on the Big Horn Crows. William D. Stewart and guests spent a fortnight fishing in New Fork's headwater lakes (the present Bridger Primitive Area). They then joined Andrew Dripps and the fur caravan bound for St. Louis.

Uncle Jack Robertson wrote (Green River, Rocky Mountains, August 3, 1837) to his mother at Owens Station, Missouri that, "favored by the politeness of Captain Stewart," he was sending $1,000 by Drips for deposit with William Sublette. Uncle Jack also said he trapped last year in "Mexican Provinces," and was starting "tomorrow" for the same country (lower Green River and beyond).[8]

[7] Marvin C. Ross, *The West of Alfred J. Miller*, 159.
[8] Stone, *Uinta County*, 43–44, and the illustration.

JAMES BRIDGER was the pilot and Lucien Fontenelle the commander of the seventy-five-man company that marched northward from Green River rendezvous in August, 1837. The American Fur Company was in the saddle; the Rocky Mountain Fur Company had become a memory. Osborne Russell had departed in another company by way of Two Ocean Pass to begin trapping on the high country of Stinking River. They would meet Fontenelle on Clark's Fork in mid-October to winter.[1]

Trapping the Henry Lake–Madison River region was slow because of downed timber; consequently the Fontenelle-Bridger outfit was trapping on the Judith and Musselshell rivers when October came along. They had seen three surprises: beavers were scarce, buffalo were coarser, and Blackfeet were scarcest of all for some reason. At the Big Horn in November, Fontenelle learned that Russell had been frightened out of the country by news of smallpox among the Blackfeet.

Russell was goaded to greater haste by the appearance of a war party of Crows on November 1 at the Big Horn. These Indians were from the Wind River village of Chief Long Hair, an old friend of Bridger's, which fact was hastily mentioned. Night-crawling Crows had already stolen three of Russell's horses, with saddles and bridles.[2] After an apologetic, apparently friendly, visit at the Big Horn, the tricky Crows stole the rest of Russell's horses. He was proceeding

---

[1] Russell, *Journal of a Trapper*, 61–62. Russell's dates seem to be in conflict with those of William H. Gray. The supply train arrived July 18, 1837. Russell's departure on July 20, 1837, appears not only too soon, but rather early in the season. Gray departed July 25, 1837, long before the returning fur caravan started to St. Louis. See also Victor, *River of the West*, 214, 223–24. Meek's dates should be 1837, 1838.

[2] Russell, *Journal of a Trapper*, 64.

on foot when he met Little Soldier, who said he was sorry the "dogs" had stolen the horses.

"I mounted my horse to come to your assistance," Little Soldier assured Russell. "If you will go with me I will get your animals, and give you some saddles and robes; you can stay with me until the Blanket Chief [the name they gave Bridger] comes."

Distrusting the Crows, Russell and his men declined. Little Soldier was tearful: "I am very sorry. What shall I tell the Blanket Chief? How can I hold my head up when I meet him; and what shall I do with your things?"

"We told him to give them to the Blanket Chief; then we got out of his reach," concluded Russell.

Neither Bridger nor any of his men saw Little Soldier when they crossed the Big Horn and followed the drifting buffalo to the upper Powder River plains for the winter. But Bridger evidently knew how to deal with the Crows. Later Fontenelle told Russell, at Fort William, that the stolen property had been recovered.[3]

Robert Newell reports that shortly after he arrived among the Crows in the late summer of 1837, "Came the news that the small pox was at Fort Van Buren [mouth of Tongue River], the Crow trading post . . . conducted by Samuel Tullock for the American Fur Company. The fear of that complaint," continues Newell, "set the Crows running from it so very hard, it wore out several hundred horses, before we stopped the retreat.

"We went from the Little Horn, to the head of Powder River, to the Big Horn, up to Wind River, and to its head, where they stopped to recruit their animals. . . . I went down to Fort Van Buren for safety . . . arriving November 9, 1837."

December 13, 1837: "I thought best to hunt for our camp, and left with four men, one woman and child [his family]. . . . Next morning found our horses were gone. . . . Our goods we put under ground, and returned to Fort Van Buren on foot. . . . Men took dogs and brought our baggage. Dogs are used here in winter to pack and haul."

December 29, 1837, again: "I left Fort Van Buren with five men, one woman and child [his family]. . . . Over to Tongue . . . . On to Powder River . . . where we found Fontenelle's camp. . . . Mr. Fon-

[3] *Ibid.*, 70–72, 80–81. (Russell's "Black Hills" are the present Laramie Mountains.)

tenelle had gone with twenty-five men for supplies, but has not yet returned. . . . Our camp is eighty strong . . . 22d of January, 1838."[4]

"In that neighborhood," says Meek (meaning several miles south, near the present Kaycee), "a company of Bonneville's men under the command of Antoine Montero, had established a trading post . . . but he could not hold his own against so numerous and expert a band of marauders as Bridger's men, assisted by the Crows. . . . By spring Montero had little property remaining."[5]

Kit Carson says the smallpox was among the Blackfeet, and they had gone north of the Missouri. On Powder River: "It was one of the coldest I ever experienced. We kept the animals in a corral. Their feed was cottonwood bark which we would pull from the trees, then throw it by the fire. We had to keep the buffalo from our camp by building large fires in the bottoms. They came in such large droves that our horses were in danger of being killed, when we turned them out to eat the branches of the trees which we had cut down."[6]

Russell reports that Fontenelle reached Fort William on December 20, 1837, one month after Russell's party had arrived. On January 28, 1838, Russell started for Powder River with supplies for the main camp (under Bridger), leaving Mr. Fontenelle at the fort. "On the 7th day of February we reached [Bridger's] camp. . . . They were living on the fat of the land . . . so crowded with buffalo it was difficult to keep them from the horses, which were being fed on sweet cottonwood bark."[7]

Newell admits: "We have lost several horses and mules by hard weather this winter . . . our time was principally spent peeling cottonwood bark for our horses. . . . On the North Fork of the Platte times is hard; about five trading houses to eight hundred lodges of Sioux . . . . Times is getting hard all over this part of the country; beaver scarce and low; all peltries are on the decline."

Bridger led his men away from Powder River on March 29, crossing the Big Horn at the mouth of the Little Horn. "Getting the necessary information from Mr. Bridger concerning the route he

[4] Newell, *Memoranda*, 34–36.

[5] Victor, *River of the West*, 223–34.

[6] Carson, *Own Story*, 39. (1837 should read 1838.)

[7] Russell, *Journal of a Trapper*, 80–81.

intended to take, we all started in a gallop in a westerly direction," wrote Russell on April 18. Making quick work of Pryor's, Clark's, Rocky, Bodair's, and Twenty-Five-Yard rivers and scouting the Gallatin, they reached the Madison on June 1, 1838.

According to Russell, Bridger noticed he was following "a trail made by a village of Blackfeet [who were] . . . to all appearances occasionally dying of smallpox. . . . That day we passed an Indian lodge . . . which contained nine dead bodies." Continuing on their trail, June 3: "Mr. Bridger, having charge of the Camp, tried to avoid them by taking into the mountains, but the company remonstrated; and he encamped on a branch that ran through a box canyon."

"Our leader ['The same Old Iroquois'] was no military commander; therefore no orders were given." After securing the property, about fifteen mounted men made a dash for the village. Russell's group opened fire, bringing warriors into counterattack. Eight or ten Indians were killed.[8]

Trapper Mansfield was pinioned by his falling mount, and the savages were not neglecting him. He felt sure a tomahawk was being hurled at him, and in an appealing moan, he called out to a disappearing world: "Tell Old Gabe [Bridger] that Old Cotton [his own soubriquet] is gone!" But his horse eased the weight, and Mansfield was able to deliver the message himself.[9]

Meek says the mount of one of the Blackfoot women was shot down, and Meek tried to take an unusual prisoner. "The woman was saved by seizing hold of the tail of her husband's horse, which carried her out of danger."

A few days later, at Henry's Lake, Bridger had a talk with Little Robe, chief of the Piegans. The Chief complained that his people [Blackfeet] were perishing from smallpox communicated to them by the whites. Bridger reminded Little Robe that it was the Mandans and other Indians who persisted in crowding around the boat that brought smallpox to Fort Union and Fort Van Buren. Bridger and Little Robe parted as friends after some trading of horses and hides. Bridger led his men to Snake River and thence to rendezvous.

Newell's words are few but precious: "We are at this time on

[8] *Ibid.*, 86–88.
[9] Victor, *River of the West*, 230–32.

Snake River, June 12, 1838. Three men left this morning to hunt the Flathead village. 12th, the missionaries taking Indians out of their Country . . . Bridger with the Camp."[10] Proceeding by way of Pierre's Hole and Jackson's Little Hole to Horse Creek, they found a note directing them to the Wind River–Big Horn junction. Here Bridger and his men relaxed.

Newell is careful to identify the site. Added in pencil, obviously at a later date but in Newell's handwriting, is this: "At Riverton, Wyo., on Wind River."[11] At another time Newell says the camp was at the "mouth of the Popo Agie," which is the same place.

[10] Newell, *Memoranda*, 37.
[11] *Ibid.*, 38.

As the top-ranking mountaineer at the Wind River Rendezvous of 1838, James Bridger was a welcoming host, answering questions about the country, the route, the Indians, the wild animals, and the mountaineers. In fact he was, himself, the answer to most questions!

Captain Andrew Drips of the American Fur Company reached Wind River, June 22, 1838, with eighteen cartloads of supplies, in care of forty-five men and using two hundred horses and mules. Accompanying the train were the missionary party of William H. Gray, Cushing Eells, Elkanah Walker, and Asa B. Smith, their four wives, and three missionary assistants. Traveling with the missionaries were William Drummond Stewart and a party of five, also Johann August Sutter.

Mrs. Myra F. Eells reports the Independence Day celebration: "July 5, 1838: Captain Bridger's Company comes in about ten o'clock with drums and firing—an apology for a scalp dance. After they had given Captain Drip's Company a shout, fifteen or twenty Mountain men and Indians came to our tent, with drumming, firing and dancing.

"If I might make a comparison, I should say that they looked like the emissaries of the devil, worshipping their own master. They had the scalp of a Blackfoot Indian, which they carried for a color, all rejoicing in the fate of the Blackfeet, in consequence of the smallpox."[1] However, by invitation, James Bridger, Robert Newell, and others were mealtime guests of different missionaries.

Francis Ermatinger of Fort Hall arrived July 8, 1838, with an

[1] Le Roy R. Hafen and F. M. Young, *Fort Laramie*, 54–56 (quoting from Myra F. Eells's "Journal").

eastbound party of fourteen, including Jason Lee, P. L. Edwards, and F. Y. Ewing. The rendezvous suddenly became a "Grand Central Station" of activity, with everyone writing letters to be carried by the returning caravan.

James Bridger sponsored the most important documents, revealing his recent earnings, and possibly his future plans and affiliations. The documents follow:[2]

Wind River Rendezvous, July 13, 1838.

Wm. L. Sublette, Esq.,

Dr. Sir: Attached herewith you will find a power of attorney from myself to you, giving authority to collect from Pratte Chouteau & Co., the full amount due from them to me for services rendered, and hope you will use every exertion to obtain it for me, and deposit it in some safe keeping, subject to my future disposal, in the meantime using it for your benefit if you think proper. Accompanying this power is an acknowledgement from Mr. Drips of the amt. due me by the Company. I am unable to obtain from him a draft or order in legal form, but hope you may be able to collect the money.

My best respects to my old friend, R. Campbell, and accept for yourself the warm esteem of,

Your friend and obt. servt.,
His
James X Bridger
Mark

Wind River 13 July 1838.

Know all men by these presents, that I, James Bridger, late of Illinois, and now in the Rocky Mountains, have constituted and appointed and do hereby constitute and appoint William L. Sublette of St. Louis, Missouri, my true and lawful attorney with full power in my name to do and perform all my business transactions as fully and as perfectly as though I were personally present hereby confirming the same. And I do by these presents, fully authorize said William L. Sublette to receive all moneys due me and in my name to give receipts therefore; to institute suits at law for the securing the paying of all debts due me.

And especially, whereas Pratte Chouteau & Co. of St. Louis, Mis-

[2] Courtesy of Missouri Historical Society, St. Louis, Missouri.

souri, are due me a sum of money of which the accompanying instrument of writing is their acknowledgement and which reads as follows viz:

Messrs Pratte Chouteau & Co,
    Gentl.
There will be due James Bridger on his arrival at St. Louis three thousand three hundred and seventeen dollars and thirteen cents for services rendered the R. M. Outfit for the two last years services,
Andrew Drips, Agt. For Pratte Chouteau & Co., Rocky Mountains.

Wind River J. 13, 1838.

Now I do by these presents authorize said William L. Sublette to receive the said sum of money of said Pratte Chouteau & Co. and to take all legal measures for enforcing the payment thereof as fully and as perfectly as though I were personally present and transacting the same, hereby confirming to all intents and purposes the acts all and severally of my aforesaid attorney.

In testimony whereof I have hereunto set my hand and seal this thirteenth day of July in the year of our Lord one thousand eight hundred and thirty eight.

James [His X Mark] Bridger.
Witness: Wm. Preston Clark,
    John Radford.

The phrase "on his arrival at St. Louis" in the preceding is a veiled hint that Bridger had a little extra traveling of his own in mind. But he wasn't the only trapper who would run away from it all. Robert Newell observed: "Men who had been in the Company for a long time, commenced leaving, owing to the Company being so hard. Some run off, stole horses, traps, and other articles of value."[3]

Russell confirms Newell's grievance: "During our stay at the rendezvous, it was rumored among the men, that the Company intended to bring no more supplies to the Rocky Mountains, and discontinue all further operations. This caused a great deal of discontent among the trappers, and numbers left the party."[4]

[3] Newell, *Memoranda*, 37.
[4] Russell, *Journal of a Trapper*, 90–91.

Trapper Joseph L. Meek was more discouraged than he cared to admit and sought to drown his troubles in drink. Instead of drowning them, however, he preserved them. His act so disgusted his Nez Percé wife that she left him, taking their two-year-old Helen Mar Meek. Ermatinger would leave them with relatives at Walla Walla.[5]

Others, possibly for want of resources, clung to the life like matted cockleburs. "Mr. J. Walker went to the [Little] Snake country with a part of Drips' camp, thirty or forty men; some in other directions."[6] Kit Carson went with seven men to Fort David Crockett (Brown's Hole) and took employment as hunter, "keeping twenty men provisioned."[7] Fontenelle and Harris led the eastbound caravan out of camp on July 20, 1838.

Breaking camp at the same time, Drips and Bridger departed with eighty or ninety men and the usual Indian following. Their route was up Wind River, through Union Pass, down the Gros Ventre to Jackson Hole and Snake River, reaching Pierre's Hole on August 5, 1838.[8] Thereabouts came a general dispersal. Newell took his "woman and two little boys" (the latest born March 30, 1838) to Fort Hall, then returned "and joined Mr. Drips in Pierre's Hole." Bridger lodged his family with his wife's people, who were returning for the winter to the Flathead village on the Salmon.

While all were near Missouri Lake (Hebgen), Meek reports that they had a buffalo hunt; in brief: "It was the work of half an hour to slay two thousand or maybe three thousand animals. Here and there and everywhere, lay the slain buffalo. Occasionally a horse with a broken leg was seen, or a man with a broken arm . . . or worse. . . . Now came out the women of the Indian village to help us butcher and pack up the meat. . . . By night the camp was full of meat, and everybody was merry. Bridger's camp, which was passing that way, traded with the village for fifteen hundred buffalo tongues."[9]

After the buffalo hunt, Meek found beavers plentiful on the Gallatin, and while crossing Burnt Hole, he proudly inscribed the fact on a whitened buffalo skull for Bridger's jealous eyes. But Meek's

[5] Victor, *River of the West*, 238–39.
[6] Newell, *Memoranda*, 38.
[7] Carson, *Own Story*, 42.
[8] Newell, *Memoranda*, 38.
[9] Victor, *River of the West*, 248–49.

mischievous threat to market his bulky bundle at the hated Fort Hall boomeranged with a sting. Bridger suspected a trick from the incorrigible freeman, but Commander Drips made such ugly threats that when they came together in Pierre's Hole, Meek meekly produced a sales receipt from Drips's own Joseph R. Walker.[10]

Meek then joined the Indian traveling village, to obtain from the Nez Percé chief a replacement for the wife he recently lost downriver. Incidentally he drove a right good bargain, gaining a lifetime helpmeet and becoming Newell's brother-in-law.[11]

Newell's "Memoranda" says: "I then left Fort Hall and joined Mr. Drips in Pierre's Hole. Went from there to the head of Green River. Commenced winter quarters . . . November 20, 1838. Captain Drips left in December for Wind River, with his camp," piloted by James Bridger. After settling the main camp in the friendly, chinook-warmed Wind River–Big Horn valley, Captain Drips, Bridger, and a substantial number of men who were quitting the mountains proceeded to Fort William, where Drips had left his family. Bridger was contemplating future plans.

Bridger's ruminating was evidently along this line: Louis Vásquez and Andrew Sublette had maintained a trading post at Clear Creek (Denver) from 1834 to 1836, moving in 1837 to Fort Vásquez (Platteville), ten miles below Lancaster P. Lupton's new post. Philip Thompson, William Craig, and St. Clair grubstaked Uncle Jack Robertson at Fort David Crockett in 1837.

Peter A. Sarpy and Henry Fraeb erected Fort Jackson near Fort Vásquez in 1837, but were closing it in 1838. Fraeb then moved westward to a branch of Little Snake River, and built a log hut within a picketed enclosure. Hiram M. Chittenden says this project had James Bridger's aid and approval.[12]

Bridger had a seventeen-year-old date with the city of St. Louis; he had told Captain Raynolds in 1859 that he once went seventeen years without tasting bread. That could have been only from 1822 to 1839.[13]

There is evidence that late in 1838, or early in the year 1839,

[10] *Ibid.*, 251.
[11] *Ibid.*, 252–53, 256.
[12] Chittenden, *Fur Trade*, 971.
[13] Raynolds, *Exploration of the Yellowstone*, 77.

Bridger fell in with Louis Vásquez and Henry Fraeb, probably at Independence, Missouri, and that they talked one another into some sort of partnership, journeying on to St. Louis to set the scheme to incubating.

Summarizing from the Louis Vásquez biography: The license to "Vasquez and Sublette" was issued in 1837, apparently sponsored by the American Fur Company, Bridger's new affiliation. James P. Beckwourth was employed by them at Fort Vásquez, in 1838. And: "Jim Bridger had visited his old friend Louis, at Fort Vasquez, in 1839."[14]

From other inferences, it appears that James Bridger was an interested bystander at Independence, Missouri, April 15, 1839, when Pratte, Chouteau and Company's mountain supply train departed, led by Moses B. Harris and a crew of eight. In the emigrant section were missionaries Asahel and Mrs. Munger and John S. and Mrs. Griffin, with Paul Henderson as guide, and two laborers. A separate group of four was headed by Dr. F. A. Wislizenus, all destined for the Green River rendezvous, which Bridger would attend only in spirit.[15]

One of the most appreciative men that Bridger met on this trip to St. Louis was the Catholic missionary priest, Father Pierre Jean De Smet. The priest was sent up the Missouri River to Fort Union, April 15, 1839, and returned that autumn. He was "to gain knowledge of the disposition of the savages, and of the success that might probably be looked for from founding a mission among them." De Smet saw Bridger on the way.

Father De Smet did not keep a journal or a diary, but at various times he wrote letters relating anecdotes and incidents of travel to superiors, associates, and friends, most of whom were abroad. He had become more definitely oriented towards his new assignment by the 1839 trip, especially through his interviews with James Bridger and other mountaineers, of which interviews far too little has been preserved.

By marriage Bridger was a prominent member of the Flathead

---

14 Lauren C. Bray, "Louis Vasquez, Mountain Man," *Westerners Roundup*, July–August, 1959, 12–13. Hereafter referred to as Bray, "Louis Vasquez."

15 Asahel and Eliza Munger, "Diary 1839," *Oregon Historical Society Quarterly*, December, 1907, 387–405.

Nation, son-in-law of Chief Insala, and tribal "brother" of the Indians who first visited Captain Clark in St. Louis to inquire about the white man's "Book of Heaven."

Father De Smet once wrote of the West: "In several places you can see steam and sulphurous flames escaping from the bosom of the earth; and I learned from a traveler, who had been all over this region for a number of years, subterranean noises are often heard." De Smet's editors (Chittenden and Richardson) conclude that this "traveler" was James Bridger, and that on De Smet's return to St. Louis (1839) he sought Bridger out for further conversations.

At the Fort Laramie Peace Conference of 1851, the worthy priest interjected James Bridger's description of the Yellowstone, which De Smet had previously given, in part, in a letter. He says: "Between the sources of the Madison and Yellowstone Rivers . . . bituminous, sulphur and boiling springs are numerous. The hot springs contain a large quantity of calcareous matter, and form hills more or less elevated (cones or formations).

"Gas, vapor and smoke are continuously escaping by a thousand openings from the base to the summit of the volcanic pile. The noise at times resembles the steam let off by a boat. Strong subterranean explosions occur. The hunters and the Indians speak of it with superstitious fear. . . . Near Gardner River there is a mountain of sulphur [Mammoth Hot Springs]. I have this report from Captain Bridger, who is familiar with every one of these mountains."[16]

During that summer and autumn of 1839, Bridger was surprised at the quantity of news filtering in from the mountains to the Sublette, Pratte, and other merchandising and freighting firms. Many adventurers were coming and going.

To the reminiscing Bridger, seeing St. Louis in its growing pains, "Main Street" seemed as if it were being devoured by strange new interests, expanding from Broadway, Chestnut, and Market streets. They all lost their charm in the presence of the seething Levee or Front Street. Here a fringe of steamboat chimneys, with smaller boats nudging their way around as if they were afraid of the Mississippi River, gave depressing notice of the fact that there was, in

[16] Hiram Chittenden and Alfred Richardson, *Life, Letters, and Travels of Pierre Jean De Smet*, 661. Father De Smet wrote in 1863 of his journey to the Laramie peace conference of 1851.

Bridgers' tongue: "Nary dang set for a beaver trap anywhurz!"

Captain Sublette and Robert Campbell could make Bridger feel at ease, but they could not make him feel at home. He was a mountaineer, wearing a mountaineer's garb, having a mountaineer's habits, with a mountaineer's appetite. Left to himself on the street, the lump in his throat "wouldn't swaller down"; he was "plumb" homesick. As time dragged on in that plush environment, there was a possibility he could learn to like the "grub," even "dough bread." The corn bread and sorghum were "shore exciting."

But the deep, soft bed-ticks of rye straw or cornhusks were tiresome, not restful. At one "flop-house" a late-arriving patron was instructed to crawl in bed with the mountaineer. The patron asked Bridger, "Don't you take your britches off?"

"Haint yit!" Bridger assured him. In the upshot, Bridger gave up the bed, borrowed a "buffler-hide" and "quiled right down on the floor and slept."—"Kin hear more, and git up quicker," Bridger told the man.

JAMES BRIDGER and Henry Fraeb left St. Louis in the early spring of 1840 to join Moses B. Harris and the mountain supply train at Independence. Louis Vásquez and Andrew Sublette had left the previous August (1839) with a stock of goods for Fort Vásquez. They traveled by steamer to Independence and by their own wagon train from there. Vásquez and Sublette joined Philip Thompson, who was transporting a pack load for his post at Fort David Crockett, and passed Lupton with six heavy wagons for his post. They reached Fort Vásquez on September 18, and Fort David Crockett the first of October.[1]

Bridger and Fraeb with a small party, including young James Baker, were traveling companions of Protestant missionaries Harvey Clark, A. T. Smith, P. B. Littlejohn, and their wives; Catholic missionary Father Pierre Jean De Smet and his party; and Oregon emigrant Joel P. Walker, his wife, and their five children. On the way the travelers picked up further details of the last year's happenings in the mountains.

At the Platte River, Bridger learned that E. Willard Smith had already gone downstream in a Mackinaw flatboat thirty-six feet long and eight feet wide, loaded with seven hundred buffalo hides and three hundred buffalo tongues from Fort Vásquez. They had left the post on April 26, 1840,[2] and relayed news that touched Bridger's heartstring.

Hungry hunters from Fort Crockett had levied on one hundred buffalo on Little Snake River, and retaliating Sioux had helped themselves to as many Fort Crockett horses. Itinerants drove off

---

[1] E. Willard Smith, "Journal with the Fur Traders, 1839–40," *Oregon Historical Quarterly*, September, 1913, 250–79.

[2] *Ibid.*, 250–79.

a herd of Fort Hall horses and then robbed an old man as they neared Fort Crockett. Denied a welcome at Fort Crockett, these robbers fled to Fort Uinta, followed by Joseph R. Walker at the head of an angry posse of regulars, including Craig, Meek, Carson, and Newell. The posse recovered the horses and ridded the country of the rowdies.

Other scenes and pictures came to a homesick Bridger, along with the nagging suggestion of past years, made by Uncle Jack Robertson, that he establish a trading post and make it a home. After Robert Newell had parted with Bridger and Drips, in December, 1838, Newell had "spent the balance of the winter down on Green River, over to Ham's Fork . . . . [On March 1, 1839] on to Black's Fork, one of the best places for wintering in the Rocky Mountains," as Bridger had probably told him.[3]

Brown's Hole, or Fort David Crockett, was a popular place, although off the main-traveled road. Thomas J. Farnham found it, the week of August 12, 1839, "a hollow square of one-story log cabins, with roofs and floors of mud. . . . Here also are the lodges of Mr. Robinson [Uncle Jack Robertson], trader . . . . His skin lodge was his warehouse; and buffalo robes were spread upon the ground and counter, on which he displayed his butcher knives, hatchets, powder, lead, fish-hooks and whiskey. , , , He receives beaver skins from trappers, money from travelers, and horses from Indians. . . . A white man has no business here."[4]

Dr. Wislizenus camped on Black's Fork in mid-August, 1839: "It is a rushing brook, overgrown with cottonwood, willows and wild currants; we found splendid pasturage and grass for the horses. The ground is loamy sand." More reasons why Uncle Jack Robertson homesteaded nearby.

A week or so later, on the Little Snake, Dr. Wislizenus "met Captain Walker, whom we had met at rendezvous; and some trappers and Indians, who had come here for dried meat.

"Captain Walker is an original among the mountain loafers. He has taken such a fancy to this life that it is unlikely that he ever returns to civilization. We found him with a pipe in his mouth, and clad with nothing but a blanket, for which he excused himself to us,

[3] Newell, *Memoranda*, 38.
[4] Thomas J. Farnham, *Travels in the Great Western Prairies*, 252-53.

because his shirt was in the wash. He had sufficient fresh buffalo meat, and invited us to the rib of a fat cow."

Reaching the South Platte, September 3, 1839, Wislizenus wrote: "Three Forts here [Lupton, Vásquez, and Bent] . . . . Much rivalry . . . . I met the well known [Thomas] Fitzpatrick, who had passed through many an adventure during his life in the mountains. He was a spare, bony figure, a face full of expression, and white hair; his whole demeanor reveals strong passion."[5]

James Bridger and Henry Fraeb, with Moses B. Harris and the 1840 supply train, were joined at Fort William on June 4 by Andrew Drips who was in charge of the fort. Drips's affectionate leave-taking of his family recalled Wislizenus' reference to Drips's and Walker's wives at the rendezvous a year earlier. It was a fair appraisal of the wife that Bridger was soon to meet: "Their Indian wives . . . quite passable as to their features, appeared in highest state, their red blankets, with silk handkerchiefs on their heads. . . . They behaved most properly; took care of the horses; pitched a tent; and were alert for every word of their wedded lords."

It was a momentous occasion when Drips, Harris, and company filed into Green River's Horse Creek rendezvous on June 30. Competitor Ermatinger had, a fortnight before, deposited an eighty pack-horse load of suppiles at Fort Hall in a determined effort to succeed where Wyeth had failed.[6]

After selling his furs at Fort Hall, Robert Newell proceeded to the rendezvous on Horse Creek. "Mr. Drips, Fraeb and Bridger, from St. Louis with goods. But times was certainly hard. No beaver, and everything dull. . . . While at rendezvous I had some difficulty with a man by the name of Moses Harris. I think he intended murder; he shot at me, about seventy or eighty yards."[7] Harris had guided the missionaries to Green River, and there lost the job to Newell.

Bridger seems to have traveled ahead of the caravan from Fort William to meet his Indian people and escort them to the rendezvous. Kit Carson wrote, in the autumn of 1839: "A chief of the Flatheads and some of his tribe, joined us and we traveled on to Big Snake River, for winter quarters, and passed this winter without being

[5] Dr. F. A. Wislizenus, *A Journey to the Rocky Mountains in 1839*, 137.
[6] Russell, *Journal of a Trapper*, 111.
[7] Newell, *Memoranda*, 39.

molested by Indians. In the spring [1840] Bridger and party started for rendezvous on Green River. Jack Robinson [Robertson] and myself departed for the Utah country to Robidoux's Fort, and there disposed of the furs we had caught."[8]

Father De Smet says he was met at Green River by a deputation of ten Flathead Indians, apparently led by James Bridger, who had come to escort De Smet to their village. "I stayed four days on Green River to allow my horses time to recover from their fatigue. On the 4th of July [sixth in other letters], I left with the Flatheads [and presumably Bridger and Baker], ascending Green River and crossing the divide to Little Jackson Hole.

July 10, 1840: "The stream was a torrent of prodigious height; but the horsemen swam it with their mounts. To get me over they made a kind of sack of my skin tent; and put all my things in and set me on top of it. The three Flatheads who had jumped in to guide my frail bark by swimming, told me, laughing, not to be afraid; that I was on an excellent boat. This machine floated on the water like a majestic swan; and in less than ten minutes I found myself on the other bank. The next day we went through Teton Pass to Pierre's Hole . . . to the main camp of the Flatheads,"[9] and held religious services.

Under date of December 30, 1841, Father De Smet spoke of this visit again: "A Flathead showed me the scars left by the balls and arrows of the Blackfeet. . . . One of them bore the scars of four balls which had pierced his thigh; another had his arm and breast pierced by a ball; a third, beside some wounds from a knife and spear, had an arrow five inches deep in his belly. . . .

"I expressed a desire to know the medicines which they used in such cases; they, much surprised at my question, replied, laughing 'we apply nothing to our wounds; they close of themselves.' This recalled to me the reply of Captain Bridger in the past year. He had had, within four years, two quivers-full of arrowheads [two arrowheads?] in his body. Being asked if the wounds had been long suppurating, he answered humorously: 'In the mountains the meat never spoils!' "[10]

8 Carson, *Own Story*, 48.
9 Chittenden and Richardson, *Life and Travels of Father De Smet*, 221.
10 *Ibid.*, 1012.

Father De Smet's subsequent statements indicate that Bridger accompanied him at least part of the way on the 1840 excursion. De Smet says: "We ascended Henry's Fork of Snake River, and on July 22, 1840, came to Henry's Lake. Nearby . . . is the head of the Missouri."

Proceeding leisurely the entire village settled in Three Forks Valley on August 21. Father De Smet tells a friend why: "In this great and beautiful plain were buffalo in numberless herds. From Green River to this place our Indians made their food of roots and the flesh of such animals as the red and black tailed deer, elk, gazelle, big horn or mountain sheep, grizzly and black bear, badger, rabbit and panther; killing also occasionally such feathered game as grouse, prairie hens, swans, geese, cranes and ducks; fish also from the rivers, particularly salmon. But cow meat is the favorite dish of all the hunters.

"Finding themselves therefore in the midst of abundance, the Flatheads prepared to lay in their winter supply. They raised willow scaffolds about their lodges for drying meat, and everyone made ready his firearm, his bow and arrows. Four hundred horsemen, old and young, mounted on their best horses, started early in the morning for their great hunt. I chose to accompany them in order to watch this striking spectacle from near at hand.

"At a given signal they rode at full gallop among the herds. Soon everything appeared confusion and flight all over the plain. The hunters pursued the fattest cows, discharged their guns and let fly their arrows, and in three hours they killed more than 500. Then the women, the old men and the children came up, and with the aid of horses, carried off the hides and meat, and soon all the scaffolds were full and gave the camp the aspect of a vast butcher shop."

Arranging for the Flatheads to meet him at Fort Hall in a year, Father De Smet departed on August 27, "seventeen warriors being deputed to serve as my escort" beyond the country of the Blackfeet. Their route was through Bozeman Pass (first called Bridger Pass), now gored by a 3,600-foot railroad tunnel. Proceeding by way of Fort Union, De Smet reached St. Louis on January 31, 1841.[11]

After the grand buffalo slaughter, James Bridger returned to Green River with his family and a few of his Flathead people. Re-

11 *Ibid.*, 233.

joining Fraeb and his determined men, Bridger visited the Little Snake country to find winter meat and to appraise the site as a trading post, since much of the travel was on that route. They learned, and quickly, what they had hoped they would not learn. Prowling war parties of Cheyennes were touring in force, herding the newcomers back to Green River.

Joseph L. Meek, Robert Newell, and William Craig were going to Oregon to become farmers. Uncle Jack Robertson, Kit Carson, St. Clair, and Philip Thompson, along with others, were crowding one another in Fort Crockett, waiting for opportunity to knock. Meanwhile Osborne Russell was facing a dull winter at Salt Lake with a village of half-bloods. We next hear of James Bridger on Black's Fork, through the cruel circumstances that made it Hobson's choice for a wilderness home.

IF THE ANNUAL SUPPLY CARAVAN, returning with furs, was the heartbeat of the fur trade, that unique business well-nigh perished in 1841, for there was no supply train and no rendezvous that year. Instead, a one-way cavalcade of independent overlanders, numbering about 90, with about 20 carts or wagons and 150 horses or mules, left Westport, Missouri, May 10, 1841.

Among the group were John Bartleson, John Bidwell, Father De Smet, and Joseph Williams, with Thomas Fitzpatrick as guide. Some of the travelers were using pack animals and most of them had mounts, while Father De Smet's men, largely French Canadians, had five or six Red River carts, each drawn by two mules hitched in tandem.

Parson Joseph Williams, an itinerant Hoosier minister of Methodist persuasion, though traveling in his sixty-fourth year on horseback, overtook the caravan near the Platte River and promptly fellowshipped with everybody—except: "There were some as wicked people among them," he confided to his diary, "as I ever saw in my life!" May 31, 1841: "Our leader, Fitzpatrick, is a wicked, worldly man, and is much opposed to Missionaries going among the Indians."[1]

Traveling to Fort Laramie and South Pass, Williams writes on July 23, 1841: "We lay on Green River bottom, where we fell in with Mr. Fraeb, who was on a hunting expedition. This man, with nine or ten of his company was afterwards killed in a skirmish with the Sioux Indians. His company was mostly composed of half-breeds, French and Dutch, and all sorts of people collected together in the mountains; and were a wicked, swearing company of men.

[1] Joseph Williams, *Narrative of a Tour, Indiana to Oregon, 1841–1842, and Return*, 34.

194

... Leaving Mr. Fraeb's company, we continued on our journey, down Green River."[2]

July 27: "We camped on Black's Fork. We are now among the Snake nation and Flathead Indians. ... 28th. On Ham's Fork of Green River. One of our wagons broke down today. 30th [traveled] towards Bear River .... Next night we lay on Black's Fork .... August 2, 1841 ... we came to Bear River .... Here we rested and waited for the Snake Indians to come and trade with us."

The Flatheads named by Williams were not outlaws, but in-laws, relatives of James Bridger by marriage. The wagon broke down quite opportunely; Fitzpatrick and De Smet were overdue for a long conference with Bridger. It lasted almost a week.

When Williams reached Fort Hall, about August 14, he wrote: "Here news came to us that about two hundred Sioux had attacked Fraeb's company, mentioned in a former part of my narrative."[3]

As the death of Fraeb was the turning of the semaphore on James Bridger's career, we may examine Bidwell's version, written from memory after many years: "Guided by Fitzpatrick, we crossed ... South Pass. Approaching Green River, it was found that some of the wagons, including Captain Bartleson's, had alcohol on board; and that the owners wanted to find trappers ... to whom they might sell it. This was a surprise to many of us, as there had been no drinking on the way. John Grey was sent ahead to see if he could find a trapping party; and he was instructed, if successful, to have them come to a certain place on Green River.

"He struck a trail and overtook a party on their way to the buffalo region, to lay in provisions, i.e. buffalo meat; and they returned, and came and camped on Green River, very soon after our arrival, buying the greater part, if not all, of the alcohol, it first having been diluted so as to make what they call whiskey—three or four gallons of water to a gallon of alcohol.

"Years afterwards we heard of the fate of that party; they were attacked by Indians the very first night after they left us, and several of them were killed, including the Captain of the trapping party, whose name was Fraeb."[4]

[2] *Ibid.*, 42.
[3] *Ibid.*, 46.
[4] John Bidwell, *In California Before the Gold Rush*, 23–24.

Basil Clement (Claymore), after sixty years, tried hard to recall under the cross-examination of Charles Edmund DeLand, his affiliation with Henry Fraeb and James Bridger, beginning with the spring of 1841. With respect to their encampment, Clement merely outlined the route: from the mouth of Grand River (South Dakota), Fort Pierre ("with Bridger's partner, Old Vasquez"), Fort Laramie, Sweetwater, Sandy, Big Sandy, Green River, Ham's Fork, Henry's Fork (Muddy?), to Black's Fork, in that order.

"Old Vásquez" drops out of Clement's narrative at Fort Laramie. Clement continues: "From there [Black's Fork] to Little Snake Creek. Old Frapp [Fraeb] was killed there. He was one of three partners. We went there on a buffalo hunt to make jerked meat. We got meat of the Sioux and Cheyennes, with forty-seven men. After we had plenty of meat they made a dash for us. We defended ourselves . . . . We fought them from morning till dark.

"They killed ten of our men; and killed 110 head of horses that belonged to us; and of the forty-five head of horses alive, there was only five not wounded. All that we had to protect us was dead horses; and we made a Fort of them. . . . Then we made a cache and put the dried meat into it. This was my first year with Bridger. Bridger was not with us in the fight; he was at Fort Bridger, on Black's Fork."[5]

Another version is by James Baker. Maggie Kilgore, of Savery, Wyoming, Baker's old home, gathered it from neighborhood traditions after Baker's death.[6] From this, and Baker's own statements, it appears that young Baker accompanied James Bridger from St. Louis, in 1840, on Baker's second excursion to the mountains. On Laramie Plains, "the Indians were thick as bees," Baker always said. The travelers were "stopped many times and subjected to examination. Two or three councils were held . . . . Thanks be to Bridger for our safety, because . . . of his great . . . ability to treat with the redskins."

Baker seems to have accompanied James Bridger, Father De Smet, and the Flatheads into winter quarters. Baker wrote the Utah

[5] Basil Clement, *The Mountain Trappers* (ed. by Charles E. De Land), vol. XI, *South Dakota Historical Society Collection*, 290–366.

[6] Maggie Kilgore, "Life of Jim Baker," Cheyenne *Tribune*, July 23, 1917; see also *Latter-day Saints Millennial Star*, June 24, 1897.

Pioneer Jubilee Commission, May 19, 1847, that he had visited Utah Valley [Utah Lake] for the first time in 1841: "When I came in from Montana, with forty other men and seven Shoshone Indians."

Traveling by way of Bear River, Baker's party appears to have visited the Green River country at that time, meeting Fitzpatrick and his emigrant train, which had halted for his visit with James Bridger. Hearing further reports of rampaging Sioux and Cheyennes from Fitzpatrick, Bridger was justly uneasy and sent a small party, express, to put Fraeb on his guard. Young Baker was with the party, which, however, arrived after Fraeb's initial skirmish. Baker was not engaged in the fight, but knew of its details. In due course, he returned to Black's Fork with the gruesome news. He told the Jubilee Commission he went, by way of Utah Valley, to Arizona to trap for the winter.

James Bridger told Captain Stansbury, September 18, 1850, that Henry Fraeb and a party of freemen "were encamped about two miles from where we then were, with their squaw partners, and a party of Indians. Most of the men being absent hunting buffalo, a band of five hundred Sioux, Cheyennes and Arapahoes, suddenly charged upon their camp, killed a white man, an Indian, and two women, and drove off 160 head of horses.

"Intelligence of this onslaught reached Major Bridger, then occupied in erecting a trading post on Green River [Black's Fork]. He sent Fraeb advice to abandon his post at once, for fear of worse consequences. The advice, however, was neglected, when about ten days after, as Fraeb's party was on their way to join his partner, they were attacked by another large party of Savages.

"Fraeb had but forty men; but they instantly 'forted,' in the corral attached to the trading post, and stood their defense. The assault lasted from noon until sundown, the Indians . . . losing forty men. Fraeb himself was killed, with seven or eight of his people."[7]

Henry Fraeb was probably killed about August 7 or 8, 1841, as the events may be placed between the two known dates given: Fraeb's meeting with Fitzpatrick on July 23, 1841, and the news of his death, which appeared in Parson Williams' journal on August

[7] Howard Stansbury, *Exploration and Survey of the Valley of the Great Salt Lake*, 239-40.

14. Fraeb's working unit, which met the first attack, may have preceded him to the region.

Fraeb's proposed trading post was located about half a mile above the junction of Battle Creek and Little Snake River (then St. Vrain's Fork) in Wyoming, very near the state boundary and about eighteen miles southwest of Bridger Peak on the continental divide. The post was burned by Indians shortly after Fraeb's death. James Baker settled on a homestead about three miles southwest of Savery and twelve miles west of Battle Creek in 1873. His quaint two-story, fortified log cabin was moved to Cheyenne in 1917.

FORT BRIDGER was in the making. In spite of the disorganized exodus from the mountains, men were still available to trap the streams and trade with the Indians. Most of the fur men recognized James Bridger's seniority. But a competing frontier merchant was at Fort Hall, and Fort Bridger was already suffering from a malady peculiar to its proprietor-partner—wanderlust. The place would just have to grow up! Much as we would like to describe its growing pains in detail, there is a dearth of documentation.

It is significant that, in baptizing Bridger's son, Felix, in January, 1854, Father De Smet recorded: "born in December 1841, son of Captain Bridger of Salt Lake."[1] The next reference is in the revealing dairy of parson Joseph Williams, returning from Oregon in 1842. At Whitman's Waiilatpu, the Williams party was joined by Captain Richard Grant, chief trader at Fort Hall, with a pack-horse caravan of goods.

June 1, 1842: "We stopped on Snake River, at Fort Boise," Williams writes. "This day I heard some dreadful oaths from Captain Grant, about some threats which he had heard from Mr. Bridger, one of the American Fur Company, against Fort Hall; and respecting some goods which had been stolen by Mr. Bridger's Company from the Hudson's Bay Company."[2]

July 3: "We reached Green River . . . found nothing there but one dog. We had expected some company to the United States. . . . From Green River we turned out of our intended route and went about a southwest course, in order to avoid the Blackfeet Indians." July 3 (6?): "Reached Bridger's Fort. Company had left for the United States, about thirty days before, and we saw nothing there

---

[1] Missouri Historical Society, St. Louis, Missouri.
[2] Williams, *Tour to Oregon*, 1841-42, 74.

but three little starved dogs. We saw the grave of an Indian woman, who had been killed by the Cheyennes."[3]

A few bright dogs may have been in charge of Fort Bridger, but the fact was soon to be learned that both Bridger and Fitzpatrick were on the road, eastbound, with a caravan of furs. Dr. Elijah White and Lansford W. Hastings, leading more than one hundred Oregon emigrants, sojourned at Fort Laramie to exchange ox teams for horses, expecting later to abandon the wagons and use pack horses, if needed.

Miss Allen says, "They spent a week refitting for the rest of the journey. . . . At last they started, and had proceeded scarce a mile on their way, when, to their joy, they met Mr. Fitzpatrick, who was escorting Mr. Bridger and a party who occupied a post near the base of the opposite side of the mountains, and who was now on his way to the States, with a large quantity of furs." Dr. White engaged Mr. Fitzpatrick to pilot his party to Fort Hall for $500.[4]

Bridger continued eastward. John C. Frémont, on his first expedition, met and had much to say about "Mr. Bridger." Marching up Platte River and nearing the forks (present Ogallala) July 6, 1842, Frémont, with an escort, detoured up the South Platte, while chief topographer Charles Preuss led Frémont's main party (Kit Carson as guide) up the North Platte. The two parties would meet at Fort Laramie. Mr. Preuss writes, July 8, 1842:

"Nothing occurred to break the monotony until about 5 o'clock, when the caravan made a sudden halt. There was a galloping in of scouts and horsemen from every side—a hurrying to and fro in noisy confusion; rifles were taken from their cover; bullet pouches examined: in short there was the cry of 'Indians,' heard again. I had become so much accustomed to these alarms, that now they made but little impression on me; and before I had time to become excited, the newcomers were ascertained to be whites. It was a large party of traders and trappers, conducted by Mr. Bridger, a man well known in the history of the country. As the sun was low, and there was a fine grass patch not far ahead, they turned back and encamped

[3] *Ibid.*, 77–78.
[4] *Ten Years in Oregon (1838–1847) Travels and Adventures of Dr. E. White and Lady* (compiled by A. J. Allen), 153–54.

for the night with us. Mr. Bridger was invited to supper; and, after the *table cloth* was removed, we listened with eager interest to an account of their adventures. What they had met, we would be likely to encounter; the chances which had befallen them, would probably happen to us; and we looked upon their life as a picture of our own. He informed us that the condition of the country had become exceedingly dangerous. The Sioux, who had been badly disposed, had broken out in open hostility, and in the preceding autumn his party had encountered them in a severe engagement, in which a number of lives had been lost on both sides. United with the Cheyenne and Gros Ventre Indians, they were scouring the upper country in war parties of great force, and were at this time in the neighborhood of the *Red Buttes*, a famous landmark, which was directly on our path. They had declared war upon every living thing which should be found westward of that point; though their main object was to attack a large camp of whites and Snake Indians, who had a rendezvous in the Sweetwater Valley. Availing himself of his intimate knowledge of the country, he had reached Laramie by an unusual route through the Black Hills, and avoided coming into contact with any of the scattered parties. This gentleman offered his services to accompany us so far as the head of the Sweetwater; but the absence of our leader . . . rendered it impossible for us to enter upon such an arrangement. . . . this news had thrown . . . all into the greatest consternation in our party, to my surprise. . . . All night long, groups assembled around the fires were listening eagerly to exaggerated details of Indians hostilities. . . . A majority of them were disposed to return, but Clément Lambert and five or six others professed their determination to follow Mr. Frémont to the end of his journey."

July 10, 1842: "In the course of the day we met some whites, who were following along in the train of Mr. Bridger; and, after a day's journey of twenty-four miles, we encamped at the Chimney rock."
July 13: "We reached Fort Laramie."

Resuming Lieutenant Frémont's text: "There are twenty men at the post, several with Indian wives and children. In the course of conversation [with Bridger] I learned the following particulars:
"The Cheyennes and Sioux have become more hostile to the

Whites. In August, 1841, they had a severe engagement with a party of sixty men under command of Mr. Frapp [Fraeb], of St. Louis. The Indians lost eight or ten warriors; and the Whites had their leader and four men killed. . . . It was this party, of Fraeb's survivors, on their return under Mr. Bridger, which spread so much alarm among my people.

"The emigrants to Oregon and Mr. Bridger met here, a few days before our arrival. Division and discouragement appeared among the emigrants, because of wearisome hardships of travel; the feet of their cattle were so badly worn they traveled with difficulty. The travelers were told the countryside was entirely swept of grass, and that there were few buffalo for food; finally, that their weakened animals could not draw their wagons over the mountains ahead.

"Under these circumstances they disposed of their wagons and cattle at the forts. . . . Mr. Boudeau [in charge of the post] informed me that he had purchased thirty, and the lower Fort eighty head of fine cattle, some of the Durham breed. Mr. Fitzpatrick had reached Laramie in Company with Mr. Bridger; and the emigrants were fortunate to obtain his services as guide as far as Fort Hall, leaving here July 4, 1842. We then heard that the Gros Ventre Indians had united with the Oglallahs and Cheyennes, to oppose the Whites, and their allies the Snakes and other Indians.

"I was not surprised at the alarm among my own men. Kit Carson, one of the best and most experienced mountaineers, fully supported the opinion given by Bridger of the dangerous state of the country, and openly expressed his conviction that we could not escape without some sharp encounters with the Indians. In addition to this he made his will; and among the circumstances which were constantly occuring to increase their alarm, this was the most unfortunate; and I found that a number of my party had become so much intimidated, that they had requested to be discharged at this place."[5]

[5] John C. Frémont, *Report of the Exploring Expedition to the Rocky Mountains, 1842*, pp. 37–42 ("Frémont incorporated in his *Report* the happenings during his absence from July 6 to July 13, with the statement that he was including an 'extract from the journal of Mr. Preuss' [pp. 36–39]. Since there is no evidence that Preuss kept a 'journal' in addition to his diary, we can guess that Preuss gave Frémont the necessary information and Frémont wrote the 'extract' to harmonize with the style of his detailed, elaborate *Report*. Allan Nevins did not reprint this material in his new

William L. Sublette wrote William Drummond Stewart in September, 1842, from St. Louis, disclosing certain activities of Vásquez. "In April last [1842] I left St. Louis for the upper counties on the Missouri River, in order to collect and wind up the concern of Sublette and Campbell, where we had large amounts standing out. . . .

"While above I met with Bridger who had just got in from the west side of the mountains from South Snake River [Little Snake], that is, Green River or Sateskiddee. You recollect Bridger and Fraeb left here two years since with about thirty men, trading and trapping on the waters of the Columbia River. Last fall Fraeb, with three others, whilst out making meat from the fort, was killed by the Sioux Indians; and Bridger has come in with about twenty men and thirty packs of beaver [autumn 1842]; and also Louis Vasquez, who remained behind [in St. Louis] to settle up the business of Vasquez & Sublette. V. & S. made rather a sinking business of it. Brother A. W. Sublette is now on the farm, and Vasquez and Bridger has left here lately with about thirty or forty men, fitted out by the American Fur Company, to trap on the waters of Missouri, near the Three Forks. . . . I got back from Independence the 1st of September. . . . found many old houses had failed in St. Louis, and business completely prostrated. Such times I have never seen."[6]

Robert Campbell wrote to William L. Sublette (then at Lexington) on May 23, 1842: "Andrew has just come in from the farm. . . . Vasquez arrived some days ago, and Andrew and him had a private interview . . . to determine some settlement. . . . Vasquez has a note of Locke, Randolph & Co., for $800, part belonging to himself, and part to Vásquez & Sublette. . . . Times continue very bad and everything looks gloomy, even worse than when you left—I hope you will force collections everywhere. . . . Whilst I now write you, Vasquez and Sublette are in conversation in the store." Same June 24, 1842: "Mr. Vasquez leaves today to try and collect the money for the note he received in payment for the Fort &c; he will write you, where he may learn you are, on going up the River." Same, June 25,

edition of Frémont's *Report*." Quoted from Charles Preuss, *Exploring with Frémont*, translated and edited by Erwin G. and Elizabeth K. Gudde, 23.); Frémont's *Memoirs of My Life*, 108–11, 113–15. This quotation is paraphrased in parts.

[6] Robert Campbell, "Correspondence of Robert Campbell," *Missouri Historical Society Glimpses of the Past*, January–June, 1941, pp. 42–43.

1842. "Vasquez has been detained longer than I anticipated, and I therefore write you so that you may be sure to hear from me, at different points." (This letter evidently was taken by Vásquez).[7]

Nearly a year later, May 17, 1843, Campbell wrote Captain Sublette: "I had a letter from Louis Vasquez, dated on Green River, December 12, 1842, stating they were all well." Father De Smet reached St. Louis on July 29, 1842.

The following receipt is in the account book of Andrew Drips for 1819–20 (now in the Bancroft Library, according to Dale L. Morgan): "Received of JAMES BRIDGER, sixty-five dollars in silver and gold, September 3, 1842; the above paid to Mr. E. Chouteau."

[7] *Ibid.*, 31–33, 40–41, 55–56.

JAMES BRIDGER and Louis Vásquez left Missouri outposts rather late with a small pack load of goods, reaching the unfinished Fort Bridger about November 1, 1842. Uncle Jack Robertson and Joseph Reddeford Walker, with their Indian families and following, had moved over from Fort Davy Crockett for the Fort Bridger housewarming. The principal business that winter, however, was chasing beaver skins, as hard to get as greenbacks fluttering in the wind.

In the early summer of 1843, Vásquez would travel eastward with the load of furs. Bridger and his crew were being lured to far-away Milk River under the vigilant scrutiny of the Blackfeet. Some of the news for 1843 originates with Bridger's best friends, William L. Sublette and Sir William Drummond Stewart, whose sporting procession reached Green River at the end of July, after Bridger had gone north.

Captain Sublette and Sir William were on a farewell junket to the Old West in the "Old Way." They must have succeeded, for Johnson and Winter complained, "The great scarcity of buffalo . . . was attributable . . . to the presence of Sir William Stewart, with his pleasure party, and fifty or sixty fine horses . . . who kept ahead of us, killing, and driving the game out of reach."[1]

William Clark Kennerly, one of Sir William's guests, agreed: "Leaving Fort Laramie, we continued our slaughter of buffalo and also found more antelope, elk, deer, grizzly, and black bear than we could possibly use."[2]

Nearing the Sweetwater a day or two behind the leaders, Johnson and Winter report: "On the 20th [July, 1843] we met Messrs. Vasquez and Walker, with a company of twenty or thirty men, coming

[1] Overton Johnson and W. H. Winter, *Route Across the Rocky Mountains*, 16.
[2] William C. Kennerly, *Persimmon Hill* (as told to Elizabeth Russell), 150.

down from the mountain, where Messrs. Vasquez and Bridger have a small Trading Post among the Shoshone or Snake Indians. They were loaded with furs and skins, which they were taking to the Forts on the Platte, where they supply themselves."[3]

Matthew C. Field, another guest of Sir William, writes July 26, 1843, from the Sweetwater: "This morning Jo Pourier, Leo Walker and Guesso Choteau left camp early on an express message to Bridger's Fort, 200 miles, to find the Snake Indians and invite them to come and meet us."[4]

On August 9, at what is now Frémont Lake, Field notes: "Travelled full ten miles on foot around the lake to camp, where we found Walker, and 7 lodges, 4 of white freemen, and 3 of Indians [including Uncle Jack Robertson and Miles Goodyear]. . . . We set the Sho-sho-nee girls to work tailoring. . . . the principal *modiste* . . . was Madam Jack Robinson (Robertson) [Bridger's neighbor]. . . . The trappings on her horse did not cost less than three hundred dollars . . . really dazzling to behold!"[5]

Young Kennerly met Uncle Jack and his "Madam," and reported: "When I made known to him my desire for a buckskin suit . . . he said a few words to her, she nodded her head, told me to stand up, then turn around . . . thus taking my measurements with her eye; picking up a butcher knife, she then proceeded to cut the garments out of the antelope hide which I had produced. By the next day they were all finished, with fringe down the sides of the trousers."[6]

On August 13, 1843, Field says he "rode from camp this morning, with Sir Wm and Choteau, and struck *"Green River"* . . . about 4 miles. . . . We were carrying a letter to Bridger, which we meant to leave on a pole for him at *'The Old Rendezvous,'* and which ran as follows—

Willow Creek, Piney Fork, Roc. Moun.
Aug. 12, 1843
The compliments of Sir Wm Stewart to Capt. James Bridger. Come and see us. We have been expecting you for several days, and shall wait

---

[3] Johnson and Winter, *Route Across the Rocky Mountains*, 15.
[4] Field, *Prairie and Mountain Sketches*, 126.
[5] *Ibid.*, 137–38, 142.
[6] Kennerly, *Persimmon Hill*, 156.

for you a few days more. Come to camp. We have commenced an extensive game of ball, and we want you to come and 'Keep the ball in motion,' come. . . . and a steed is at your service. Come—hurrah!

Sir Wm D. Stewart, per Sec.

. . . . unfortunately, it proved mail failure day, and the letter to Bridger was not dispatched."[7]

Just after the proprietors left Fort Bridger in July, hostile Indians attacked, inflicting a few casualties according to several visitors. James Bridger would probably have preferred to hear the scattered notes on the attack gathered by Matthew C. Field and paraphrased here.

Seventy-five Cheyennes came down Black's Fork, through water or willows for three or four miles. A half-blood hunter, John, had Bridger's gun and was on his knees drinking. The Cheyennes made him tell all about the fort, then took his gun and horse. They came to Martin, another hunter, who watched his chance, shot among his pursuers, and escaped.

The Cheyennes divided. They killed and scalped a Flathead horse-guard who was gambling at "hand"; speared a (Snake) woman and a boy asleep, took a girl prisoner, cut out seventy Snake horses, exchanged some of their own tired mounts for fresh ones grazing on a hill, and fled. Uncle Jack Robertson, Miles Goodyear, and five or six freemen pursued the marauders. Three miles away they met Snake hunters returning with meat. The Snakes joined in the chase, helped to rout the Cheyennes, and recovered some horses. One Snake was speared by two men at once during the battle.[8]

John Boardman arrived at Fort Bridger on August 13, 1843, "expecting to stay ten or fifteen days to make meat; but the Sioux and Cheyennes had been here, run off all the buffalo, killed three Snake Indians, and stole sixty horses."[9]

Several of the emigrant diarists of 1843 made little or no note of Fort Bridger. Peter H. Burnett, who became California's first governor, may furnish the reason in his description of distances: "From

---

[7] Field, *Prairie and Mountain Sketches*, 146–47.

[8] *Ibid.*, 141.

[9] John Boardman, "Journal, Overland Journey, 1843," *Utah Historical Quarterly*, October, 1929.

main dividing ridge of the Rocky Mountains [South Pass], to first water that runs to the Pacific, 2 miles; to Little Sandy 14 miles; to Big Sandy 14 miles; to Green River 25 miles; down same 12 miles; to Black's Fork of Green River 22 miles; to Fort Bridger [August 14th] 30 miles; to Big Muddy 20 miles; to Bear River 37 miles."[10]

Theodore Talbot, of Frémont's party, wrote, in August, 1843: "30th. Came nearly west, along Black's Fork, passing under the bluff on which Vasquez & Bridger's houses are built. We found them deserted and dismantled. They are built of logs, plastered with mud. We crossed Black's Fork and camped in the pretty valley which lies along either side of its winding course.

"Vasquez with his gallant party of mountaineers and a band of Indians came dashing into camp at full speed. . . . Vasquez had just returned from hunting in the Youta Mountains. His partner, Old Jim Bridger, the most celebrated trapper of the Rocky Mountains, has started with a party of forty men to trap on Wind River [Milk River].

"They were all attacked here a short time since by a large party of Cheyennes, of whom we were warned by Bald Chief. They drove off the cavayade [modern cavvy or remuda] belonging to the Fort, and also the horses belonging to sixty lodges of Snakes who were camped in the thick willows in the valley just below the Fort. Most of the men were out hunting at the time of the attack, but they soon set out in pursuit, and succeeded in overtaking them and getting back most of the horses.

"They say it was a beautiful sight to see the Cheyennes formed in the shape of a crescent, driving the stolen horses at full speed before them, a party of skirmishers following close behind, zigzagging, or, as it is called, 'making snake' along the line. . . . The Cheyennes were led on by Tesson and Louis Rivy, a half-breed and a Frenchman."[11]

We next hear from James Bridger, himself. His celebrated letter announcing the opening of Fort Bridger, written December 10, 1843, to "P. Chouteau & Co.," was dictated to E. S. Denig at Fort Union. It follows:

[10] Peter H. Burnett, "Letters, 1843-44," *Oregon Historical Quarterly*, December, 1902, 408.

[11] Theodore Talbot, *Journal with Frémont Expedition* (ed. by Charles H. Carey), August 30, 1843.

Fort Union, 10 December 1843

Mess. P. Chouteau & Co.,

Gent.

I arrived here some days ago from my beaver hunt having been particularly unsuccessful owing to the lateness of the season, and caught only about three packs, but I believe that a good hunt could be made in the same country, and will therefore try it next spring, when I hope to do more than present appearances would justify.

When I separated from Mr. Vasquez at the Platte, I gave him all the goods designed for the trade with the Indians, in the mountains, and he being so strongly recommended by the Company in St. Louis, as a very capable man, trust principally to him for profitable returns. As he has all the goods, and no opposition in that quarter, there is every prospect of his doing well; he has all to himself, and has traders with the Pannacks, Nez Perces, Flatheads . . . Pocans, Pend d'Oreilles, and other nations who are generally well supplied with Beaver, and I have no hesitation in advancing it as my opinion, he will make satisfactory returns.

It was an understanding between him and me, that as he had been so strongly recommended as a capable man by the Gentlemen of the Company in St. Louis, that I would give him all the goods and means of carrying on the above trade, and start myself, with a few *green horns*, and try to trap as many Beaver as possible; the calculation is that if he succeeds, as I have no doubt he will, his return will pay the whole of our equipment, and whatever I have, or will make next spring, will be a clear profit for he and I.

Therefore, as I stated before, I have fair prospects of a hunt next spring, and a perfect reliance on Mr. Vasquez for his success in the trade. I send you my order hereby for an equipment for next year, which I think is only things that are absolutely necessary for the carrying on of our business, which, if you will be so kind as to furnish, I have no doubt will be able, in due time, not only to realize a profit to you, but for myself also.

I have established a small store with a Black Smith Shop, and a supply of iron in the road of the Emigrants, on Black's Fork, Green River, which promises fairly. They, in coming out are generally well supplied with money, but by the time they get there, are in want of all kinds of supplies. Horses, Provisions, Smith work, &c, brings ready cash from them; and should I receive the goods hereby ordered, will do a considerable business in that way with them! The same establishment trading with the Indians in the neighborhood, who have mostly a good number of Beaver among them.

My present intention is to make a spring hunt and deliver up my returns, and after receiving the inclosed equipment, to make an expedition into the California, which country is now the only one remaining unexplored, and is rich with Beaver. I shall take from 30 to 40 men for that purpose to trap it thoroughly and make also a large return of Horses, Valuable shells &c, which, together with the returns that Mr. Vasquez will make, ought to realize a good profit for all concerned.

I have heretofore, through circumstances that could not be prevented, and over which I had no control, been disappointed in my expectations of doing the business that I know could be done, but fortune may perhaps, favor me this time. If it proves otherwise, I will wind up my business with you and leave it off.

The conduct of Mr. Vasquez at the Platte was not such as it should have been considering the recommendation he had in St. Louis, and I was sorry for it. The note given by him to O'Fallon, I wrote you to protest, and hope you have not paid it; the same is for the amount of $150—I bought the note of Abraham Woods from the Company of $200, with interest thereon, which together with $84 in Cash I sent by Mr. Guesso Chouteau, with orders to him to place it in the hands of Mr. Cyprian Chouteau; please inquire whether or not it has been done.

I have also bought a draft on Mr. Redman Stewart, and some cash, for the sum of $450, or thereabouts, which is at our establishment at Black's Fork. Should it be necessary for us to have our license renewed, you will be so good as to have it done, and forwarded by the equipment, as also a passport to travel in the California and return therefrom, which you can forward at the same time. The above is all that I know of at the present time, and I conclude by presenting my best respects to all the gentlemen of the Company.

(S) J. Bridger, by E. S. Denig.

William Laidlaw, in charge of Fort Union, wrote to Pierre Chouteau and Company, December, 1843: "Bridger has come in with a mountain party of thirty or forty men. He is not a man calculated to manage men, and in my opinion will never succeed in making profitable returns. Mr. Vasquez, his partner, is represented to be, if possible, more unable than he, as by drinking and frolicking at the Platte, he neglected his business."[12]

Charles Larpenteur, clerk for Laidlaw, wrote reminiscently in 1872: "Jim Bridger . . . having been told there were beaver on Milk River, went there with thirty men. . . . About November [1843] Bridger and his men came from Milk River to pass the winter with us. . . . They camped a half mile from the Fort. . . . He had been deceived; and his hunt on Milk River was a poor one. . . .

"The main substance of Bridger's conversation was his brave men, his fast horses and his fights with Blackfeet. . . . A few days before Christmas, a large war party made a raid on the band of horses belonging to the Fort, running off six of them, and wounding one of the guards in the leg with buckshot. . . . The braves mounted to pursue the Sioux.

"Bridger's clerk, who had been left in camp, came running in to the Fort out of breath, scared to death, calling: 'The Sioux are in camp! . . . Mr. Denig and I, with a few men . . . took our guns and ran to render what assistance we could. . . . In my hurry I had taken the key to the store with me. . . . Pressing demands were made for ammunition, and Mr. Laidlaw, a fiery, quick-tempered old Scotsman, smashed in a window. . . . Soon, to our disappointment, came the report a man was killed, and a mare belonging to the Opposition, was shot in the hip.

"The Opposition, who had seen Bridger's men turn out to fight, concluded to join. . . . The Sioux were on a hill, making signs for them to come on and fight. . . . Bridger's men declined the invitation. . . . The Sioux had concealed in a ravine, a small body of men ready to fly, in case the men came on . . . the leaders halting, . . . an old man put whip to his horse . . . and went by at full speed. . . . The Indians fired a volley which dropped the old man dead off his horse . . . and wounded the mare. . . . At the funeral, it was said . . . 'This burial is caused by the cowardice of Bridger's party'—that is, if some of Bridger's men had been killed, the old man wouldn't!'"[13]

As a postscript to James Bridger's letter ordering supplies for the new Fort Bridger, H. Picotte wrote to Pierre Chouteau, January 4,

---

12 Photostats, courtesy, Missouri Historical Society, St. Louis, Missouri.
13 Larpenteur, *Forty Years a Fur Trader,* 211-15.

1844: "In which he objects to furnishing Bridger and Laidlaw with new equipment, as the balance due by them is more than they can pay; 'their order is too heavy!' "[14] Bridger must have received the bad news while still at Fort Union. The "new equipment" which was not sent was to be a very tangible influence on the character and destiny of Fort Bridger.

[14] Ellen G. Harris, Manuscript Library, Missouri Historical Society, St. Louis, Missouri.

Fort Bridger in 1849–50, looking west. From Captain Howard Stansbury's *Report*.

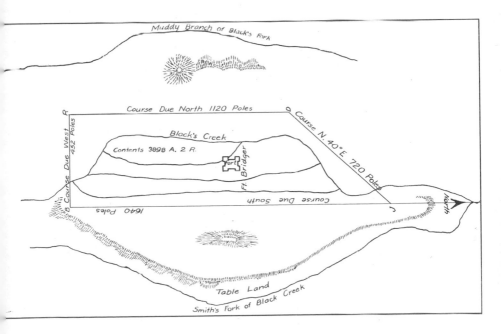

Muddy Branch of Black's Fork

Course Due North 1120 Poles

Course N. 40° E. 720 Poles

Black's Creek

452 Poles

Course Due West

Contents 3898 A. 2 R.

Ft. Bridger

Course Due South

1640 Poles

North

Table Land

Smith's Fork of Black Creek

J. M. Hockaday's Survey of Fort Bridger, 1853.

Fort Bridger, Utah Territory, after the army acquired it in 1858. Fort Bridger symbolized the shift of the mountain men from trapping to the business of supplying Western emigrants.

WITH ALL of Fort Bridger's promise of opportunity and its subsequent historical acclaim, one is astonished at the number of contemporary visitors who failed to find James Bridger at home; who were critical of the establishment and of the facilities offered; who reported competing traders at or near the fort; or who passed Fort Bridger in complete disregard of its existence. Only a few representatives need be mentioned.

John Minto wrote: "August 30 [1844]. We lay over for the day at Fort Bridger. . . . James Bridger [Vásquez or Walker?] was doing his own trading. . . . Quick and sharp at a bargain, he said, as soon as I had shown him the gun, and stated that I wanted deerskins for it: 'Young man, I can't do it; we get few deerskins here. I'll give you ten goatskins; that's the best I can do.'

"August 31 [1844]. We drove away late from Fort Bridger, up the narrow valley of a small stream called the Muddy. An old Irishman [Fitzpatrick?], just arrived at Fort Bridger, came into our camp late at night, as trader for Bridger. We judged the Ford & Saunders Company . . . to be very little behind us, as the old trader came with the Ford Company. . . . September 1. We start with a rush this morning . . . reached the divide between Green and Bear rivers a little past noon."[1]

The Reverend Edward E. Parrish wrote: "Friday, August 30, 1844 . . . . About half past three o'clock camped near the Green River fort known as Bridger's Fort. The water and grass are fine. We expect to stay here tomorrow. Captain [Joseph Reddeford] Walker kindly conducted us to the place of encampment, and then returned to his own wigwam among his own Indians of the Snake

[1] John Minto, "Travel Diary," *Oregon Historical Quarterly*, June and September, 1901, 165–66, 209–10.

Nation. . . . Mr. Walker has taken some pains to pilot this Company from Fort Laramie to Fort Bridger."[2] (Walker left Lieutenant Frémont at Bent's Fort, July 1, and Fitzpatrick left Frémont some weeks earlier.)

James Clyman says he moved up the valley of Black's Fork, arriving at the Bridger and Vásquez Trading Post early in the afternoon of August 31, 1844. He describes it as "a temporary concern, calculated for trade with the Shoshones and Utahs, which is not very valuable. This place is likewise the general rendezvous for Rocky Mountain hunters and trappers. That once numerous class of adventurers are now reduced to less than thirty men, which started out under the Command of Mr. Bridger yesterday, on an excursion through the mountains of northern and Central Mexico. This Fort is also within the limits of Mexico. . . . We here met Mr. Robidoux from the Arkansas, with horses, mules and other articles to catch our trade.

"September 1, 1844 . . . . Our route through this Green River Valley . . . might be made to save about fifty miles. . . . The only object of this zig zag road is to pass the trading house, which, however, is some convenience, as we were able to trade every extra article we had, for moccasins and leather clothing. Exchanged all our worn-out mules and horses," wrote Clyman.[3]

James Bridger dropped out of sight for a while and may have visited California. His interest in California was first stimulated by Jedediah S. Smith, but he mentioned it himself in his letter of December 10, 1843, to Pierre Chouteau, citing his interest especially in beavers, but also in horses and shells. At that time he planned to go "after receiving the inclosed equipment," which was conjectural, and on receipt of "a passport to travel in the California and return therefrom," which was not afterwards mentioned.

J. J. Warner vaguely recalled that "between 1832 and 1840, Fraeb, Bridger and Fitzpatrick . . . each came to California one or two times with trapping parties." But Bridger was located elsewhere during those particular years.[4]

---

[2] Edward E. Parrish, "Travel Diary," *Oregon Pioneer Association Transactions*, 16th Annual Reunion, 1888, 104–105.

[3] *James Clyman, Frontiersman*, 99.

[4] Warner, "Reminiscences," pp. 176–93.

Bridger's sweeping references to the Gila and southern California as "the most delightful spot that ever God made for man" are undoubtedly hearsay and omit much that is not delightful. But his suggestive mention to Captain Gunnison of a visit to "Oregon and the interior of [northern] California," has some corroboration.[5]

Bridger's daughter, Mary Ann, was in the Whitman mission school (Walla Walla), while Joseph L. Meek, Robert Newell, and other former trapper associates had moved to Oregon.

William B. Lorton saw Bridger on August 1, 1849: "He has crossed the Sierra Nevada Mountains, and says the snows fall generally not before November; and we are early enough."[6] Bridger subsequently told H. J. Clayton that he once visited the Sacramento River,[7] and he told the Mormon Pioneers, June 28, 1847: "There is a splendid range of country on the north side of the California Mountains [Oregon?], calculated to produce every kind of grain and fruit; and there are several places where a man might pass from it over the [Siskiyou] Mountains to the California settlements in one day. There is a vast abundance of timber . . . north of the California Mountains, that is, walnut, oak, ash, and hickory."[8]

Specifically mentioning Sevier Lake (Utah) and its streams in his travels, Bridger "thinks the Utah Lake is the best country in the vicinity of the Salt Lake. . . . He passed through that country a year ago last summer, in the month of July [1845]." Newmark says of Elijah T. Moulton, a Canadian: "In 1844 he had joined an expedition to California, organized by Jim Bridger."[9]

Therefore, Bridger did probably visit first Oregon and then California, making his rather hasty exit over the Sierras to the south of Lake Tahoe and keeping to the higher lands of middle Nevada and Utah, reaching Fort Bridger about August 1, 1845. It was not an exceptional excursion.

Joel Palmer, July 17, 1845, westbound on the Sweetwater, wrote: "We found here a celebrated mountaineer [Joseph Reddeford] Walker, who was traveling to Bridger's Fort . . . July 25, 1845,

[5] Gunnison, *A History of the Mormons*, 151–52.
[6] Dale L. Morgan, Bancroft Library (Unpublished diary of W. B. Lorton, 1849). See Note 7.
[7] *James Clyman, Frontiersman*, 324–25.
[8] Clayton, *Journal*, 276.
[9] Harris Newmark, *Sixty Years in Southern California*, 171.

crossed the creek several times and encamped near Fort Bridger. This is a trading fort owned by Bridger and Bascus [Vásquez]; it is a shabby concern. Here are about twenty-five lodges of Indians, or rather, white trappers lodges, occupied by their Indian wives.

"They have a good supply of robes, dressed deer, elk and antelope skins; coats, pants, moccasins and other Indian fixins, which they trade low for flour, pork, powder, lead, blankets, butcher-knives, spirits, hats, ready-made clothes, coffee, sugar, etc. . . . They had a herd of cattle; twenty-five or thirty goats, and some sheep. They generally abandon this Fort during the winter months. The bottoms are covered with good grass. Cottonwood timber in plenty. The stream abounds in trout. . . . 26th. Remained at the Fort. 27th. Reached Little Muddy."[10]

Jacob R. Snyder commented, July 26, 1845: "Moved our encampment to the opposite side of the creek, and near Fort Bridger. Here are a number of lodges, and a temporary place for trade, and a trapper rendezvous. The location is, in every respect, the best for a trading post that I have yet seen on the route. 27th. Remained at Bridger, arranging to commence packing. 28th. We were very much indebted to Captain Walker and Mr. Vasquez, for their kind attention and assistance, this mode of travel [packing], being entirely novel to us. . . . Encamped ten miles from Bridger."[11]

A sidelight comes from A. R. Bouis's letter of August 31, 1845, Fort Pierre, South Dakota, to Joseph Picotte at Fort John (Laramie): "Vasquez writes from Black's Fork [n.d., August 3?], that in consequence of Bridger's party not having been heard from, he [Vásquez] will not come to Fort John this season. He has traded five packs of beaver; 600 ditto deerskins, &c. He is very sanguine in his expectations and thinks Bridger will make a first rate man [presumably as a partner at Fort Bridger]."[12] Bridger must have appeared at Fort Bridger forthwith.

This brings us to the obscure but specific and contemporary statement that Bridger had been to California. It is in A. R. Bouis's

[10] Joel Palmer, *Journal of Travels Over the Rocky Mountains in 1845–1846*, July 17–26, 1845.

[11] Jacob R. Snyder, "Journal, 1845," vol. VIII, *Society of California Pioneers Journal*, 1930–31.

[12] A. R. Bouis, "Letter, 1845," vol. IV, *South Dakota Historical Society Collections*, 1920.

letter of September 17, 1845, written from Fort Pierre to his employer at St. Louis, Pierre Chouteau, Jr. He reported his visit to Joseph Picotte, a brother factor at Fort John:

"Mr. James Bridger arrived at Fort John [Laramie] on the 2d instant, and delivered Mrs. Jos. Picotte 840 beaver skins and castorem; 675 dressed deerskins; 25 mules; 24 horses; 1400 California sea shells; H. C. [his credit?], the whole amounting to about $5,000, exclusive of the California shells, as I do not know what Mr. Picotte will allow for them. . . . Mr. Bridger was in California, and plenty of beaver there, but he wouldn't trap, as the Indians stole the traps as soon as the hunters set them. Vasquez has gone with ten men to hunt on Wind River Mountain."[13]

Mr. Bouis had written the day before, September 16, to the firm of Bridger and Vásquez: "Mr. Bridger's letter of the 3d inst. has been duly received and contents noted. A copy of what was furnished Mr. B. at Fort Union, November, 1843, was received at this place in December of the same year, and charges made in conformity with said account. . . . You have been credited with everything delivered to Mr. Jos. Picotte at Fort John on the 22d inst.; but I cannot fix prices for the California sea shells until I see Mr. Honore Picotte on the subject."

Then on November 9, 1845, Bouis wrote to P. D. Papin: "It is to be regretted that Mr. Picotte has not yet arrived; as in that case I could answer your several inquiries respecting Ward's California shells."[14] This undoubtedly refers to Elisha B. Ward. (Ward's Lake, Idaho, became Payette Lake.)

James W. Waters went to California on the Santa Fe Trail in 1843–44. He chartered a boat at San Pedro and coasted to Lower California for a quantity of abalone shells. These he packed on mules and took east. He exchanged them at Bent's Fort or Fort Laramie, in 1845, for beaver skins and buffalo robes which he marketed in St. Louis.[15] But Waters' biographer does not connect Bridger and Waters at any time.[16]

[13] Courtesy, Will G. Robinson, *South Dakota Historical Society Collections*, (1918), 209–10.

[14] Elisha B. Ward, see page 255 below.

[15] *James Clyman, Frontiersman*, 324–25.

[16] Arthur Woodward, "Trapper Jim Waters," Los Angeles Westerners *Keepsake Publication* Number 23, 1860, 16.

Piecing together the events of James Bridger's life, we may surmise that his Flathead first wife died about this time, probably in the winter of 1845–46. She passed away soon after the birth of her third child, whom they christened Mary Josephine in 1853. Mary Ann was in the Whitman mission school and Felix Francis was a toddler of four.[17]

As a mark of respect for a faithful wife and a good mother, the characterization of Patrick Gass (1805) should be quoted. "To the honor of the Flatheads . . . we must mention them as an exception; as they do not exhibit those loose feelings of carnal desire, nor appear addicted to the common customs of prostitution; and they are the only Nation on the whole route where anything like chastity is regarded."[18]

James Clyman, eastbound, made a futile call at Fort Bridger on June 7, 1846: "Arrived at the old deserted trading house. Judge of our disappointment . . . finding this spot solitary and alone . . . without human being having visited it for at least a month. What the cause, could not be certain, except that Bridger and his whole company had taken the road down Bear River."[19]

Clyman hadn't read his morning newspaper. The *Missouri Republican* of July 7, 1846, interviewed P. D. Papin who had just returned from the Laramie forts with 1,100 packs of buffalo robes, 10 packs of beaver, and 3 packs of bear and wolf skins consigned to Pierre Chouteau, Jr., and Company. The paper reported that "Messrs Vasquez & Bridger had arrived at Fort John [Laramie] before Papin left there [early June]."[20]

A few bright, fresh furs may have topped the shipment. James Gemmell says he was in a trapping party led by James Bridger to Jackson Hole and West Thumb of Yellowstone Lake in 1846. But they were back at Fort Bridger in time for the summer migration.[21]

Joseph E. Milner, "California Joe," says that he worked as horse herder at the age of eighteen for Bridger and Vásquez, presumably

[17] Courtesy, Missouri Historical Society, St. Louis, Missouri.

[18] Patrick Gass, "Journal," in *History of the Expedition of Meriwether Lewis and William Clark in 1804–1806*, 204.

[19] *James Clyman, Frontiersman*, 220.

[20] *Missouri Republican*, July 7, 1846, vol. XX, in *Nebraska Historical Society Publications*, 159–60.

[21] *Contributions to the Montana Historical Society*, 1896.

the winter of 1845–46. Reporting five horses missing on one occasion, Milner says: "Bridger at once sounded the alarm and twenty men were soon on the trail of the thieves, young Joe being one of the party. After a chase of several miles, with Jim Bridger in the lead, the thieves . . . were overtaken. The stolen horses were recovered and six Indians were killed. . . . One White man was killed, and another badly wounded, but recovered."[22] Like many other Indian fights, this one cannot be corroborated.

We are indebted to Edwin Bryant for an excellent description of Fort Bridger and its people, July 14, 1846: "We struck the Big Sandy River, an affluent of the Green. Greenwood's Cut-off leaves the old trail [via Fort Bridger] at this point. It is said to shorten the distance to Fort Hall fifty or sixty miles [by missing Fort Bridger]."

July 17, 1846: "We camped near the camp of Messrs. Hastings and Hudspeth, who left California the last of April, and explored a new route south of Great Salt Lake, shortening the distance 150 to 200 miles. My impressions are unfavorable to the route, especially for wagons and families.

"Fort Bridger (nearby) is a small trading post, established and now occupied by Messrs. Bridger & Vasquez. The buildings are two or three miserable log cabins, rudely constructed, and bearing faint resemblance to human habitations. It is in a handsome, fertile bottom, about two miles south of the old wagon trail. . . . There is the finest quality of grass in great abundance. The stream is pure and cold, and abounds in spotted mountain trout. There are clumps of cottonwood trees. Fort Bridger is distant from Pacific Springs about 133 miles.

"There are numbers of traders here from the neighborhood of Taos, with dressed buckskins, buckskin shirts, pantaloons and moccasins to trade with the emigrants. The emigrant trade is a very important one to the mountain merchants and trappers.

"The countenances and bearing of these men, who have made the wilderness their home, are generally expressive of a cool, cautious but determined intrepidity. In a trade they have no conscience, taking all the 'advantages'; but in matters of hospitality or generosity, they are open handed, ready, many of them, to divide with the needy what they possess. . . . Captain Joseph Reddeford Walker is

22 Joseph E. Milner and E. R. Forrest, *California Joe* (Milner).

now on his return from California . . . driving 400 or 500 California horses. . . . He spoke discouragingly of the new route to the south of Great Salt Lake. Several emigrant parties have arrived here, and others have left, by Fort Hall."

July 18, 1846: "We determined to take the new route; Mr. Hudspeth to guide us as far as the Salt Plain. . . . I wrote several letters to my friends among the emigrant parties in the rear advising them NOT to take this route. . . . We were mounted on mules, had no families, and could afford to hazard experiments. They could not.

"During the day I visited several of the emigrant corrals. Many of the trappers and hunters now collected here were lounging about, making small trades for sugar, coffee, flour and whiskey. Several Indians visited our camp. An old man and two boys sat down near the door of our tent this morning, and there remained without speaking, but watchful of every movement for three or four hours. When dinner was over we gave them some bread and meat, and they departed without uttering a word.

"Circles of white-tented wagons may now be seen in every direction, and the smoke from the campfires is curling upwards, morning, noon and evening. An immense number of oxen and horses are scattered over the entire valley grazing upon the green grass. Parties of Indians, hunters and emigrants are galloping to and fro and the scene is almost one of holiday liveliness. It is difficult to realize that we are in a wilderness, a thousand miles from civilization.

"July 20, 1846, all companies moved off from Fort Bridger,"[23] the celebrated Donner party to its ruin.

The St. Louis *Missouri Republican* of October 26, 1846, carries a letter dated Fort Bridger, July 19, 1846. The letter was rephrased by the *Republican* editor, hence the perspective: "Fort Bridger is said to be a miserable pen, occupied at times by Messrs. Bridger & Vasquez, and resorted to by a number of loafing trappers, to exchange furs and moccasins for flour, bacon and whiskey."[24]

James F. Reed, of the ill-fated Reed-Donner party, wrote from Fort Bridger, July 31, 1846: "We have arrived here safe, with the loss of two yoke of my best oxen. . . . I have replenished my stock

[23] Edwin Bryant, *What I Saw in California*, 135, 142–44.
[24] Photostats, courtesy, Missouri Historical Society, St. Louis, Missouri.

by purchasing from Messrs. Vasquez & Bridger, two very excellent and accommodating gentlemen, who are the proprietors of this trading post. The new road, or Hasting's Cut-off, leaves the Fort Hall road here. There is, however, or thought to be, one stretch of forty miles without water. . . .

"Mr. Bridger and other gentlemen here who have trapped that country say that the Lake has receded from the tract of country in question. There is plenty of grass which can be cut and put into wagons for our cattle while crossing it. . . . Mr. Bridger informs me that the route we design to take, is a fine, level road, with plenty of water and grass, with the exceptions before stated. . . .

"I want you to inform the emigration that they can be supplied with fresh cattle by Messrs. Vasquez & Bridger. They now have about 200 head of oxen, cows and young cattle, with a great many horses and mules; and they can be relied on for doing business honorably and fairly. Mr. Bridger will go to St. Louis this fall and return with the emigration in the spring, and will be very useful as a pilot. He will be found during the winter in St. Louis at Mr. Robert Campbell's."[25]

Reed, a survivor of the disaster, wrote in the *Pacific Rural Press*, March 25, 1871, a little more concerning his stop at Fort Bridger: "Several friends of mine, who have passed here with pack animals for California, had left letters with Mr. Vasquez—Mr. Bridger's partner—directing me to take the route by way of Fort Hall, and by no means to go the Hastings Cut-off. Vasquez, being interested in having the new route traveled (otherwise the emigration would use the Greenwood Cut-off and miss Fort Bridger), kept these letters. This was told to me after my arrival in California."[26]

A further quotation from Reed's letter of July 31, 1846; follows: "The independent trappers who swarm here during the passing of the emigrants, are as great a set of sharks as ever disgraced humanity, with few exceptions. Let the emigrants avoid trading with them. Vasquez & Bridger are the only fair traders in these parts."

Even with Reed's encouraging recommendation, Bridger's native

25 J. Roderic Korns, "West from Fort Bridger," *Utah Historical Quarterly*, XIX, 1951, pp. 192–94.

26 *Ibid.*, 193.

diffidence must have hampered him disappointingly in his efforts to sell himself to such natural leaders as James F. Reed. We only know that he did not go to St. Louis that autumn and did not lead an emigrant caravan across the mountains in 1847.

THE FORT BRIDGER collection of hides and furs was not especially large, but Bridger had begun to market them in wagons, instead of by pack train. Orson Pratt, of the Mormon pioneer party, was the first traveler to mention an encounter with the Bridger party two miles below Fort John, on June 2, 1847.

"By a small party from Fort Bridger . . . we learned the snow was two feet deep on the Sweetwater. They were obliged to leave their wagons, in charge of a portion of their company, and rush through with their horses to this place to find grass to sustain them. Most of them had just left on their return for the wagons." June 8, above Fort Laramie: "About one mile from our encampment a small company of wagons loaded with peltries and furs from Fort Bridger . . . were encamped; they were going to Fort Laramie."[1]

Brigham Young and the Mormon pioneers chanced to meet James Bridger near the mouth of Little Sandy. A granite monument bearing a bronze plate, in the town of Farson, Wyoming, marks the "Site of the Bridger-Young Conference" of June 28, 1847.

The journal of William Clayton, secretary to the Mormon Church Presidency, gives the most detailed account of their travels. Monday, June 28, 1847; "Many of the brethren are trading with Mr. [Moses B.] Harris, for pants, jackets, shirts etc., made of buckskins, and also the skins themselves. . . . He will take rifles, powder, lead, caps or calico, and domestic shirts in exchange; but puts his own price on both sides, and it is difficult to obtain a fair trade."

After they crossed Little Sandy: "Elder G. A. Smith introduced us to Mr. Bridger of Bridger's Fort, on his way to Fort John, in company with two of his men. Mr. Bridger, being informed that

---

[1] Orson Pratt, "Journal with Mormon Pioneers, 1847," vols. 11 and 12, *Latter-day Saints Millennial Star*, June 2, 1847. Hereafter referred to as Pratt, "Journal."

we had designed to call at his place to make some inquiries about the country, he said if we would turn off the road here and camp, he would stay with us till morning. . . .

"A while after we camped, The Twelve [Apostles] and several others went to Mr. Bridger to make some inquiries concerning our future route, and the country. It was impossible to form a correct idea of either, from the very imperfect and irregular way he gave his descriptions, but the general items are in substance as follows:

"We will find better grass as we proceed farther on. His business is to Fort Laramie. His traders have gone there with robes, skins, &c, to fill a contract; but having started later than they intended, the men at Laramie have taken advantage of the delay, and he is going to see to the business himself.

"There is no blacksmith shop at the Fort at present. There was one but it was destroyed. . . . There was a man opened a farm in the Bear River valley [Ogden, Utah]. The soil is good, and likely to produce corn, were it not for the excessive cold nights, which he thinks would prevent the growth of corn. . . .

"The Utah [Indians] abound . . . near Salt Lake . . . but we have no need to fear them . . . he would not kill them; he would make slaves of them." (Most of Bridger's descriptions deal with Utah generally and with what is now Arizona and California.)

"Supper had been provided for Mr. Bridger and his men; and the latter having eaten, the Council dismissed, Mr. Bridger going with President Young to supper, the remainder retiring to their wagons, conversing over the subjects touched upon."[2]

Howard Egan adds: "After supper I went down to where Mr. Bridger was encamped, and from his appearance and conversation, I should not take him to be a man of truth. . . . He crossed himself a number of times . . . said he had made sugar . . . where Harris said there were no trees."[3]

Clearly Clayton did not have supper with Bridger and Brigham Young. This may account for a certain famous comment which was attributed to Bridger on that occasion, but which no contemporary scribe recorded. Without a written source, it has appeared in a

[2] Clayton, *Journal,* 272–78.
[3] Howard Egan, *Pioneering in the West,* 89.

variety of forms, all saying about the same thing—that Bridger would give $1,000 for any ear of corn the Mormons would grow in Utah.

Being unfamiliar with Bridger's diction, President Young himself may have understandably been put to it to recapture Bridger's precise words.

Dr. Willard Richards, Mormon church historian at the time, and a member of the pioneer party, made the following entry in his own diary which was transferred to the "Manuscript History of Brigham Young," 1847: "June 28th. . . . Met Capt. James Bridger. . . . he said he would give one thousand dollars for a bushel of corn raised in the Basin."[4]

Two years later, on July 9, 1849, President Brigham Young declared in a sermon: "Mr. Bridger said he would give $1000 per bushel for all the corn we could raise in the valley."[5]

Speaking in Wellsville, Utah, on June 7, 1860, President Young said: "Bridger said to me: 'Mr. Young, I would give a thousand dollars if I knew that an ear of corn could be ripened in these mountains.' "[6]

And again, on May 29, 1870, President Young spoke in Salt Lake City: "When we met Mr. Bridger on the Big Sandy River, he said: 'Mr. Young, I would give a thousand dollars if I knew an ear of corn could be ripened in the Great Basin.' "[7]

While President Young gave three or four slightly differing versions, speakers and writers who have relayed this popular quotation at second hand are chiefly responsible for its infinite variety.

The journal of Wilford Woodruff, then an apostle and later president of the Church of Jesus Christ of Latter-day Saints, says: "We met in council with Mr. Bridger . . . and found him to be a great traveler, possessing an extensive knowledge of nearly all Oregon and California [which then included Utah and Idaho], the mountains, rivers, lakes, springs, valleys, mines, ore &c. He spoke more highly of the Great Basin for a settlement than Major [Moses B.] Harris

[4] Page 95.
[5] Manuscript History of Brigham Young, Index 3.
[6] *Latter-day Saints Journal of Discourses*, June 7, 1860.
[7] *Ibid.*, May 29, 1870.

had done. He said it was his Paradise, and that if these people settled in it he would settle with them; and that there was but one thing that would operate against it's becoming a great grain country, and that would be frost, as he did not know but the frost might affect the corn. . . . Mr. Bridger remarked that it would not be prudent to bring a great population to the Basin until we ascertained whether grain would grow or not."[8]

Appleton Milo Harmon, employed at the Mormon Ferry (Casper, Wyoming), journalized: "July 3 . . . Mr. James Bridger of Bridger's Fort, arrived about 11 A.M., and brought a line from President Young, as follows:

> June 29, 1847, Little Sandy.
> Mr. Thomas Grover and Company:
> We introduce to your notice Mr. James Bridger whom we expected to have seen at his Fort. He is now on his way to Fort Laramie. We wish you to cross him and his two men on our account, because he was going to Laramie and expected to return to his Fort in time to pilot the Pioneers through to Salt Lake. He said that he could take us to a place that would suit us.

"There were four of our soldiers from Brown's detachment [Mormon Battalion] that came back with Mr. Bridger on a furlough and were going to the States. . . . I wrote a line by the request of Captain Grover to our next Company, notifying them that we were keeping a ferry and intended to stay until they came up; giving them all the latest news we had from the Pioneers, and sent it by Mr. Bridger to Laramie."[9]

Bridger may have misunderstood; at any rate, he did not return to pilot Brigham Young and the Mormon pioneer party into the Salt Lake valley. Had he done so, it is safe to assume that they would have avoided the much more difficult and unnatural route through Emigration Canyon, and that "This Is The Place" monument would have risen a few rods farther south, at Parley's Canyon.

President Woodruff said, July 7, 1847, at Fort Bridger: "In the

[8] Wilford Woodruff, *Journal and Life History of Wilford Woodruff* (ed. by M. F. Cowley), June 27, 1847.

[9] Appleton M. Harmon, *Appleton M. Harmon Goes West* (ed. by Maybelle Harmon Anderson), 39.

afternoon I went to Bridger's House and traded off my flint-lock rifle for four buffalo robes, which were very large, nice, and well dressed. I found things generally at least one-third higher than I had ever known."[10]

When they reached Fort Bridger, Orson Pratt added, July 7, 1847: "Nine Indian lodges stood a few rods distant, occupied by the families of the trappers and hunters, who have taken squaws for wives. Some few half-breed children were playing about the lodges. Bridger's trading post is situated half a mile due west of these lodges on an island. . . . We passed over four branches of Black's Fork without any road but a foot-path. Three-quarters of a mile brought us to the door of Bridger's. We here turned to the south, and crossing three more branches, camped within half a mile of the post. . . .

"Bridger's Post consists of two adjoining log houses, dirt roofs, and a small picket yard of logs set in the ground, about eight feet high. The number of men, squaws and half-breed children in these homes and lodges may be about fifty or sixty. . . . 8th. Our blacksmiths are busily engaged in setting wagon tires, shoeing horses, etc. . . . 9th. We again resumed our journey."[11]

The Reed-Donner party of 1846 attempted to save time and distance by crossing the Salt Desert, but the Sierra winter snows caught them there. Several members perished and Fort Bridger lost the expected business of the party. The doldrums set in at Fort Bridger and, as it turned out, remained permanently.

Chester Ingersoll, an emigrant, got the bad news from Bridger, as it is presumed others did also, to go by way of Fort Hall, without seeing Fort Bridger. "July 15, 1847. On the 11th we had the pleasure of meeting Capt. Bridger. He informed us that there was part of a company lost last year going to California. They left their pilot and lost their way, and 70 out of a hundred perished. And, also, twenty wagons were lost on the Oregon road. . . . 18th, Thence up Black's Fork to Bridger's Fort, 25 miles, road good and grass plenty. . . . This Fort is only a trading post with the Snake Indians."[12]

On November 29, 1847, Rev. Marcus Whitman, his wife, and eleven men were killed by Cayuse Indians at Walla Walla, and about

[10] Wilford Woodruff, *Journal and Life History*, July 7, 1847.

[11] Pratt, "Journal," July 7–8, 1847.

[12] Chester Ingersoll, *Overland to California in 1847*, July 15, 1847.

fifty men, women, and children were taken captive, many of whom were never rescued or returned. Among these were Mary Ann Bridger, aged eleven, daughter of James Bridger, and Helen Mar Meek, daughter of former trapper Joseph L. Meek. Both girls had been registered at the Whitman mission school. In time the tribal leaders were induced to identify and surrender the guilty Indians, and, ultimately, the raiders were found guilty. They were hanged on June 3, 1850, by the one and only Joseph L. Meek, at that time a U. S. marshal.

The news of the Whitman massacre, singularly enough, was brought to James Bridger by Joseph L. Meek, on April 9, 1848, as Meek traveled to Washington, D. C., carrying memorials for the territory of Oregon. We can only speculate on the greeting, conversation, and parting of these two old trapper cronies. Bridger was to learn, later, that Mary Ann had died in March, 1848.[13] The visit with Meek gave Bridger a great many things to think about, not the least of which was the importance to which Meek had risen. Meek was a new man with far-flung horizons; Bridger's environment was clinging to him like a vine.

Obviously Bridger needed assistance—a helpmeet. Consequently another little-known incident occurred about this time—his marriage to a Ute Indian woman. Sorry, we cannot even give the date, much less describe the gown she wore.

The Latter-day Saints' *Emigrants' Guide*, prepared by William Clayton, was issued in March, 1848, to show intermediate mileage by "Roadometer." The *Guide* shows the junction of the Utah-Oregon roads (Greenwood Cut-off) twenty miles west of the South Pass summit, and ninety-eight miles from Fort Bridger. At the junction is the note: "Take the left hand road." From that moment, as from that point, the "left hand road" through Fort Bridger became the Mormon or Salt Lake road.

The Utah emigrants forded Green River just halfway from the junction to Fort Bridger. Then, according to the *Guide*: "You cross four rushing creeks, within half a mile, before you reach the Fort; and by traveling half a mile beyond the Fort, you will cross three others, and then find a good place to camp. The Fort is composed of

[13] For Mary Ann Bridger's death, we are accepting Dr. Clifford M. Drury's statement in *Henry Harmon Spalding*, 352.

four log houses, and a small inclosure for horses. Land exceeding rich—water cold and good; considerable timber."

"I knew Jim Bridger," John R. Young wrote his grandson. In the summer of 1848, Young's father went east with teams to assist "Uncle Brigham's Company, and I went along. We lay at Fort Bridger two weeks. Every day I watched the Indians run horse races and gamble. One day Bridger gave me five dollars. I bet it and won. Then Bridger said: 'My Boy, don't you ever gamble again, for I have noticed that gamblers nearly all die with their boots on, and you are too fine a boy to die that way.' I never gambled again. I never saw him laugh, yet he loved humor and fun.

"One day a vagabond Mormon boy came along and claimed to be a trusted, secret messenger of Brigham Young. Bridger looked him over, then said: 'If you will stay here and marry the Indian squaw that I will pick out for you, I will give you a tent and make an Indian trader out of you.' The dude accepted the offer, the tent was pitched, night came on, and the Indian woman was sent to the tent. At the camp fire where the Indians were gambling, the mountaineers gathered around the 'new fledged trader,' congratulated him on his good fortune, and bade him good night.

"He retired to his lodge and silence reigned. In a few minutes were heard yells of pain, and a white man in his shirttail burst from the tent, with an angry squaw, armed with a heavy quirt, following close upon his heels. The mountaineers roared with laughter, but Bridger laconically said: 'He has just remembered that secret message Brigham had entrusted him with.' Father got one of the men to go get his breeches and take them to him. We saw no more of the 'trusted messenger.' "[14]

Fewer emigrants visited Fort Bridger in 1848 because of the new shortened road to Bear River, which missed the fort by a few miles. Apparently reduction in the number of visitors gave the owner time for his building work. When Brigham Young arrived, September 12, 1848, with the first large Mormon train of the year, John D. Lee wrote in his journal: "The Fort consists of eight block houses, and a small inclosure, picketed in." The traffic to Utah was fairly heavy— one reporter estimating the Mormon wagon train at "six hundred miles and forty days in length." Three of the larger companies

14 John R. Young, "Letter, 1848," *Utah Historical Quarterly*, July, 1930, 84.

totaled 2,417 people and 792 wagons. They were all passing Fort Bridger, but doing little or no business there because of the relief trains sent from Utah to meet them.

We are not sure where Bridger spent the winter of 1848–49. An early fur trapper who became one of the "Progressive Men of Montana" was Charles Chouquette. He says that with Antone Busette and Louis La Breche he joined James Bridger and an enormous party of eighty men on the spring hunt of 1849. In April, on the site of Great Falls, they were attacked by four hundred Blackfeet and had a long, hard fight. Forty-seven Indians were left dead on the field.[15] There is no confirmation of the story nor is there good reason to doubt it. Bridger may well have been there.

[15] Charles Chouquette, "Fort Benton Journal, 1854–56; Fort Sarpy Journal, 1855–56," vol. X, *Contributions to the Montana Historical Society*, 126n.

WHEN WILLIAM KELLY reached the Sweetwater, he met "Vasquez, who had gone out to trade with the emigrants. . . . He is a Frenchman, the partner of Mr. Bridger in the trading post. . . . Vasquez came here with a number of horses, hoping to find custom. . . . We exchanged three of our most cripped nags, giving boot, which he was eager to get in flour and coffee, but these we could not spare. . . .

"The U. S. Government has made them a proposition to purchase the Fort as a military station, then keep the Savages in check. . . . We reached Fort Bridger [about June 14, 1849] . . . and got good water, together with the luxury of a little milk for the invalids, and we all felt better.

"I cannot imagine how the term 'Fort' came to be applied to these trading stations, for they have no one point of resemblance to such a structure, Fort Bridger being even more completely destitute than the others of any such feature. It is simply composed of a few log huts, closely huddled together, without as much as a loophole to discharge a musket through.

"In one of these Mr. Bridger lives, with his Indian wife; Mr. Vasquez's family occupied another; a third was a store; and the fourth contained a good forge and a rude carpenter shop. We stopped a day to rest . . . and for the good pasture for the horses. Mr. Bridger permitted us to use his workshops . . . but we postponed it till we got to Salt Lake. We purchased a small, fat beef for $20 . . . and enjoyed the luxury of some regular roast joints, having been given the use of the kitchen.

"Mr. Bridger, though only forty-five years of age, has had more experience as a mountaineer than any other dweller amongst them; and not only traded with the Indians at the Fort, but taking a pleasure

231

himself in the sport of trapping, was in the habit of leaving his partner as the home manager, and spending a great deal of his time in roaming through the wilderness.

"He was excessively kind and patient with me in laying down the route to Salt Lake, taking the trouble of drawing a chart with charcoal on the door . . . pointing out a new line that had never yet been attempted, which would be a short cut of thirty miles. But as we were traveling by wagons, he did not think it advisable we should use it. . . . We left Fort Bridger early in the morning of the third day, wonderfully recruited and recovered."[1]

The next day, June 17, 1849, William G. Johnston and party arrived. A week earlier on the Sweetwater, Johnston had halted "near to the camp of a temporary trading post, established within a week past, by Mr. Vasquez, one of the proprietors of Fort Bridger. He was accompanied by a considerable party of trappers, most of whom, had with them, their Indian wives and children. They occupied lodges made of skins sewed together, and stretched over poles about fifteen feet in height, a small opening being left at the top for the escape of smoke, as in all, there were fires.

"There was something weird about the appearance of many of the trappers, the hair of their heads and eyebrows being white from exposure, while their skin resembled parchment in color and texture. Their women were engaged in making fabrics of buckskin: coats, leggings, moccasins, etc., while their children, all small, fat and hearty, toddled about, excepting some who were being nourished at maternal founts. Most of the trappers were French Canadians. The same untidiness as to housekeeping and personal toilet was noticeable as that observed at Fort Laramie among the Natives.

"Mr. Vasquez was a fine, portly looking gentleman of medium height, about fifty years of age; and made an impression of being intelligent and shrewd. The object of the temporary post was for purposes of trade with the emigrants. The goods on sale consisted of buffalo robes, deer skins, and buckskin goods in process of making, besides horses and mules. . . . Our mess traded some bacon and a lot of beads, trinkets, etc., and a mule for a horse. . . .

"Mr. Hudspeth, at Independence, advised . . . by all means, to

[1] William Kelly, *Across the Rocky Mountains from New York to California,* 146–47.

follow the trail via Sublette's Cut-off [Greenwood's Cut-off, missing Fort Bridger]. . . . Mr. Vasquez, on the contrary . . . insisted the more desirable route was by Fort Bridger and Salt Lake. . . . Taking paper and pencil he sketched the two routes . . . and piled argument on argument. . . . The latter advice prevailed! In the sequel . . . we learned that an object in establishing the temporary trading post was to divert the tide of emigration in the direction of Fort Bridger.

"Sunday, June 17, 1849, We came to Fort Bridger . . . at the foot of the Uintah Mountains, which loom up grandly above the beautiful, fertile valley, surrounding the trading post, one of the most attractive spots thus far seen. . . . There are several log buildings, surrounded by a high picket fence, and having a heavy, wooden entrance gate. . . . I visited several of the apartments of the Fort, among others, the rooms occupied by the families of the proprietors, through which we were conducted by Mrs. Vasquez, who entertained us in an agreeable and hospitable manner, notably by inviting us to 'sit on chairs'!

"Opening upon a court were the rooms occupied by the Bridger family. Mr. Bridger, with a taste differing from that of his partner (who has a wife from the States), made his selection from among the ladies of the wilderness, a stolid, fleshy, round-headed woman, not oppressed with lines of beauty. Her hair was intensely black and straight, and so cut that it hung in a thick mass upon her broad shoulders. In a corner of Mrs. Bridger's room was a churn filled with buttermilk, and dipping from it with a ladle, Mrs. Vasquez filled and refilled our cups, which we drank until completely satisfied. . . .

"In the course of the conversation, Mrs. Bridger mentioned the loss of a skillet lid; and her inability, thus far, to replace it. . . . Our own skillet had been fractured and thrown away . . . but for some reason we had treasured that skillet lid . . . and before one could say 'Jack Robinson,' it was transferred to Mrs. Bridger's kitchen. Fifty skillet lids would not have been worth the smile which greeted us. . . . As we turned to leave . . . we were given a roll of freshly churned butter, of a rich golden yellow, and glistening as it were, with drops of dew.

"In a store room of the Fort was a considerable stock of buffalo robes, one of which I purchased for the sum of $5. It was an exceptionally large, fine robe, with long, silky hair, and its equal, I have rarely seen . . . Other store rooms were nearly bare of goods. In one was a keg of whiskey, a jar of tobacco, and a box of clay pipes, but little else. . . . Some long, red stone pipes of St. Peters' Rock, from the upper Mississippi . . . are sold at $5; Mr. Bridger informed me there is a ready sale for them."[2]

Mrs. Bridger's enjoyment of the skillet lid was of short duration. Only eighteen days later, on July 4, 1849, she died at the birth of a baby girl. The baby was named Virginia Rosalie—later to become Virginia Bridger Wachsman Hahn.

Captain Howard Stansbury, U. S. topographical engineer, wrote: "Saturday, August 11, 1849; A drive of thirty-two miles brought us to Fort Bridger. . . . It is built in the usual form, of pickets, with the lodging apartments and offices opening into a hollow square, protected . . . by a strong gate of timber. On the north, and continuous with the walls, is a strong, high picket fence, inclosing a large yard, into which the animals belonging to the establishment are (may be) driven for protection.

"We were received with great kindness and lavish hospitality, by the proprietor, Maj. James Bridger. . . . Several of my wagons needing repair the train was detained five days for the purpose, Major Bridger courteously placing his blacksmith shop at my service.

"At that time," writes Stansbury, "there were two or three emigrant routes from Fort Bridger: 1. Via Bear, Portneuf, Raft and Humboldt rivers. 2. Echo, Weber, Emigration or Parley's canyons to Salt Lake, but rounding Great Salt Lake to the North. 3. Echo and Weber Canyons, missing Salt Lake City." The Captain "therefore determined . . . accompanied by Major Bridger . . . to seek a more direct route," but he did not find one.

"I was detained until the 20th, by the absence of the partner of Major Bridger, who was on a trip . . . and without whose presence, Major Bridger did not deem it prudent to leave the Fort." Stansbury's report may be briefly summarized. He did considerable examining of possible routes, but in the main he traveled west from Fort Bridger, disregarding established trails. He probed Lost Creek (Pumbars) and Ogden Hole, coming out at the mouth of Ogden

[2] William G. Johnston, *Experiences of a Forty-Niner*, June 10–18, 1849.

River. Bridger returned home and Stansbury proceeded to Salt Lake for the winter.[3]

John Wilson, newly appointed Indian agent "at Salt Lake, California," visited Fort Bridger about that time in order to size up his job and his Indians "through the assistance," he informs us, "of Mr. Vasquez, (Mr. Bridger not being at home). . . . The Utah Indians should cease their accustomed depredations on the Whites. . . . Most of the country is too high for crops. . . . water freezes in the tents of the Natives every month. . . . Only wild hay can be grown. . . .

"Black's Fork, Ham's Fork and tributaries, among which is Fort Bridger, is perhaps, next to this [Salt Lake] valley, the most extensive and most beautiful as to pasturage. It will unquestionably become the Government's duty, at as early a day as possible, to extinguish by treaty, the Indian's title to Salt Lake, Cache, Fort Hall and other valleys; and negotiate for a highway through Indian lands to Fort Bridger, where, in my opinion, without delay, there ought to be established, a military post.

"Captain Stansbury, under the guidance of Mr. Bridger, has already traced out a road direct from Fort Bridger, via Blacksmith's Fork, so as to cross Bear River just above where it flows into Great Salt Lake." A more direct route from Fort Bridger to Fort Laramie can be opened at a lower elevation, farther south than South Pass, in which case "all travel hereafter to Oregon and California which comes up the Platte will unquestionably pass by Fort Bridger. Even this year more than half of the California emigrants passed by Bridger. Thus you will see at once the great importance of the position of Fort Bridger, and the inevitable propriety of making it the great military post of this country."[4]

James Haley White spent half a day with Bridger at his fort in 1849. Bridger had lived a mountain life for twenty-seven years, and, according to White, "knows little of and cares less for civilization. He thought he deserved better treatment from the Mormons than they had given him. He described the Utah Valleys to them, and

[3] Stansbury, *Exploration of Salt Lake Valley*, 74.
[4] 31 Cong., 1 sess., *Ex. Doc. 17* (John Wilson, August 22, 1849). This quotation is paraphrased in part.

told them how to get there. But they were his worst enemies and on many occasions threatened to take his life."[5]

Captain Gunnison reported: "The Utahs are frequently at war with the Shoshones. The Mormons are partly between them. A better site for a commanding influence over all the mountain tribes, is Fort Bridger, which is between the Shoshones, Crows, Sioux, Apaches and Utahs. And no more influential person could be found, than the man already there, as owner, trader, erst-while wide-west traveler, James Bridger, who is connected with them by marriage."[6]

Mrs. Martha M. Morgan's party reached Fort Bridger on the first of October, 1849: "We lay in camp all day. The next morning, with some others, I visited the Fort, found Captain Bridger in good spirits, a frank, open-hearted mountaineer. He is a Virginian by birth, has lived in the mountains for the last twenty-eight years; has visited the States but twice, and sixteen years of this time he assures me that he never tasted bread. He has a squaw, or several of them, for his wife. We then went to an Indian camp, one mile off. Here we found six or eight Frenchmen, who have lived with the Indians many years, hunting and trading. Through the day we exchanged corn, flour and other rations, for dressed skins, ready made antelope and elk pants and moccasins."[7]

Bancroft's historians, drawing on the extensive Mormon church files, wrote: "In the autumn of (1848) they [Ute Indians, Provo, Utah] began to steal the grain and cattle of the white man [Mormons], one of their number being killed. . . . Hostilities broke out. . . . Vasquez and Bridger wrote to Brigham on the 17th of April, 1849, that the Utes were badly disposed toward Americans, and that Chiefs Elk and Walker were urging the Utes to attack the [Mormon] settlements in Utah Valley [Provo]."

In a footnote Bancroft quotes Brigham Young. "I believe that Old Bridger is death on us, and if he saw that 400,000 Indians were coming against us, and any man were to let us know, he would cut his throat. . . . His letter [above] is all bubble and froth. . . . Vasquez is a different man."[8]

[5] Missouri Historical Society Manuscript Files, St. Louis, Missouri.
[6] Gunnison, *A History of the Mormons*, 150.
[7] Martha M. Morgan, *A Trip Across the Plains in 1849–1850*, 12–13.
[8] H. H. Bancroft, *History of Utah*, 309.

The end of the episode is in Bancroft's *History of Utah*: "On the 31st of January, 1850 . . . settlers reported the Indians in Utah Valley (Provo) had stolen fifty or sixty head of cattle or horses, threatening further depredations, and asked permission to chastise them, which was granted. . . . In this war, Big Elk and twenty-seven warriors were killed; one white man was killed and six were wounded."[9]

The various recommendations for establishing a federal military post at Fort Bridger may have been agreeable to the Mormon leaders, but to their notion the wrong people were to sponsor and have charge of it. Territorial Governor Brigham Young, in his message to the legislature of December 2, 1850, declared in part: "We have spared no expense, endeavoring to break the Indians of their pilfering habits. But it becomes us to be prepared to repel sudden invasions. To this end I recommend a more efficient organization of the Territorial Militia, and a more uniform distribution of public service." The Governor then explains that this was to include Green River Precinct, (now Wyoming) and the entire Fort Bridger Indian frontier.

A news item of passing import, dated November 21, 1849, appeared in the *Latter Day Saints Millennial Star*, Liverpool, England, May 1, 1850, saying that "Louis Vasquez, associated with James Bridger at Fort Bridger, had opened a branch store in Salt Lake City."

Captain Stansbury, with James Bridger as guide, had a look at the "new route" east from Fort Bridger on his way home. Their travel was mainly along the present Union Pacific railroad route across southern Wyoming. The following quotes are from Stansbury, the rest paraphrased from the same source.

September 5, 1850. "From its position with regard to several powerful Indian tribes . . . Fort Bridger offers many advantages for a military post. . . . A competent force at this point would have great influence in preventing bloody collisions between hostile tribes.[10]

"Our trunks and heavy baggage were left in charge of Major Bridger, to be forwarded by a Mormon train from the city, Governor Young, having kindly engaged to see that they were safely

9 *Ibid.*, 309–10.
10 Stansbury, *Exploration of Salt Lake Valley*, 228–34.

transported to St. Louis. Major Bridger . . . offered his service as guide. . . . The offer was accepted. We left Fort Bridger September 10, 1850."

Since the death of Bridger's Ute wife, the children had been in the care of a Shoshoni housekeeper. As she had proved to be satisfactory, Bridger arranged for her and the children to journey east in that same wagon train. It was the beginning of a new domestic life for them all.

Bridger and Stansbury ascended Bitter Creek, "which was formerly a rendezvous for trappers and traders on account of the abundance of buffalo. None are to be seen now." September 17. Muddy and Little Snake; September 18, St. Vrain's Fork, near Fraeb's last fight. September 19, spot where fourteen fur traders under Mr. Vásquez had "forted" against forty Sioux. September 20, 1850, crossed Continental Divide at "Bridger's Pass"; September 21, Sage Creek; September 23, North Platte River and Medicine Bow River; September 24, Laramie Plains and Laramie River.

Indians were approaching; Major Bridger, shouldering his rifle, "walked out towards them and made various signs to a party that came to meet him. . . . They recognized him . . . and commenced a race for our camp . . . holding out their hands to shake. They were Oglallahs, several hundred of them."

Major Bridger, who was personally known to many of the visitors, was seated among them. "He was unable to speak either the Sioux or Cheyenne language . . . notwithstanding this, he held the whole circle, for more than an hour, perfectly enchained, and evidently most deeply interested, in a conversation and narrative, the whole of which was carried on without the utterance of a single word. The simultaneous exclamations of surprise and interest, and the occasional bursts of hearty laughter, showed that the whole party perfectly undertood."[11]

September 28–30: "The train was directed to move forward under the charge of Major Bridger." It continued through the Black Hills and Cheyenne Pass into Chugwater Valley, where Captain Stansbury overtook it. Here the Captain suffered a fall that delayed him two weeks. He left Fort Laramie on October 16, "the train being in charge of Lieutenant Gunnison."

[11] *Ibid.*, 252–54.

It is significant to note that both Stansbury and Gunnison approved of "Bridger's Pass" over the continental divide for the Pacific Railroad.

Stansbury drops only the slightest hint of what became of James Bridger. Appended to his description of Chimney Rock is this comment: "It is the opinion of Mr. Bridger that it was reduced to its present height by lightning or some other sudden catastrophe, as he found it broken on his return from one of his trips to St. Louis, though he had passed it uninjured on his way down." Bridger was not with Stansbury on the way west.

JOINING HIS FAMILY en route, Bridger reached Independence about the end of October. In this busy place, overflowing with frontiersman, half-Indian families, and gaily dressed Mexicans, the Bridgers seemed to be at home. Depositing the family in temporary quarters, probably with a married tribeswoman, Bridger, in hunter fashion, drifted southward through a magnificent landscape of alternating pasture and forest lands. He closely scrutinized the locality so often recommended to him and soon found what suited him: a spreading tract of richly fertile land, "For Sale," holding a few tilled fields as if in loving embrace. A log house, which he and a workman quickly erected, provided the threshold over which Bridger may have borne his new bride—with her several adopted children.

General Dodge was told by Bridger himself or by one of his family: "In 1850, Bridger took as his third wife a Snake [Shoshoni] woman. He bought a little farm near Santa Fe, Missouri, and moved his family there from Fort Bridger that year [including Mary Josephine, aged six, Felix Francis, aged eight, and Virginia Rosalie, aged one]." At a much later date, Virginia Rosalie said: "Father gave three horses and a couple of blankets for the Shoshone wife. . . . They moved from Fort Bridger in 1850, and came back to Jackson County. He bought the big Thatcher farm, three and a half miles northeast of New Santa Fe, near Dallas. Father had 375 acres under cultivation, and several hundred more in timber." George Kemper, a neighbor, helped Bridger erect a log house.[1]

The final purchase involved a trip to St. Louis, of course. Robert Campbell, by now a leading banker and businessman, had been custodian of the Bridger funds at his Missouri State Bank since the death of William L. Sublette in 1845. Bridger was much interested

[1] E. R. Schauffler, in Kansas City *Star*, March 2, 1941.

to learn that Campbell was participating in plans for an Indian peace parley in 1851 at or near Fort Laramie, hub of the Indian country involved.

Father De Smet planned to move up the Missouri as far as Fort Union and use his influence on all branches of the Sioux and Cheyenne tribes to get them to attend the council. Bridger was on hand to instruct the priest how best to reach Fort Laramie from Fort Union by way of the Yellowstone and Powder rivers, then make his way to the Overland emigrant road near Independence Rock. Thomas Fitzpatrick, for several years identified with the Indian agencies for the upper Platte and Arkansas (Colorado), was already busy assisting Indian and army officers, dispatching runners to all tribes concerned, and urging widespread attendance from all of them.

Bridger's special friends, the Shoshonis, and their distinguished leader, Washakie, along with their neighbors, the Crow Indians, were being formally invited. As Robert Campbell and Thomas Fitzpatrick were joining the official party proceeding from Fort Leavenworth, Bridger went on ahead to urge, if necessary, a good showing by his beloved Shoshonis at the council. He reached Fort Laramie in early July, having learned the details of Washakie's plans.

Assembled at Fort Laramie by early August, although the council would officially begin on September 1, were several Plains Indian villagers, as well as numbers of more distant natives, chiefly Sioux, Cheyennes, and Arapahoes. Some of the more docile southern tribes had declined, fearing depredations by the Sioux and Cheyennes. The escort or policing force of less than three hundred armed soldiers could maintain peace only if ten times that many Indians chose to behave themselves. A number of gratuities were promised, and a large attendance was expected.

Indian Commissioner (Colonel) D. D. Mitchell, with a large staff, was in charge, to designate the encamping and attendance space and positions, to carry out the planned program, and to conduct and record the actions taken. The Colonel depended on such mountaineers as Bridger and Fitzpatrick to interpret for all participants, and especialy to see that feuding tribes were placed a good distance apart.

Percival G. Lowe, a soldier, recalling the occasion after fifty years, recaptured the scene: "It turned out that Major Bridger, the interpreter, had reported to headquarters the approach of the Snakes [Shoshones, about August 28]; and he had been directed to lead them down near our camp. . . . Boots and Saddles had sounded, so as to be ready whatever happened; as the Sioux and the Snakes were enemies. . . . Just below was a large Sioux camp. . . . When the Snakes reached the brow of the Hill . . . a Sioux sprang upon his horse, bow and arrows in hand, and rushed towards them. . . . A Frenchman, interpreter, was instantly in pursuit. . . . The Chief . . . [of the Snakes] raised his gun ready to fire, just as the Frenchman . . . pulled the Sioux from his horse, disarmed, and stood over him.

"Here I met Bridger for the first time. He . . . told Lieutenant Hastings . . . that the Shoshones had been assigned a position near his troop, and asked where they could camp without interfering with the dragoons. Hastings told him that I knew the ground . . . and turning to me said: 'Corporal Lowe, show Captain Bridger the limits of our camp and give him all the assistance you can.' That order was license for me to stay on Bridger's staff until a camp was made. . . . I galloped off with the great Mountaineer. . . . He was pleased with the camp assigned. I asked him if he had any objections to my staying with him until camp was formed.

" 'No, young man. These are the finest Indians on earth. Stay with me, and I'll show 'um to you.' Soon they went into camp in their own peculiar way. Every prominent point was dotted by a sentinel, quietly wrapped in his blanket, gun ready for use. Bridger said:

" 'Well, you seen that fool Sioux make the run, didn't you?'

" 'Yes Sir.'

" 'Well, . . . [the interpreter] saved that fellow from hell. My Chief would 'er killed him quick; and then the fool Sioux would 'er got their backs up, and there wouldn't have been room to camp 'round here for dead Sioux. . . . They see how these Shoshones are armed. I got them guns for 'um: and they are good ones.' Colonel Mitchell requested Captain Bridger to call. I delivered the message and returned with Bridger, who spent some hours with the Commissioners' party. . . . Some how, I had conceived a great liking for and felt a great confidence in Bridger."[2]

[2] Percival G. Lowe, *Five Years a Dragoon*, 79–84. This quotation is paraphrased in part.

Lowe heard the Shoshoni preacher (medicine man, Bridger interpreting) exhort his people to kindness, honesty, and brotherly love.

"Now," says Bridger, "I don't know nothing about religion . . . but me and the Shoshonis don't have no trouble with what he says."

Bridger pointed out a Shoshoni warrior with a special coup. Sioux raiders ran off a lot of Shoshoni horses and took one scalp. This man and several others went in pursuit, but they all returned in about a week, excepting this man. While he was being mourned as dead, he rode into camp driving the lost Shoshoni horses and six Sioux mounts, with six Sioux scalps dangling from his bridle and belt!

The last soldiers arrived at the council on September 1, without the expected gifts; and, on recommendation of the manager of Fort Laramie, the entire assemblage moved on September 4–5 to Horse Creek, thirty-five miles down the Platte, for better forage and campsites. The Crow Indians, with Robert Meldrum, interpreter, in charge, arrived on September 10, followed next day by Father De Smet, Alexander Culbertson, and a few Sioux Indians from Fort Union.

The most vexing task of the council was mapping the boundaries of the territory claimed by each tribe. The Sioux, for example, recognized the Platte as their southern boundary, but they also claimed the southern shores as hunting grounds. Then came the reading, interpreting, and accepting, sentence by sentence, of the treaty in its final form, and its signing by the proper authorities. The treaty was completed by September 17.

The renewing of tribal peace treaties, all duly sanctioned and celebrated at formal dog-roasts, was an almost endless chore requiring the studied assistance and diplomacy of the interpreters. James Bridger was especially concerned when the Shoshonis and Cheyennes finally came together, ostensibly as friends. The Shoshoni wits, possibly prodded by Bridger, recalled the cowardly horse-stealing raid on Fort Bridger in 1843 when the post was occupied only by a few women and children.

Merrill J. Mattes, journalist extraordinary, has discovered five unpublished scratch maps made by Pierre Jean De Smet. Four of them are in the St. Louis University. The fifth one, dated 1851, was prepared for, and presented to Colonel Mitchell. The map was made on the spot "from scraps then in my [Father De Smet's] possession," and was "made use of by that gentleman [Colonel Mitchell] in Council" at Horse Creek.

These maps "are documents of signal import, which should inspire renewed respect for the ubiquitous Bridger; and yet increase the stature of the versatile and indefatigable De Smet," Mattes assures the eager readers of the *Mississippi Valley Historical Review* for September, 1949.

"The draftsmanship of the first three, while not striking, is respectable. . . . The fourth map . . . depicts that remarkable region . . . the headwaters of the Yellowstone, the Wind, the Green, the Snake, and the Missouri Rivers. . . . This 'Bridger's Map,' is crude and smeary; and it has all the earmarks of being sketched in the field, without benefit of desk or blotter. In view of De Smet's express testimony, that the most famous trapper of all, supplied him with his geographical data, at least for the 'Yellowstone Park' section, it is a fair guess that this map was drawn by De Smet, with Bridger at his elbow. . . .

"All the principal features are in evidence: 'Volcanic country' [Geyser Basins]; 'Sulphur mountain, near Gardiner's Cr.' [Mammoth Hot Springs]; a lake '60 x 9 miles'; 'Hot Springs'; 'Grand Canyon'; 'Falls 290'; 'Steam Springs'; 'Two Ocean Pass'; and 'Coulter's Hell,' on Stinking [Shoshone] River. The Fifth map contains all the features of the Fourth, with refinements." It is in the government files in Washington, D. C.[3]

The editor of the *Missouri Republican*, B. Gratz Brown, wrote in the November 9, 1851, issue: "Letter From The Editor: Treaty Ground, near Fort Laramie, September 12, 1851: This entire day was given up to an attempt to designate on the map the territory of each [Indian] Nation. In this effort the Commissioners had the assistance of the Rev. Father De Smet . . . he has carefully collected and embodied in a number of small maps . . . all that he has seen and gathered. . . .

"In addition the Commissioners had the assistance of Mr. James Bridger, the owner and founder of Bridger's Fort, in the mountains. This man is a perfect original. He is a Kentuckian [Virginian] by

3 Merrill J. Mattes, "Behind the Legend of Colter's Hell," *Mississippi Valley Historical Review*, September, 1949, pp. 277–79.

birth, but has been in the Indian country since he was sixteen [eighteen] years of age. He was with General Ashley in his early trapping expeditions, and afterwards with various companies, and finally, roamed over the country on his own hook, in the capacity of trapper, hunter, trader, or Indian fighter, as the emergency demanded. He has traveled the mountains East and West, and from the northern boundary of the United States to the Gila River.

"He is not an educated man, but seems to have an intuitive knowledge of the topography of the country, the courses of streams, the direction of mountains, and is never lost, wherever he may be. It is stated by those who have had him in their employ that in the midst of the mountains when the party of trappers wished to move from one stream to another, or cross a mountain to any stream or place, or when lost or uncertain of the proper direction, they would always appeal to Bridger.

"He would throw his gun carelessly over his shoulder, survey the country awhile with his eye, and then strike out on a course, and never fail to reach the place, although he had several hundred miles to traverse over a country which he never traveled, and to a place he had never seen. To this seemingly intuitive knowledge of the country, he adds the singularly retentive memory of peculiarities and of every incident in his own history and that of his companions.

"In his own rude way, he can lay down nearly every stream that empties into the Missouri, or Yellowstone, or that flows down the western slope of the Rocky Mountains, and describe how these streams interlock with each other. He showed us, and his information in this respect was confirmed by others, how it was practical to go by water from the Missouri River into the Columbia River, or from the Atlantic to the Pacific Ocean, without portage at any place except where the Rivers are impassable because of rapids. There is a lake in the Rocky Mountains from which the waters flow on the one side into the Missouri, and on the other into the Columbia River. Everything Bridger has seen, he recollects with entire precision, and in his wild life (he is now advanced in years) he has traversed the whole country in many directions."[4]

An echo of the Laramie council comes from Chief Washakie of

[4] B. Gratz Brown, editorial correspondence in the *Missouri Republican*, November 9, 1851. Photostats by courtesy of Missouri Historical Society, St. Louis, Missouri.

the Shoshonis, who may have been better at minding his own business than at working with others or making records and reports. James S. Brown found him still nursing a grievance in 1854 for having been slighted at the council of 1851. Washakie said he had gone to Laramie as chief of *all* the Shoshonis, but the agents of the Big Father in Washington called another man to be head of the Shoshonis, and through him they gave out the blankets and other goods. The Shoshonis called him "Tavendu-wets" (the White Man's Child).[5]

While attending the peace council, James Bridger seems to have arranged with Robert Campbell to enter the young Bridgers in a parochial school. Father Pierre Jean De Smet wrote from St. Louis University, September 27, 1852, to Reverend P. J. Verhagen, S.J., St. Charles, Missouri: "I will thank your reverence for an immediate answer to the following. Captain Bridger, an old Rocky Mountain friend of mine, has sent his two children (half-breeds) to the States to be educated. One is a girl about seven years old; the boy is a little over eight. They have never been baptized, at least I think so, and shall enquire on the subject. He has left means with Colonel Robert Campbell for their education and clothing. Enquire of Madam Hamilton whether she will admit the little girl? And at what price? Will Madam Barada admit the boy as a boarder, pay for his schooling at your school, and how much per year. Please answer without delay. I am afraid the Protestants will try to get them; the sooner they are away from here, the better."

Father De Smet wrote again from St. Louis University, April 1, 1853. "Mr. J. Bridger, Fort Bridger and Vasquez, Dear Friend. Our good friend Colonel R. Campbell, acquainted me yesterday that a departure for the mountains was about to take place, and I avail myself of this opportunity of writing a few lines to you. A few days ago I had the pleasure of paying a visit to your children who reside at present in St. Charles. They appeared to be well pleased, and are certainly well taken care of. Felix frequents our school and is making progress. His sister lives in the Academy and under the immediate care of the ladies of that well conducted establishment, who have every regard for her that good mothers could have for their own children. Both have been somewhat sickly during the

[5] James S. Brown, *Life of a Pioneer*, 318–19.

winter, but are now doing well. You may rest assured that all shall be done to make them comfortable and happy.

"You have promised me a letter with regard to the Flatheads, and I have anxiously expected it during the whole course of last year. Should you see them, remember me to them, and assure them that I daily address my prayers to the Lord for their welfare and happiness; but to attain this end, they must remain faithful to God, and not listen to bad counsel, and to ill-disposed persons. It would be for me the height of happiness to learn that they still cherish the idea of seeing a Blackgown in their midst; and were this the case, of which I wish to be informed, I would do all I can to see this, their desire, accomplished. I send you by this occasion a couple of pistols and a knife, as a present to my dear friend Insala [Michael] whose remembrance I shall always cherish. Remember me to all, etc."[6]

[6] Copies of Pierre Jean De Smet's letters kindly furnished by the Missouri Historical Society, St. Louis, Missouri.

JAMES BRIDGER'S last days at Fort Bridger found him quiet, friendly, and helpful, as if unaware that the ranch was being pulled from under him.

Mrs. B. G. Ferris, wife of the newly appointed secretary of Utah Territory, wrote: "On the evening of the 19th [October, 1852] we encamped at Fort Bridger—a long, low, strongly constructed log building, surrounded by a high wall of logs, stuck endwise in the ground. Bridger came out and invited us in, and introduced us to his Indian wife, and showed us his half-breed children—keen, bright-eyed little things.

"Everything was rude and primitive. This man strongly attracted my attention; there was more than civility about him—there was native politeness. He is the oldest trapper in the Rocky Mountains; his language is very graphic and descriptive; and he is evidently a man of great shrewdness. He alarmed us in regard to our prospects of getting through; said the season had arrived when a heavy snow might be looked for any day; urged us to stay with him all winter; showed us where we could lodge, guarded against the cold with plenty of buffalo skins; and assured us that he could make the benefit of our society, and the assistance of Mr. Ferris in his business, more than compensate for the expense of living. This was a delicate way of offering the use of his establishment without remuneration.

"His wife was simplicity itself. She exhibited some curious pieces of Indian embroidery, the work of her own hands, with as much pleased hilarity as a child; and gave me a quantity of raisins and sauce berries—altogether it was a very pleasant interview. He told us, if we were determined to go, to make as little delay as possible; and made a very acceptable addition to our larder, in the shape of fresh potatoes and other vegetables. We left Bridger's early in the morning of the 20th."

Mrs. Ferris moved from Salt Lake City to the Pacific coast in the spring of 1853, when her husband retired. At Bear River (Corinne, Utah) she wrote on May 10, 1853, that their train was supposed to start from Salt Lake City the twenty-fifth of April, and a Mr. Livingston had sent his wagon-master and a clerk to Fort Bridger to procure extra cattle. After the time for their return had come and gone, Livingston went himself and found them at Fort Bridger in bad condition, having suffered dreadfully in the severe cold and deep snow. "About the same time, a party of Mexicans came in from the Rio Colorado [Green], and reported several of their companions frozen to death some twenty miles from the Fort."[1]

William A. Hickman left his home in the Salt Lake Valley about the same time Livingston departed and managed to reach Green River crossing for a summer stand, in early May, 1853. He moved later to Pacific Springs. There he was prepared to do horseshoeing, wagon repairing, and horse trading, offering fresh, strong draft and riding animals for weak or worn-down stock. He claims to have done an extraordinary business, especially in whisky.[2]

James Linforth, an English Mormon bound for Salt Lake City, reached the "California ferry" on Green River (above the Sandies) on August 3, 1853. He backtracked and reached the Utah crossing on August 4, 1853. "There was a trading post there, and crowds of traders, gamblers and Indians, who, of course, live on the emigrants." There they met "Elder Bigler," a relative of Linforth's partner.

On August 6, Linforth "traveled about seventeen miles over an excellent road to Fort Bridger, on Black's Fork, a short distance west of a bluff, very prettily dotted over with cedar. . . . It is merely a trading post, belonging to Major James Bridger, one of the oldest mountaineers in this region. The Fort is built in the usual form of pickets, with lodging apartments opening into a hollow square. A high picket fence incloses a yard into which the animals of the establishment are driven for protection, both from wild beasts and Indians.

1 Mrs. B. G. Ferris, *The Mormons at Home*, October 19, 1852 and May 10, 1853.
2 William A. Hickman, *Brigham's Destroying Angel*, 88–92.

"The grass in the neighborhood is abundant, but about a mile and a half from the Fort, Mr. Bridger had erected a board, on which was written a request for emigrants to keep a mile away from his place. The road from Fort Bridger, described in Clayton's Guide, leads to the west of the bluff west of the Fort; but the new road, the one altogether traveled now, leads to the right."[3]

Bridger's signboard was erected at his property line. Only Mormons were using the road, and they were not patronizing Fort Bridger, except to use its pasturage. California and Oregon emigrants used the road farther north. Thus the business for which Fort Bridger was established no longer existed.

The Utah legislature had Fort Bridger in mind when, on March 3, 1852, it created Green River County (now in Wyoming) and placed it under existing Salt Lake County officers. "The Sheriff of Great Salt Lake County is hereby authorized to organize Green River County, whenever the inhabitants . . . call for it, or circumstances render it expedient."

J. H. Holeman, Indian agent, Utah territory, wrote to the Honorable Luke Lea, United States commissioner of Indian affairs in Washington, from Great Salt Lake City, April 29, 1852:

"Mr. James Bridger, who was the interpreter for the Snake Indians at the Treaty of Laramie [1851], and who is very favorably noticed in the communication of Colonel D. D. Mitchell, informed me that the Utah Indians, residing in Uwinty Valley, had frequently expressed their dissatisfaction, in the strongest terms, against the Mormons making settlements on their lands; that they had understood they intended to do so, and were anxious to know what they should do, or if they had the right to prevent it. This was stated to me in such a manner that I could not hesitate to believe it.

"I subsequently met a delegation of the Uwinty Utes who confirmed the information I had received, and expressed their decided disapprobation to any settlement being made on their lands by the whites, and more particularly by the Mormons. They requested that I send them traders, and pledged friendship in the strongest terms.

"I sent them two different companies of traders; one from Fort Bridger, whom they treated with great kindness and respect. The

[3] James Linforth and Frederick Piercy, *Route from Liverpool to Great Salt Lake City*, 97–98.

others went from this city. The Indians immediately demanded to know if they were Mormons, such was the feeling of hostility expressed towards the Mormons. The Shoshones or Snakes were equally opposed, and expressed their disapprobation to the Mormons settling on their lands."[4]

Joseph H. Porath, of Salt Lake City, recently noticed this significant document sequestered in the Salt Lake County Recorder's files: "$400. August 28, 1852. Received of James Bridger, in full, four hundred dollars, for the right and title of five houses and location in Utah Territory, situated one mile and a quarter from Fort Bridger, on the south side of Black's Fork, extending three miles up the river and three down. Witnesses: William F. Shortridge, Edward Lynch. Signed Charles (His X Mark) Sagenes."

During the winter of 1852–53, the Utah legislature granted a charter to Hawley, Thompson and McDonald, a Utah firm, to install and operate a ferry on Green River for the use of emigrants (in what is now Wyoming).

The Utah valleys were rapidly being settled, and the Ute Indians and their game were being forced into the mountains. Because of the resulting hunger and suffering, the Indians raided the herds of the whites, and on July 17, 1853, the so-called "Walker War" (Ute Indian chief) was on in earnest, the Utes against the Mormon settlers. The burden of the blame was placed by the Mormons on Mexican slave traders, who, they claimed, had taken Ute Indian women and children into slavery.

Brigham Young, governor of Utah and ex-officio superintendent of Indian affairs in Utah, informed his chief in Washington, Indian Commissioner Manypenny, "I issued a revocation of all licenses to trade with Indians . . . to prevent trading of guns, powder and lead to our enemies." Though rather far from the war, in central Utah, Fort Bridger was subject to this declaration.

On August 26, 1853, Dr. Thomas Flint, an emigrant, journalizes: "One mile below the Fort [Bridger] camped. 27th. Moved to a small creek . . . opposite the Fort. . . . White went to the Fort for ammunition, but found the Fort in possession of the Territorial Officers, Mormons, who had, 24 hours before, driven Old Man Bridger out and taken possession.

[4] 35 Cong., 1 sess., *H. R. Ex. Doc. 71* (The Utah Expedition), 144–47.

"Fort made by setting in the ground two parallel lines of high posts and filling in between with gravelly clay. 29th. Here we found a camp of forty Mormons, out hunting Indians, and to assist their emigrants. Forty more were at Fort Bridger."[5]

Isaac C. Haight wrote Franklin W. Richards (both Mormons) on August 31, 1853: "We met a large posse going out to arrest Bridger and some of his gang, that resisted the authorities of Utah. They have stirred up the Indians to commit depredations upon our people; and some of our people have been killed."

Hickman had a long ear for gossip, if not a tendency to launch it. He says that while he was at Pacific Springs that summer, "a difficulty took place between the ferrymen and mountain men. The latter had always owned and run the ferry across the Green River. But the Utah legislature granted a charter (exclusive) to Hawley, Thompson & McDonald, for all ferries there.

"The mountain men, who had lived there for many years, claimed their rights to be the oldest, and a difficulty took place, in which the Mountain men took forcible possession of all the ferries but one. ... When the ferrying season was over, the party having the charter brought suit against them for all they had made during the summer, 'some thirty thousand dollars'!

"About this time it was rumored that Jim Bridger was furnishing the Indians with powder and lead to kill Mormons. Affidavits were made to that effect, and the Sheriff was ordered out with a posse of 150 men, to arrest him, capture his ammunition, and destroy his liquors. I was sent for, to come to Brigham Young's Office. He told me he wanted me to go with the Sheriff, James Ferguson and party, as I had been out there that summer, was acquainted with those Mountaineers, and might be of special service.

"I accordingly went; Bridger had heard of this and left, no one knew where to. We searched around several days for him. Finally one of the party who had taken the ferries, came to Fort Bridger, and was arrested. No ammunition was found; but the whiskey and rum, of which he had a good stock, was destroyed by doses."[6]

[5] Thomas Flint, "Diary of Dr. Thomas Flint," August 26–29, 1853, *Historical Society of Southern California Annual Publications*.

[6] Hickman, *Brigham's Destroying Angel*, 91–92.

William L. Marcy elicited the story from Bridger himself: "He remained secreted for several days, and through the assistance of his Indian wife was enabled to elude the search of the Danites and make his way to Fort Laramie, leaving all his cattle and other property in possession of the Mormons."[7]

In his history of Colorado and Wyoming, Bancroft says of Fort Bridger: "He [Bridger] abandoned it in 1853, being warned by the Mormons, who did not desire a hostile Fort in the neighborhood of their settlements."

The *Missouri Republican* of November 5, 1853, reports: "Theodore Winthrop, of New York, arrived from Puget Sound. Mormons had accused Jim Bridger of selling ammunition and arms to Indians hostile to them, whereupon forty of them were sent by Governor Young to arrest him. He fled to the mountains. They took his Fort, and lived on his provisions, but soon returned home. Soon Bridger, with his wife and children, started east, and would probably arrive at Westport next week."[8]

The figure of James Bridger, appropriately enough, rose out of the confusion about November 1, 1853, after Hickman's posse had "poured" its last drink. Bridger was with John M. Hockaday, a government road surveyor, who had been engaged by Bridger to survey his land holdings at Fort Bridger. On November 6, 1853, the survey was completed:

"A survey of land made for James Bridger, November 6, 1853, in the Territory of Utah, and county of Green River. Beginning at the corner (marked J on the plat, about two miles north by northeast of Fort Bridger) on north side of Black's Fork, seventy-two poles [rods], on a due south line from said stream, running thence due south one thousand six hundred and forty poles to a stone corner on east side of said Black's Fork (marked B on the plat), one hundred and sixty poles from said stream on a due west line; thence due west four hundred and fifty-two poles to a stone corner (marked R on the plat); thence due north one thousand one hundred and twenty poles to a stone corner (marked D on the plat), on north side

[7] Randolph B. Marcy, *Thirty Years of Army Life on the Border*, 401.

[8] *Missouri Republican*, November 5, 1853 (*Nebraska Historical Collections*, vol. XX, 1922, 252).

of Black's Fork (marked J on the plat). Contents three thousand eight hundred and ninety-eight acres, two roods. Surveyed by John M. Hockaday."[9]

"Lewis [sic] Vasquez, Charles LaJunesse, and James Bridger, settled upon the land within site of Fort, as stated by Mr. Bridger.

"A true copy of the original [filed] General Land Office, Washington, D. C., March 9, 1854. John Wilson, Commissioner."[10]

The six square miles thus inclosed in the survey was 1.4 miles in width, 5 miles in length on the east side, and 3.5 miles in length on the west side, the sloping end at the north being 2.25 miles in length. With the survey in hand, neither hiding nor hurrying, Bridger returned to the Missouri farm and spent the winter (1853–54) with his family.

The Mormon leaders greatly feared that the image of James Bridger meant as much to the Indians as that of Brigham Young meant to the Mormons. Such a domination could be dangerous. Thus the Mormons continued their devious efforts to establish themselves as equal or superior to Bridger.

The so-called special mission to the Indians in the vicinity of Green River (now Wyoming) was set apart by the General Authorities of the Mormon church on October 8, 1853, with Orson Hyde as sponsoring apostle; John Nebeker, president and captain (for military duties); John Harvey, first counselor and lieutenant; and James S. Brown, second counselor and lieutenant.

Brown says they were to erect an outpost near Fort Bridger and preach civilization among the Indians, in order to prevent trouble for Mormon emigrants and settlers. "We were to identify our interests with theirs, even to marrying among them, if we would be permitted to take the young daughters of the Chief and leading men," as Bridger had done. At a final meeting November 1, 1853, in Salt Lake City, with apostles Orson Hyde, Parley P. Pratt, and Ezra T. Benson, "we were also told that some of us might have to take Indian wives."

Thirty-nine men (no women or children) left Salt Lake City on November 2, 1853, in twenty wagons, with 110 cattle, horses, and

[9] The Fort Bridger Survey appears in the Salt Lake County Recorder's office, Records Book B, 68.

[10] 52 Cong., 1 sess., *Senate Report 625* (Hockaday Survey of Fort Bridger).

mules. They reached Fort Bridger on November 15. "Twelve or fifteen rough mountain men . . . seemed to be very surly and suspicious of us. . . . We passed over to Smith's Fork . . . followed up the creek (ten or twelve miles) and selected a site, November 27, 1853. The writer made plans for a block-house, which was built with four wings . . . two stories high. . . . All the rooms were provided with portholes. . . . In two weeks the house was ready for occupancy."

Fifty-three men in twenty-five wagons joined the "missionaries" in late November, making a total of ninety-two men, all of them well armed. "Elisha B. Ward, an old mountaineer and trapper, and his Indian wife, Sally, assisted us in our studies of the Shoshone dialect," while other Shoshonis camped around the blockhouse. "Yet with all these opportunities, there were only about six of us, out of the Ninety-two, that made even fair progress" with the Shoshoni language.

The Shoshonis "begged until they became a nuisance." It was a trying time. Many cattle died of hunger and cold, "and we were, and had been for some weeks, living on bread alone." Little wonder that "a reaction of spirit . . . or another spirit, came upon the camp— a spirit of great discontent. For a time it seemed as if it would break up the Mission; but finally it was overcome," Elder Brown revealed.

Someone with foresight gave the blockhouse and its acres the prophetic name, Fort Supply, keeping the Mormon emigration in mind. But cold weather was against it, and during its brief occupancy, Bridger's alleged warning to the Mormon pioneers came back to him from Fort Supply as a mocking echo: "We would give $1,000 for a crop of corn!"

Apostle Hyde arrived on May 8, 1854, with twenty-five new men. He selected four men to visit Washakie's Shoshoni village on the headwaters of the Platte, including James S. Brown and Elisha B. Ward, mountaineer. Chief Washakie bluntly asked: " 'Who are you? . . . and what is your errand?' . . . We told him we were Mormons . . . sent by the Big Mormon captain . . . that we might be friendly . . . learn the Indian dialects, manners, and customs. . . . Teach Indians to till the earth; raise stock; and build houses, so Indian women and children would not suffer. . . .

"We said that some of us might want to come out into his country and marry some of their good daughters, and rear families by them.

. . . One old wise counselor said: 'No, for we have not daughters enough for our own men. . . . But we are willing to give an Indian girl for a white girl. I cannot see why a white man wants an Indian girl. They are dirty, ugly, stubborn and cross; and it is a strange idea for white men to want such wives. But I can see why an Indian wants a white woman!'

"Chief Washakie, however, said the white men might look around; and if any one of us found a girl that would go with him, it would be all right; but the Indians must have the same privilege among the white men."

That rather awkward incident marked the beginning of the end of the "mission." On June 1, 1854, Brown wrote: "We reached the Middle Ferry on Green River, Green River County, Utah [now Wyoming]. There we met W. I. Appleby, probate judge; Hosea Stout, prosecuting attorney; William Hickman, Sheriff; Captain Hawley, Ferryman, his family and some others." Judge Appleby and the officers had only recently arrived from Salt Lake City to organize the county.

Brown took employment with the ferry company as interpreter, and noted: "As the 'court' was new, it was difficult for the Sheriff to serve a writ without a posse to aid him. . . . I was summoned to take charge of a posse. . . ." A man crossed four thousand cattle and then applied to the ferrymen for a lost calf, abusing and threatening them for not paying. Hearing of this, Judge Appleby ordered Sheriff Hickman to bring the man in dead or alive. Brown accompanied Hickman. The two ran into a hostile camp of twenty-four armed men. In the argument, Hickman warned them, "We have between seventy-five and one hundred men just over those hills [at Fort Supply]." The leader agreed to answer for his man.

The upper ferryman, ten miles above, informed the Judge that twenty-eight mountaineers had run him off, taken charge of his ferry, and were pocketing the money. The Judge ordered the Sheriff to arrest the mountaineers and bring them to court. Sheriff Hickman summoned James S. Brown to take the posse of fourteen men up the opposite side of the river. "We will get them drunk," said Hickman, "then I think we can manage them."

"To our surprise, we found their leader, L. B. Ryan, apparently in a drunken stupor." There was a little fighting, then the Sheriff arrested Ryan (but not the mountaineers) and bonded him for $10,000. "We went back to the Middle Ferry . . ." and on July 7, 1854, Brown's "missionary labors seemed to have come to an end in that part."[11]

Hickman explains that Ryan had previously owned and operated the upper ferry and was only reclaiming what was his own property when he was hauled into the carpetbagger court.[12]

The intensely confused ferry situation may explain why neither Vásquez nor Bridger is known to have operated a ferry on Green River.

[11] James S. Brown, *Life of a Pioneer*, 304-45. This quotation is partly paraphrased.

[12] Hickman, *Brigham's Destroying Angel*, 105-107.

JAMES BRIDGER'S winter (1853–54) with his family on the Missouri farm gave him an opportunity to establish himself as a householder, to visit old friends in St. Louis, and to plan his business ventures. Among his moves, he must have authorized the following, from the Baptismal Register, Sacred Heart Academy, St. Charles, Missouri: "On the 6th of January, 1854, I, the undersigned, baptized Felix Francis Bridger, born in December, 1841, son of Captain Bridger of Salt Lake. Godfather, Walter McGavin.—Js. Fr. Van Assche, S. J."

Father Pierre Jean De Smet wrote as follows: "Saint Louis University, [Saint Louis, Missouri], March 11, 1854. Reverend Father Verhaegen, S. J., Reverend and Dear Father;—We are all enjoying good health at the University, and Father O'Loughlin has recovered. I spoke to Mr. [Robert] Campbell the other day about the little Rocky Mountain Felix, and told him that I had written to your Reverence to procure the necessary clothes for the child, for which he thanked me and said it was all right.

"His father will probably soon arrive in St. Louis, and may again proceed to the mountains, taking his two children along with him. All expenses incurred for Felix up to the day of his departure, Mr. Campbell has promised, shall be settled; but in the doubt that he may perhaps not be left in St. Charles, does not like to pay in advance. This much was said to Mrs. Barada, but has not been well understood by her. You may assure her that all is right.

"I hope Major Bridger will find his children in good health at his arrival in St. Charles. He has spent upwards of thirty years among the Indians, and is one of the truest specimens of a real trapper and Rocky Mountain man. He has been always very kind to us; and as he has much influence among the various tribes of the far West, he may still continue to exercise it in our favor. I hope he will call on your Reverence."[1]

While visiting St. Louis in the spring of 1854, Bridger met Sir George Gore, who was organizing a big game safari, and who forthwith hired Bridger as his pilot and guide. With Bridger's assistance Gore completed his retinue and his outfit of equipment at St. Louis and Westport. With Henry Chatillon and his brother, local guides, Gore then set out for Fort Laramie. He wisely wished to try out his organization and ready himself for larger trophies by wintering at Fort Laramie, possibly making a short autumn expedition to the Medicine Bow Mountains.

Bridger returned to the farm for some heavy work during the autumn and winter of 1854–55. Clearing a commanding site near the crest of a ridge just south of Indian Creek, he laid the foundation of a spacious dwelling. It would face north (towards the present Kansas City business district some nine or ten miles distant), "the sort of hilltop lookout a Mountain Scout would naturally select for his home," observed E. R. Schauffler, while locating the place for the Kansas City *Star* (1941).

Local tradition insists that Bridger bought the house in Westport, and moved it eight or nine miles south to the farm, probably late that year of 1854. It was a two-story house with commodious middle hallways on each floor, each hall having openings to two big rooms on each side, every one of the eight rooms having a fireplace served by two tall double chimneys. A one-story porch extended across the front of the house. For a long time it was one of the largest homes

---

[1] The letters and baptismal records were kindly furnished by the Missouri Historical Society, St. Louis, Missouri. The following transcripts were also supplied:

"Elizabeth Bridger was at the Sacred Heart Academy. St. Charles, Missouri, October, 1852, to November 15, 1853.

"On the 21st day of April, 1853, I, the undersigned, baptized Mary Josephine Bridger, a half-breed Indian girl, aged about seven years. Godmother, Olivia Emmerson. P. J. Ver Haegen.

"On the 10th of May, 1854, I baptized John Bridger, about four years old; and Virginia Bridger, about six years old, children of Major James Bridger, and of his Indian wife of the Shoshone or Snake Nation in the Rocky Mountains. Godfather, Alexander to Louis (sic); Godmother, Rosalie Richard, his wife.—P. J. De Smet, S. J."

We find no other evidence, however, that Elizabeth, Mary Josephine, or John Bridger (Bridges, or an orphan?) were James Bridger's children. Virginia Bridger, born July 4, 1849, would have been nearly five at the recorded time of baptism, and her mother was a Ute, not a Shoshoni.

in the Big Blue Valley and was a popular place for dances, parties, and holiday gatherings. Painted white, it was as conspicuous then as its descendent flock of handsome suburban homes are today, with their white paint and green shutters.[2]

Completing his land purchases, which seem to have constituted one square mile of land, Bridger signed papers on April 2, 1855, for the purchase of a piece of land from James W. Manion. Across a field, a gravestone in a private burial ground bears the legend, "J. P. Thatcher, Born May 9, 1789; Died September 9, 1853." Mrs. Hahn said Bridger's first purchase was "the Thatcher farm."

But Bridger had an appointment at Fort Laramie in two weeks.

One of the specialists employed by Sir George Gore, Henry Bostwick, recalled the salient features of the expedition, after twenty years, for F. George Heldt.[3] (Some of the details are given here:) Then about sixty years of age, Sir George collected a retinue of 40 men, and supplied them with 112 horses—some very fine ones—12 yoke of cattle, 14 dogs, 6 wagons, and 21 carts. (Marcy says that there were secretaries, stewards, cooks, fly-makers, dog-tenders, hunters, servants, etc.)[4]

In the spring of 1855, Sir George's cavalcade rolled northward into the Black Hills of Dakota. Approaching *Inyan Kara* Mountain, G. K. Warren, a later traveler, wrote: "We were near the place where Dakota Indians plundered Sir George Gore in 1855, for endeavoring to proceed through their country; and one of them was actually [in 1857] mounted on one of Gore's best horses, taken at the time. Sir George's party was only about half as numerous as mine. . . . These Indians [who blocked Warren's way] were herding the buffalo nearby, for the fur to grow enough to make robes, not killing any."[5]

After being challenged by the Dakota Indians, Sir George journeyed to the lower Powder River, the home of the buffalo.

---

[2] E. R. Schauffler, in the Kansas City *Star*, March 3, 1841.

[3] F. George Heldt and Henry Bostwick, "Sir George Gore's Hunting Expedition, 1854-56," *Contributions to the Montana Historical Society*, No. 1, 1876, pp. 128-31; see also Alter, *James Bridger*, 268-70.

[4] Marcy, *Thirty Years of Army Life*, 402.

[5] 35 Cong., 2 sess., *Serial 975* (G. K. Warren, "Explorations in Nebraska," Utah War of 1858), vol. I, 631.

Dividing his camp, Sir George stationed himself and his principal men in shelters at the mouth of Tongue River. The rest of the command, with a share of the animals, encamped about eight miles up Tongue River. Dakota's Black Hills to the east, the Big Horn Mountains to the south, and the Absaroka Range to the west were good big-bear lands, and it was a busy winter.

Indian Agent A. J. Vaughan, Fort Union, July, 1856, complained to Commissioner William Clark: "The English Gentleman [Gore] ... will return in a month or so ... having been in the Indian Country since the passport was issued by you 24th May 1854. ... He has most palpably violated it [the passport]. [With his men] forty-three in number, he built a Fort in the Crow country some 100 feet square and inhabited the same nine months, trading with the Crows. ... He and his men also state that he killed 105 bears and some 2,000 buffalo; Elk and Deer, 1,600 ... purely for sport. ... The Indians have been loud in their complaints. ... What can I do? ... Nothing, I assure you, beyond apprising you!"[6]

Bridger had reason to be doubly safe in this encampment, for on October 7, 1855, the leaders of the great Blackfoot Nation, at the behest of Governor Stevens of Washington Territory, signed a treaty of peace with the Nez Percés, the Flatheads, and the whites at the mouth of the Judith River.[7]

Sir George visited a Crow Indian village on the Rosebud River in the spring of 1856, and Bostwick remembered "several vagabond Whites residing with them." But by that time, Sir George's cup of hunting adventures was filling rapidly, and the expedition returned to the camp at the mouth of Tongue River. There Gore constructed two flatboats for himself and a few boatmen to descend the Yellowstone to Fort Union. Most of the party went by land with the wagons and teams. Lieutenant G. K. Warren says: "I made an examination of the Yellowstone River in August, 1856, and in carrying this out I was fortunate in being able to purchase the means of land transportation from Sir George Gore, who was returning from an extensive hunting excursion. ... We left the mouth of the Yellowstone July 25, and traveling leisurely up the left bank, reached a point a hundred

6 *Contributions to the Montana Historical Society*, 1940.

7 A. J. Partoll, "Blackfoot Peace Council of October 1855," *Frontier and Midland*, Spring, 1937; Historical Reprint No. 3, 3–11.

miles from the mouth, beyond which it was impossible to advance with wagons."[8]

While Gore was arranging for the construction of two Mackinaw boats at Fort Union for the Missouri River voyage, a misunderstanding arose about the terms on which the wagons and other supplies would be accepted by Culbertson, the factor. In that disagreement, the goose that was about to lay the golden egg for Culbertson, died a glorious death.

"Gore accordingly burned his wagons and all his Indian goods and supplies, in front of the Fort, guarding the flames from plundering by both Whites and Indians." In the night he threw the iron parts of the wagons and carts into the Missouri River. "His cattle and horses he sold to the vagabond hangers-on . . . or gave them away; and with his two flat-boats . . . descended the Missouri to Fort Berthold, where he wintered among the Indians, 1856–57. He departed for St. Louis by steamer in the Spring."

After seeing Sir George securely established at Fort Berthold (above Bismark, North Dakota), James Bridger proceeded by canoe downstream on the Missouri River to spend the winter with his family on the farm at Little Santa Fe.

Claiming attention here is an important note by Captain John B. Colton, who collaborated with General Dodge on the James Bridger memorial monument project in 1904. Identifying a small copy of a well-known picture (opposite p. 148) Colton writes: "Captain James Bridger. . . . Photograph taken in St. Louis in 1857. . . . His grave is at Dallas, Mo." A presentation note to General Dodge is added (in (1902?): "This I had saved for you; ever your old friend, Mrs. Virginia R. Wachsman." The original photograph may have been sponsored by Robert Campbell and by Sir George Gore. Campbell told G. K. Warren that Bridger was in the Campbell counting room about April 1, 1857.[9]

---

[8] 35 Cong., 2 sess., *Serial 975* (G. K. Warren, "Explorations in Nebraska," Utah War of 1858), vol. I, 627. (Warren had just written, "I have been fortunate in meeting with Mr. James Bridger, Mr. Alexander Culbertson, Mr. Robert Campbell, and others, well acquainted with the character of the country from personal experience, and have the assurance of the services of Mr. Bridger, if the exploration should be ordered." 621.)

[9] John B. Colton, "Inscription on Bridger's photograph," Yale University, New Haven.

The rest of the available story of Sir George Gore's extraordinary hunting expedition comes from General Randolph B. Marcy, who met Sir George in St. Louis and James Bridger at Fort Laramie, both for the first time, in 1857. Sportsman Gore told Marcy "that during his protracted hunt he had slaughtered the enormous aggregate of forty grizzly bears, twenty-five hundred buffaloes, besides numerous elk, deer, antelope and other *small* game." He had the trophies to confirm the killings.

General Marcy wrote of the two men: "Bridger, when I first met him, was . . . tall, thin, and wiry, and with a complexion well bronzed by exposure; with an independent, generous and open cast of countenance. . . . His history . . . interested me. . . . engaged for many years in trapping . . . From the headwaters of the Missouri . . . he wandered south into California, and ultimately established himself on Black's Fork. . . . Here he erected . . . Fort Bridger . . . prosecuting a profitable traffic with both the Indians and the California emigrants.

"At length, however, his prosperity excited the cupidity of the Mormons, and they intimated to him that his presence in such close proximity to their settlements, was not agreeable, and advised him to pull up stakes and leave forthwith. Upon his questioning the legality or justice of this arbitrary summons, they came to his place with a force of 'avenging angels,' and forced him to make his escape to the woods in order to save his life. He remained secreted for several days and through the assistance of his Indian wife, was enabled to elude the search of the *Danites*, and make his way to Fort Laramie, leaving all his cattle and other property in possession of the Mormons.

"From Laramie . . . he returned to the States, and laid his case before the authorities at Washington; and he was on his return, when I met him. . . . Bridger had been the guide, interpreter and companion of Sir George Gore, who possessed an income of some $200,000 per annum. . . .

"Bridger often spoke to me about Sir George Gore, and always commended him as a bold, dashing and successful sportsman, a social companion, and an agreeable gentleman.

"Sir George's habit was to sleep until about ten or eleven o'clock in the morning, when he took his bath, ate his breakfast, and set out generally alone for the day's hunt; and Bridger says it was not unusual for him to remain out until ten o'clock at night, and he seldom returned to camp without augmenting the catalogue of his exploits.

"His dinner was then ordered, to partake of which he generally extended an invitation to my friend Bridger, and after the repast was concluded, and a few glasses of wine had been drunk, he was in the habit of reading from some book, and eliciting from Bridger his comments thereon. His favorite author was Shakespeare, which Bridger 'reckin'd was a leetle too highfalutin for him'; moreover, he remarked that he 'rayther calculated that thar big Dutchman, Mr. *Full-stuff* was a leetle bit too fond of lager beer, and suggested that probably it might have been better for the old man if he had imbibed the same amount of alcohol in the more condensed medium of good old Bourbon whiskey.

"Bridger seemed deeply interested in the adventures of Baron Munchausen, but admitted, after the reading was finished that 'he be dogond ef he swallered everything that thar *Baren* Mountchawson said, and he thout he was a durned liar.' Yet, upon further reflection, he acknowledged that some of his own experiences among the Blackfeet would be equally marvelous, '*ef writ down in a book.*'

"One evening Sir George entertained his auditor by reading to him Sir Walter Scott's account of the battle of Waterloo, and afterward asked him if he did not regard that as the most sanguinary battle he had ever heard of. To which Bridger replied, 'Wall, now, Mr. Gore, that thar must 'a bin a considdible of a skrimmage, dogon my skin if it mustn't; them Britishers must 'a fit better thar than they did down to Horleans, whar Old Hickry gin um the forkedest sort of "chainlightnin'" that prehaps you ever did see in all yer born days!' And upon Sir George's expressing a little incredulity in regard to the estimate Bridger placed upon this battle, the latter added, 'You can jist go yer pile on it, Mr. Gore—*you can*, as sure as yer born.' "[10]

Vásquez, meanwhile, wasn't having much success with his new store at Salt Lake City, and in August, 1855, he sold his interests at Salt Lake City and Fort Bridger and moved his family to an eighty-acre farm in Missouri "situated between that of Jim Bridger on the south and William Bent on the north," according to his biographer Bray, "which he bought in 1852. His partnership with Bridger had

[10] Marcy, *Thirty Years of Army Life*, 400–404.

been terminated." He remained there until his death in 1868.[11]

James Bridger's differences with the Mormons, aside from the loss of his business and the loss of his property, merely placed him in a large class. The Mormons were having differences, mostly religio-political in nature, with their Indian agent, territorial secretary, courts, judges, and attorney and surveyor generals. Singularly enough, when President Buchanan appointed a replacement for Brigham Young in the office of governor of Utah Territory, Brigham Young continued as the governor of the people.

[11] Bray, "Louis Vasquez," 18.

ESCORTING the new governor of Utah and his staff were 2,500 United States Army troops, 312 wagons comprising 12 supply trains, and 3,250 oxen handled by 360 civilians. A loose herd of 800 beef cattle attracted the buffalo-hungry Cheyennes on the Platte. That is where James Bridger joined the force as guide and interpreter at five dollars a day. Lieutenant P. W. I. Plympton, quartermaster, engaged him at Fort Laramie on July 16, 1857.

Bridger had already led advance units through South Pass and returned when Captain Marcy met him at Fort Laramie, August 18, 1857. In September Bridger became guide for Colonel Alexander, the interim commander. Captain Van Vliet had been dispatched to Salt Lake City to assure Brigham Young that President Buchanan was only establishing a military department in Utah, as in other territories, and that the army was under strict orders to fight only in self-defense.

Governor Young distrusted the entire proceeding and, on September 15, 1857, issued a "Proclamation of War" forbidding entry to all armed forces and instructing his militia, of some 6,000 men, to harass and repel any invasion. The Mormon settlers at Fort Bridger and Fort Supply swept up all movable property, burned all inflammable improvements, and fled to Salt Lake City. Only a hundred-foot-square cobblestone wall, built by the Mormons, remained.

Colonel Alexander and James Bridger came up to the advance supply trains at Ham's Fork on September 30. Here they were stopped and served with Governor Young's ultimatum. It said that the army would be allowed to winter at Fort Bridger only after surrendering all arms to Louis Robison, Utah's quartermaster-general.[1]

[1] 35 Cong., 1 sess., *H.R. Ex. Doc. No. 71*, 30–35.

Colonel Alexander could only defer to his superiors and reject Governor Young's terms. It was a signal for Utah guerrillas and scouts to annoy the army's supply trains, "stampede or capture their stock; burn the wagons and supplies; blockade the roads; destroy the river crossings; and set fire to the forage." During the first week of these operations three supply trains were burned, all near the Sandies.

Bridger's intimate knowledge of the roads, the terrain, river crossings, grazing areas, and fuel and water supplies was all-important to the army leaders at that moment. A conference of officers was held October 10–11, 1857, at which Bridger recommended Bitter Creek, Henry's Fork, and intervening areas as suitable for grazing. Army headquarters were established at Camp Scott, chosen by Bridger, near the ruins of Fort Bridger on November 2, 1857. Bridger was then dispatched eastward to accompany the new permanent commander, Colonel Albert Sidney Johnston. Transferred to Captain Dickerson, Bridger was nevertheless kept in the Colonel's mess at five dollars a day.

Having made five trips during the season, Bridger had seen the forage dwindle, and now the winter was on in earnest. Naturally, he was "relentless in pronouncing there was no grass . . . but promised grass and shelter two miles farther."[2] More than half of the horses were lost from starvation and freezing, and problems mounted.

General Fitz-John Porter says: "Near the Rocky Mountains, snowstorms began to overtake us, but Bridger, the faithful and experienced guide, ever on the alert, would point in time to the 'Snowboats,' which, like balloons sailing from the snow-capped mountains, warned us of storms; and would hasten to a good and early camp in time for shelter before the tempest broke upon us. At South Pass a cold and driving snowstorm barred progress for a few days, but permitted the gathering of trains, which assured protection."[3]

William Drown, chief bugler, wrote from Ham's Fork on November 3, 1857: "Our old guide has received a regular appointment this evening from Colonel Johnston, as principal guide through Utah; and is to rank as Major. As I am not in the humor of sleeping this evening, I will try and give a short description of this Mr. or Major Bridger, as he is now called.

[2] *Ibid.*, 96–97.

[3] W. P. Johnston, *Life of General Albert Sidney Johnston.*

"He is a man about fifty-five years of age, about six feet in height; has been a quite stout, powerful man, although he is now quite thin, and has the appearance of a man who has been through considerable hardship. . . . He established a trading house, where he realized a considerable fortune, trading with the Utahs and other Indians. . . . A few years after the Mormons established themselves near Salt Lake, they came to him and gave him his choice—to receive from them $8,000 for his place here, leaving all his cattle and everything as it was, or to be forced to leave, although the stock he had here at the time was well worth the amount proffered. . . . He is allowed by all Mountaineers to be the best and most experienced guide in the country."[4]

From the center of the controversy, as if to cultivate an ally, Governor Brigham Young wrote to his official superior, the Honorable James W. Denver, commissioner of Indian affairs, in Washington, D. C., one of the briefest and best sermons ever delivered on Indian management: "I have proven that it is far cheaper to feed and clothe the Indians than to fight them." But the axiom contained a boomerang.

Commissioner Denver wrote to Brigham Young on November 11, 1857: "This department has information from reliable sources, that, so far from encouraging amicable relations between the Indians and the people of the United States, outside of your own immediate community, you have studiously endeavored to impress on the minds of the Indians that there was a difference between your own sect, usually known as Mormons, and the Government and other citizens of the United States—that the former were their friends, and the latter their enemies."

Concerning delays, disallowances of voucher payments, and gifts to the Indians, Denver concluded: "It could never have been intended by Congress, that the money should be used in arousing the savages to war against our own citizens."[5]

James Bridger, for himself and Louis Vásquez, and John H. Dickerson, for the government, signed "Articles of Agreement" on November 18, 1857, providing for a ten-year lease of the Fort Bridger land, as described in the Hockaday survey and plat. The govern-

4 Theophilus F. Rodenbaugh, *From Everglade to Canyon*, 204.
5 35 Cong., 1 sess., *H.R. Ex. Doc. No. 71*, 185–86.

ment would pay $600 a year, payments to commence when Bridger could establish his title. Any buildings remaining would go to Bridger, while the government would have the right, at any time, to purchase the land for $10,000.

In transmitting the lease, Dickerson said, Bridger "bases his claim to the land on some Mexican or Spanish law, similar to the pre-emption laws of the United States. I think it exceedingly doubtful whether his title is good."[6]

Captain Marcy was dispatched to Fort Massachusetts (in south-eastern Colorado), on November 24, 1857, for animals, men, and foodstuffs. His party consisted of 40 enlisted men, 20 mountaineers, and 120 pack and riding animals, in case the Mormons intercepted them. Many chose to go with Marcy rather than stay at Fort Bridger. Quite a few men at Camp Scott were on sick report because of frost-bite, caused by their wearing common leather shoes when they should have had warm, buffalo overshoes such as the mountaineers wore.

William A. Carter wrote to his wife on November 26, 1857, that Bridger was "remarkable for his intimate knowledge of all the country. . . . At first his conversation was very interesting, but I soon became wearied by his excessive egotism. He tells wonderful stories of fights with Indians, etc. . . . thinks himself entitled to credit for all explorations west of Missouri." Robert S. Ellison concludes that Carter soured on Bridger because of the ridiculous "Arkansas traveler tales" Bridger told the pestering army privates.[7]

During the late autumn and early spring of 1857-58, half a dozen engineer units traveled, examined, or improved all or parts of the proposed route from the forks of the Platte (Nebraska), along Lodge Pole Creek, Cheyenne Pass, Laramie Plains, Bridger's Pass, and Bitter Creek to Fort Bridger. Nearly all the leaders conferred with Bridger before making the reconnaissance or making their reports. The route was sixty or seventy-five miles shorter and the crest elevation about five hundred feet lower, but the final decision was against it because of the scarcity of water and forage.

General Johnston reported to Washington, April 22, 1858: "The

[6] 52 Cong., 1 sess., *Senate Report No. 625* (Fort Bridger Lease. Reproduced in Alter, *James Bridger*, 298-99).

[7] Robert S. Ellison, *Fort Bridger*, 67-68.

Editor of the *Deseret News* [Salt Lake City], makes to inflame the people against the Army, and more directly against me. Indian Agent [Garland] Hurt writes and sends affidavits that contain a refutation of the charges, and show that persons among them, by their own improper conduct, have brought the hostilities they complain of upon themselves."

An investigating committee composed of W. M. F. Magraw and James Bridger reported by letter on April 28, 1858, to Major Fitz-John Porter: "The *Deseret News*, April 14, 1858, charged Col. A. S. Johnston, Commander of this Army, with having incited the Utah and Pannack Indians against the Mormons, through Dr. Hurt and B. F. Ficklin, respectively.

"We know that such has not been the policy of Col. Johnston toward the Indians. As early as October, 1857, he sought and obtained through one of us [Magraw] an interview with Wash-a-kee, the principal chief of the Shoshones; the other [Bridger] acting as interpreter. On this occasion Col. Johnston desired Wash-a-kee to go with his people [Indians] to the buffalo and procure food and clothing, and not connect himself and people with the difficulties that existed between the Government and the Mormons.

"Wash-a-kee complained bitterly of the wrongs which had been perpetrated on his people by the Mormons, charging them with taking their lands from them, and driving their friends from the ferries on Green River. He also charged the Mormons with constantly attempting to prejudice him and his people against the government and all persons who were not Mormons; and that when Brigham Young sent them any presents they always told them that they were gifts of the Mormons.

"He [Wash-a-kee] spent one night in Colonel Johnston's Camp, and was accompanied by one of us [Bridger] to Fort Thompson, situated on the Popo Agie, one of the tributaries of Wind River, where he joined his people, and started in a few days in pursuit of the buffalo, and has not been seen since.

"We feel free to say, that if Colonel Johnston had given Wash-a-kee the least encouragement he would have at once commenced open hostilities against the Mormons. . . . About the 13th of March, 1858, we met in Col. Johnston's quarters, Ben Simons, Delaware Indian, and Little Soldier, a sub-chief of the Shoshones, with twenty of their men. We were present during the entire interview, about two hours. "They complained of the wrongs done by the Mormons, and related inducements held out by the Mormons, to form an alliance with them against the Government, offering a full share of the spoils, if they would assist in capturing supply trains intended for the Army in the spring. Colonel Johnston advised them to have nothing to do with existing difficulties; that the Great Father did not wish them to connect themselves in any way with this Mormon trouble. . . .

"Colonel Johnston's conduct, and his policy, as expressed to us on more than one occasion, forbids even the supposition that he is in any way, guilty of the charge complained of by the Mormons."[8]

Captain Gove wrote in June, 1858: "General [Albert Sidney] Johnston has the following gentlemen in his mess: Major Fitz-John Porter . . . Captain John Newton . . . Lt. L. L. Rich, and Mr. Bridger, a guide. . . . Old Mr. Bridger is quite a modest and retiring man, but will sometimes, like all mountaineers, tell a story."[9]

Captain Marcy returned on June 9, 1858, with five companies of infantry and mounted riflemen and 1,500 pack and riding animals. The army set out for Salt Lake City on June 13. In camp on Bear River (Evanston), Colonel Johnston reported to headquarters on June 16; "Captain Newton, of the Engineer Corps, was detached yesterday, with an escort of an officer and thirty men, and the most experienced Guide of the mountains, James Bridger, to examine thoroughly the country from this point."

Captain Newton's report, dated July 17, 1858, indicates that he and Bridger rambled along the ridge routes examining prospective wagon roads from the head of Yellow Creek (Duck-Saleratus). They inspected Pumbar's (Lost Creek), the rimlands of Ogden Hole, and Cache Valley and its passageways eastward, particularly Blacksmith's Fork–Big Creek (to Randolph, Utah). Returning through Ogden Hole, they proceeded up Bauchanin's Fork (East Canyon), rejoining the army in Emigration Canyon and entering Salt Lake City after ten days' travel of 222 miles (by pedometer). Captain Newton's report is strewn with such phrases as: "This

8 35 Cong., 2 sess., *Serial 975* ("The Utah War of 1858"), vol. I, 82–84.
9 Jesse A. Gove, *The Utah Expedition,* 273–74.

Canyon is reported by my guide to be very bad for two miles; after that for nine miles, the sides of the canyon flare into gentle hills."[10]

The army marched in funereal solemnity through the empty streets of Salt Lake City on June 26, 1858. Brigham Young was not there to welcome or good speed them. As an amazing gesture of disapproval, he had ordered the Mormons of northern Utah to move south at least as far as Utah County (Provo), leaving their cities and communities largely depopulated. The troops camped by the Jordan River (Salt Lake City). They then moved to Camp Floyd. The site, designated by Brigham Young and accepted by the army, lay thirty-six miles south and was not occupied by Mormons. The mobile Mormons then returned to their homes, crops, and occupations.

James Bridger's discharge as guide was dated July 20, 1858, from Camp Floyd, Utah. He started at once on the long, lonesome journey home to his family and farm at Little Santa Fe, Missouri.

He was returning almost empty-handed. The buildings and fences at Fort Bridger had been burned; the livestock and loose property had been confiscated; he had no established homestead right to the land; his wages had been paid and sent home; and it looked as if the door to the Rocky Mountains was closing to him forever.

We find no record of an accounting for the business done at Fort Bridger, at the ferries, at the roadside stands, or at the Salt Lake City store, and no record of payment or settlement between Bridger and Vásquez. All the bookkeeping was, of course, done by Vásquez, as only he could write.

These were not Bridger's only sorrows. At Little Santa Fe a new son, William, born October 10, 1857, was held out to him by strange hands. The family had but recently been deprived of a mother, and the Old Scout made a widower for the third time. In the ensuing adjustment, Mr. and Mrs. George London were engaged as housekeepers in the big house to care for the three children. Presumably they would also attend to the share-cropping of the arable land.

[10] 35 Cong., 2 sess., *Serial 975* ("The Utah War of 1858"), vol. I, 202–206.

AS CHIEF TRADER at Fort Bridger, Louis Vásquez may have neglected business more than he attended to it. His emigrant roadside
stands in midsummer and his temporary store in Salt Lake City were
worthy attempts to increase the trade and to prolong the trading
season. James Bridger wrote Pierre Chouteau on December 10,
1843, that Vásquez was by mutual consent the Fort Bridger trader,
though no traveler "noticed" Vásquez there in 1845, 1846, 1849,
or thereafter.

There may have been a reason. Sublette and Campbell sued
Vásquez's company in 1842 for a merchandise indebtedness of
$2,751.77 and, after much leniency, foreclosed on a fractional
eighty- acre tract of land near St. Louis in 1845.[1] In December, 1843,
as one businessman to another, William Laidlaw wrote disparagingly
to Chouteau of Vásquez's drinking and neglect of business. On that
occasion Bridger also mentioned it, saying he was sorry, for he
realized it might affect the credit which the firm of Bridger and
Vásquez was seeking.

Passing over the hiatus of Vásquez's nine-year absence from the
fort, we chance upon him in a visit to Salt Lake City. A special cor-
respondent in Great Salt Lake City for the San Francisco *Daily
Evening Bulletin* mailed a report, dated October 11, 1858, and published October 29, 1858, part of which follows:

"I have had the pleasure of meeting, during the past week, Major
Vasquez, the oldest mountaineer in this country, and the discoverer
of Great Salt Lake. He first entered this valley 36 years ago. In the
fall of 1822, he, with a company of trappers, arrived in Cache Valley,
where they determined to spend the winter, and trap in the numerous streams with which it abounds. The winter, however, became

[1] Sunder, *Bill Sublette*, 158.

so severe—the snow falling to the depth of 8 feet—they found it necessary to hunt out a better valley in order to save their animals.

"Accordingly, Major Vasquez, with one or two of his party, started out, and crossing the divide, entered this valley, and discovered Great Salt Lake. This they at first took to be an arm of the Pacific Ocean. They found the valley free from snow, and well filled with herds of buffalo. Returning to their party, they guided them over into this valley, when they divided—one party, under Weber, wintering on the river which now bears his name; the other party wintering on Bear River, near its mouth.

"The following spring Vasquez built a boat, and circumnavigated this sheet of brine, for the purpose of finding out definitely, whether it was an arm of the sea or not, and thus discovered that it was in reality merely a large inland lake, without an outlet. Since that time the lake has been gradually receding.

"Mr. John Owens, of Fort Owens, in the Bitter-root Valley, Washington Territory [now Montana] and Indian Agent for the Flathead tribe of Indians in that valley, is also on a visit to this city, purchasing goods for his agency."[2]

From that dispatch comes quite an array of misinformation and the one fact that Vásquez was "on a visit." Noting the generosity with which he shares the discovery and subsequent exploration of Great Salt Lake, we may be ready for his sale of the "Brooklyn Bridge," that is, Fort Bridger.

The Mormon church historians, from evidence satisfactory to them, made the following entry in the manuscript "Journal History," under date of October 18, 1858 (including documents dated 1855): "Louis Vasquez of the firm of Bridger and Vasquez, executed a bill of sale of Fort Bridger and acknowledged receipt of $4,000 on August 3, 1855, and $4,000 this day—also acknowledged before Samuel A. Gilbert, Clerk of 3rd District Court, that Hiram F. Morrell, was his lawfully appointed Agent and that he fully approved of the acts and doings of said Morrell in the sale of said property."

Joseph H. Porath, of Salt Lake City, found this document at the Salt Lake County Recorder's office in Records Book "B" (page 128).

Sale of Fort Bridger: Fort Bridger, Utah Territory, Green River

[2] Bancroft Library, Berkeley, California, kindly furnished a photostat.

County, August 3, 1855. This indenture, made and entered into, this day and date above written, witnesseth that Bridger and Vasquez, of the first part, for and in the consideration of the sum of Eight thousand dollars, one-half in hand paid, and the other half to be paid in fifteen months from this date, have this day, bargained, sold and conveyed, and by these presents do bargain, sell and convey to Lewis Robison, of the second part, all the right title and interest, both real and personal, to which we have any claim in said Green River County, Utah Territory, consisting of the following property—To wit—Twenty miles square of land (more or less), upon which is situated the hereditaments and appurtenances, the buildings known as Fort Bridger Buildings, consisting of the Ranch and Herd ground, together with all the right, title and interest of the said property of the first part to all and every article of property belonging to said post including cattle, horses, goods, groceries, etc.—

Now if the said party of the second part shall well and truly pay to the said party of the first part the sum of four thousand dollars in fifteen months from this date, then this bond to be in full force and effect in law; otherwise to be null and void, and the property above described to revert back to the said party of the first part.

In witness whereof we have hereunto set our hands and seals this day and date above written
in the presence of

Almerin Grow, and
Wm. A. Hickman.

Recorded October 21, 1858

his
Jas X Brdger
mark
Louis Vasquez,
per *H. F. Morrell,* Agent

Strangely enough, Mr. Porath found another "Sale of Fort Bridger," dated three years later, in the same Records Book B (125–27):

This indenture, made the eighteenth day of October, in the year one thousand eight hundred and fifty-eight, between Louis Vasquez, of the city of St. Louis in the state of Missouri, of the firm of Bridger and Vasquez, (formerly of the County of Green River and Territory of Utah), of the first part; and Lewis Robison of the City of Great Salt Lake and Territory of Utah, (Formerly of Green River County, in the Territory of Utah), of the second part—

Witnesseth that: For and in consideration of the sum of Four Thousand Dollars, lawful money of the United States, in hand paid to

275

the party of the First Part by the party of the Second Part, at or before the ensealing and delivery of these presents, and for and in further consideration of the sum of Four Thousand Dollars, which the party of the First Part, acknowledges to have been paid in lawful money of the United States, at Fort Bridger, in Green River County, and Territory of Utah, on the third day of August, one thousand, eight hundred and fifty-five to James Bridger, then acting as his full and lawful Agent, and partnership owner with him in the property personal and real, and claims to lands and improvements hereinafter mentioned, by the above named party of the Second Part, the receipt of which sums (Eight Thousand Dollars) is hereby acknowledged; said party of the First Part hath remised, released, conveyed and forever quit-claimed, and by these presents doth remise, release, convey and forever quit-claim,—and doth hereby further, fully endorse the acts and doings of the aforesaid James Bridger, his partner and Agent, in the transfer and quit-claim by him made in an Indenture bearing date at Green River County, in the Territory of Utah, the Third day of August, one thousand, eight hundred and fifty-five (which Indenture is hereby made a part of this and attached thereto) to all the right, title and interest, both real and personal by him claimed individually, and for the firm of Bridger and Vasquez, in the County of Green River and Territory of Utah, consisting of the following, to wit:

Twenty miles square of land more or less, in which is included the plat of land surveyed by John M. Hockaday on the sixth day of November, one thousand eight hundred and fifty-three (the plat of survey of which are hereby made a part of this indenture), together with all and singular the tenements, hereditaments, and appurtenances thereunto belonging or in anywise appertaining; also the building known as Fort Bridger, situated on said plat of land, together with all and every article of property belonging to said Fort, and claimed by the aforesaid firm of Bridger & Vasquez, including cattle, horses, groceries, drygoods, and the reversion, and reversions, remainder and remainders rents, issues and profits thereof; and also all the estate right, title, interest, property, possession, claim and demand whatsoever, as well in law as in equity, of the said party of the first part, as well as the said firm of Bridger & Vasquez, of, in, or to the above described premises, and every part and parcel thereof, with the appurtenances, to the aforesaid party of the Second Part, and to his heirs and assigns forever.

To have and to hold all and singular, the above mentioned and described premises, together with the appurtenances, unto the said party of the Second Part, his heirs and assigns forever, and to warrant and defend the same against all claims of the said Party of the First Part, or the said firm of Bridger & Vasquez, and of the heirs or assigns of either or both of the parties of said firm forever.

In witness whereof, the said Party of the First Part hath hereunto set his hand and seal the day and year first above written.

> *Louis Vasquez*
> *Bridger & Vasquez*
> *Per Louis Vasquez.*

Territory of Utah,　　　)
County of Great Salt Lake) SS

Personally appeared before me, Samuel A. Gilbert, Clerk of the United States Court, for the Third Judicial District of Utah Territory, Louis Vasquez, who, being duly sworn, says that: Hiram F. Morrell was his lawfully appointed Agent, and as such was authorized to sign the indenture referred to in the indenture hereto attached and bearing this date; and that he, the deponeth, doth fully approve of the acts and doings of the said Morrell in the above premises as if done by himself in his own proper person.

Deponent further says that he is duly authorized to act for and in behalf of James Bridger, aforesaid, and for him to sign the preceding indenture.

> *Louis Vasquez*

In testimony whereof I have hereunto set my hand and seal of Court at Great Salt Lake City, in the Territory and County above named, this eighteenth day of October, one thousand eight hundred and fifty-eight.

> *Samuel A. Gilbert*, Clerk.

Recorded October 21, 1858.

Territory of Utah　　　)
Great Salt Lake County) SS.

Personally appeared before me, Samuel A. Gilbert, Clerk of the United States Court, for the Third Judicial District of Utah, Louis Vasquez whose name appears to the above conveyance, for himself and as the agent of Bridger & Vasquez, and acknowledged the same to be his free act and deed, and that he executed it for the purposes therein mentioned. He also acknowledged that the erasure of the word "Formerly" in the fourth line from the top, and its insertion in the

fifth line, was done by mutual consent of the parties to the instrument.
In testimony whereof I have hereunto set my hand and affixed my official seal at Great Salt Lake City, this, the twentieth day of October, A. D. 1858.

Samuel A. Gilbert, Clerk

Although the 1855 document was not recorded until 1858, the spirit of confirmation is furnished from the Mormon church business letter file:

Great Salt Lake City,
August 9, 1855

Louis Robinson, Esqr.
Dear Brother: . . . We are glad the purchase is made. You are right, also, in remaining while Brother Butler is absent putting up hay. . . . [A list of supplies being sent, to be sold at the fort]. . . . The account is open with Bridges Ranch [*sic*].

All flour in small quantities for twenty-five cents per lb. Sell beef, when you can, to trains at a high price, say 10 or 12½ cents;. . . . I do not see any way for you . . . than to stay there a good share of the time for the present, to make it as profitable as possible.

Signed: *Brigham Young*
D. H. Wells

In the same letter file is a letter from Heber C. Kimball to Franklin D. Richards: "The Church have bought out Bridger's Ranch, and one hundred head of horned cattle, some 7 or 8 horses, some flour, and goods that he had, and paid $8,000 for it, and Bridger is gone."

From John Pulsipher's unpublished diary: "Tuesday, September 14, 1855: I went down to Fort Bridger on business, and to see our new neighbor, Lewis Robison, who has bot the old mountaineer's claim for the Church, and he is to take charge of it."[3]

Hiram Vásquez, stepson of Louis and twelve years of age at the time of the sale, often spoke in later years of the pile of gold (coins?) on the table at Fort Bridger. It appears also that about July 3, 1878, twenty years later, Louis Robison and an attorney visited Fort Bridger and made formal demand of William A. Carter, resident,

[3] Jerry F. Twitchell, "The Latter-day Saints History of Bridger Valley," 41–42.

for the Fort Bridger premises. They requested Carter to transmit the demand to Washington, but he did not comply.[4]

Judge Carter wrote, in 1878, that after Johnston's army left only a small command at Fort Bridger in 1858, Louis Vásquez reached Fort Bridger in September with a wagon train of United States Army freight. Vásquez had a sub-contract with Russell, Majors and Waddell. He stopped at Carter's place while unloading some of the freight, and Carter purchased the empty wagons from Vásquez.

Carter's manuscript says that Vásquez had with him copies of Hockaday's plat of Fort Bridger grounds and Dickerson's lease from James Bridger, and that he intended to complete the sale and obtain the second $4,000 when he reached Salt Lake City. When Vásquez returned, he informed Carter that he had the money and had transferred the army contract to Brigham Young.

Andrew Jenson, assistant church historian, reviewing the history of Fort Supply, states that Governor Alfred Cumming at one time attempted to restore Fort Bridger "to the citizens who had been dispossessed," but was unsuccessful.[5]

Finally, William A. Hickman wrote: Fort Bridger "was then, [1857] and had been for two years, owned by the Church . . . and in possession of Mr. Robison, who had charge of the same from the time of its purchase, I having been one of the carriers of the heavy load of gold it took to purchase said place, with the stock and goods thereon [$4,000 in gold coins would weigh nearly sixteen pounds]."[6]

Bridger, on the way home from Camp Floyd to Little Santa Fe, should have met Vásquez and his freighting train in the neighborhood of Fort Laramie if Judge Carter's dates are correct.

James Bridger was with Sir George Gore on a hunting expedition on August 3, 1855, and did not sign the sale agreement. Vásquez is said to have had Bridger's authority to affix Bridger's signature. That power of attorney should have been shown by a document. If Vásquez signed for Bridger, why did he imitate "His X Mark"? Why did he misspell both of Bridger's names in the signature but not in

[4] Ellison, *Fort Bridger*, 34.

[5] Andrew Jenson, "History of Fort Bridger and Fort Supply," *Utah Genealogical Magazine*, January, 1913, 39.

[6] Hickman, *Brigham's Destroying Angel*, 118.

the document? Why did Morrell sign for Vásquez? Who are: "*We who have hereunto set our hands and seals*"? In this strange document Vásquez acknowledges receipt of $4,000 paid to James Bridger. And Vásquez does "fully endorse the acts and doings of the aforesaid James Bridger," though the evidence is that James Bridger did not fully endorse the acts of Louis Vásquez.

On the face of it, the document would appear to have been signed only by Morrell for all three signers. The *ex post facto* delegating of authority bears some analogy to an overdraft at the bank; the lenient banker will avoid the uglier name for it. According to the document the property is to revert if the second four thousand dollars is not paid by November 3, 1856. The payment was not made; yet there was no penalty, no explanation, for this violation. If Louis Robison was acting for the church and not for himself, he should have had proper documentation to avoid another transfer. "Twenty miles square of land" is four hundred square miles, but the Hockaday survey for Bridger calls for only six square miles. Warranty deeds are not usually so inexact, nor do they include "every article of property," unspecified and undescribed.

The October 18, 1858, "Sale" purports to describe the same property as the sale of August 3, 1855; yet the later description is far too involved and pedantic for clarity. One of the witnesses, William A. Hickman, said he was studying law. One may suspect some student was "practicing" law in preparing that wordy instrument.

As they stand, these documents and the transaction as effected are not even up to frontier standards, and by no means are they in accord with the usual Mormon standards of integrity and quality. The only conclusion possible is that both Bridger and the church were imposed upon by men who were being trusted more than they deserved.

There is ample evidence, much of it in these pages, to indicate that Bridger had no knowledge of the sale of Fort Bridger. The only inkling he ever had was in 1853, when Mormon bouncers sought to oust him for illicit trade with the Indians. He told William Drown in November, 1857, that he had refused $8,000 and was forced out as an alternative.

Every vestige of authentic contemporary firsthand information about James Bridger, whether good, bad, or indifferent, has been faithfully presented herein. From this collection of facts and characterizations, it is very difficult to charge him with duplicity or dishonesty in his dealings with the Indians or the Mormons.

Long afterward Bridger's heirs were awarded $6,000 for the improvements at Fort Bridger which the Mormons burned when the army approached in 1857. The amount seems reasonable in view of the time elapsed before payment.

Heading the Utah officers who forced Bridger into hiding from his fort was William A. Hickman, who also "witnessed" the transaction of the "buying" of the fort by the church in 1855, and who participated in the delivery of the cash to Vásquez. Hickman and Bridger were none too friendly afterward. Hickman apostatized a little later and became aggressively hostile to the church in many vexing ways.

WHEN THE ARMY projected the exploration of "the headwaters of the Yellowstone and Missouri rivers, and of the mountains in which they rise," it was inevitable that Captain William F. Raynolds, commander, should interview Pierre Chouteau and Company, leading outfitters to mountaineers, and that James Bridger should be employed not only as the "best guide available," but as the "best guide" period.

The official order provided for seven scientists, such as astronomer, topographer, geologist, meterologist, botanist and naturalist, and a guide, each of the eight to be paid $125 a month and "found." There were also a military escort of thirty infantrymen, under a lieutenant, and a party of seven Congressional guests.[1]

Leaving St. Louis, May 28, 1859, they moved up the Missouri River by steamer with annuities for the Indians and supplies for the fur men. The boat was heavily loaded after taking on the escort, with its herd of draft mules, many packs, carts, wagons, and supplies, at Fort Randall. The sojourn at Fort Pierre, June 18–28, allowed Raynolds to organize the overland caravan and to consign supplies, by steamer, to the upper Yellowstone River.

A local Sioux Indian guide was employed to accompany Raynolds to the Black Hills, the boundary between the Sioux and Crow Indians. There, on the north slope of the Black Hills, Raynolds wrote that on July 20, "our guide was missing," together with a mule, bridle, and saddle. He was afraid of the Crows, who were enemies.

For the first time Raynolds writes the name: "Bridger and some of the soldiers . . . returned, having killed three [buffalo] cows each." July 21, 1859: "My American Guide, Bridger, is now on familiar

[1] Raynolds, *Exploration of the Yellowstone* (dated daily journal).

ground and appears to be entirely at home in this [Little Missouri–Powder River] country."

There is no intimation or likelihood that Bridger discovered gold at this time around here, as implied by Colorado's historian, Frank Hall, and others.

July 23: "Our Guide, Bridger, favored following the bank, but gullies forced the wagons to follow the ridges." Buffalo stampeded a "six mule team." On July 25, 1859, scarcity of forage put them "to hewing down cottonwood trees and allowing the animals to feed on the bark. . . . Bridger asserts that, in case of necessity, animals can be subsisted on this bark an entire winter."

July 31, 1859: Lieutenant Maynadier, with the heavy wagons, and Lieutenant Smith, with the escort wagons, traveled down Powder River until "Bridger declares it will be impossible to follow it much farther. . . . I have almost determined to accept Bridger's advice, and strike across the country for Fort Sarpy," eighteen miles below the Big Horn on the Yellowstone, to meet the supplies.

August 1: "After reaching camp, Bridger started in search of a route . . . towards Tongue River. . . . Bridger returned late at night after a six hours ride, and makes a rather discouraging report; but thinks we can cross the Mizpah." August 5: "The stream upon which we are encamped is called by Bridger Pumpkin Creek . . . from a species of wild gourd . . . on its banks. . . . The point of junction of Tongue River and the Yellowstone was pointed out by Bridger . . . twelve or fifteen miles distant.

"Bridger now advises that we travel up Tongue River some distance, before crossing. . . . This is not in accordance with my preconceived plan, but I shall accept his advice out of deference to his remarkable knowledge of the country." August 8: "Bridger calls it the Canyon of Tongue River." August 9: "The ravines on each side of us were impassable, and the selection of the road proved Bridger's excellence as a guide."

August 10: "After reaching camp, Bridger examined the country to the west . . . and reports a good road." August 11: "Bridger calls the stream we are now on, Emmel's Fork." August 13: "Mr. Hutton, with the guide and interpreter . . . left camp at an early hour . . . in the afternoon the party returned. . . . Years have elapsed since our

Guide passed through this special region; and he has forgotten some of its minutiae, though he seems perfectly familiar with its general features." Fort Sarpy had been erected at a new site since he was there.

August 23: Bridger's old friend, Robert Meldrum, in charge of Fort Sarpy, came into camp and spent the afternoon and evening in conversations. August 24: "Six wagons started this morning" to meet the supply boats; they returned next day. August 29: the party gathered into Fort Sarpy.

"The Fort is an inclosure about one hundred feet square, of upright cottonwood logs fifteen feet high, the outer wall also forming the exterior of a row of log cabins which are occupied as dwelling houses, store houses, shops and stables. The roofs of these structures are nearly flat, and formed of timber, covered to the depth of about a foot with dirt. . . . The entrance is through a heavy gate."

Leaving Fort Sarpy August 31, Raynolds turned up the Big Horn on September 2; "the Guide states that the best route . . . is on the west side." September 6: Near the Little Horn "a herd of buffalo was discovered and Bridger's skill with the rifle added two cows to our larder." Crossing to the east side, they came to a small stream "which Bridger, who seems to know every square mile of this section, calls Grass Creek." Raynolds added later, "We found it entitled to the name!" He also noted that "the trappers' names for most places are translations of the Indian titles, which Bridger pronounces readily."

Above Soap Creek the Big Horn "is large, deep and nearly three hundred feet in width. . . . Its remarkable canyon is famous throughout the west. . . . It was decided to visit this natural curiosity. . . . The Canyon is one of the most remarkable sights on the continent. The River here narrows to a width of less than one hundred and fifty feet, and bursts out through reddish tinted walls of perpendicular rock over three hundred feet in height. Bridger claims to have descended the lower Canyon of the Big Horn some years since on a raft, during his service as a trapper."

September 9: After camping up Soap Creek, Raynolds noticed a huge elk in a thicket. Bridger went for the elk. About dark he returned, having shot the animal about a mile from camp, saying it was one of the largest elk he had seen. The head and horns were removed so the carcass could fit in a cart.

September 11: "Dr. Hayden and Mr. Snowden wished to visit a bluff . . . but as Bridger was very decided as to the danger of parties going abroad alone . . . the project was abandoned." September 12: "Bears are very numerous"; a dozen had been seen, "and one, a yearling cub, was brought down by Bridger's rifle." September 13: "While Bridger was in advance of the train today he discovered five or six Indians . . . in the distance, apparently watching our march" and trying to steal animals or articles.

Septmber 14: Crossed Tongue River, forty feet wide and one foot deep. They passed De Smet Lake, a small pond three or four miles long, apparently without an outlet; "Bridger and Meldrum agree in saying it has none." September 22: "A thick fog closed around us, shutting off all view" and embarrassing travel. "Our Guide, however, did not falter but pointed out our course with every mark of complete confidence."

September 26, 1859, near Middle Fork of Powder River: "Bridger and myself turned our faces downstream [present Kaycee area]. . . . After a ride of fifteen miles we came to the ruins of some old trading posts, known as the Portuguese Houses. . . . Erected many years ago by a Portuguese trader named Antonio Mateo [Montaro]. . . . Only one side of the pickets remains standing. . . . Bridger recounted a tradition that at one time this post was besieged by the Sioux for forty days."[2]

September 27, 1859, in camp: "Bridger made a short excursion . . . to select a route. . . . Unfavorable. . . . But as he strenuously insists, I shall follow his advice." Smith, Hayden, Bridger, and Stephenson went downstream in quest of Maynadier on the twenty-eighth and returned on the thirtieth without him. October 1: "We left for the Platte . . . the Guide claiming he knows the country perfectly."

October 3, 1859: An area impassably rocky, rough, and cut with deep ravines; "as Bridger says we shall not find water for nearly ten miles I ordered" camp. October 4: Boulders, which originally strewed the trail, "had been carefully and systematically piled in low pyramids on the side, leaving a road of comparative excellence.

[2] Irving, *Captain Bonneville*, 365–66, and note.

Bridger claims, however, that . . . no Indian would have been guilty of such a sensible work." October 10: "The soil covered . . . several inches with a white salt, or, as Bridger calls it: 'Alkali.' "

October 11, 1859, they reached Platte River near the Red Buttes. "I had, in my ignorance, asked Bridger if there was any danger of crossing the [Overland Stage] road without knowing it. I now understand fully his surprise, as it is as marked as any turnpike in the East." Turning eastward on this "turnpike" past Richards' Trading Post at Platte Bridge (west edge of present Casper, Wyoming), Raynolds' party settled for the winter with Major Twiss, Indian agent, on Deer Creek. They made use of some unfinished huts abandoned by the Mormons fleeing Johnston's army.

Frequent way stations on the much-used road and a growing settlement at Fort Laramie provided contacts with civilization. Short expeditions of inquiry, formal interviews with Indian claimants or residents, and the daily care of the draft and riding mules and horses were necessary tasks. "The Pony Express was established while we were in winter quarters, and by it we several times received interesting items of news but three days old."

Artist-meterologist Schonborn measured and melted the snow that fell from December to March, an exceptional amount, though temperatures and winds were not severe. Thus there was time to talk about the weather and themselves. The frequent clashes among the military men resulted in an entirely new escort for the worst of the expedition, which was yet to come. For the mountaineers the winter was a usual routine.

"From all I hear," wrote Raynolds, "I conclude, in the palmy days of the fur trade . . . the trappers . . . were little more than white Indians, having Indian wives, and all the paraphernalia of Indian life, moving from place to place . . . and subsisting, like the Indians, upon the products of the country.

"Bridger says that at one time he did not taste bread for seventeen years.

"Is it surprising, that men leading such a life . . . should beguile the monotony of camp life by spinning yarns, in which each one tries to excel the others? Some of the Munchausen tales stuck me as too good to be lost.[3]

[3] Raynolds, *Exploration of the Yellowstone*, 76–77.

"One was to this effect: In parts of the country petrifactions and fossils are numerous. As a consequence, in a certain locality, a large tract of sage is petrified, its leaves and branches all stone, while the rabbits and sage hens are still there, all perfectly petrified. . . . More wonderful still, these petrified bushes bear diamonds, rubies, sapphires and emeralds, some as large as walnuts.

"Another story: A party of whites was pursued by Indians; the enemy being so close the whites were forced to hide during the day and travel only at night; but in this they were aided by a huge diamond on the face of a neighboring mountain, by the light of which they traveled for three nights.

"I will end these specimen tales by one from Bridger, which partakes so decidedly of a scientific nature, that it should not be omitted. He contends that near the headwaters of the Columbian River [tributary of Lewis or Snake], in the fastnesses of the mountains, there is a spring gushing forth from the rocks near the top of the mountain. The water when it issues forth is cold as ice, but it runs down over the smooth rock so far and so fast that it is *hot at the bottom!*"[4]

Defending Bridger, Nathaniel P. Langford wrote on September 19, 1870: "I forded Firehole River a short distance below our camp. . . . Taking off our boots and stockings, we selected for our place of crossing what seemed to be a smooth rock surface in the bottom of the stream, extending from shore to shore. When I reached the middle of the stream I paused a moment and turned around to speak to Mr. Hodges, who was about to enter the stream, when I discovered from the sensation of warmth under my feet, I was standing upon an incrustation formed over a hot spring, that had its vent in the bed of the stream. I exclaimed to Hodges: 'Here is the River which Bridger said was *hot at* the bottom!' "[5]

4 *Ibid.*, 77. This quotation is partially paraphrased.
5 Nathaniel P. Langford, *Discovery of Yellowstone Park*, 174–75.

JAMES BRIDGER'S advice often became Captain Raynolds' order. "Early in March . . . I knew that it would be necessary to take all our supplies in packs, as it would be impossible for our wagons to accompany us," wrote Raynolds. He left Deer Creek on May 10, 1860, in the face of two formidable deterrents: a record-breaking winter snowfall and his own choice of routes: the shortest, but also the highest, approach to the Yellowstone. Traveling up the Sweetwater and crossing the divide low to Wind River Junction, Raynolds commented: "May 22, 1860: The Big Horn is formed by the junction of the Popo-Agie and the Wind River at this point. . . . By the trappers, however, it is always spoken of as Wind River until it enters the Canyon some thirty miles below here."[1]

May 26, 1860, ascending Wind River Canyon: "Soon after leaving camp a bear was discovered on the opposite side of the stream, which Bridger's accuracy with the rifle promptly killed, and some of the men brought the carcass into camp. The Guide had been previously complaining of illness, and was reluctant to leave camp in the morning; but the sight of game produced a sudden and remarkable convalescence."

The horsemen reluctantly took turns with "the single pair of wheels we use for the odometer." May 28: "I gave orders to leave our odometer wheels behind." But at the evening camp, "I sent back for the wheels."

May 30, 1860: "It was my original desire to go from the head of Wind River to the head of the Yellowstone, keeping on the Atlantic slope. . . . Bridger said at the outset that this would be impossible. . . . Directly across our route lies a basaltic ridge, rising not less than

[1] Frost, "Notes on General Ashley," 61. Thus Wind River, between the present Riverton and Shoshoni, as Potts correctly says, is running east-northeast.

five thousand feet above us, its walls apparently vertical with no visible pass nor even canyon. . . . Bridger remarked triumphantly and forcibly to me upon reaching this spot: 'I told you, you could not go through; a bird can't fly over that without taking a supply of grub along.' I had no reply to offer; and mentally conceded the accuracy of the information of 'The Old Man Of The Mountains.' . . .

"The head of Wind River forms a natural amphitheatre. . . . We saw abundant buffalo sign . . . tending to confirm the statement, that the Snake Indians keep buffaloes penned up . . . and kill them as their necessities require."[2]

May 31, 1860. Bridger said that the camping ground for the night would be upon the waters of the Columbia and within five miles of Green River. Nearing the summit, "we soon found ourselves floundering in the snow. Bridger, for the first time, lost heart and declared it would be impossible to go farther."

To the left, some ten miles, is a bold conical peak which "I regard as the topographical center of the continent, the waters from its sides [as Bridger had informed him] flowing into the Gulf of Mexico, the Gulf of California, and the Pacific Ocean. I named it Union Peak, and the Pass, Union Pass."

June 1, 1860: "We are now on . . . what Bridger says . . . is Gros Ventre Fork. . . . My Guide seems more at a loss than I have ever seen him. Our object now is to keep as near the crest as possible, and recross as soon as we are able, to the headwaters of the Yellowstone."

It was an impossible task; no wonder Bridger was baffled, or that, on the fourth, "a spirit of insubordination and discontent was manifest among the men . . . in their determination to abandon the odometer wheels." June 5, 1860: "I counted at one time twenty-five mules plunged deep in the mud, totally unable to extricate themselves."

June 6, 1860: "I started with Bridger. . . . the labor was excessive. . . . the summit was reached. . . . Bridger immediately declared we were on the wrong route [the ravines still trending towards the Pacific]. . . . The crossing of the spur was of course useless . . . and resulted from a mistake of Bridger's. These little errors in matters of detail upon his part are not remarkable, as it is fifteen years since he visited this region."

2 35 Cong., 2 sess., *Serial 975* (G. K. Warren, "Explorations in Nebraska," Utah War of 1858), vol. I, 631.

For several miserable miles, unbearably cruel hours, and impossibly painful pages, Captain Raynolds fought snow, mud, water, hidden boulders and timber, discouragement, injuries, exhaustion, ill temper, illness, hunger, disobedience, blasphemy, and hostile insubordination with his own naked will power. Even the worst days of the past began to seem bearable, but not these. With the entire body of men seething and grumbling, only Bridger outwardly seemed to keep trying to please the young, ambitious commander. Bridger had previously learned about military leaders, and imperious Indian chieftains, so he worked with his mouth shut and a heavy lid on his temper.

"June 7, 1860: I started in the morning with nine men for a last attempt. . . . My companions were the Guide, James Bridger; Dr. Hayden; Mr. Hutton; Mr. Schonborn; and four men. . . . We ultimately reached . . . the dividing crest of the [Wind River] Range." The prospect was grandly appalling and discouraging, with undulating, ivory-smooth snow draping the entire horizon. "To bring the party to where we stood . . . would result in the certain loss of our animals, if not the whole party. I therefore very reluctantly decided to abandon the plan . . . after one prolonged, disheartening view!"

From the grassy floor of Jackson Hole, the Grand Tetons were more glowering than glorious. Snake River, in front of the Raynolds' party, was booming brimful, affording no crossing for a distance of twenty-five miles; yet cross it they must!

A raft was "a complete failure. Before this, however, I had resolved to try Bridger's ingenuity, and had ordered him, with such men as could be spared, to construct a boat. After the raft fiasco, I found that he had made good progress, and I immediately put all hands to work on the undertaking.

"The framework was, of course, easily constructed, but our great difficulty was to devise a covering, there being no skins in our possession, and our gutta-percha blankets . . . being almost worthless. We were compelled to make use of them, however, protecting them by a lodge skin of Bridger's; and to render them more completely impervious to water, I had large quantities of resin gathered from the pine in the vicinity, and thickly coated them with this substance.

"By night a very respectable boat was completed, rude in appearance, but promising to be serviceable. Its length was 12 ½ and its beam 3 ½ feet; and it was remarkable for the fact that it was constructed entirely without nails or spikes, the framework being bound together with leather thongs, and the covering fastened on by this common device of the traders in this section.

"At the crossing point, there are three channels, about a hundred yards in total width. Two of these a loaded horse can swim . . . but the third is too deep and swift. 14th. We launched our boat at 9 A.M. . . . manned by four of our best swimmers, laden with a few goods, and this succeeded. . . . It will thus be necessary to load her lightly and make many trips."

June 15, 1860. "One detachment carried the goods from camp nearly a mile through the marshes . . . to the boat. In crossing, the craft would reach the opposite shore a quarter of a mile . . . below. She would then be carried . . . upstream, and again launched, reaching our shore . . . below us. . . . Carried up and reloaded. . . . The round trip consumed but three quarters of an hour, and we made seventeen during the day. 16th: The herd of mules was driven to the channels . . . divided into bands . . . and induced to follow the leader [all swimming across]. In ten trips all persons and effects were ferried across, save the odometer wheels, which I have decided to abandon [since, they were already lost from the raft]."

Bridger's own version of the ferrying enterprise may be repeated in A. J. Shotwell's reminiscent article: "Another laughable incident was related to me by Bridger himself. . . . He was with an exploring party . . . under the command of a young officer, fresh from West Point. . . . At a river swollen from melting snows, Bridger suggested a plan for crossing the turbulent stream. He was curtly told he was employed only as a guide. The fresh young West Pointer ordered two mounted men to ride in and fasten a line to the opposite shore. The horses lost their footing in the swift current and one of the men was drowned. Then, in humiliation, the West Point youth appealed to Bridger, to take the crossing in hand. This Bridger did. . . .

"And here comes the laughable part. . . . On resuming his Command the youth asked the Chaplain to assemble the expedition and return thanks to Providence for the safe crossing. Here Bridger's eyes sparkled as he told how the Chaplain had fallen on his knees, and in a loud voice thanked the Lord for bringing the troops over in safety. And darn his skin, Old Jim concluded to me, he never mentioned Bridger once!"[3]

Captain Raynolds led his party over Teton Pass June 17, 1860, and through Pierre's Hole. "The Grand Tetons have shown off on our right; while ahead, to the north, a lofty snow-clad peak was visible, which Bridger declared is at the head of the Jefferson. We were aiming for the Madison."

In the dense forests of the continental divide area, progress was laborious and slow because water was everywhere and fallen timber snagged the packs. Unfamiliar streams in flood stage coursed the land, giving Bridger grave concern and extra reconnaissance travel. A swollen, unrecognizable Henry's Fork confused Bridger and a crossing boat was half-finished when a scout discovered a ford for tall animals, which the smaller ones could also swim without loads. A branch stream equaled Lake Fork in size, while Spring Fork was also in disguise. Prairie lands provided a welcome relief. They reached Great Falls on July 12 and Fort Benton on July 15, too late for the eclipse expedition.

Raynolds wrote regretfully: "The Valley of the Upper Yellowstone is yet a terra-incognita. . . . Although it was June, the immense body of snow baffled our exertions, and we were compelled to content ourselves with listening to marvelous tales of burning plains, immense lakes, and boiling springs, without being able to verify these wonders.

"I know of but two white men who claim to have ever visited this part of the Yellowstone Valley—James Bridger and Robert Meldrum. The narratives of both these men are very remarkable, and Bridger, in one of his recitals, described an immense boiling spring that is a perfect counter-part of the Geysers of Iceland. As he is uneducated, and had probably never heard of the existence of such natural marvels elsewhere, I have little doubt that he spoke of that which he had actually seen.

"Bridger also insisted that (not far from) the point at which we made our final effort (in the snow) there is a stream of considerable size which divides, and flows down either side of the watershed, thus discharging its waters into both the Atlantic and the Pacific Oceans.

[3] A. J. Shotwell, "Recollections," Freeport, Ohio, *Press*, May 3, 1916.

Having seen this phenomenon on a small scale in the highlands of Maine, where a rivulet discharges a portion of its waters into the Atlantic, and the remainder into the St. Lawrence, I am prepared to concede that Bridger's 'Two-Ocean-River' *may* be a verity."[4]

Captain Raynolds arranged to descend the Missouri by boat, but "James Bridger, Guide, Dr. F. V. Hayden, Naturalist, A. Schonborn, Artist-Meterologist, and W. D. Stewart, Topographer, and a crew of packers" were directed to attach themselves to Lieutenant John Mullins, of the military escort, and proceed overland from Fort Benton to the mouth of the Yellowstone. They left July 20, 1860, using Indian trails both old and new, as Bridger indicated. Mullins' diary offers some information.

July 24, 1860: "I observed a band of Indians approaching. . . . I sent an advance party with my Guide, to ascertain who they were. They proved to be the 'Little Robes,' a band of Blackfeet Indians. They were delighted to meet me, and I accompanied them to their village, half a mile distant, where, to my surprise, I saw waving from the top of the Chief's tent, the 'Star Spangled Banner.' I counted 54 lodges, and estimated the number of Indians to be about 150 or 200.

"They insisted on my stopping with them, saying they wished to smoke, eat and talk with their White brethren. I concluded it was best to stop, and after selecting a good position for defense in case of treachery, I ordered out a stronger guard than usual, and had the animals hobbled within gun-shot of camp, and the packs, parfliches, saddles, etc., piled up in such a manner as to form a defense work, to be used if necessary.

"The Chief invited me to his tent and set out something to eat, of which I partook; although it was not very palatable in its nature, still I did not want to offend the feeling of our red brothers. I was enabled to talk with them through my Guide and interpreter, James Bridger, who spoke the Flathead language, and was readily understood, as there were several members of the band who were Flatheads, and could interpret the rest."

Accurately hitting the low passes between the watersheds and locating pasturage, game, water, and campsites, Bridger didn't know that Mullins made such entries as these in his journal: "I consider

[4] Raynolds, *Exploration of the Yellowstone*, 10–11.

myself very fortunate in striking this [Indian] trail. . . . I changed my course this morning. . . . I selected a good camp. . . . I sent out my hunters. . . . I arrived at Yellowwater Creek, and determined to camp here, as my Guide informed me that it was 25 or 30 miles to the next water."[5]

Some of Captain Mullins' commands were merely paraphrases of James Bridger's mountaineer English, duly clothed in authority.

August 3, 1860. "I discovered, by aid of my glass, a large body of Indians approaching us rapidly. I selected a camp in the timber, under cover of the cottonwood trees and dead timber. Very soon about twelve Indians galloped up to the crest of the hill above my camp and halted, as if to reconnoitre my position. I sent out the Guide, James Bridger, to ascertain what they wanted, and in the mean time had all my animals hobbled and tied up close to camp. . . . Bridger soon returned, bringing the Indians into camp, saying they were Crows, and friendly."

Reaching Fort Union August 11, 1860, Mullins closed his report to Raynolds: "I cannot conclude, sir, without expressing my appreciation of the services of James Bridger, the Guide, whose reputation is not confined to our country . . . and to Doctor Hayden . . . Mr. Schonborn . . . and Mr. Stuart."

Raynolds' consolidated party left Fort Union on August 15. The properties were largely stowed into two special river boats, named, respectively the *Jim Bridger* and the *Bob Meldrum*, and manned by competent crews. Captain Raynolds and the main body of men, with James Bridger as guide and interpreter, proceeded overland. There was much unrest among the Indians and local guides were not available; consequently Bridger's background and good sense would serve instead of local familiarity.

Heading more directly across country, they reached Fort Pierre September 7 and left on the tenth, arriving in Omaha on October 4, 1860. Here the expedition disbanded. James Bridger proceeded to his unfamiliar, but not estranged family on the Little Santa Fe farm south of Independence.

[5] *Ibid.*, 161–70.

RETURNING MOUNTAINEERS were usually good story sources, but Bridger had a limited reputation as a raconteur. General Dodge wrote that a famous journalist of that day, Colonel E. Z. C. Judson, using the nom de plume, "Ned Buntline," got enough adventures out of Bridger that winter of 1860–61 to keep him writing the rest of his life.

Judson may have accompanied Bridger to Denver in 1861, for General Dodge says: "Bridger took him across the plains. . . . Not long afterwards the Jim Bridger stories commenced. . . . One of these was printed every week, and Bridger's companions used to save them up and read them to him. Buntline made Bridger famous and carried him through more hairbreadth escapes than any man ever had!"[1]

These stories must have appeared as the alleged experiences of fictitious characters. None have been found that are definitely identifiable as Bridger's adventures or narratives.

Noting the requirements of family and home, Bridger found that he needed money. Louis Vásquez, his former partner and present neighbor, was in Bridger's debt, but Louis was assisting his nephew, A. Pike Vásquez, in establishing a grocery store in Denver. Louis and Pike had for some time been partners in the fur trade. James P. Beckwourth had recently visited Louis, as he was also interested in the Denver store.[2] Bridger wrote Beckwourth in Taos for aid in settling with Vásquez.

Six months later, in Denver, Bridger issued to Beckwourth a power

[1] Dodge, *Biographical Sketch*, 7; see also Alter, *James Bridger*, 518. Dodge may have mistaken the hack's name; John C. Van Tramp, Frank Triplett, E. S. Ellis, Rufus B. Sage, Emerson Bennett, and many others did the same.

[2] Bray, "Louis Vasquez," 10, 18.

of attorney, directing legal action on certain property in west Denver (Auraria) on Ferry Street.[3] Frank Hall's history of Colorado says that Kit Carson and Jim Beckwourth reached Denver from New Mexico that spring, adding the colorful news that David H. Moffat, telegraph agent, "arrived from Omaha with a wagon load of books and stationery . . . which was exposed for sale, in a not very pretentious building on Ferry Street, west Denver, opposite the Old Vasquez house [the new grocery store]."[4] As no action appears, Bridger's gesture must have produced results.

The explosive growth of settlements in the West stimulated the quest of a shorter route than the Overland Stage–Pony Express route through Wyoming and the Butterfield route through New Mexico. Torch bearers for a shorter route were Colorado interests. Denver's *Rocky Mountain News* reported that Bela M. Hughes, new president of the Central Overland California and Pike's Peak Express Company, had arranged for James Bridger (his neighbor on the Missouri River frontier) to assist the company's chief engineer, E. L. Berthoud, in locating the route west of Denver.

Bridger arrived in Denver by overland stagecoach May 8, 1861. In an interview the *News* quoted Bridger: "They [the early fur trappers] found gold everywhere in this country in those days, but thought it unworthy of their notice to mine for it, as beaver [then worth $8.00 a pound] was the best paying gold they wanted to mine for in the creeks and rivers."[5]

Bridger had supported the stage company in recommending the move from central Wyoming to the Laramie Plains–Bridger Pass route, but, after a conference with Colorado interests, Hughes asked Bridger to join Berthoud in an exploration for a direct route, to make the decision conclusive. Ascending Denver's Clear Creek, they stopped first at the forks at "Camp Bridger." On May 12, 1861, while Bridger reconnoitered to the southwest, Berthoud examined the North Fork and there discovered what has since been known as Berthoud Pass, elevation 11,314 feet.

[3] Nolie Mumie, *James Pierson Beckwourth*, 71–73 (credited to Fred A. Rosenstock, Denver, Colorado). Margaret Carrington, in *Ab-Sa-Ra-Ka*, noted, "Once he was wealthy, and his silver operations in Colorado might have been very lucrative, but he was the victim of misplaced confidence." 113–14.

[4] Frank Hall, *History of Colorado*, I, 253–54.

[5] Le Roy R. Hafen, *Overland Mail*, 220–23 and note.

Hastily descending westward by way of Fraser River and the Colorado, they returned to report. The company forthwith decided to send "Major Bridger and E. L. Berthoud to review, locate and mark out this new road from Denver to Salt Lake City." (*Rocky Mountain News*, June 19, 1861). Berthoud, Bridger, and party left Denver July 6, 1861, to make a preliminary survey.

At middle elevation they crossed the divide from the Colorado to the Yampah River and, near the mouth of the Little Snake River, swung the new route over to White River, thence westward to a Green River crossing. Bridger eagerly told the surveyors of the Green River canyons in the Uinta Mountains on the upper river and of other gorges toward the junction of the Green and the Colorado.

Berthoud wrote Frederick S. Dellenbaugh: "Bridger would tell in camp of the Canyons of the Colorado and Green River; and of the almost utter impossibility of getting water from either canyon, although in full sight of an abundance of it, which I bitterly experienced when trying to explore down Green River, south of White River, in Utah, in 1861."

West of the Green, Bridger led the Berthoud engineers up the Duchesne and Strawberry and down the Provo to Provo City, thence north to Salt Lake City. They returned promptly by the same route for a few verifications and amendments. Berthoud was quoted. "A good wagon road ... can be quickly and cheaply built to Provo, Utah," about 425 miles, for $100,000 (*Rocky Mountain News*, October 12, 1861). Bridger seems to have remained silent. He knew too well that they had surveyed only a midsummer route which, during the rest of the year, would be closed by snow in Berthoud's Pass, a mile higher than Bridger's Pass only a few miles to the north.

Bridger returned to his Missouri farmstead for the winter (1861–62), probably traveling by stagecoach as guest of the company that employed him. The Pony Express and regular mail stages, pestered by Indians in exposed places, moved during the late summer of 1862 from the South Pass to the Bridger's Pass route. The change omitted Fort Laramie and the rest of the stage stations between South Platte and Fort Bridger. Unwittingly the Old Scout witnessed or participated in some of this change-over "as Guide, U. S. Army, at $5 per day."

The Collins papers imply that Bridger was employed by the United States mail service as a guard for troops leaving Fort Leavenworth in May, 1862. Colonel William O. Collins was in command. His eighteen-year-old son went along for his health. Both were making their first journey over the route and were dependent on a good guide. The cavalcade reached Overland City (Julesburg) on May 23, 1862. At Scott's Bluff, May 25, 1862, Colonel Collins wrote to his wife:

"The Platte is nearly a mile wide, shallow, and full of quicksand; it was also at a high stage, but we had a magnificent crossing. On arrival the night before, I took a detachment of about twenty picked men, all on horseback, the Guide [Bridger] and myself leading, feeling our way, and learning the channels, which are constantly shifting, as the stream is a moving mass of sand and water. To cross, we put ten or twelve mules to a wagon. Everything went like clock work."

During a stop at Fort Laramie on May 30–31, 1862, the son, Caspar Collins took up the busy father's pen at Sweetwater Bridge, Sunday, June 16: "This is the worst country for winds I ever saw (about a mile below Independence Rock) . . . Our other Guide, Major Bridger, went off this morning up in the mountains to get out of the wind. He says he is going to get in some canyon and make a large fire.

"Yesterday, Mr. Pallady [hunter-interpreter, employed as guide] shot an antelope near the camp, and he and I and Louis . . . dragged him to the tent before my father and Major Bridger were up. . . . There is no one messing [eating] with us now but the two Guides. . . . The Indians keep stealing stock from the mail stations and now and then shoot a man. . . . Mormon trains loaded with provisions are going to Denver. . . . Emigrants are going to the gold mines in Washington Territory [Idaho]."

Caspar continues the news to his mother on June 30, 1862, at Camp High Land, South Pass (last crossing of Sweetwater). "Yesterday a teamster of Lieut. Glenn, who was left back to guard a provision train, came into camp with the word that they were attacked by Indians. In about an hour my father left camp with over a hundred picked men. They got there too late, the Indians having left, after killing two emigrants. . . . One Indian shot three arrows at Lieut. Glenn, one of them passing between his arm and body, and hitting a rock behind him. There was about four hundred Indians, and Glenn and thirty men chased them all."[6]

Another version of this affair emphasizes James Bridger's part: William S. Brackett, who was in the escort for two new Utah judges, says: "James Bridger was ordered to go along . . . and make a report. . . . I was riding with Bridger over a long hill when we came upon the wagon that had been attacked, and the horribly mutilated bodies of the two men. . . .

"Bridger calmly dismounted, knelt on the ground and closely examined the footprints around the body. Then he pulled three arrows from the old man's corpse and closely examined them— 'Arapahos and Cheyennes' he said. . . . At the wagon we found . . . the Indians had got the harness off the horses by cutting nearly every strap. At one side lay the body of a young man. . . . In his hand was a Colt revolver, with four chambers empty. . . . Three bullets had pierced his body, and he was scalped and mutilated.

"When Bridger saw the pistol he walked around the wagon in a circle, carefully examining the grass and sagebrush. Suddenly he stooped and siezed a piece of sagebrush and broke it off. On it was a speck of blood. Widening his search he found more blood, and came back, saying: 'The boy hit one of the scamps, anyway.'[7] . . . a silent old fellow, he was" concludes Brackett, "Close-mouthed with all except the Commander of our force."

Caspar Collins finished his letter of June 30, 1862, to his mother: "Here is the kind of house we live in. . . . My father's square tent, with the fly to sit under as a porch in hot weather, and a Sibley tent . . . for seventeen. In it we eat, and Mr. Pallady sleeps. Major Bridger and my father sleep in the Little Lodge, as the Major calls it; and our cook sleeps in another tent.

"These old Mountaineers are curious looking fellows. . . . They nearly all wear big, white hats with beaver around it; a loose white coat of buck or antelope skins, trimmed fantastically with beaver fur; buffalo breeches, with strings hanging for ornaments along the sides; a Mexican saddle, moccasins, and spurs with rowels two inches long, which jingle as they ride. They have bridles with,

---

[6] Spring, *Caspar Collins*, 106, 117, 119, 121, 122, 124–31.

[7] William S. Brackett, "Bonneville and Bridger," vol. 3, *Contributions to the Montana Historical Society*, 1900; see also Alter, *James Bridger*, 394–98.

sometimes, ten dollars' worth of silver ornaments on; Indian ponies, a heavy rifle, a Navy revolver, a hatchet and a Bowie knife. They all have a rawhide lasso [lariat] tied on one side of the saddle, to catch and tie their ponies."

Caspar, the ebullient youth, wrote again on July 6, 1862. This letter was written at High Land Camp, South Pass, and was addressed to his mother. "Lieut. Vananda has just got back from escorting the Judges of the U. S. Court to Utah. . . . Before long we are going on a hunting, fishing and scouting expedition among the Wind River Mountains fifty miles from here (it is twenty miles from South Pass to Atlantic Peak; and sixty miles to Riverton)."

Writing his mother again on August 13, 1862, at the upper crossing of Wind River, Caspar says: "We—that is, my father, Adjutant Glenn, Dr. Regner and I—have been on an expedition to Wind River, around the mountains; there were two guides and twenty-two men along; the wagonmaster, and three teamsters with two wagons [carts? They were hunting elk, deer, rabbits, ducks, sage hens, snipe, and fish].

"We crossed Green River at a new ferry . . . And camped that night on what the Mountaineers call Horse Creek." The party then apparently ascended New Fork, crossed to the headwaters of the Sweetwater, and descended Little Popo Agie to the Wind River–Big Horn (Riverton).

On the mountain, "we had to cut our way through a pine forest for over five miles," and then all hands, with the lariats, let the wagon down a two-hundred-foot slope too steep for the horses and mules. "My Father slept in a tent with twenty-six; and we could have slept there too; but some of the men have vermin, and it was so close we could not stand it.

"It was amusing to see Old Major Bridger cooking his supper. He would take a whole jack rabbit, and a trout about eighteen inches long, and put them on two sticks, and set them up before the fire, and eat them both without a particle of salt; and drink about a quart of strong coffee. He says when he was young, he has often eaten the whole side of ribs of a buffalo.

"A person cannot hunt by himself, for there are Indians lurking all through the country. They would bark like prairie wolves around our camp. . . . In the Wind River valley there is neither rain nor snowfall, the mountains around catching it all. Wind River is called Big Horn, one of the headwaters of the Yellowstone, which runs into the Missouri."

Among the Collins papers is a memorandum made by Colonel Collins which indicates he must have been taking notes from Bridger's talks. Collins' precise recapitulation gives distances from Sweetwater to Salt Creek, Thomas Fork, Bear River, Ham's Fork, Green River Ferry, and Big Sandy; also the nine intermediate stops, with distances, to Fort Hall, with estimates of traveltime, size of party, and availability of forage and game.

In a final report before leaving the Sweetwater country, Caspar wrote his mother, August 31, 1862, from Sweetwater Bridge: "We have made a journey to Green River lately; we were gone only six days. My father, Lieut. Vananda, Major Bridger, Mr. Peck, the operator for the telegraph Company, and myself, were in a mess together. . . . Shipley's and Mackay's Companies are over on the new route running up the South Platte, and from there across to Ham's Fork."

The military was unusually busy that autumn and winter with two routes of travel to patrol, one of them requiring constant attention regardless of the season or the weather. James Bridger appears again in Casper Collins' letters to his mother that autumn. Bridger was engaged by Colonel Collins at Fort Laramie, about September 20, to pilot his party to Fort Halleck, at Elk Mountain in the western part of the Laramie Plains. They were back at Fort Laramie October 7, 1862. "We had Major Bridger with us as Guide. He knows more of the Rocky Mountains than any living man. . . . He is totally uneducated, but speaks English, Spanish and French, equally well, besides nearly a dozen Indian tongues, such as Snake, Bannock, Flathead, Nez Perce, Pend d'Oreille, Ute, and one or two others I cannot recollect. He has been in many Indian battles and has several arrow wounds, besides being hit so as almost to break his neck."

Caspar wrote to his uncle on December 15, 1862, from Ft. Laramie, saying that they had encamped on the Little Laramie River coming back from Fort Halleck and found "beaver dams so thick that one would back water to the falls above it, for ten miles, with few exceptions."[8]

[8] Spring, *Caspar Collins*, 148–50.

Bridger spent the winter with his family on the farm, but returned to Colonel Collins at Fort Laramie in 1863. Colonel Collins and his son Caspar had visited their Ohio home to collect more recruits. They returned promptly, bringing Mrs. Collins with them. Bridger's reappointment was dated August 18, 1863, at Fort Laramie, and War Department files indicate that he was again contracted on October 1, 1863.

Lieutenant J. Lee Humfreville, Company A, Eleventh Ohio Volunteer Cavalry, set out on a scouting expedition in September, 1863, to South Park, Colorado. The detachment consisted of a few cavalrymen, a handful of armed and mounted Arapaho Indians, and James Bridger as guide. Humfreville described Bridger's handling of a tense situation:

"After a sharp engagement with a war party of much greater numbers than ours, we withdrew to a hillside. Some of the enemy warriors dismounted; and hiding in the grass and bushes, began firing upon us. . . . Bridger challenged an Arapahoe to join him in a close-up reconnaissance. The Arapahoe refused, and Bridger abused him soundly by means of the sign language. At last the Arapahoe took Bridger's hand and they proceeded. . . . I heard a shot; and in a few minutes Bridger returned with a warm, bloody scalp.

"I then ordered our Arapahoes to go forward and fire the grass. They refused, until Bridger ridiculed them. Then the whole party accompanied him and fired the grass. Indians previously concealed fled in great numbers. Bridger insisted, however, that under no circumstances, must we leave our present position. . . . In a short time they attacked; and Bridger picked off the first Indian who got within range of his deadly rifle. The troopers then used their Spencers to good effect. Thus the Indians were prevented from getting near us; and in a few hours they withdrew."

However, Humfreville's western anthology, compiled after twenty-five years, contains several dubious tales concerning Bridger. His alleged trading of a yoke of somebody's oxen to a (nonexistent) winter emigrant for a book he could not read is hardly consistent with more careful characterizations and doesn't square with Colonel Collins' official report: "There is a Post Library of six hundred books, and a reading room . . . with newspapers and magazines, all circulated to other posts as needed."

Some of Humfreville's slightly less apocryphal text is concerned with Bridger's habits: "I occupied the same quarters with Bridger one whole winter. If he grew sleepy in the afternoon, he went to bed; and when he awoke, he would make a fire, roast meat, and eat it (in apparent disregard of Army routines, though he was on duty). He never ate until he was hungry.

"Bridger's suit of buckskin became infested with vermin; and he asked me how to get rid of them. [Bridger well knew that, in the summertime he could spread the garments on an ant-hill for a quick and complete dry-cleaning job]. Spreading his garments on the ground, I poured a ridge of powder down all the seams, then burned the vermin. It also burned the buckskin clothing badly. 'I'm going to kill you for that!' was Bridger's vigorous reaction."

When on the march "Bridger was always in front. It was necessary at all times for the Guide to be acquainted with and on the lookout for traps laid by the wily savages; and to know how to guard against them to prevent the troops from being outgeneraled."[9]

The Civil War was on; the Indians were becoming more desperate; the business of the country was chaotic; and even army pay checks were delayed excessively, along with food supplies. More work than usual faced the soldiers, who must guard the new mail route (by way of Bridger's Pass) as well as construct and service it. The only man on familiar ground that winter was James Bridger, and his enormous shadow sheltered a great many inexperienced men.

[9] J. Lee Humfreville, *Twenty Years Among Our Hostile Indians*, 462–70.

JOHN S. COLLINS, post trader at Laramie, from 1872 to 1882, first halted there in April, 1864, on his way to the Montana mines, traveling via Fort Hall. At Fort Laramie, April 26, 1864, he "met Jim Bridger, organizing an emigrant train, to open a new route to the gold fields by way of the Big Horn mountains." Collins recollected that he heard Bridger talking to green soldiers, saying that when he first came there, Laramie Peak was a hole in the ground.[1]

Bridger was granted a temporary release from army service on April 30, 1864, to allow him to pilot a company of emigrant miners to the Montana gold fields. A much-traveled route from Fort Laramie had circled around the Big Horn Mountains to the north (the present Sheridan route), but Bridger advocated a shorter, easier, safer route to the south of the Big Horns (the present Thermopolis route) in order to avoid the hostile Sioux.

Others thought the same way; General Dodge wrote to General Connor, June 10, 1865: "You are aware that . . . an appropriation exists for a road from Fort Laramie to Virginia City, by way of Powder River and Big Horn."[2]

The Reverend L. B. Stateler kept a journal, wrote letters, and preserved speeches relating to an expedition to Montana that season. From these the Reverend E. J. Stanley has prepared a *Life* of Stateler. A lively chapter in the work relates to James Bridger.

About May 1, 1864, Stanley wrote, "A large company was preparing to start to Montana's new gold fields from Denver." They traveled near what is now Cheyenne, Wyoming, reaching Fort

---

[1] John S. Collins, *Across the Plains in 1864.*

[2] Le Roy R. Hafen, *Powder River Campaigns, and Sawyer's Expedition of 1865,* 33.

Laramie for final organization before proceeding into the Indian country.

Stanley continues: "The emigrant company numbered about three hundred persons, with sixty-two wagons. They were regularly organized under the guidance of Major Bridger, the famous mountaineer, and travelled in military order. Mounted men went before, and followed behind. In the morning the horses were harnessed and the oxen yoked and hitched up; and they would make one move or drive each day, traveling until about 3 or 4 o'clock in the afternoon.

"Upon arriving in camp, the wagons were driven close together, the front wheels of one wagon close to the hind wheels of the other, in a circular, or diamond shape, with the wagon tongues and the teams inside, thus making a strong corral, sufficient to hold all the stock, and constituting a strong bulwark for defense, should they be attacked by Indians.

"When they camped the horses were unharnessed, the cattle unyoked, and sent out under a strong guard to graze. About sundown all the stock—horses and cattle—were driven inside the corral, the gate or opening closed by a cordon of ox yokes and chains, or by a wagon being drawn into the gap, where they were kept until morning. When it was dark, guards were posted all around the camp to prevent surprise by an enemy. At daylight the animals were sent out again and grazed until about 7 o'clock. By this time breakfast would be over, tents struck, and baggage packed away; the stock would be driven in, hooked up and the march resumed for another day.

"During the afternoon, when the day's journey was ended, the camp presented a scene of activity. The men who were not on guard, were busy preparing wood, bringing water, mending harness, or greasing wagons; the women (and some of the men too) were baking bread, cooking, and doing their laundry work; while the children were engaged in their youthful sports. . . ." There we have the James Bridger version of "A Day with the Cow Column."[3]

When the party left the Oregon Trail at Red Buttes and headed for the Big Horn River, they found the Wind River Mountains to their left and the Big Horn Mountains to their right.

[3] E. J. Stanley, *Life of L. B. Stateler*, 175–76.

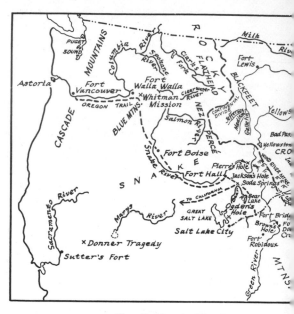

Jim Bridger's Territory:

"Before reaching the Big Horn River . . . in a fine place for a camp . . . we found we were within a mile of a large band of Indians. . . . They had come in during the night. . . . Major Bridger, our Captain, went with a small Company of unarmed men in the direction of the Indian camp, for an interview. The Chief, seeing them approach unarmed, came, with a company of his braves in the same manner.

"Presently the Indians changed their manner, began to shout 'Bridger! Bridger!' at the top of their voices, and came galloping up to the White men. They were Shoshone or Snake Indians, from about Old Fort Bridger, and recognized our Captain as their old friend. They had come across the mountains on a buffalo hunt.

"The Chief was a particular friend of Bridger. When we found out who they were, and what it all meant, there was great rejoicing. We made them a feast, gave them some presents, and Major Bridger gave the Chief a paper showing that they were friends of the White people. The Chief's name was Wash-a-kie."[4]

[4] *Ibid.,* 180–81.

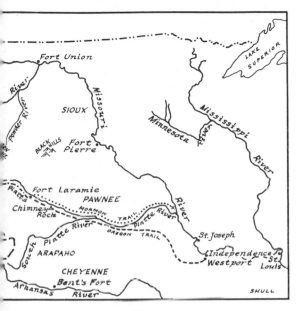

The American West of 1836–48

The Big Horn River was in flood stage, too deep to ford and impossible to bridge. The emigrants felled trees and whipsawed the lumber to construct a ferry boat. The horses and cattle were forced to swim. Stateler's journal indicates that they crossed the Yellowstone River on July 4, 1864. By that time several other trains had overtaken them, and the entire company numbered about one thousand persons, all bound for the new El Dorado.

The Stateler-Bridger party left the Yellowstone near present Livingston, "crossed the mountains through a gap that has ever since retained the name of Bridger Pass [in the diarist's time only; it has since been called "Bozeman Pass"], and camped near the site of the present city of Bozeman." Continuing on, they encamped at Madison River July 8, 1864, and reached Virginia City environs about July 10–12, 1864.

Cornelius Hedges and company were behind Bridger's company, having come through Fort Laramie on May 25, 1864. Hedges recorded their progress: "At Deer Creek, June 2, paid our share for pilot; camped on Bridger's ground. 5th, Our train now over a hundred. Guide drunk; wrangling all afternoon. 7th, passed several

307

old camps. Bridger six days, and Jacobs three days ahead. Train lagged, no Guide.

"June 11, Saturday, 1864. Wind River [Big Horn] quite a stream. Boat built by Bridger's train, buried on other shore. Went to work on boat. 12th, Ferry took over two wagons at a time. 13th, started from Ferry, after burying the boat. 15th, Camped on Grey Bull River. 17th, Met two of Bridger's men, and found they were only twelve miles ahead. 18th, Crossed Stinking Water. Bridger's and Jacob's trains near us. All sorts of stories. 206 miles on Cut-Off.

"June 19, Sunday, 1864. Train meeting in evening; didn't settle the Guide money question. July 2, Saturday, 1864. Struck Yellowstone. 3d, road lay up the Yellowstone, 4th, waited till Jacob's train passed then pushed on to the Ferry. We are up with Bridger and all. We forded. Ferry charge $2.50. 5th. Passed the Camp on the Yellowstone.

"July 6, Wednesday, 1864. We have been ahead all day of most of our train. Caught up with Bridger's advance about 4 o'clock and camped in a splendid meadows. Snow mountains all around us. 7th, passed the headwaters of the Yellowstone and struck those of the Gallatin. 8th, Saw Jacob's camp; he came out ahead of Bridger's by going around; our train was out of the Canyon. Our team was the last of the train. Got down to Creek at noon; found log houses and settlements, etc.

"July 9, Saturday, 1864. Camped on west side of Gallatin River. Couldn't get off till most had gone. Walked on; 20 miles to Madison River. 10th, Sunday, Camped near Hot Springs. Started out for Virginia City; estimated fifteen miles, found it forty, and much uphill at that. Reached [Virginia] City about 2:30. Met Jim Clark's brother; and some who were with us on the Platte, and went around —got through sooner than we by ten days. 11th, reached the city about 10 a.m. 12th. Prospects look poor; claims are very high [priced]; chances for work not numerous; we are tramping, eating up what little we had."[5]

This may explain why Bridger, like Brigham Young, preferred farming to the risky business of mining. Bridger was only on leave from the army, however, and he promptly returned to Fort Laramie.

[5] Cornelius Hedges, "Diary, Iowa to Montana, 1864." Photostat, courtesy of the Montana State Historical Society.

The War Department record shows that on August 3, 1864, Bridger was re-employed at five dollars a day, this time by Lieutenant H. E. Averill, acting assistant quartermaster. This service was brief, expiring August 31, and may have been for an Indian conference.

Captain Eugene F. Ware saw Bridger at Fort Laramie in August, 1864. "Every night he was out in front of the Sutler's store sitting on the benches. . . . He readily responded to questions; and would talk as long as he was talked with. . . . When told that visiting Indian women ate the entrails of freshly slaughtered beeves, feeding the choicer morsels to the little Indian children, Bridger declared: 'It's all right. . . . I have cleaned up that kind of stuff and eaten it myself, when I had to!' "

Bridger said that the Indians believed that like parts of the animal nourished like parts of man. And that when stealing horses, the Indians called up their dogs, which ran along with the party. When they camped, the horses grazed, and the Indians ate the dogs. "Thus there is no comissary, no baggage to bother."

"Bridger knew everything that an Indian knew," says Ware, "and he could do anything that an Indian could do. . . . He wasn't an egotistic liar. . . . He never in my presence vaunted himself, about his own personal actions. He never told about how brave he was, nor how many Indians he had killed."[6]

The lodestone in Bridger's mind, after his discharge, was the family on the farm near Little Santa Fe, and there he settled for the winter of 1864–65.

[6] Eugene F. Ware, *The Indian War of 1864*, 203–206, 253–54.

JAMES BRIDGER, sequestered on the Missouri farm, was not forgotten by the United States Army. "I found him there," said General Dodge, "when I took command of that country in January, 1865, and placed him as Guide of the Eleventh Ohio Cavalry, in its march from Fort Riley to Fort Laramie [appointment date not known]."[1]

During the close of the Civil War, formal Indian treaties were dissolved through sheer neglect and political expediency—for roads, mining, hunting expeditions, trading posts, and especially for emigrants and settlers. Nearly all the Indians were desperately fighting the disappearance of game, pasturage, and watering places.

The Cheyennes were particularly destructive along the overland telegraph line from Fort Kearny to the Sweetwater. Enraged by Colonel Chivington's massacre of a Cheyenne village in Colorado (November 29, 1864), they retaliated frequently and violently. General Dodge was new; he placed General Connor of Denver in charge of the new District of the Plains. He also rushed available troops to Fort Laramie. Units of the Eleventh Ohio Cavalry were attended by James Bridger, who was being assigned to the new district commander.

The contagion of hatred spread from the Southern Cheyennes to the Northern Cheyennes and to their affiliates, the powerful Oglala Sioux. When the relief forces arrived at Fort Laramie on May 3, 1865, Colonel Thomas Moonlight, post commander, set out with about five hundred men to pacify or punish the aggressors. The party was depending largely on the guidance of James Bridger, who knew the Indians they sought, as well as the country in which they would operate.

[1] Alter, *James Bridger*, 515.

The hostile bands were not yet organized, however, and the reconnaissance through the Powder and Wind River areas was fruitless. Sergeant I. B. Pennick, writing on May 14, 1865, near Independence Rock, noted that "Bridger, the Old Pioneer Guide (also Colonel Moonlight) took supper with us."[2]

Subsequently, Mrs. Sarah L. Larimer, recuperating at Fort Laramie from Sioux captivity, reported that "Two-Face" and "Black Bear" (Black Foot?) brought in two captives, Mrs. Ewbanks and Miss Roper, for reward.[3] Instead of being rewarded, however, these Indians and Black Crow were publicly hanged by Colonel Moonlight, who was enraged at the cruelties suffered by the women during captivity. The Indians' bodies were left dangling in chains for several days. Colonel Moonlight was relieved of his command because of this. Finn Burnett's biographer said: "Jim Bridger . . . prophesied that this hanging would lead to dreadful consequences later on the trails."[4]

Bridger's army service record shows that he was promoted to chief guide, at ten dollars a day, on July 6, 1865. He was to serve until September 30, 1865, with the Powder River expedition under General P. Edward Connor. According to Captain H. E. Palmer, the expedition consisted of about 480 soldiers, 75 Pawnee Indians, 70 Winnebago and Omaha Indians, six companies of cavalry (250 men), and 195 teamsters and wagon masters, with 185 supply wagons.

Palmer said that James Bridger had six assistants: Nick Janisse, James Daugherty, Michael Bouyer, John Resha (Richard), Antoine Le Due, and James Bordeau. Colonel Connor and the guides reconnoitered the proposed river crossings. They examined Bridger's Crossing, just below the present Orin Junction (called also the Mormon Crossing, according to Burnett), and the La Bonte Crossing, seven or eight miles upstream.

But the freshet caused by melting mountain snows had washed away or submerged all signs of the crossings—along with the reputations of the guides, whose first real task was a failure. Burnett says

2 Grace Raymond Hebard and E. A. Brininstool, *The Bozeman Trail.*

3 Sarah L. Larimer, *The Capture and Escape*, 133.

4 David, *Finn Burnett*, 43.

the sutler's wagons had crossed at Bridger's Ferry a month earlier.

Moving out of Fort Laramie on July 30, 1865, the main cavalcade soon reached the expected river crossings, and, as Palmer explains: "I found the General [Connor] thoroughly discouraged, and more than disgusted with his Guides." Palmer noticed a buffalo crossing nearby, however, where the entire train crossed safely to the north bank of the Platte.

August 5, 1865, Captain Rockafellow wrote: "Major Bridger, on scout yesterday, discovered the trail of a thousand Indians, which was two days' old. . . . 8th: General Connor, Lieutenant Jewett, Major Bridger, Janisse and Brennan, Guides, started at 6:30 A.M. on a hunt for buffalo and water." They found plenty of antelope and a few buffalo bulls. They also found Major Bridger's wagon trail of ten years ago, which General Connor decided to use.

The party separated, however, "old Major going up it while we went down," says Rockafellow. They again reached Bridger's Trail but "could see only tracks of animals which he drove tandem," presumably hitched to a cart. But Bridger wasn't lost; he got in after dark.

August 14, 1865, Jewett, Bridger, and party having found no better site on a trip upriver, the lofty, well-wooded banks of Powder River were chosen for the new post. "Major Bridger says that this is the point where the various Indian tribes meet to fight their battles." Workmen remained to construct Fort Connor, but most of the command proceeded, reaching Crazy Woman's Fork on August 22, Lake De Smet three days later, and Peno Creek on August 26.

Bridger told Palmer that Peno took its name from a French trapper, who shot and wounded a buffalo bull there. The bull rushed Peno to "the steep bank of the Creek. . . . Mr. Bull caromed on his rear and knocked Peno into the Creek, the bull tumbling after him. . . . The fall was more disastrous to the bull than to the man. . . . Such is the story as told to me by Major Bridger."

At the mouth of Peno Creek, Burnett heard Bridger tell the party: "On our next day's march . . . we would cross a small spring stream that was poison; and cautioned us not to drink it."

While ascending the ridge between Powder and Tongue rivers (August 26), Palmer rode with Bridger: "I was riding in the extreme advance, in company with Major Bridger. . . . He had been telling me about himself. . . . We were close friends. His family lived at Westport, Missouri. His daughter, Miss Jennie [Virginia] had married [February 25, 1864] a personal friend of mine, Lieutenant Albert Wachsman; and during the winter of 1863 [after Bridger's son, Felix, had enlisted in the Civil War] I had contributed to the help of the family [men at remote stations did not get their checks regularly], all of which the Major knew (Mr. and Mrs. George London, of Westport, were keeping the three children, probably in the Bridger home).

"The Old Major was sitting upon his horse, his eyes shaded with his hands. . . . 'Do you see those 'ere columns of smoke over yonder . . . by that saddle . . . fifty miles away?' For the life of me, I could not see any columns of smoke, even with a field-glass. The atmosphere appeared hazy . . . but there were no columns of smoke. When the General [Connor] came up with his staff, and was informed of the smoke, the General raised his field glass and scanned the horizon carefully. . . . He then remarked, there were no columns of smoke to be seen.

"The Major quietly mounted his horse and rode on. . . . To satisfy curiosity, and to give our guides no chance to claim that they had shown us an Indian Village, and we would not attack it, Captain Frank North and seven men were dispatched to reconnoitre.

"I galloped on and overtook the Major; and as I came up to him, I overheard him remark about 'These dam paper-collar soldiers,' telling him there were no columns of smoke. . . . It afterward transpired that there was an Indian village in the immediate locality designated. Bridger understood well enough it was a favorable locality for Indians to encamp."

Moving cautiously up the Tongue valley on August 29, General Connor's advance scouts suddenly discovered an Arapahoe village in the act of decamping. The Indians were apparently on a routine, meat-making expedition. Connor's troops, in electrical reaction, "dashed across the meadow and attacked in pell mell, non-military fashion. There were hand-to-hand struggles with Indian men, women, and even children, alike, in an indescribable scene."

"The Indians made a brave stand for their families," and actually

313

repulsed the soldiery in about two hours' fighting, the Indians far outnumbering the attackers. "Desultory firing continued until after dark." It was subsequently learned that a chief and 63 warriors had been slain, 1,100 ponies captured, and 250 Indian lodges with their contents burned, along with a large quantity of buffalo meat. That left the remaining Indians practically leaderless, empty-handed, on foot, and hungry.

The soldiers, after cremating their own dead to prevent mutilation, tramped towards Fort Connor, possibly not without disturbed consciences. "Ever since we left Fort Laramie our camp had been surrounded with thousands of wolves that made the nights hideous with their infernal howling; but not until tonight, have we heard the 'Medicine Wolf,' which Old Bridger claims to be a supernatural sort of animal, whose howling is sure to bring trouble to camp.

"Bridger, Nick Janisse, and Rulo [guides], being very superstitious, were so frightened at this peculiar howling that they took up their blankets and struck out for a new camp, which according to their theory, was the only way of escaping from inpending danger; they went down the river about half a mile and camped in the timber by themselves."[5]

A. J. Shotwell, after fifty-odd years, tried to remember Bridger on that expedition. "Bridger made his camp alone, beside our own, so as to be near the Scout who messed with our party. Few had conversation with him, so prone was he to hold himself aloof. He would cook his frugal meal, and as soon as darkness approached, wrap himself in his blankets for the night. But with the first peep of day he was astir, and after a hasty cup of coffee, and some jerked meat, he would saddle up, and after calling on General Connor, quietly ride away."[6]

With the Indians at the soldiers' throats, General Dodge, department of Missouri, was grimly goaded into a do-or-die policy. His investigating cavalcade reached Fort Connor (at that time under construction) on September 7, 1865. Only the day before, wrote

[5] Hafen, *Powder River Campaigns of 1865,* with Captain H. E. Palmer's "Summary," 103–52; Captain Rockafellow's "Diary," 153–203; and Finn G. Burnett's "Recollections," 204–17.

[6] A. J. Shotwell, "Recollections," Freeport, Ohio, *Press,* May 3, 1916.

Dodge, "Connor, hearing nothing from Cole, sent out Major North with a couple of Indian scouts, and with Bridger as Guide."[7] Cole's beleaguered men were soon found and brought to Fort Connor. Convinced by what only James Bridger could have told him, General Dodge decided that he would concede the Indians' rights to the Powder-Big Horn-Yellowstone country and run the new railroad across far-away southern Wyoming.

General Dodge was gravely concerned about the Indians nominally in his care; he refused to believe that "the only good Indian is a dead Indian." He was also dedicated to the building of the Pacific railroad, of which he was soon to become chief engineer. On delving deeply into these matters at first hand, the General would discover that James Bridger, an unlettered, Indian-reared man, had the answers to most of the questions asked. Bridger was, indeed, a living encyclopedia of the country and its inhabitants.

At the General's request, Bridger accompanied the Dodge party to Fort Laramie for a week of studying the eastern approaches to the Black Hills (Laramie Mountains) for a railroad location. General Dodge explained the need: the line must be the shortest, straightest, and lowest, with the fewest uphill and downhill grades, through the Black Hills. Platte River, the lower Lodgepole, Laramie Plains, and Bridger's Pass had already been approved.

Having trapped the Black Hills and criss-crossed them in many travels, always taking note of the climb, Bridger assured the General that, as he had told Captain Stansbury fifteen years earlier, the railroad line should switch over, at a convenient place, from Lodgepole to Crow Creek (present Hillsdale-Archer-Cheyenne area) and continue westward over the Crow Creek (Sherman Hill) Red Butte trail. The surveys were accordingly ordered, with check runs over alternate bits of the way. A year later a booklet of thirty-two pages was issued showing all elevations, distances, grades of ascent and descent, conclusions, and recommendations concerning the route roughly designated by Bridger.[8]

[7] Grenville M. Dodge, *The Battle of Atlanta*, 92. See also J. R. Perkins, *Trails, Rails, and War; The Life of General G. M. Dodge*, 184; George Bird Grinnell, *The Fighting Cheyennes*, Chapter XVI.

[8] Grenville M. Dodge, "Report, Union Pacific Railroad, on Lines Crossing the Rocky Mountains." (In the seventy-seven years of steady improvement shown by

Captain Eugene F. Ware "met down on the Platte, a man named Morgan, on the preliminary survey of the Union Pacific. He had run a trial line up past [Fort] Laramie; but Bridger told him that the Cheyenne Pass, at the head of Lodgepole, was a lower pass." Mr. Morgan found by his instruments that "this was a fact."[9]

Bridger's discharge as chief guide came on November 30, 1865. He caught a ride from Fort Laramie with the army mail ambulance, then with a train of empty wagons. He luckily fell in with friends at Fort Kearny, Nebraska.

A feature writer for the local newspaper, (Fort Kearny semi-weekly *Herald*), Legh R. Freeman, interviewed Bridger for the edition of January 6, 1866. After sketching Bridger's career to date, he added, for the readers' interest: "Colonel Bridger . . . is fully six feet high, rawboned, blue eyes, auburn hair (now somewhat gray), is very active and communicative. . . . He has no faith in mounted expeditions against Indians. He says . . . the Indian ponies can travel steadily for weeks together, and subsist on cottonwood bark only; and their riders will build fires of the huge piles of buffalo chips, found where the herd wallows.

"He thinks that our mode of hunting savages with mounted men and wagon trains is simply absurd, since it results only in heavy loss of animals, and unnecessary exposure of troops, who are compelled to return for rations, or halt for their train to overtake them, which gives the savages exultant triumph, leaving the warriors smoking their pipes, whose bowls are tomahawks, and the helves thereof the stems.

"The Colonel is now enroute for Washington [St. Louis?]. He wants to tell the authorities how to manage the Indians; that if they will let him select a party of men, he will follow the Indians on foot, week after week, faring as they do, and will eventually overtake and surprise their villages. He is of the opinion that troops unaccustomed to the frontiers, are stampeded by the yell of the Indians, when the enemy is in small force and might easily be managed by experienced 'Dodgers.' He thinks that the expedition of the Eighteenth U. S.

---

the time tables of 1882 and 1959, the line from Omaha to Ogden has been shortened by forty-four miles, with less than one mile saved between Cheyenne and Laramie. The line remains today approximately along the line laid down by Bridger.)

[9] Ware, *The Indian War of 1864*, 203.

Infantry, now moving against the Sioux, is planned more sensibly than any before fitted up in the country, since their wagon train is to establish a temporary base from which pack mules will supply the troops."[10]

[10] Legh R. Freeman in the Kearney, Nebraska, *Weekly Herald*, January 6, 1866; see also James B. Carrington, "Across the Plains with Bridger as Guide," *Scribner's*, January, 1929.

JAMES BRIDGER found himself among friends at Fort Kearny. Colonel Maynadier, the commander, introduced the Old Scout to Colonel Henry B. Carrington, who was outfitting for the Powder River country, where he would succeed General Connor.

Mrs. Carrington, whose diary was being kept as General Sherman had suggested, was much comforted by General Dodge's eager interest and assistance. The General was leaving his position as commander of the armies in Kansas and the territories to become chief engineer of the Union Pacific Railroad, but his hand clearly appears in Mrs. Carrington's last sentence, describing Colonel Carrington's new command: "As Chief Guide, Major James Bridger . . . assisted by H. Williams, who had been Guide" for General Dodge in Kansas.[1]

Bridger was on duty at Fort Kearny, January 25–31, 1866, as "Chief Guide for Headquarters" at seven dollars a day. His service record shows a new appointment, dated March 5, 1866, with salary adjusted to five dollars a day. But here again the hidden hand of General Dodge supports that of Colonel Carrington, and when Bridger was mistakenly discharged, he was, instead, retained at double pay.

Colonel Carrington's cavalcade drew nonchalantly out of Fort Kearny on May 19, 1866, with twenty-two teams of mules. The loosely organized assemblage (including a thirty-piece brass band, plenty of easy chairs, and quite a few officers' wives) reflecting the general attitude, was lamentably out of line with James Bridger's

[1] Margaret I. Carrington, *Ab-Sa-Ra-Ka*, iii, 44; see also Henry B. Carrington, *Special Commission Hearings, Indian Operations on the Plains, Special Order No. 40*, 54. Spring, 1867, Fort McPherson, Nebraska.

grave fears for such an apparently reckless invasion. As a result came Special Order No. 5, June 11, 1866:

"The troops and trains of this Command will be camped and parked, forming one closely locked square, and ropes stretched across any opening so that no animal may escape. After sunset all animals must be within the square." Special Order No. 6, was issued on June 12, 1866, discontinuing all "straggling" for hunting, visiting ranches, or other purposes; "the regimental band will not stray," rifles were to be carried uniformly ready for use, and "Silence" must be observed after 9 P.M. Most revolutionary of all was the order of June 13, 1866: As the soldiers were to preserve peace, it would be considered a grave offense for a soldier to wrong or insult an Indian; every soldier must treat every Indian kindly, with formal courts-martial for certain violations.[2]

The story of this campaign is well documented, Colonel Carrington's files having been presented at the hearings of the Special Commission, in the spring of 1867, at Fort McPherson, Nebraska. The popular versions were those written by Margaret I. Carrington, wife of the Colonel, and Frances C. Grummond, wife of Lieutenant George W. Grummond. Each woman kept a journal and published a book, Mrs. Grummond's book coming out after she had become the second wife of Colonel Carrington. Margaret Carrington says her book was prepared by "gathering many of its details from officers of the posts, from Major Bridger, and others, as each day's experience unfolded." Some of her facts and expressions, shown herein, are merely copied down as Bridger's utterances.[3]

United States Indian commissioners were holding a "peace conference" at Fort Laramie with the Sioux and the Northern Cheyennes. The commissioners were asking the Indians for full right-of-way for the emigrants to Virginia City, Montana, but the Indians balked at everything except the gifts. Carrington and Bridger were invited to a few of the earlier sessions, but then they had orders to push on. "Major Bridger told us that he had seen kegs of powder distributed to Indians and carried away on their ponies."[4]

[2] Henry B. Carrington, *Hearings*, 3–4.
[3] Margaret I. Carrington, *Ab-Sa-Ra-Ka*, xix.
[4] *Ibid.*, 76; see also Henry B. Carrington, *Hearings*, 15.

Red Cloud, Sioux chief, angrily bolted the conference, leaving everyone uneasy. Already the military signs were posted forbidding all dealings with the Indians, but leading Indians were to be given free access to military leaders for talks. Carrington left Fort Laramie on June 17, 1866, with some misgivings about the conference. "Bridger's good sense was rarely at fault; and he never had any confidence in the success of the conference."

As Colonel Carrington was leaving Fort Laramie, General P. St. George Cooke at Omaha (who had approved game-hunting plans for the officers, wives accompanying the officers, and a military brass band for the expedition) telegraphed instructions to curtail costs by discharging the chief guide. The War Department record shows, however, that Colonel Carrington endorsed the order "Impossible of Execution," and, from that date, June 16, 1866, Bridger was employed as chief guide at ten dollars per day until the end of the campaign.[5]

Crossing the Platte at the so-called Bridger Ferry (present Orin), the expedition found a flatboat in service as a ferry. It was attached to a cable spanning the stream, and hitched in such a way as to use the water current to carry the boat from one bank to the other. The ferry was located at or near "Bridger's Ford," the buffalo crossing used by Colonel Moonlight and General Connor in 1865. We find no confirmation of the belief that Bridger was owner or part owner of the ferry.

Rambling officers and their women, amusing themselves by studying the startling, repeating echoes of pistol shots between canyon walls, were gently chided by "Old Bridger, in his peculiarly quaint and sensible way. 'Better not go *fur*. There is *Injuns* lying under wolf-skins, or skulking on them cliffs, I warrant! They follow ye always. They've seen ye, every day; and when ye don't see any of 'em about, is just the time to look out for their devilment.'"

Sure enough, that very day the Indians had driven off the ferryman's livestock. "Mr. Mills, the proprietor of the Ferry ranche (his

[5] Frances C. Carrington, *My Army Life on the Plains*, 129; see also Henry B. Carrington, *Hearings*: "Upon my earnest remonstrance to General Cooke, asking whether I must discharge James Bridger and all the Guides who knew the country in which I was operating, he modified the order, giving me discretion to employ in certain cases." 35.

wife a Sioux), and an Indian who was in his employ, recovered part of the stock.

"Major Bridger and Mr. Brannan claimed, as they had at Laramie, that we were advancing directly in the face of hostilities; and Major Bridger went so far as to affirm that the presents, which were made to the Indians at Laramie, were given to positive enemies, or to those who had no influence at all, over the warlike bands of the Big Horn and Powder River country."[6]

Proceeding north from the Platte on June 23, 1866, Mrs. Carrington reported that "James Bridger had a head full of maps and trails and ideas all of the utmost value to the expedition." At Fort Reno (Fort Connor), June 28, 1866, a company of Winnebago Indians had possession of the fort, but many of them had left and others wished to leave for a very good reason. "It was generally understood and was distinctly affirmed by Major Bridger, that some of the Sioux at Laramie expressly demanded, as a condition of their consent to peace, that the Winnebago Indians, being deadly enemies, should leave the country."[7]

Moving out of Fort Reno on July 9, 1866, to a camp on Crazy Woman's Fork, Carrington passed Lake De Smet and, on July 13, reached Big Piney Fork, which appeared to be an inviting site for the new post. Fort Phil Kearny was to become the headquarters of the new Mountain District. The chief guide was uneasy, knowing that they were in the choicest of the Sioux homelands. "On the 14th . . . I started to Goose Creek and Tongue River valleys, having received very flattering reports as to their resources from my Chief Guide, James Bridger. After a ride of thirteen hours, and nearly 70 miles, I found less cottonwood on the streams, and that the pine region would be 18 miles distant."[8]

In their absence a couple of white traders called at the encampment to deliver a peremptory order from the Sioux for the soldiers to make no crossings of their land, to build no forts, and to get out of the country. Lurking Indian braves waited for the return of the messengers. The Colonel missed the visitors, having "crossed buttes

[6] Margaret I. Carrington, *Ab-Sa-Ra-Ka*, 83–85.

[7] *Ibid.*, 94–95.

[8] Henry B. Carrington, *Hearings*, 14.

and ridges nearer the mountains for the purpose of testing Major Bridger's recommendation that a new and shorter road should be opened to Tongue River Valley."

The day's events precipitated the construction of Fort Phil Kearny as a four-company post. The work began Sunday, July 15, 1866, on a mesa near the main camp, and, on the same day, the chiefs and leading Indians were called to a conference in the tented army headquarters. But it was a poor day for "smoking." To this session came "Black Horse," "Little Moon," "Dull Knife," and several other Cheyenne leaders, gaily dressed (or undressed) to match the gold braid the officers fished from the baggage for the occasion.

"In front of them all, and to the left of the [flag-draped] table, sitting on a low seat, with elbows on his knees, and chin buried in his hands, sat the noted James Bridger, whose forty-four years on the frontier, had made him as keen and suspicious of Indians as any Indian himself could be of another. The Old Man, already somewhat bowed by age . . . and having incurred the bitter hatred of the Cheyennes and Sioux alike, knew full well that *his* scalp [Bridger was called Big Throat because of his goiter] would be the proudest trophy they could bear to their solemn feasts; and there he sat, or crouched, as watchful as though old times had come again, and he was once more to mingle in the fight. . . .

"To us he was invariably straightforward, truthful and reliable. His sagacity, knowledge of woodcraft, and knowledge of the Indian, was wonderful, and his heart was warm and his feelings tender wherever he confided or made a friend. . . . Near Major Bridger stood Jack Stead, the interpreter. . . . With a Cheyenne wife . . . watchful as Bridger, himself, to take care of his own scalp."[9]

The Cheyennes were derided by the Sioux for sitting with the whites. Next morning Indians drove off some of Major Haymond's horses, cut down one or two men, and, in a subsequent melee, killed French Pete, his Sioux wife, his children, and his hired help at the trading station. In spite of this show of unrest, Captain Burrows was sent back to Fort Reno with foot soldiers on July 19 for much-needed provisions. Guided by James Bridger, they were well on the way when camping time came.

For the rest of this story, we turn to S. S. Peters. Besides the

[9] Margaret I. Carrington, *Ab-Sa-Ra-Ka*, 113–15.

Winnebago Indians who had been left at Fort Reno, there were several "Galvanized" soldiers (Rebel prisoners who preferred to fight, for pay, on the Indian frontier), some of whom had deserted for the Montana mines. There were also the stand-bys of regular soldiers, eager to be active at something useful. One of them was S. S. Peters, who left Fort Reno on July 20, 1866, in an outfit of twenty-six men and seven wagons for the new post, Fort Phil Kearny.

Nearing Crazy Woman's Fork on July 21, they were attacked by a swarm of Indians from surrounding hills. Advance scouts rushed back, and the wagons were forted and a corral formed for the animals, but several horses came in with Indian arrows in their bodies. As this was a forced dry camp, groups crawled to the stream for water. More than half of the detachment was injured within a few minutes; several were incapacitated, and a few were killed.

After an "eternity" of fearful fighting, "a solitary horseman was observed coming over the little ridge to our left. Before he reached the ravine he was ordered to halt. He did so and shouted that he was a 'friend.'

" 'What's your name?'

" 'Jim Bridger.'

"And so it was. He was shown a crossing through the ravine and came on up to the corral.

" 'I knew there was hell to pay here today at Crazy Woman,' said he to a group of officers. 'I could see it by the signs the Indians made on the buffalo skulls. But Captain Burrows and two hundred soldiers are coming down the road there about two miles away. . . .'

"Burrows had intended to make the usual overnight camp at Clear Creek, but Bridger . . . reported that he had discovered several signs made by Indians on buffalo skulls, that a battle was to be fought at Crazy Woman today, and advising all Indians to gather there. . . . Burrows then decided on a forced march to the Crazy Woman camp. . . . So [with Burrow's arrival] our little Command was saved from annihilation." After a short period of recuperation, both parties proceeded on their way.[10]

Colonel Carrington's files show a message from Burrows on July

[10] Frances C. Carrington, *My Army Life*, 73–81. This quotation is partially paraphrased.

24, 1866, requesting armed assistance for the Dillon and Kirkendall emigrant trains. Carrington dispatched Coloney Kinney "with 60 infantry, a howitzer, and wagons, for relief." Kinney joined Burrows before daylight. With the first emigrant wagons was a small command under Lieutenant G. M. Templeton, Eighteenth Infantry. On their arrival at Crazy Woman, late July 31, their Lieutenant Daniels, reconnoitring in advance, was "killed, stripped and scalped."[11]

With Bridger's sanction, Captain Burrows took this crippled train back with his supply train to Fort Reno. In due time they all returned by way of Crazy Woman's Fork to headquarters, at Fort Phil Kearny. It was a serious situation, and Bridger was deeply uneasy. Said Mrs. Carrington, "Bridger would walk about constantly scanning the opposite hills that commanded a view of the fort."[12]

On August 3, 1866, Colonel Carrington dispatched Brevet Lieutenant Colonel Kinney, with Captain Burrows and two companies of soldiers, to select a site on the Big Horn River for a new post, originally Fort Ransome but now changed to C. F. Smith, on the direct line to the Montana mines. In a short time, "they reported a village of Crow Indians seven miles out, another on Pryor's Fork, and another on Clark's Fork, all friendly.

"I immediately sent James Beckwith [mulatto] who claimed to have lived with the Crows as a chief among them, and who married with them, to communicate my views and wishes, and to learn their disposition towards the whites . . . and to induce them, if possible, to communicate with "Red Cloud" quietly, and learn the disposition of himself and the Sioux of Tongue River Valley.

"I also sent James Bridger, my Chief Guide, and especially familiar with the Crow Indians, to have an interview with them for the same purpose.

"The substance of their report is given in the following communication to Department Headquarters, which is introduced here, although not in order of date, but as nearly concurrent in actual date of fact:"

Fort Philip Kearny, Dak., Nov. 5, 1866.[13]
I sent James Bridger, Chief Guide, and Guide Williams to examine

[11] Henry B. Carrington, *Hearings*, 11–12.
[12] Frances C. Carrington, *My Army Life*, 96.
[13] This quotation consists of excerpts from the report.

the whole line hence to Virginia City, with view to an exact report of its condition and resources, and no less its susceptibility of being shortened by proper cut-offs. I shall embody their reports in map form by next mail.

Lieutenant Bradley, in charge of escort to Captain Hazen, . . . has also returned from Fort Benton.

2. Lieutenant Bradley's party, returning from Fort Benton, and about 30 miles from Fort C. F. Smith, were attacked by a large force of Sioux about noon. Mr. Brennan, Guide, detached for special duty on the trip, while leading the advance with Acting Assistant Surgeon McCleary, was suddenly attacked by a party of Indians. Brennan was killed and scalped. Dr. McCleary had his horse shot, and escaped. . . .

3. Bridger and Williams visited the Crow Indians as instructed. This was at Clark's Fork. The village numbered 500 men. "White Mouth," "Black Foot," and "Rottentail," [chiefs] insisted that they were at peace and wished to be always. The young men in some cases wished to join the Sioux, and compromise their old title to this country, of which they had been robbed by the Cheyennes and Sioux.

"Red Cloud" had visited their village, and they had returned the visit, but declined to join them on the War Path against the Whites

The Crow chiefs report that it took a half a day's ride to go through the villages of the war parties on Tongue River. The Sioux chiefs said they would not touch the new Fort on Powder River [Reno] but would destroy the two new Forts, in their hunting grounds, meaning Phil Kearny and C. F. Smith. Thus they will have two big fights.

4. Beckwith, mulatto guide, has made a visit to the same band of Crows. They sent for him as he was formerly with them. . . . He talks much; I doubt his influence with them, but shall soon know the result of his visit; Mr. Bridger thinks them ready to enlist.

5. The Crows represent that a treaty was made with them on the Upper Missouri on board the steamer *Ben Johnson*, whereby, for the sum of $25,000, they surrendered a route to Montana south of the Big Horn Mountains. . . . It is not unlikely that an attack will be made (By Sioux) this winter early.

"Fort Philip Kearny, Dak., Sept. 17, 1866. Messenger from Fort C. F. Smith brings message that at request of Mr. Bridger a party of Crows visited that post, reporting 500 lodges of Sioux in Tongue River Valley, all hostile. Cheyenne chiefs 'Black Horse' et al. . . . with whom I held council in July . . . brought me the same report."

September 21: "Guide Brennan . . . was scalped near Fort Smith; but Guides Bridger and Williams, sent by me to the Crows, and through to Virginia City to initiate a new survey of the route, visited a Crow Village of 500 warriors at Clark's Fork. . . . The foregoing, in substance, was confirmed by their subsequent interviews with other bands of Crows between Clark's Fork and the Big Horn; and information from Beckwith (mulatto guide). . . . Bridger said that 250 young Crows would go on the War Path during the winter if I wished it. [Having already hired much of my quota] I could not accept their proposition.

"Beckwith died in their village, without giving me the result of his visit."[14] Carrington thus ingloriously terminates an illustrious career. Lieutenant George M. Templeton's diary, at Fort C. F. Smith, does a little better.[15]

James Bridger had gone on to Virginia City on his route survey. Finding that the emigrants themselves had been making cut-offs, Bridger and Williams made rather quick work of it and were back to Fort C. F. Smith in late September. They reached Fort Phil Kearny in October, which is about the date given for Beckwourth's demise.

It may have been on this occasion, in Virginia City, that Bridger met the man who was to become one of his best friends. Nathaniel P. Langford writes: "I first became acquainted with Bridger in the year 1866 [1865?]. He was then employed by a wagon road company, of which I was president, to conduct the emigration from the states, to Montana by way of Fort Laramie, the Big Horn River, and Emigration Gulch.

"He told me in Virginia City, Montana, at that time, of the existence of hot, spouting springs in the vicinity of the source of the Yellowstone and Madison Rivers, and said that he had seen a column of water as high as the flagpole in Virginia City, which was about sixty feet high."[16]

Others seem to have at least tried to enlist Bridger's assistance on

---

[14] Henry B. Carrington, *Hearings*, 20–21, 30.

[15] Henry R. Wagner and Charles L. Camp, *The Plains and the Rockies*, no. 272, Beckwourth's death, in Lieutenant George M. Templeton's diary.

[16] Langford, *The Discovery of Yellowstone Park*, 17.

emigrant roads. A feature story on emigrant roads in the Montana *Post,* Virginia City, April 18, 1865, reported that Nathaniel P. Langford was president of the Missouri River and Rocky Mountain Wagon Road and Telegraph Company, which consolidated with the Bozeman City and Fort Laramie Wagon Road and Telegraph Company. Thus: "Messrs Bridger and Bozeman have joined their interests in their respective roads, with this [Langford] Company, and have been employed to conduct the emigration from Fort Laramie."[17] At that particular time, Bridger was at Fort Laramie serving as guide for Colonel Thomas Moonlight.

Bridger's road report to Colonel Carrington in late October, 1866, was paraphrased and condensed by Mrs. Carrington, who supplied the distances as later measured by an odometer:

Fort Phil Kearny to Fort C. F. Smith	91 miles
(Using Bridger's Cut-off)	
Fort C. F. Smith to Clark's Fork	63 miles
(Ferry, timber, grass and water)	
Clark's Fork to Yellowstone Ferry	90 miles
(Immel's Fork and other crossings)	
Yellowstone Ferry to Bozeman City	51 miles
(In the mountains)	
Bozeman City to Virginia City	70 miles
(Mountain-meadows and farms)	
	365

Bridger's route, Mrs. Carrington noted, "is twenty miles less than Colonel Sawyer's route. The course of travel adopted by Major Bridger confirms his opinion that nearly thirty miles more can be saved by construction improvements."[18]

But the new road was not a way out of the difficulties caused by the Carrington "invasion." The ominous threat uttered by "Red Cloud," in a conversation with "Black Horse," seemed to haunt Margaret Carrington's rooms. In July, 1866, "Black Horse" had said to "Red Cloud": "Let us take the White man's hand and what he gives us, rather, than fight him longer and lose all." "Red Cloud"

[18] Margaret I. Carrington, *Ab-Sa-Ra-Ka,* 252 (250–258).
[17] Virginia City newspaper photo-copied by Montana Historical Society.

answered angrily: "White man lies and steals. My lodges were many, but now they are few. The White man wants *all*. The White man must fight, and the Indian will die where his fathers died."

Bridger was psychic enough to feel Red Cloud's hate, and the Old Scout's warning kept ringing in the sensitive woman's ears: "Where there ain't no Injuns, you'll find 'em thickest." And they did![19]

[19] *Ibid.*, 183–85.

THAT THE SIOUX meant business is shown by the many clashes recorded in Mrs. Carrington's diary: eight raids or attacks in July, five in August, and thirteen in September, continuing in early winter.[1] James Bridger, "the Colonel's confidential Guide, at all times seemed instinctively to know, the invisible as well as the visible operations of the Indians." This was at once the white's greatest comfort and their greatest fear.

"The nights were made hideous at times, by the hungry wolves which gathered in hordes about the slaughter yard of the Quartermaster. The only comfort was the statement of Bridger, and others, that Indians were rarely near, when many wolves were present; and that they could distinguish the howl of the wolf from the cry of an Indian, by the fact that the former produced no echo [because it was moving].[2]

"After random skirmishes and frequent pursuits of stock-stealing parties, there had been a pitched fight to increase the intensity of the Commander's assurances, backed up by the Guide, Bridger, that the enemy was increasing in force, and was watchful of every exposure or recklessness of parties leaving the Fort for whatsoever purpose, to destroy us utterly."[3]

Chief Two Moons (Siouan family) said that "he and a small party of friendly Cheyennes, were sent to the fort [Phil Kearny] as spies to see if it could be taken by storm. Here Two Moons saw Old Bridger . . . and had quite a nice visit. When Two Moons returned to the hostile camp he reported the post too strong to be taken without great loss."[4]

1 Margaret I. Carrington, Ab-Sa-Ra-Ka, 121–28.
2 Frances C. Carrington, My Army Life, 97, 128.
3 Ibid., 135.
4 Ibid., 161–62.

Bridger took pains to show Two Moons and his men that Fort Phil Kearny was impregnable. What followed, said Mrs. Carrington, "proved the value and integrity of Major Bridger and his statements, and no less showed the wisdom of a settled policy, not to precipitate or undertake, a general war, while there was but a handful of men at the Post.[5]

"Shortly after Captain William J. Fetterman arrived at Fort Phil Kearny, impressed with his own opinion, to which he had often given language, that 'a company of regulars could whip a thousand; and a regiment could whip the whole array of hostile tribes,' he was permitted to make the experiment of lying in the cottonwood thicket of Big Piney from 2 o'clock till 10 o'clock in the morning, using hobbled mules for live bait to decoy the aborigines.' "

The Indians displayed their canniness by not appearing. In a speech made later, Colonel Carrington quoted Captains Fetterman and Brown: " 'I can take eighty men and go to Tongue River through all the Sioux forces.' To this boast, my Chief Guide, the veteran James Bridger, replied in my presence: 'Your men who fought down South are crazy! They don't know anything about fighting Indians.' "[6]

From mid-July to mid-December the official reports show that the Indians killed 91 enlisted men, 5 officers, and 58 civilians and got away with 306 oxen, 304 mules, and 161 horses in fifty-one raids or attacks. The situation certainly was touchy, and the crafty Sioux, under the personal leadership of Red Cloud, had carefully set their plans on a hair trigger. The Indians would draw the garrison out, detachment by detachment, and surprise them—a plan which would succeed if the recent recklessness shown by some troops in attempting to recover stock could be taken as a measure of their ability.

Thus it was a part of a major plan to attack the wood train, with its fifty-odd woodcutters and its military guard, at 11:00 A.M. on December 21, 1866. When scarcely two miles from the fort, the party was attacked, and the picket on an intervening lookout swiftly signaled the news to the fort. Captain Fetterman's company rushed to the rescue, halting only long enough for Colonel Carring-

[5] Margaret I. Carrington, *Ab-Sa-Ra-Ka*, 209.
[6] Frances C. Carrington, *My Army Life*, 253.

ton's instructions: "Support the wood train; relieve it; and report to me; do not engage or pursue Indians at its expense; under no circumstances pursue over Lodge Trail Ridge." Lieutenant Grummond's command followed almost immediately.

When Captain Fetterman's company approached the wood train, the Indians sent a carefully picked handful of mounted men to decoy Fetterman into the hills—and the ruse succeeded. Fetterman followed and the savages swarmed upon him from all sides. Lieutenant Grummond's command must have yielded to a similar ruse in violation of James Bridger's ceaseless warning, phrased for an officer by Colonel Carrington, not to follow an Indian too far.

The heaviest firing, or so it sounded at the fort, began about noon. A terrifying silence came at 12:45 P.M., when the last man of all three groups had been slain, and the Indian victors began to appropriate the soldier's clothing and to mutilate the naked bodies in demoniac glee before departing. It was just after dark when Captain Ten Eyck returned to Fort Phil Kearny with forty-nine of the bodies and made the crushing announcement that the other thirty-two men had been killed and would be brought in on the next trip.

It was a day to add age to any man's shoulders, and James Bridger, whose advice should have prevented it all, was bearing the greater share of misery.

General Philip St. George Cooke, department commander, acting impulsively after reading the news dispatches, removed Carrington by quick-tempered telegram, ordering him to Fort Caspar, there to patrol the telegraph and overland stage lines.

Colonel Carrington and his unhappy family trudged out of Fort Phil Kearny on January 23, 1867, "under lead of Bailey, our intrepid Guide; Bridger, old and infirm, had been left behind," was Frances (Grummond) Carrington's lament.[7]

A little later, when General Sherman read his copy of Carrington's report of the massacre, he removed General Cooke and put General C. C. Augur in command of the department of the Platte. Augur, quite as promptly, changed Carrington's orders, while Carrington was on the way, to read "Fort McPherson" (present North Platte), where both Indian and railroad business was busiest.[8]

[7] *Ibid.*, 183.
[8] Margaret I. Carrington, *Ab-Sa-Ra-Ka,* 225n. (1878 edition).

Major Alson B. Ostrander says Bridger was still at Fort Phil Kearny, April 23, 1867. About that time, however, Bridger seems to have been ordered to report to General C. C. Augur, Department of the Platte, Fort Laramie. He would be available to appear at the Senate Committee Hearings in Fort McPherson (North Platte), but was mostly needed for conferences with General Grenville M. Dodge, chief engineer in charge of nearby Union Pacific railroad construction.

General Dodge was also hosting several adventuring politicians, financiers, and government officials. The railroad builders and allied workers, following the end-of-track, were besieged by enraged Cheyenne Indians. Lodgepole Creek was in heavy flood; and Indians pulled up the survey stakes, stole the work animals, destroyed equipment, consumed supplies, and killed everyone not closely guarded by armed soldiers, thus discouraging labor and delaying work.

General Dodge had grave doubts about the military protection. While his visitors were conferring on the scene, they were almost swept off their feet by one hundred attacking Cheyennes. General Dodge, revolver drawn, hurried to the end-of-track nearby, yelling orders to the graders, who were too frightened to obey. Dodge whirled around and told his government guests: "We've got to clean these damn Indians out, or give up building the Union Pacific Railroad. The Government may take its choice."[9]

A few days later the sprawling city of Cheyenne began to take form with its satellite, Ft. D. A. Russell (now Ft. Warren) to hold the Indians in check. The Indians didn't appreciate the compliment of naming the city "Cheyenne," but they never misunderstood the fort nearby, which General Augur manned at full strength.

It was the last time General Dodge was to see James Bridger. With twinges of rheumatism in his stiffening legs and blank stares in his dimming eyes, Bridger had humbled the distinguished army generals with such recommendations as abandoning the northern forts, running the railroad across southern Wyoming, and leaving the Indians alone in their own territory.

Bridger did not forget that the supply train for Phil Kearny was due to leave Fort Laramie in early July, 1867, and he was there to accompany it.

[9] Perkins, *Trails, Rails, and War*, 208–10.

Reaching Phil Kearny in early July, Bridger was disturbed by the proximity, numbers, and restlessness of the Sioux. Notwithstanding, Mattes found the new commanding officer saying of Bridger: "He is not needed here, one guide for this post being enough. . . . I pay no heed to rumors about attacks on posts, except to put the Post in good condition as possible for a fight."[10]

Red Cloud was still enraged over the invasion of the whites, and war parties were everywhere. Bridger foresaw the worst. On August 1, 1867, several hundred Cheyennes attacked a dozen civilian haymakers and a nineteen-man armed escort near Fort C. F. Smith. This eight-hour Hayfield Fight (before artillery reinforcements from the post routed the Indians) resulted in three white men dead and three wounded; Indian losses: "A great many."

On August 2, 1867, timber cutters and sawyers, with an ample escort, left Fort Phil Kearny in fourteen heavy wagons for the pinery, seven or eight miles distant. Their main encampment was established on an open plain a mile or so distant from the pinery entrance. As only the wagon gears were needed for hauling, the fourteen heavy boxes were arranged in an oval corral on rising ground in the center of the camp, commanding a view of the entire horizon.

It was not by chance that thirty-five new Springfield repeating rifles with an abundant supply of cartridges were in these wagon boxes, or that sundry barrels, boxes, bales, and bags barricaded the outer walls of the wagon boxes for the protection of rifle marksmen.

The first wagon train of timber started back to Fort Phil Kearny about the same time another crew reached the pinery; both had vigilant escorts. The Indian signal smokes around the horizon did not mean a buffalo surround was in progress. The two wagon trains were hardly out of sight, when, galloping madly toward the stationary wagon-box camp, came the vanguard of two or three thousand angry Indians, from practically every point of the compass.

Major J. Powell, officer in charge, was enjoying a bath in the creek, but managed to reach the wagon-box corral ahead of the nearest savages. He instantly placed his own eager men, twenty-six soldiers and seven civilian assistants, at the firing holes and in positions for handling guns and ammunition. Powell managed also to

[10] Merrill J. Mattes, *Indians, Infants, and Infantry*, 130–34.

hold his marksmen in check, asking them to wait until they were sure of their target before firing.

After the first round of shots, which felled a ring of attacking braves, the howling Indians, expecting a lull while the guns were being reloaded, came on in waves. They were met with an even more deadly barrage from the new repeating guns. In the fast and heavy exhibition firing that followed, dead and wounded Indians lay literally in piles around the wagon-box corral, though many wounded were dragged away by surviving horsemen.

After about four hours, there came a break in the ranks of the attackers, and their invincible leader, Red Cloud, was seen moving away. The howitzers from the fort were attacking from the rear; the fort had been able to rush aid to the pinery through the working of an efficient signal warning system.

Long afterward, Red Cloud regretfully related that Indian casualties at the wagon-box fight were 1,137 dead or wounded. Only three whites were killed and two or three wounded at the corral.

While the Sioux and Cheyenne survivors licked their wounds and a segment of public opinion comforted them, the army noted that emigrant travel to the Montana mines was diminishing over the Bozeman Trail and increasing along the westward moving Union Pacific end-of-track. Bridger remained at Fort Phil Kearny for a few weeks, assisting in assuring the Indians that the government would close the forts; that emigrants would cease traveling across their lands; and that the Indians would have uncontested use of their beloved Yellowstone River country.

But if Bridger had been asked, he could doubtless have predicted some such vengeful retaliation as the Custer Massacre, which came within ten years. The Massacre took place within seventy-five miles of that death-dealing corral, and many of the same warriors participated in it.

Another peace conference at Fort Laramie was being announced by couriers bearing gifts of tobacco, as usual. The Sioux and Cheyennes belittled and berated the meeting, but the Crows would attend with Pierre Chien (Fort C. F. Smith) as interpreter. As they were friends of Bridger's, he would probably go with them.

Bridger's Hawken rifle, in the Exhibit Room of the Montana State Historical Society at Helena, was said to have been purchased from the Old Scout himself by Pierre Chien for sixty-five dollars. The gun was presented to J. J. Allen of the Crow Agency and then to the Historical Society. Bridger may have sold the gun in 1867; he could not see the sights well any more, and he would not need it where he was going.[11]

M. Simonin celebrated the advent of steel rails at Cheyenne, Wyoming, November 13, 1867, and then covered the peace conference at Fort Laramie on November 14.[12] The peace council followed the course predicted by Bridger. Only the Crows took part, and they complained of their impoverishment and of nonpayments on preceding treaties. They demanded removal of the northern forts; then they stalked out, refusing to sign.

Pierre Chien did not "shine" as an interpreter, Simonin reported, but he knew a good gun when he saw one. Hawken guns were also carried by William Henry Ashley, Edwin T. Denig, Christopher (Kit) Carson, and James Clyman, according to Russell; but Bridger's Hawken had a thirty-four-inch barrel. Other sources indicate that Bridger had other guns. Plate 102 of John Grace Wolfe Dillin's *The Kentucky Rifle* bears this legend: "By John Shuler, Liverpool, Pa., 1830, superposed double barrel rifle, both barrels rifled, property of the great Plainsman, Jim Bridger, from whom it passed to a man named Clarke, who later was killed by Indians while piloting a wagon train from Missouri to the California Gold fields in 1849." We find no corroboration, and no contradiction of this statement.

Bridger's discharge was dated September 23, 1867, at Fort Laramie, and he seems to have gone directly to his family on the Missouri farm. John Hunton says Bridger was still there in October, 1867; but Bridger soon caught a ride home.

The St. Louis *Missouri Republican* of November 18, 1867, quoting a writer in the Kansas City *Advertiser* of November 16 said: "We met the other day, James Bridger, the trapper. . . . Mr. Bridger had but just returned, when we met him, from a trip to Fort Laramie and Virginia City [Montana], on which he had acted as a Guide to Federal troops, locating a military road and military posts. He has served the Government in a similar capacity for many years."

11 Russell, *Guns on the Early Frontiers*, 74–75.

12 M. Simonin, "Fort Laramie Peace Commission, 1867," *Frontier and Midland*, January, 1931, 6–12.

On his return to the mountains the following spring, Bridger was restored to duty as guide at five dollars a day, May 15, 1868, at Fort Laramie. On May 22, he was assigned to Lieutenant P. F. Barnard, of the Fourth Infantry, who went back to Forts Reno, Phil Kearny and C. F. Smith to gather up the remaining property and move it to the Platte River posts. Wagon master F. G. Burnett commented: With Bridger along "we always knew what sort of camp the one ahead would be; and what kind of country we would travel over to reach it . . . though his eyesight was failing."

On the completion of that detail, which involved no difficulty with the Indians, Bridger was transferred to Colonel Darling, assistant quartermaster at Fort D. A. Russell (Cheyenne), and "by him paid and discharged" on July 21, 1868. Thus ends the official record of the scouting service of the Old Plainsman, with the following minor exception.

After his first ride behind a locomotive from Cheyenne, in the summer of 1868 and a brief visit with his family, Bridger was called into consultation with a group of army officers, headed by General Philip H. Sheridan, who was scheduled for a winter campaign against the southwestern Indians.

"The end of October [1868] saw completed the most of my arrangements," wrote the General, "though the difficulties to be encountered had led several experienced officers of the Army, and some frontiersmen, like Mr. James Bridger, the famous scout and guide of earlier days, to discourage the project. Bridger even went so far as to come out from St. Louis to dissuade me. But I reasoned as the soldier was much better fed and clothed than the Indian, I had one great advantage, and that, in short, a successful campaign could be made. . . .

"To see to this I decided to go in person. . . . We started on the 15th of November, and the first night out, a blizzard struck us and carried away our tents. . . . I took refuge under a wagon and there spent such a miserable night that, when at last morning came, the gloomy predictions of Old Man Bridger and others rose up before me with greatly increased force."[13]

[13] Philip H. Sheridan, *Memoirs*, vol. 2, 308.

Two-Ocean Creek, looking north. The man at the left is pointing to the Pacific Creek; the man at right to the Atlantic Creek.

JAMES BRIDGER
1804 1881
CELEBRATED AS A HUNTER, TRAPPER,
FUR TRADER AND GUIDE. DISCOVERED
GREAT SALT LAKE 1824, THE SOUTH
PASS 1827. VISITED YELLOWSTONE LAKE
AND GEYSERS 1830. FOUNDED FT. BRIDGER
1843. OPENED OVERLAND ROUTE BY
BRIDGER'S PASS TO GREAT SALT LAKE.
WAS GUIDE FOR U.S. EXPLORING
EXPEDITIONS, ALBERT SIDNEY JOHNSTON'S
ARMY IN 1857, AND G.M. DODGE IN U.P.
SURVEYS AND INDIAN CAMPAIGNS 1865-66.
THIS MONUMENT IS ERECTED AS A
TRIBUTE TO HIS PIONEER WORK BY
MAJ. GEN. G. M. DODGE

Monument commemorating Bridger's accomplishments, erected by General Grenville M. Dodge in Mount Washington Cemetery, Kansas City, Missouri.

WHEN JAMES BRIDGER returned to his farm, he carried on his stooping shoulders his own uneasy load of worries. Finished now with uniforms, with Indians, and with traveling and frontiering, he needed only some sort of security and subsistence, which most men spend a lifetime in providing. That sense of security was to come in part through a son-in-law, Captain Albert Wachsman, already endeavoring to establish himself, but especially through the ministrations of a loving, faithful daughter, Virginia Bridger Wachsman. To the devoted Wachsmans, though he was but a frail shadow of his former self, James Bridger was still a great man.

After spending her school years under the care of the Londons, Virginia married Captain Albert Wachsman in the big house on February 25, 1864, and in a few years had taken full charge of the place and the family cares. Bridger saw little of his son, Felix Francis, for he enlisted in the Missouri Artillery in the spring of 1863, serving to the end of the war in 1865. Felix then served under General George A. Custer, in the southwestern Indian campaigns, from 1866 to 1871. He then returned to the New Santa Fe farm, to remain.

On August 21, 1869, Captain Wachsman assisted Bridger in inquiring about a possible claim on the army for the lease of Fort Bridger in 1857. The army reminded him, however, that he had not shown proof of title. On October 27, 1873, when Bridger was "getting old and feeble, and . . . a poor man," Bridger took the matter up with United States Senator B. F. Butler. Sixteen long, slow years later, and eight silent years after the Old Scout's death, the Bridger heirs were granted $6,000 "for the improvements" at Fort Bridger, which the Mormons had burned in 1857.[1]

We have only glimpses of James Bridger's life in retirement, all

[1] Dodge, *Biographical Sketch;* see also Alter, *James Bridger,* 475–92.

from kindly, sympathetic folk. Visiting local writers, chiefly for the Kansas City *Star*, made frequent mention of Wornall Road, east of the Bridger home, High Drive, to the west, and the state line a little farther west. One Hundred and Seventh Street (east-west) of the present Kansas City is a few rods north of the old Bridger home-site. Only a half-filled foundation and a dry cistern hole remained in 1941 to mark the spot, the house having been torn down about 1908, according to E. R. Schauffler.

The inquiries of the author and a news photographer stimulated the memories of the people they met; Edgar Watts, Mrs. Lizzie Watts Cummins, and Mrs. Robert T. Davis had known the Old Scout in their childhood, and the Davis family lived for a time in the Bridger residence. The Stubbins Watts farm adjoined the Bridger farm, and the families were close friends.

"Once when Bridger was down at our house, he got mad at his horse and cussed the horse out. I never heard such a fancy job of language," shuddered Mrs. Cummins. "My, my! . . . After Bridger left, my little brother Edgar thought it would be all right to talk that way to his pony." "And Mother gave me a good tanning!" interjected Edgar, in vivid recollection.

Mrs. Cummins remembered Bridger's telling her father (Stubbins Watts) that people said he was a liar when he told of seeing springs of boiling water in the Yellowstone. "Why, Stubbins," Old Jim would say, "they said I was the damndest liar ever lived!"

"He used to ride a white-faced, roan horse, with two white feet," Edgar Watts recalled. "The horse was named Ruff; and even after Bridger's sight left him, he kept on riding that horse. Sometimes he got the reins crossed, and the horse went wrong; but it always came either to our house or to Bridger's own home, safely."

William Bridger, Jim's youngest son, lived for a while in a log house at Wornall and 103d Street. Miss Emma, one of the Vásquez family, remembered James Bridger's reluctance to sit on a chair if a rail fence, wood-pile, or space to squat on his heels was available. She heard her grandfather ask Bridger once how his crops were doing. Bridger replied disgustedly, "Perfect damn failure! Perfect damn failure!"

"I shall always remember Bridger's kindly, blue-gray eyes," said

Mrs. Wright, who, at ten or twelve years of age, lived across the road from the Bridgers and was a playmate of the Bridger children. "I would often go over to see Mr. Bridger. He was always very hospitable, and liked to have the children of the neighborhood come to see him. His son, Bill, played the violin, and the whole neighborhood used to come to dance at the Bridger home.

"I often saw him riding on horseback or walking over his land, feeling his way along with his stick, accompanied by two or three of his fox hounds. If they started a rabbit, the Old Man would get greatly excited, and halloo the hounds on to the chase.

"He would sit out on the porch, resting his chin on his cane, with his face towards the West—a lonely figure. He liked to talk of his life on the Plains, and I remember his saying once, at a time when his eyesight was almost gone, 'I wish I was back there among the mountains again—you can see so much farther in that country.' He was proud of this apple orchard, and used to send basketfuls of apples to his neighbors."[2]

Mrs. Wachsman wrote to General Dodge in 1904: "In 1873 father's health began to fail him, and his eyes were very bad, so that he could not see good, and the only way father could distinguish any person was by the sound of their voice; but all who had the privilege of knowing him were aware of his wonderful state of health at that time; but later, in 1874, father's eyesight was leaving him very fast, and this worried him so much. He has often-times wished that he could see you. At times father would get very nervous, and wanted to be on the go. I had to watch after him and lead him around to please him, never still one moment.

"I got father a good old gentle horse so that he could ride around, and have something to pass the time, so one day he named this old horse 'Ruff.' We also had a dog that went with father; and named this old faithful dog 'Sultan.' Sometimes father would call me and say: 'I wish you would go and saddle Old Ruff for me; I feel like riding around the farm'; and the faithful Old Dog would go along. Father could not see very well, but the old faithful horse would guide him along; but at times father would draw the lines wrong, and the horse would go wrong, and they would get lost in the woods. The

2 E. R. Schauffler, in Kansas City *Star*, March 2, 1941.

strange part of it was, the old faithful dog, Sultan, would come home and let us know that father was lost. The dog would bark and whine until I would go out and look for him, and lead him and the old horse home on the main road.

"Sometimes father wanted to take a walk out to the field, with Old Sultan by his side, and cane in hand, to guide his way out to the wheat field; would want to know how high the wheat was; and then father would go down on his knees and reach out his hands to feel for the wheat; and that was the way he passed away his time.

"Father at times wished that he could see, and only have his eyesight again, so that he could go back out to see the mountains. I know he, at times, would feel lonesome, and long to see some of his old mountain friends, to have a good chat of olden times, away back in the fifties. Father often spoke of you and would say: 'I wonder if General Dodge is alive or not; I would give anything in the world; if I could see some of the old Army officers once more, to have a talk with them of olden times; but I know I will not be able to see any of my old time mountain friends any more. I know that my time is near. I feel that my health is failing me very fast, and see that I am not the same man I used to be.' "

Guiding hands led James Bridger to the funeral of his son, Felix Francis, in 1876. The burial plat was in Watts's burial ground, near what is now 101st and Jefferson streets. A decade later the thirty-year-old William was laid beside Felix, a choice space nearby being held in reserve.

James Bridger died, July 17, 1881, and was buried in that grassy space beside his sons on July 19. Modest gravestones were erected, the larger of which was later removed to storage. "If they want to bring it back, we will provide a place for it, from which it need never be moved," was Mrs. Wilson's (Schauffler's) blessing. "That's where it really belongs," added Mrs. Cummins. "He liked it here!"

General Grenville M. Dodge remembered James Bridger the rest of his life, and when most men would have forgotten, nearly forty years later, General Dodge gave his time, his skill, his influence, and his money to preserve that memory. December 11, 1904, in the hundredth year after Bridger's birth, General Dodge had Bridger's body removed to a select site in Mount Washington Cemetery,

Kansas City. The grave was marked by a seven-foot monument listing the principal events in Bridger's life, including service as guide for "G. M. Dodge in U. P. Survey and Indian campaigns."

At the dedication of the monument General Dodge said:

"I found Bridger a very companionable man. In person, he was over six feet tall, spare, straight as an arrow, agile, rawboned, and of powerful frame; eyes gray, hair brown and abundant, even in old age; expression mild, and manners agreeable. He was hospitable and generous, and was always trusted and respected. He possessed in a high degree, the confidence of the Indians. . . . Naturally shrewd, and possessing keen faculties of observation . . . he became one of the most expert hunters and trappers in the mountains.

"Eager to gratify his curiosity, and with a natural fondness for mountain scenery . . . he familiarized himself with every mountain peak, every deep gorge, every hill, and every landmark in the country. . . . No object of interest escaped his scrutiny, and when once known, it was ever after remembered. He could describe with minute accuracy, places he had visited but once, and that many years before; and he could travel in almost a direct line from one point to another . . . always making his goal. . . . He never lost his bearings.

"Unquestionably Bridger's claim to remembrance rests upon the extraordinary part he bore in the explorations in the West. As a Guide he was without an equal, and this is the testimony of everyone who ever employed him. He was a born topographer; the whole West was mapped out in his mind, and such was his instinctive sense of locality and direction, that it was said of him, that he could smell his way where he could not see it.

"He was a complete master of plains and woodcraft. . . . In all my experience I never saw Bridger . . . meet an obstacle he could not overcome. He could make a map of any country he had ever traveled over, mark out its streams, mountains and obstacles correctly. . . . He never claimed knowledge of the country that he did not have.

"He was a good judge of human nature. His comments upon people that he had met and been with were always intelligent, and seldom critical. He always spoke of their good parts, and was universally respected by the mountain men, and looked upon as a leader.

He was careful to never give his word without fulfilling it. . . .
He felt very keenly any loss of confidence in him or his judgement:
. . . And when he struck a country or trail he was not familiar with,
he would frankly say so. . . . So remarkable a man should not be
lost to history!"

➳ BIBLIOGRAPHY

CONGRESSIONAL DOCUMENTS

19 Cong., 1 sess., *H. Doc. 117* (Atkinson-O'Fallon Expedition of 1825).

20 Cong., 2 sess., *Sen. Doc. 67* (Ashley to Benton, November 12, 1827).

21 Cong., 2 sess., *Sen. Ex. Doc. 39* (Ashley Trapper Travel Routines; Pilcher's Expedition 1827–30; and Smith, Jackson and Sublette, by Smith).

31 Cong., 1 sess., *H. R. Ex. Doc. 17* (August–September, 1849, John Wilson, Indian agent, Salt Lake City, Utah).

33 Cong., 1 sess., *H. R. Ex. Doc. 129* (Warren's Memoir, early maps of North America).

35 Cong., 1 sess., *H. R. Ex. Doc. 71* (The Utah Expedition, Washington, 1858).

35 Cong., 2 sess., *Serial 975 and Serial 976* (The Utah War of 1858, Washington, 1859).

39 Cong., 2 sess., *Ex. Doc. 45.*

40 Cong., 1 sess., *Ex. Doc. 77.*

52 Cong., 1 sess., *Senate Report 625* (Fort Bridger Survey by J. M. Hockaday). *Indian Service Reports 1825, Serial 136.*

GENERAL SOURCES

Allen, Miss A. J. (compiler). *Ten Years in Oregon* (travels and adventures of Dr. E. White and Lady, 1838–47). Ithaca, 1848.

Alter, J. Cecil. *James Bridger, Trapper, Frontiersman, Scout and Guide.* Salt Lake City, 1925; Columbus, 1950.

Anderson, William M. "Narrative of a Ride to the Rocky Mountains in 1834," edited by Albert J. Partoll, *Frontier and Midland,* (Autumn), 1938.

Ashley, William H. "Diary and Accounts, 1825," edited by Dale L. Morgan, *Bulletins of the Missouri Historical Society* (St. Louis, Mo.), October, 1954, and January and April, 1955.

——. "Narrative, 1824–1825." See Harrison C. Dale.

"Atkinson-O'Fallon Expedition, Up the Missouri River, 1825," *North Dakota Historical Society Quarterly*, October, 1929.

Baker, James. "Letter to Utah Pioneer Jubilee Celebration Committee, Salt Lake City," in *Latter-day Saints Millennial Star* (Liverpool, England), June 24, 1897.

Baldwin, Leland D. *The Keelboat Age on Western Waters*. Pittsburgh, 1941.

Ball, John. *Autobiography*. (Compiled by Kate Ball Powers, Flora Ball Hopkins, and Lucy Ball. Grand Rapids, 1825.

Bancroft, H. H. *History of Utah*. San Francisco, 1899.

Bidwell, John. *In California Before the Gold Rush*. Los Angeles, 1848.

Boardman, John. "Journal, Overland Journey, 1843," *Utah Historical Quarterly*, October, 1929.

Bonner, T. D. *The Life and Adventures of James P. Beckwourth* (1798–1867). New York, 1856; and Charles G. Leland edition, London, 1892. All footnote references are to the Leland edition.

Bouis, A. R. "Letter, 1845," *South Dakota Historical Society Collections*, IV. Pierre, 1920.

Brackenridge, H. M. *Journal of a Voyage up the River Missouri in 1811*. Second edition, revised and enlarged, Pittsburgh, 1816.

Brackett, William S. "Bonneville and Bridger," *Contributions to the Montana Historical Society*, III. Helena, 1900.

Bradbury, John. *Travels in the Interior of America in 1809–11*. Vol. V in Thwaites' *Early Western Travels*, q.v.

Bray, Lauren C. *Louis Vasquez, Mountain Man (1798–1868)*. Kansas City, 1958. Also in *Westerners Roundup*, July–August, 1959.

Brown, B. Gratz. Correspondence in the *Missouri Republican*, November 9, 1851.

Brown, David L. *Three Years in the Rocky Mountains*. Reprinted from the Cincinnati *Atlas*, September, 1845. New York, Eberstadt, 1950.

Brown, James S. *Life of a Pioneer*. Salt Lake City, 1900.

Bryant, Edwin. *What I Saw in California*. New York, 1848.

Burnett, Peter H. "Letters, 1843–44," *Oregon Historical Society Quarterly*, Vol. III (December, 1902).

Burton, Richard F. *City of the Saints*. London, 1861.

California Society of Pioneers, publications and files, San Francisco.

Campbell, Robert. "Correspondence of Robert Campbell, 1834–1845," *Glimpses of the Past*, January–June, 1941.

Cannon, Miles. *Waiilatpu: Its Rise and Fall, 1836–1847.* Boise, 1915.

Carrington, Frances C. *My Army Life on the Plains; and the Fort Phil Kearny Massacre.* Philadelphia, 1910.

Carrington, Henry B. *History of Indian Operations on the Plains; Hearings before Special Commission.* Fort McPherson, Nebraska, 1867.

Carrington, James B. "Across the Plains with Bridger as Guide," *Scribner's,* January, 1929.

Carrington, Margaret I. *Ab-Sa-Ra-Ka (Home of the Crows): The Land of Massacre.* Philadelphia, 1868; reprint, 1878, with some changes.

Carson, (Christopher) Kit. *Carson's Own Story of His Life.* Edited by Blanche C. Grant and Charles L. Camp. Taos, 1926.

Carter, William A. "Journal, 1857–58," *Annals of the Wyoming Historical Society.* Cheyenne, 1939.

Catlin, George. *Letters and Notes on the Manners, Customs, and Condition of the North American Indians.* 2 vols. London, 1841; reprint, Philadelphia, 1913.

———. *The George Catlin Indian Gallery.* Edited by Thomas C. Donaldson. Washington, 1886.

Chittenden, Hiram. *History of the American Fur Trade of the Far West (1807–1843).* 2 vols. New York, 1902.

———. *History of Early Steamboat Navigation on the Missouri River; the Life and Adventures of Joseph La Barge.* 2 vols. New York, 1903.

———. *The Yellowstone National Park.* Cincinnati, 1921.

Chouquette, Charles. "Fort Benton Journal, 1854–1856; Fort Sarpy Journal, 1855–1856," *Contributions to the Montana Historical Society,* X. Helena, 1940.

Clayton, William. *The Latter-day Saints' Emigrant Guide.* St. Louis, 1848.

———. *Journal, 1846–1847,* (with the Mormon Pioneers, Nauvoo, Illinois, to Utah). Salt Lake City, 1921.

Clement, Basil. "The Mountain Trappers," edited by Charles E. De Land, *South Dakota Historical Society Collections,* XI. Pierre, 1922.

Clyman, James. *James Clyman, American Frontiersman.* San Francisco, 1928. Also definitive edition, Portland, 1960. All footnote references are to the second edition.

Collins, John S. *Across the Plains in 1864.* Omaha, 1904.

Colton, John B. "Inscription on Photograph of James Bridger." Yale University, New Haven.

Cooke, Philip St. George. *Scenes and Adventures in the U. S. Army.* Philadelphia, 1859.

Coutant, C. G. *History of Wyoming.* Laramie, 1899.

Dahlquist, Laura. *Meet Jim Bridger.* Fort Bridger, 1948. Also collection "Bridgerana."

Dale, Harrison C. *The Ashley-Smith Explorations.* Cleveland, 1918.

David, Robert B. *Finn Burnett, Frontiersman.* Glendale, 1937.

Dellenbaugh, Frederick S. *Frémont and '49.* New York, 1914.

De Smet, Pierre Jean. *Life, Letters, and Travels of Pierre Jean De Smet.* Edited by Hiram M. Chittenden and Alfred Richardson. 4 vols. New York, 1905.

De Voto, Bernard. *Across the Wide Missouri.* Boston, 1947.

Dillin, John Grace Wolfe. *The Kentucky Rifle.* Washington, 1924.

Dodge, Grenville M. *Biographical Sketch of James Bridger.* New York, 1905.

———. *Report, Union Pacific Railroad, on Lines Crossing the Rocky Mountains.* New York, 1867.

———. *The Battle of Atlanta and Other Campaigns.* Council Bluffs, 1910.

Drury, Clifford M. *Elkanah and Mary Walker.* Caldwell, 1940.

———. *Henry Harmon Spalding.* Caldwell, 1936.

Dunn, John. *History of the Oregon Territory, and the British Northwest Fur Trade.* London, 1884.

Eells, Myron F. *Marcus Whitman.* Seattle, 1909.

Eells, Mrs. Myra. "Journal," *Transactions of the Oregon Pioneer Association,* 1889. Also in Hafen and Young, *Fort Laramie, q.v.*

Egan, Howard. *Pioneering in the West.* Richmond, Utah, 1917.

Ellison, Robert S. *Fort Bridger, Wyoming: A Brief History.* Casper, Wyoming, 1931.

Farnham, Thomas J. *Travels in the Great Western Prairies.* London, 1843. Also in vols. XXVIII and XXIX of Thwaites' *Early Western Travels, q.v.*

Favour, Alpheus H. *Old Bill Williams.* Chapel Hill, 1936; new edition, Norman, 1962. All footnote references are to the 1936 edition.

Ferris, Mrs. B. G. *The Mormons at Home.* New York, 1856.

Ferris, Warren Angus. *Life in the Rocky Mountains.* Denver, 1940; also Salt Lake City, 1940.

Field, Matthew C. *Prairie and Mountain Sketches.* Collected by Clyde and Mae Reed Porter. Edited by Kate L. Gregg and John Francis McDermott. Norman, 1957.

Flagg, Edmund. "History of a Western Trapper," *Literary News-Letter* (Louisville), September 7, 1839.

Flint, Thomas. "Diary of Dr. Thomas Flint," *Annual Publications of the Historical Society of Southern California*, XII (1923).

Freeman, Legh R. Kearney, Nebraska, *Weekly Herald*, January 6, 1866.

Frémont, John C. *Report of the Exploring Expedition to the Rocky Mountains . . . 1842 and to Oregon . . . 1843-44*. Washington, 1845.

——. *Memoirs of My Life*. Chicago and New York, 1887.

Frost, Donald McKay. "Notes on General Ashley," *American Antiquarian Society Proceedings*. Worcester, 1945.

Gass, Patrick. "Journal," in the Hosmer edition of the *History of the Expedition of Meriwether Lewis and William Clark Expedition, q.v.*

Glass, Hugh. "The Missouri Trapper," *Port Folio* (Philadelphia), March, 1825; reprinted in Salt Lake City edition of Warren Angus Ferris, *Life in the Rocky Mountains, q.v.*

Gove, Jesse A. *Letters, 1857-1858: The Utah Expedition*. Concord, 1928.

Gray, William H. *A History of Oregon*. Portland, 1870.

——. "Unpublished Journal of William H. Gray, 1836-1837," *Whitman College Quarterly* (Walla Walla, Washington), June, 1913.

Grinnell, George Bird. *The Fighting Cheyennes*. Norman, 1956.

Gunnison, John W. *A History of the Mormons*. Philadelphia, 1852.

Hafen, Le Roy R. *Overland Mail*. Cleveland, 1926.

——. *Powder River Campaigns, and Sawyer's Expedition of 1865*. Glendale, 1961.

—— and F. M. Young. *Fort Laramie*. Glendale, 1938.

Hall, Frank. *History of the State of Colorado, 1858-1890*. 4 vols. Chicago, 1889-95.

Harmon, Appleton M. *Appleton M. Harmon Goes West*. Edited by Maybelle Harmon Anderson. Berkeley, 1946.

Hebard, Grace Raymond, and E. A. Brininstool. *The Bozeman Trail*. Cleveland, 1922.

Hedges, Cornelius. "Diary, Iowa to Montana, 1864," Montana Historical Society files (Helena).

Heldt, George F., and Henry Bostwick. "Sir George Gore's Hunting Expedition in 1854-56," *Contributions to the Montana Historical Society*. Helena, 1876.

Hickman, William A. *Brigham's Destroying Angel, Being the Life, Confessions and Startling Disclosures of the Notorious Bill Hickman*. New York, 1872.

Holmes, Reuben. "Five Scalps (Edward Rose)," *Glimpses of the Past*, 1938.

Houck, Louis. *A History of Missouri.* Chicago, 1908.
Hulburt, Archer B., and Dorothy P. Hulburt. *Marcus Whitman, Crusader.* 3 vols. Colorado Springs, 1936, 1938, and 1941.
Humfreville, J. Lee. *Twenty Years Among Our Hostile Indians.* New York, 1897.
Ingersoll, Chester. *Overland to California in 1847.* Chicago, 1937.
Irving, Washington. *Adventures of Captain Bonneville.* Edited by Edgeley W. Todd. Norman, 1961.
James, Thomas. *Three Years Among the Indians and Mexicans.* St. Louis, 1916.
Jenson, Andrew. "History of Fort Bridger and Fort Supply," *Utah Genealogical Magazine,* January, 1913.
Johnson, Overton, and W. H. Winter. *Route Across the Rocky Mountains.* Lafayette, Ind., 1848; Princeton, 1932. All footnote references are to the latter edition.
Johnston, William G. *Experiences of a Forty-Niner.* Pittsburgh, 1892.
Johnston, W. P. *Life of Albert Sidney Johnston.* New York, 1878.
Kelly, William. *Across the Rocky Mountains from New York to California.* London, 1852.
Kennerly, James, "Diary," *Collections of the Missouri Historical Society,* St. Louis, 1928.
Kennerly, William C. *Persimmon Hill.* As told to Elizabeth Russell. Norman, 1948.
Kilgore, Maggie. "Life of Jim Baker," Cheyenne *Tribune,* July 23, 1917.
Korns, J. Roderic. "West from Fort Bridger," *Utah Historical Quarterly,* XIX (pp. 192–94), 1951.
Langford, Nathaniel P. *The Discovery of Yellowstone Park.* St. Paul, 1923.
Langworthy, Franklin. *Scenery of the Plains, Mountains, and Mines.* Ogdensburg, 1855.
Larimer, Sarah L. *The Capture and Escape.* Philadelphia, 1870.
Larpenteur, Charles. *Forty Years a Fur Trader.* Edited by Elliot Coues. 2 vols. New York, 1898.
Latter-day Saints Journal of Discourses. 26 vols. Liverpool, 1854–86.
Ledyard, Edward M. (compiler). "American Posts," *Utah Historical Quarterly,* April, 1928 through April, 1933.
Lee, D., and J. H. Frost. *Ten Years in Oregon.* New York, 1844.
Lee, John D. *A Mormon Chronicle.* 2 vols. San Marino, 1955.
Leonard, Zenas. *Leonard's Narrative, 1831–1836.* Cleveland, 1904.

Lewis, Meriwether, and William Clark. *History of the Expedition of Meriwether Lewis and William Clark.* Edited by James K. Hosmer. Chicago, 1905.

Linforth, James, and Frederick Piercy. *Route from Liverpool to Great Salt Lake City.* Liverpool, 1855.

Lionberger, I. H. *The Annals of St. Louis.* St. Louis, 1928.

Manuscript History of Brigham. Office of the church historian, Salt Lake City.

Marcy, Randolph B. *Thirty Years of Army Life on the Border.* New York, 1874.

Marsh, James B. *Four Years in the Rockies; Adventures of Isaac P. Rose.* New Castle, 1884.

Mattes, Merrill J. "Behind the Legend of Colter's Hell," *Mississippi Valley Historical Review,* September, 1949.

———. "Hiram Scott, Fur Trader," *Nebraska History,* July and September, 1945.

———. *Indians, Infants, and Infantry.* Denver, 1960.

———. "Jackson Hole, Cross Roads of the Fur Trade," *Pacific Northwest Quarterly,* April, 1946, and January, 1948.

Merk, Frederick. "Snake Country Expedition 1824–1825," *Oregon Historical Quarterly,* June, 1934.

Milner, Joseph E., and E. R. Forrest. *California Joe (Milner).* Caldwell, 1935.

Minto, John. "Travel Diary," *Oregon Historical Quarterly,* June and September, 1901.

Missouri Historical Society, publications and files, St. Louis.

Montana Historical Society, publications and files, Helena.

Morgan, Dale L. Letter to the author concerning unpublished W. B. Lorton diary. Bancroft Library, Berkeley.

———. *Jedediah Smith and the Opening of the West.* Indianapolis, 1953.

Morgan, Lewis H. *The American Beaver and His Works.* Philadelphia, 1868.

Morgen, Martha M. *A Trip Across the Plains in 1849–1850.* San Francisco, 1864.

Mumie, Nolie. *James Pierson Beckwourth.* Denver, 1957.

———. *Jim Baker.* Denver, 1931.

Munger, Asahel, and Eliza Munger. "Diary 1839," *Oregon Historical Quarterly,* December, 1907.

Nasatir, A. P. *Before Lewis and Clark, Documents, 1785–1804.* 2 vols. St. Louis, 1952.

Nebraska Historical Society Publications, XX (newspaper accounts, 1808–61) (1922).

Neihardt, John G. *The Splendid Wayfaring*. New York, 1920.

Nesmith, James W. "Travel Diary, May–October, 1843," *Oregon Historical Quarterly*, December, 1906.

Newell, Robert. *Memoranda of Travel in Missouri*. Portland, Ore., 1959.

Newmark, Harris. *Sixty Years in Southern California*. Third edition. Boston, 1930.

Nidever, George. *Life and Adventures of George Nidever*. Edited by W. H. Ellison. Berkeley, 1937.

Ogden, Peter Skene. "Snake Country Journals, 1824–1829," edited by T. C. Elliott, *Oregon Historical Quarterly*, December, 1909, June and December, 1910; also published by the Hudson's Bay Record Society, London, 1950.

Ostrander, Alson B. *An Army Boy of the Sixties*. New York, 1924.

Palmer, H. E. "History of Powder River Invasion Expedition of 1865," *Nebraska Historical Society Publications*, II (1887; also in Coutant, *Wyoming*, and Hafen, *Powder River Campaigns*.

Palmer, Joel. *Journal of Travels Over the Rocky Mountains in 1845–1846, and Return in 1847*. Cincinnati, 1847.

Parker, Samuel. *Journal of an Exploring Tour Beyond the Rocky Mountains in 1835*. Auburn, 1846.

Parrish, Edward E. "Travel Diary," *Transactions of the Oregon Pioneer Association*, 1888.

Partoll, Albert J. "The Blackfoot Peace Council," *Frontier and Midland*, Spring, 1937.

Pattie, James O. *Personal Narrative*. Cincinnati, 1831.

Perkins, J. R. *Trails, Rails, and War: The Life of General G. M. Dodge*. Indianapolis, 1929.

Phillips, Paul Crisler. *The Fur Trade*. 2 vols. Norman, 1961.

Pratt, Orson. "Journal of 1847," vols. XI–XII, *Latter-day Saints Millennial Star*, June 2, 1847.

Rasmussen, D. I. "Beaver-Trout Relationship," *Transactions, North American Wildlife Conference*, Washington, 1940.

Raynolds, William F. *Report on the Exploration of the Yellowstone River 1859–1860*. Washington, 1868.

Reading, Pierson B. "Travel Diary," *Quarterly of the Society of California Pioneers*, III (pp. 148–98), 1930.

Rodenbough, Theophilus F. *From Everglade to Canyon, with Second Dragoons*. Edited by William Drown. New York, 1875.

Ross, Alexander. *The Fur Hunters of the Far West*. Edited by Kenneth A. Spaulding. Norman, 1956.
———. "Snake Country Journal," edited by T. C. Elliott, *Oregon Historical Quarterly*, December, 1913.
Ross, Marvin C. *The West of Alfred Jacob Miller*. Norman, 1951.
Russell, Carl P. *Guns on the Early Frontiers*. Berkeley and Los Angeles, 1957.
———. "Wilderness Rendezvous Period of the American Fur Trade," *Oregon Historical Quarterly*, March, 1941.
Russell, Osborne. *Journal of a Trapper 1834–1843*. Boise, 1921. Also in *Oregon Historical Society Publications* (edited by Aubrey L. Haines), 1955.
Schauffler, E. R. Kansas City *Star*, March 2, 1941.
Sheridan, Philip H. *Personal Memoirs*. 2 vols. New York, 1888.
Shotwell, A. J. "Recollections," Freeport, Ohio, *Press*, May 3, 1916.
Simonin, M. "Fort Laramie Peace Commission 1867," *Frontier and Midland*, January, 1931.
Smith, E. Willard. "Journal 1839–1840," *Oregon Historical Quarterly*, September, 1913.
Snyder, Jacob R. "Journal, 1845," *Society of California Pioneers Annual*, Vol. VIII, 1931.
South Dakota Historical Society, publications and files.
Spring, Agnes Wright. *Caspar Collins*. New York, 1927.
Stanley, E. J. *Life of L. B. Stateler*. Nashville, 1916.
Stansbury, Howard. *Exploration and Survey of the Valley of the Great Salt Lake 1849–1850*. Philadelphia, 1855.
[Stewart, William Drummond]. *Edward Warren*. Edited by J. Watson Webb. London, 1854.
Stone, Elizabeth A. *Uinta County: Its Place in History*. Laramie, 1924.
Sublette, William L. "Fragmentary Journal 1843," *Mississippi Valley Historical Review*, June, 1919.
Sullivan, Maurice S. *Jedediah S. Smith, Trader and Trail-breaker*. Santa Ana, 1934.
Sunder, John E. *Bill Sublette, Mountain Man*. Norman, 1959.
Talbot, Theodore, *Journal with Frémont*. Edited by Charles H. Carey. Portland, Oregon, 1931.
Thwaites, Reuben Gold. *Early Western Travels*. 32 vols. Cleveland, 1904–1907.
Tobie, Harvey E. *No Man Like Joe (Joseph L. Meek)*. Portland, 1949.

Abridged from *Oregon Historical Quarterly*, June, September, and December, 1938, and March, 1939.

Townsend, John K. *Narrative of a Journey Across the Rocky Mountains in 1834*. Philadelphia, 1839.

Twitchell, Jerry F. "The Latter-day Saints History of Bridger Valley (Wyoming)." Unpublished thesis, Brigham Young University, 1959.

Utah Historical Society, publications and files, Salt Lake City.

Victor, Frances F. *The River of the West (Joseph L. Meek)*. Hartford, 1870.

Wagner, Henry R. (revised by Charles L. Camp). *The Plains and the Rockies: A Bibliography of Original Narratives of Travel and Adventure*. Third edition revised by Charles L. Camp. Columbus, 1953.

Waldo, William. "Recollections of a Septuagenarian," *Glimpses of the Past*, April–June, 1938.

Ware, Eugene F. *The Indian War of 1864*. Topeka, 1911.

Ware, Joseph E. *Emigrant's Guide to California*. St. Louis, 1849.

Warner, J. J. "Reminiscences 1831–1846," *Historical Society of Southern California Publications*, 1907–1908.

Warren, Mrs. Eliza Spalding. *Memoirs of the West*. Portland, 1916.

Weber, John H. "Sketch," Salt Lake *Tribune*, July 4, 1897.

White, James Henry. "Emigrant of 1849," *Glimpses of the Past*, January–March, 1939.

Wilhelm, Prince Paul. "First Journey to North America 1822–1824," *Collections of the South Dakota Historical Society*, 1938.

Williams, Joseph. *Narrative of a Tour, Indiana to Oregon, 1841–1842, and Return*. New York, 1921.

Wislizenus, F. A. *A Journey to the Rocky Mountains in 1839*. St. Louis, 1912.

Woodruff, Wilford. *Journal and Life History of Wilford Woodruff*. Edited by M. F. Cowley. Salt Lake City, 1909.

Woodward, Arthur. "Trapper Jim Waters," *Los Angeles Westerners Keepsake Publication No. 23*, 1860.

Wright, Mrs. A. F. Kansas City *Star*, January 18, 1924.

Wyeth, John B. *Oregon: A Short History of a Long Journey, 1832*. Cambridge, 1833.

Wyeth, Nathaniel J. *Correspondence and Journals of Nathaniel J. Wyeth*. Eugene, 1899.

Young, John R. "Reminiscences," *Utah Historical Quarterly*, July, 1930.

Yount, George C. "Chronicles of George C. Yount," Edited by Charles L. Camp, *California Historical Quarterly*, April, 1923.

INDEX